JOURNAL FOR THE STUDY OF THE NEW TESTAMENT SUPPLEMENT SERIES

11

Executive Editor, Supplement Series
David Hill

Publishing Editor
David J.A. Clines

Department of Biblical Studies
The University of Sheffield
Sheffield S10 2TN
England

THE LETTERS
TO THE
SEVEN CHURCHES
OF ASIA
IN THEIR
LOCAL SETTING

Colin J. Hemer

Journal for the Study of the New Testament
Supplement Series 11

In memory of my mother and father

Published by
JSOT Press
Department of Biblical Studies
The University of Sheffield
Sheffield S10 2TN
England

Printed in Great Britain
by Redwood Burn Ltd.,
Trowbridge, Wiltshire.

British Library Cataloguing in Publication Data

Hemer, Colin J.
    The letters to the seven churches of Asia in their
    local setting.—(Journal for the study of the New
    Testament supplement series, ISSN 0143-5108; 11)
    1. Bible. N.T. Revelation I-III—Commentaries
    I. Title   II. Series
    228'.06   BS2825.3

    ISBN 0-905774-95-7
    ISBN 0-905774-96-5 Pbk

CONTENTS

PREFACE

This book is a shortened rewriting of a study which started life as a PhD thesis supervised by Professor F.F. Bruce and accepted by the University of Manchester in 1969. The researches on which it is based had their starting-point in the reading and preparation for an expedition to Asia Minor.

My closest academic debt is to the sure and kindly guidance of Professor Bruce, who stands in the highest traditions of British historical scholarship and has set an unfailing standard of excellence before his students.

I owe much to the companions of my two journeys in Turkey in 1964 and 1969, D. Evens, G.P. Rendle, H.P. Sitters, Mr and Mrs J. and H. Slade and C. E. Vernon, and in particular to the initiative of Mr J.P. Stunt, who organized and co-ordinated both visits, and whose friendship over many years has been a great support.

I acknowledge warm thanks to the libraries where I have worked at various times, especially to the John Rylands University Library of Manchester, the Cambridge University Library, and the libraries of the Museum of Classical Archaeology and of Tyndale House in Cambridge. My association with this last, under its successive Wardens, the Rev. F.D. Kidner, Dr R.T. France and Dr M.J. Harris, has been of special value. Financial assistance from grants of the Tyndale House Council has made the continuance of my work possible at crucial times; Tyndale's scholarly community and the resources of its library are a stimulus and delight to researchers from many lands. Dr Helge Stadelmann recently pays his tribute to this *Forschungsgemeinschaft* and its *anregende Diskussionen während so mancher Teepause*: such a commendation in a work of German theology must carry its own weight.

Many friends have encouraged me to the point of bringing this work finally into print. I owe much to many in the academic communities of Cambridge, Manchester and Sheffield, and to friends in Plymouth and elsewhere. I am grateful for the kind reference to my work in the recent books or commentaries of Dr J.M. Court, Professors R.H. Mounce and P. Prigent, the Rev. J.P.M. Sweet and Professor E.M. Yamauchi. Finally, my special thanks are due to Professor G.N. Stanton for his many helpful comments on the final typescript, and to the meticulous care of Professor D.J.A. Clines and his colleagues in preparing a difficult book for the press.

I trace the beginnings of a special interest in the Seven Churches to a spark ignited long ago by Canon E.M.B. Green and then to an early enthusiasm for the work of Sir W.M. Ramsay. This study, as first conceived, was in large measure a reassessment of Ramsay. I found he was often ignored, often followed blindly, often disparaged as speculative or as naively and polemically an apologist, but rarely re-examined dispassionately. In course of time I have developed and reshaped my work beyond that perspective, but I have not forsaken a central interest in working afresh with the primary sources. So the principal emphasis of these pages is upon the application of original evidence to the text rather than on secondary literature. It has seemed best to present my case here in the awareness of the most recent study, but without systematic interaction with views taken by the latest commentators. I have tried to spell out in the Introduction and Epilogue something of the wider implications of my theme for historical and critical study. I have become increasingly aware, for instance, of its bearing on the debate initiated by Walter Bauer's *Rechtgläubigkeit und Ketzerei*. Again, since I first developed my interests in the background of the New Testament the 'sociological' approach has become increasingly popular. I have tried to say something of the social history of the cities, for this was integral to my subject, and touches on issues of much current interest. I have in fact the warmest appreciation of the work of Professor E.A. Judge in particular, but my debt to him and his colleagues at Macquarie lies outside the central scope of this study.

I have learned much from the diverse interests of the many audiences, British, German, Chinese, Australian, Turkish and international, to whom I have presented the 'Seven Churches' visually. This is now, if not exactly 'the book of the films', at least the academic and technical substructure to which I have sought consistently to relate every oral and pictorial selection. If scholarship is to be effectively communicated, the scholarly foundation should be laid secure.

PREFATORY NOTE

Difficulty is sometimes experienced in the referencing to ancient literature. For many important authors confusing variations exist, and it is troublesome to find many incomplete, erroneous or untraceable references cited by modern writers. The greatest problem is found in the case of Aelius Aristides, whose orations are variously cited according to the wholly unrelated systems and page numbers in the editions of Jebb (1722), Dindorf (1829) and Keil (1898), all difficult of access. Few allusions to these speeches in modern works can be traced directly without extensive consecutive reading. I have accordingly worked on the principle that the value of a reference depends on the possibility of locating its source, and I have tried, at the occasional cost of a cumbrous sequence of figures, to describe an ancient passage by as full and varied a notation as may be necessary and possible from the available versions. Explanations of particular points are occasionally offered in footnotes, and an = sign inserted where a duplication might otherwise rather occasion than prevent confusion.

Greek names are generally Latinized in the forms most familiar and acceptable in English usage, but no attempt has been made to force a pedantic and rigid consistency irrespective of context. Conventional abbreviations have been used for ancient writers and their books.

LIST OF PRINCIPAL ABBREVIATIONS

ABSA   *Annual of the British School at Athens.*
AJA   *American Journal of Archaeology.*
AJSL   *American Journal of Semitic Languages.*
AJT   *American Journal of Theology.*
AS   *Anatolian Studies.*
AthMitt   *Mitteilungen des deutschen archäologischen Instituts. Athenische Abteilung.*
BA   *The Biblical Archaeologist.*
BASOR   *Bulletin of the American School of Oriental Research.*
BCH   *Bulletin de correspondance hellénique.*
BJRL   *Bulletin of the John Rylands Library, Manchester.*
BMC   *Catalogue of the Greek Coins in the British Museum.*
CAH   *Cambridge Ancient History.*
CB   W.M. Ramsay, *Cities and Bishoprics of Phrygia*, 2 vols. (Oxford, 1895).
CIG   *Corpus Inscriptionum Graecarum.*
CIJ   *Corpus Inscriptionum Iudaicarum.*
CIL   *Corpus Inscriptionum Latinarum.*
CIS   *Corpus Inscriptionum Semiticarum.*
CP   *Classical Philology.*
CR   *The Classical Review.*
CRE   W.M. Ramsay, *The Church in the Roman Empire before AD 170* (London, 3rd edn, 1894).
CSHB   *Corpus Scriptorum Historiae Byzantinae.*
DGRA   Sir W. Smith, *Dictionary of Greek and Roman Antiquities* (London, 3rd edn, 1890).
EB   *Encyclopaedia Biblica.*
EBr   *Encyclopaedia Britannica.*
EQ   *The Evangelical Quarterly.*
Expos   *The Expositor.*
ExpT   *The Expository Times.*
FGH   *Die Fragmente der griechischen Historiker*, ed. F. Jacoby (Leiden, 1954–).
HDB   *A Dictionary of the Bible*, ed. J. Hastings (Edinburgh, 1898–).

ICC	*International Critical Commentary.*
IG	*Inscriptiones Graecae.*
IGRR	*Inscriptiones Graecae ad Res Romanas Pertinentes.*
ILS	*Inscriptiones Latinae Selectae*, ed. H. Dessau.
Jahreshefte	*Jahreshefte des österreichischen archäologischen Instituts in Wien.*
JBL	*Journal of Biblical Literature.*
JDAI	*Jahrbuch des deutschen archäologischen Instituts.*
JEH	*Journal of Ecclesiastical History.*
JHS	*Journal of Hellenic Studies.*
JRS	*Journal of Roman Studies.*
JSS	*Journal of Semitic Studies.*
JTS	*Journal of Theological Studies.*
LAE	A. Deissmann, *Light from the Ancient East*, tr. L.R.M. Strachan (London, 1927).
LBW	P. Le Bas and W.H. Waddington, *Voyage archéologique en Grèce et en Asie Mineure* (Paris, ? c.1843–).
LCL	*Loeb Classical Library.*
LSh	Lewis and Short, *A Latin Dictionary* (Oxford, 1879).
LSJ	Liddell, Scott and Jones, *A Greek-English Lexicon*, New Edition (Oxford, 1940).
MAMA	*Monumenta Asiae Minoris Antiqua.*
NBD	*The New Bible Dictionary* (London, 1962).
NovT	*Novum Testamentum.*
NTS	*New Testament Studies.*
OCD	*Oxford Classical Dictionary.*
OCT	*Oxford Classical Texts.*
OGIS	*Orientis Graeci Inscriptiones Selectae.*
PEQ	*Palestine Exploration Quarterly.*
PG	*Patrologia Graeca*, ed. J.P. Migne.
PIR	*Prosopographia Imperii Romani*
PL	*Patrologia Latina*, ed. J.P. Migne.
PW	Pauly–Wissowa–Kroll, *Realencyclopädie der classischen Altertumswissenschaft.*
RA	*Revue archéologique.*
SC	W.M. Ramsay, *The Letters to the Seven Churches of Asia* (London, 1904).
SEG	*Supplementum Epigraphicum Graecum.*
SIG³	*Sylloge Inscriptionum Graecarum*, 3rd edn.
SPTR	W.M. Ramsay, *St. Paul the Traveller and the Roman Citizen* (London, 1895).

TB	*Tyndale Bulletin.*
TDNT	*Theological Dictionary of the New Testament*, ed. G. Kittel, tr. G.W. Bromiley (Grand Rapids, 1964-1976).
TLZ	*Theologische Literaturzeitung.*
TWNT	*Theologisches Wörterbuch zum Neuen Testament*, ed. G. Kittel (Stuttgart, 1933-1979).
ZNTW	*Zeitschrift für die neutestamentliche Wissenschaft.*
ZPE	*Zeitschrift für Papyrologie und Epigraphik.*

Chapter 1

INTRODUCTION

1. *The Topic Introduced*

In the words of H.B. Swete, 'The book [of Revelation] starts with a well-defined historical situation, to which reference is made again at the end, and the intermediate visions which form the body of the work cannot on any reasonable theory be dissociated from their historical setting. The prophecy arises out of local and contemporary circumstances; it is, in the first instance at least, the answer of the Spirit to the fears and perils of the Asian Christians towards the end of the first century. Hence all that can throw light on the Asia of A.D. 70-100, and upon Christian life in Asia during that period, is of primary importance to the student of the Apocalypse, not only in view of the local allusions in cc. ii–iii, but as helping to determine the aim and drift of the entire work' (*The Apocalypse of St. John*, 2nd edn, London, 1907, p. ccxviii).

Swete is surely right in stressing the importance of the historical approach to the book, and the letters to the seven churches constitute the section in which the historical situation is most explicit and approachable. Here is the key to the easiest lock in an admittedly difficult text.[1]

Due weight must be given to the primary importance of the Old Testament, with whose words and concepts the writer's mind was saturated. We find however that reminiscences of it are repeatedly applied to the particular needs of local churches. The letters have in fact a traceable *Sitz im Leben* in the local communities.

The study also raises some wider implications. The Revelation is firmly datable at a point within the crucial and obscure period in the history of the church which follows the fall of Jerusalem in AD 70. After that date the focus of Christianity shifted from Judaea and was not yet established in Rome. One of its strongest centres meanwhile was found in the Graeco-Anatolian society of the great cities of proconsular Asia. There Judaism of the Diaspora met Hellenistic and oriental culture under the authority of Rome. The information about the churches as derived from the letters is there set in a context amenable to a degree of independent historical investigation. Now some reconstructions offered by the literary-critical study of New Testament texts seem open to objection precisely because their conclusions are not independently verifiable and their chronological assumptions uncertain.[2] It will therefore be our concern in part to examine the racial, religious and social composition of the cities, their problems and ways of thought, and to seek to correlate our inferences from the text with the study of the environment. Our primary aim will be to determine what the letters meant to their original readers. In the process we may hope to find some elements to contribute to a picture of the church in the period between AD 70 and 100. We disclaim any pretension to do more: the data are too fragmentary. It will be better to place correctly a few pieces of the jigsaw than arbitrarily to reshape them to build a picture which may prove to be largely erroneous.

The following pages are written in the conviction of the importance of a careful historical method and of the need to subject texts and interpretations as far as possible to the testing of independent material drawn from classical literature, epigraphy, numismatics and archaeology. It is important that the conventional boundaries of different disciplines should thus sometimes be bridged, and the greatest variety of relevant evidence be permitted to contribute to the elucidation of the text.

2. *The Historical Problem*

a. *Some Observations on the Dating of the Revelation*
An exhaustive treatment of such perennial problems as the authorship and date of the Revelation lies outside the scope of the present work. On authorship we need only note that the writer introduces himself by the name 'John' (Rev. 1.9), and that he displays an intimate knowledge of the Old Testament and of the circumstances of the seven cities whose churches he addresses, and we may infer from his background of thought and the strange Semitisms of his style that he was of Jewish origin. Beyond that his particular identity is immaterial

for the purposes of this study. Occasional reference to him as 'John' is a matter of convenience.[3]

The problem of date, however, is a crucial factor in the historical *Sitz im Leben*. I started with a provisional acceptance of the orthodox Domitianic dating, and have been confirmed in that view by further study. It is no part of our present purpose to repeat the broad consensus of internal and external testimony on which that conclusion is based nor to expatiate upon such acknowledged difficulties as the identification of the kings of Rev. 17.9-11.[4] Some of these problems involve wider questions of the unity of the book and its possible use of unassimilated sources. The immediate issue concerns the internal evidence of the seven letters and the extent to which related passages later in the book give information which may be linked with them. Here we must anticipate the results of some subsequent discussion in asserting in general terms the literary and historical unity of the whole.

R.H. Charles (pp. xciv-xcv, 43-46) argues that the letters were originally written under Vespasian, but revised by John himself to make them suitable for incorporation in a work issued under Domitian. He maintains that except in Rev. 3.10 they contain no reference to the cult of the Caesars or to the universal martyrdom implied by the later chapters. He concludes that that one verse, together with the introductory titles and concluding formulae, belongs to the revision.

The whole trend of the historical study of the text seems to tell decisively against such a partition of the epistles. The case for their internal unity of situation, as for much else in the Revelation, must be argued cumulatively throughout our study. At this stage two particular objections may be asserted in reply to Charles: (1) that the emperor-cult is integral to the situation underlying several letters; (2) that the introductory and concluding formulae are likewise appropriate to the circumstances of the churches addressed: their unity with their epistles is in a common historical setting rather than of an artificial literary kind, as Charles supposed (pp. 25-27).

I shall defer to the next section the detailed consideration of this *Sitz im Leben* and of the topic of the imperial cult in particular, and concentrate here on a few data in Rev. 2–3 which tend to confirm our Domitianic dating of the whole. The matter requires great caution, for some allusions are to factors operative in the cities over considerable periods of their history. There are however some cases where we may suspect a correlation with a datable event or development.

(1) Rev. 3.17 has been connected with Laodicea's unaided recovery from the earthquake of Nero's reign (Ramsay, *SC*, p. 428). The evidence here might be variously read, but I argue the strong probability that the reference is to a later stage of the reconstruction, mentioned in the earlier *Sibylline Oracles* (4.108, of about AD 80), and occupying a full generation between the disaster and the time of Domitian.[5]

(2) We adduce reasons for accepting the view that Rev. 6.6 alludes to an edict issued by Domitian in AD 92 to restrict the growing of vines in the provinces (Suet. *Dom.* 7.2; 14.2) and connect this with the contemporary setting of the Philadelphian letter.[6]

(3) In Rev. 2.7 there may be reference to the abuse of the right of asylum in Ephesus, a problem known from the ostensibly contemporary letters of Apollonius of Tyana (Nos. 65, 66) to have been acute under Domitian.

(4) An explanation is offered of the 'synagogues of Satan' at Smyrna and Philadelphia (Rev. 2.9; 3.9) which links them with conflicts operative under Domitian. It is further argued that the occasion was provided by the conjunction of that emperor's policy with the insertion of the curse of the Minim in the *Shemoneh 'Esreh* about AD 90. The aftermath of the controversy may be traced in a problem passage in Ignatius (*ad Philad.* 8.2) as it affected one of the very churches under discussion.

(5) The problems of Philadelphia may have been intensified by the recent occurrence of widespread famine in Asia Minor (cf. again Rev. 6.6). There is at least an instructive parallel in an inscription of Pisidian Antioch of AD 93.[7]

(6) The Salutaris bequest in Ephesus (*BM Inscrs* 481, of AD 104) seems to mark a resurgence of paganism in the city. This may be explicable as a reaction against a revival of Christian zeal among the recipients of the Apocalyptic letter.

Certain expressions, while not to be understood as allusions to datable events, offer parallels with contemporary evidence, especially datable poems of Statius and Martial. An *aureus* of the empress Domitia depicts her deified infant son seated on a globe and stretching out his hands to seven stars.[8] Again, a comparison of Domitian with the morning star appears in a poem celebrating his entrance of his consulship in January 95 (Stat. *Silv.* 4.1; cf. Rev. 2.28). Points of this kind lend themselves to the case for believing that the

Revelation is strongly antithetical to the language of the imperial cult as current under Domitian.

Some other general indications point in the same direction. The Domitianic date will accord well with the growth of a prophetic movement in Philadelphia, represented by Ammia in the following generation (Euseb. *HE* 5.17.3-4) and later diverging into Montanism.[9] Again, comparative study of the relevant epistles of Ignatius is instructive. The case of Philadelphia is again specially illuminating. It will be argued that a Jewish opposition, impelled by the revival stemming from Jamnia, may have faced Christians with a crisis of belief and authority adumbrated in Rev. 3.7-13 and explicit in Ignatius.

Many other passages in the letters may allude to earlier events which continued to influence a local situation. But no plausible pointer seems to require either an earlier or a later date, though some would permit an earlier.[10]

We accordingly reaffirm the Domitianic date of the letters in the light of the kind of evidence here considered, while recognizing that many of these indications are uncertain. Cumulatively they align themselves with the case widely accepted on other grounds that the Revelation was written about AD 95.

b. *Some Implications of the Problem*

We have begun with the question of date because an important facet of our case is the fact that we have here a picture, however incomplete, of seven local churches in a crucial but obscure phase of Christian history.

The Revelation may be firmly placed within the problematic period between Paul and Ignatius. Other New Testament books whose evidence is sometimes pressed into service for the period 70-100 are of disputable dating. Thus the First Gospel, as a strongly ecclesiastical book, is often made a source for the condition and problems of the church in this period. I suggest that some of the results obtained by form-critical and redaction-critical approaches to this Gospel must be treated as highly conjectural unless amenable to testing by independent historical materials. I submit that the history of the church in this period is almost unchronicled and that such external materials as do exist are commonly overlooked. I question the grounds on which the *necessity* of a post-70 date for Matthew is based. This dating is a matter of probability, and it offers no secure foundation for a historical argument.

One crucial passage in Matthew (17.24-27) bears directly on a factor of importance to our present study. The incident is peculiar to this Gospel. If it could be considered as an insertion of the evangelist to give the authority of Jesus to a payment to the Romans, it might constitute prima facie evidence of a Flavian, even especially of a Domitianic, date for the Gospel.[11] The commentators however see here an early Petrine or Palestinian tradition reflecting the setting of the half-shekel Temple tax (the *didrachmon* of Jos. *Antiq.* 18.9.1.312, as in Mt. 17.24), before Vespasian diverted the proceeds to himself as earthly representative of Jupiter Capitolinus.[12]

An attempt to treat the historical problems of Matthew's Gospel is clearly far beyond the scope of our study, and would have to be considered on a far wider front. Here a digression on a point of some later relevance (see next section) draws attention to the need to formulate a problem. Some widely received judgments are open to challenge from the standpoint of insistence on the relevance of historical verification. The date of the tradition seems to be pre-70: the case for later editing in a local church environment is not established.

C.H. Dodd in an important article argues that Luke 19.42-44 and 21.20-24 are not post-70 editorial elaborations of Mark 13.14-17, but rely on an independent tradition with a wholly Old Testament background.[13]

These isolated examples from Matthew and Luke lead us into the abstruse historical problem of the significance of the fall of Jerusalem for Christianity. The event is often studied merely as a possible subject of allusion which may offer a simple criterion of date. There are few attempts to trace its historical implications.[14] Some of them may, I suggest, be traced on the political stage, and their outworkings are important for the Domitianic period.

Then, too, the study of the racial, religious and social composition of the Asian cities and churches may be expected to throw some independent light on the condition of Christianity in a focal area in this obscure period. Material of this kind may be offered as a control upon the processes of literary criticism, to introduce an element of verification and the possibility of refutation. Without some independent criterion there is no guarantee that the reconstructions which look cogent at one stage of the debate will not seem unconvincing when its fashions and assumptions have been challenged.

There are some particular areas of Christian history to which our study has a contribution to make. Such are (1) Christianity and the imperial cult, and in particular the nature of the problems the church faced under Domitian; (2) Christianity in the pagan world generally and the position of Christians in the social life of a Graeco-Roman city; (3) the relationship of the church with Judaism at this period—a point of great importance; (4) the difficult question of authority, perhaps in the context of an expanding docetism, where the historical situation suggests an incipient challenge to the Christian use both of the Jewish scriptures and of the apostolic writings. I suggest these four areas of opposition were interrelated in the circumstances of Domitianic Asia.

The present case is essentially cumulative. Many of its details are points of little individual significance. Collectively they contribute to an understanding of (1) the whole situation to which each letter is addressed; (2) the interpretation of each letter in its whole historical context; (3) the related passages elsewhere in the Revelation; and (4) some of the contemporary problems of the church in Asia and beyond. The evidences are contained in the body of the book, for the strength of the whole case is in the whole argument. Many parts are acknowledged to be tentative, if only because the fragmentary nature of the evidence precludes a false dogmatism. We shall however attempt to rest conclusions as far as possible upon the natural reading of positive and explicit materials.

The fragmentary state of the evidence in fact needs to be strongly emphasized. I have to give a partial picture, but wish to make it a balanced one. I sometimes have to employ an intricate circumstantial argument to support the tentative solution of a difficulty which may then have been recognized instantly as a plain allusion to daily life. The impact of a circumstantial case is not strengthened by a proliferation of inconclusive reasoning. Sometimes however I must in fairness state and examine the evidence in areas where any judgment must be tentative. This cannot weaken my case if its foundations are sound, but it may open a door to criticism if the difficulty of the matter is not made clear. It is open to another to explain the available evidence better. And it is better to make the attempt than simply to reinforce the sway of false assumption.[15]

c. *Some Aspects of the Historical Setting*
The effects of the fall of Jerusalem on Christianity are highly problematical. The implications for Christian thinking on subjects

like eschatology are often discussed, but remain obscure, and are perhaps overrated: the social and legal position of Christians and their relation with Roman authority and with Judaism are not often considered. Yet in this area there were certainly subtle, yet profound and complex, changes. On one point our evidence is explicit, the transference of the Temple tax to Jupiter Capitolinus.[16]

This measure is readily intelligible as offering every Jew implicitly a licence to practise his religion and an exemption from the requirements of the imperial cult on condition of payment and the implied recognition of the Roman national deity. Judaism could no longer be permitted a uniquely privileged position. Yet its intransigence made practical toleration prudent. Vespasian's formula imposed a *modus vivendi* which also helped to replenish the depleted treasury. And under his conciliatory regime the possibilities inherent in the situation were probably not developed. But in times of pressure the Jewish Christian had a potential refuge from the obligations of emperor-worship by trading on his radical and religious origin. He might legitimately argue that Paul had established before Gallio and perhaps before Nero's own court that his faith lay within the legal definition of Judaism. The Gentile Christian was presumably denied this recourse.

Before Domitian the enforcement of imperial cult against Christians probably depended on the initiative of a private accuser and the attitude of a local governor. We must next consider an important passage in Suetonius, *Domitian* 12.2: *Praeter ceteros Iudaicus fiscus acerbissime actus est; ad quem deferebantur qui vel inprofessi Iudaicam viverent vitam vel dissimulata origine inposita genti tributa non pependissent.*

It is unnecessary to postulate here two categories of persons. Suetonius is unconcerned about theological distinctions and cites representative extremes of people who might have escaped the tax.[17] Whether or not he regarded Christianity as a *Iudaica vita* he makes the point that all suspect cases were rigorously investigated. Several categories would doubtless appear in the process: Gentile proselytes and adherents, Jewish and Gentile Christians, and even apostate Jews. To the authorities these distinctions were immaterial provided the victims paid up. But the situation placed the Jewish communitites in a position of peculiar power. By disowning a Christian and informing against him, they might deprive him of his possible recourse to toleration at a price, and render him liable to the emperor-cult.

There are many indications that this may have happened extensively. When the Diaspora was reinforced, especially in the great commercial cities of Asia, by Palestinian refugees, existing racial and religious tensions became exacerbated.[18] The Jewish communities maintained their status as the exclusive chosen race even if their standing as a people was no longer recognized by Rome. A remarkable phrase in a Hadrianic inscription of Smyrna reads οἱ ποτὲ Ἰουδαῖοι (*CIG* 3148.30 = *CIJ* 742). Mommsen and Ramsay are probably right to regard this as allusion to a community which kept its ethnic identity while no longer having legal status (*SC*, pp. 272, 444n). And Smyrna is precisely the city of crucial interest to our study. For the writer of Rev. 2.9 the true Jews were a spiritual people, not an ethnic group (cf. John 8.33ff.; Rom. 2.28-9; and the closely contemporary 1 Clem. 31ff.), but the synagogue community inevitably represented visible Judaism in the eyes of authority.

About AD 90 the curse of the Minim was introduced into the 'Eighteen Benedictions'.[19] This provided a means of detecting Christians in the synagogues. The pressure of the emperor-cult explains why they sought acceptance there, and also accounts for the puzzling proselytization of Gentile Christians to Judaism at Philadelphia, as implied by Ignatius (*ad Philad.* 6.1).[20] The two cities from which the particular evidence of Jewish activity against the church is drawn are those which possessed 'synagogues of Satan' in Rev. 2.9 and 3.9.[21]

We are now in a position to suggest some of the forces at work in the Domitianic persecution, a topic on which direct evidence is scanty.[22] One factor is the emperor's insistence on the obligations of imperial cult. He required to be addressed as *dominus et deus* (Suet. *Dom.* 13; Mart. *Epig.* 9.56.3). Moreover, the specific antagonism between the church and the cult is to be seen in the growth of what Deissmann termed a 'polemical parallelism' (*LAE*, pp. 342ff.) between their titles and institutions, the evidence for which is largely derived from the great cities of proconsular Asia. This antagonism is evidently reflected in the imagery of the Revelation.

A second factor is to be seen in the part played by the Jews. The rigorous extraction of tax from them must have revealed the large number of persons anxious to avoid the obligations of emperor-cult, and many of these were disowned by the synagogues. Individual Jews may have informed against individual Christians, or the synagogues may have provided on occasion lists of bona fide members of their congregations.[23] The authorities, primarily concerned with tax-avoidance, may thus have had forced on their attention a powerful movement which appeared to defy the emperor under the guise of a Judaism which the official Jews repudiated. A systematic inquisition would naturally follow.

The Christian was faced with a cruel dilemma. His safety was assured only by preparedness, in time of need, to identify himself either with pagan society, by sacrifice to the emperor and the expected participation in the religious aspects of guilds and social life (the 'Nicolaitan' answer), or with Judaism on whatever terms would gain him acceptance in the synagogue, that is, probably, at least an implicit denial of his Lord. The first inducement was naturally strongest in those places where the pressures of authority and pagan society were most direct (Pergamum and Thyatira, and also Ephesus, where it was steadfastly rejected): the 'synagogues of Satan' brought the opposite threat against those who scorned the pagan compromise (Smyrna and Philadelphia, and perhaps the commended minority in Sardis).[24] The situation also introduced a new occasion of disunion between Jewish and Gentile Christians, on whom it impinged differently.

The scanty secular evidence will readily fit this pattern. The condemnation of the emperor's own cousin Flavius Clemens while consul in AD 95 may not be at all representative. Yet Dio's presentation of the charge (ἔγκλημα ἀθεότητος, ὑφ' ἧς καὶ ἄλλοι ἐς τὰ τῶν Ἰουδαίων ἤθη ἐξοκέλλοντες πολλοὶ κατεδικάσθησαν, Dio Cass. 67.14) implies a wider movement against persons whose connection with Judaism is described with studied vagueness. It would fit well those who denied the imperial god from a standpoint which was not acceptably Jewish. To the authorities it represented disloyalty, and its religious content was immaterial, so long as Jewish susceptibilities were not dangerously offended. Again, Pliny's letter to Trajan about the Christians (*Ep.* 10.96) refers to some who had abandoned their faith twenty (or twenty-five) years previously,[25] that is, about AD 92 (or possibly 87), perhaps under social pressures. Pliny also testifies that when investigations were prosecuted several forms of the mischief came to light and anonymous accusations spread (10.96.4-5). In a similar way we may understand the background of the legend *calumnia Iudaici fisci sublata*, which is so prominent on the coinage of Nerva. The exactions under Domitian had given free rein to informers, and his successor found it desirable to emphasize his intention to remove the abuse. The fact that such importance was attached to the point suggests that the issue had become a highly emotive and dangerous one on which any innocent citizen might be accused of an irregular Jewish affiliation which could be construed as treasonable in one who was not paying the tax. While other innocent victims doubtless suffered, the Christians were particularly vulnerable.[26]

We conclude that contemporary secular evidence accords with the Christian tradition of persecution under Domitian, but that it probably took the form of the more systematic and deliberate exploitation of pressures inherent in the situation. Nerva did not remove the danger: it might be reactivated whenever circumstances and personalities concurred.

I suggest that another related problem for the church of this period was that of scriptural authority. At about this time, though the occasion is unknown, it was declared that 'the gospel and the books of the heretics' were not sacred scripture (G.F. Moore, *Judaism*, I.243).[27] Moore sees here an indication that Christians were interpreting the fall of Jerusalem as a judgment on the Jews for their rejection of the Messiah, and also that they already claimed the status of 'scripture' for their 'gospel'. A few years later the epistles of Ignatius testify to the growth of a double threat to the church from Judaism and Docetism. The latter challenged the events whose record was now dependent on the new writings after the generation of eye-witnesses had passed. We may readily believe that Jewish attacks on these writings reinforced the inducements to wavering Christians to return to the synagogue. This may help to explain a problematic passage in Ignatius (*Philad.* 8.2).[28] We argue that many were no longer satisfied with Ignatius's traditional answers from the *euangelion*. The church was being challenged to prove its case from Jewish scriptures (if with Lightfoot we thus understand *archeia*), and its claim to be able to do so was itself in dispute. The fashion of Christian apologetic by allegorical Messianic interpretation of the Old Testament may have been both stimulated and challenged by this development.[29]

The immediate interest of the point lies in the fact that the problem is known from Philadelphia, the very place where Jews were making proselytes of Gentile Christians, and which subsequently became the probable source of Montanism, a movement concerned with the authority of new prophecy and perhaps finding its charter in the Revelation.[30] We suppose then that the curse of the Minim and the definition of the Jewish scriptures worked together to face the Christian who withdrew from emperor-cult with a combined threat of rejection and of inducement to doubt the foundations of his own faith. This provided a double reason for seeking acceptance in the synagogue.

The character of the controversy between Jews and Christians as here postulated is further illustrated both in subsequent Christian writings[31] and in the Revelation itself. Here the Jewish opposition seems to be mentioned explicitly only in Rev. 2 and 3, though the later chapters repeatedly work out the implications of the claim that the Christians are now the true Jews. The redeemed are 'out of every kindred, and tongue, and people, and nation' (5.9), but their blessings are conceived in strictly Hebraic terms. The heavenly city is the 'new Jerusalem', and the church is apparently identified with the twelve tribes who are sealed (7.4-8).[32] The term 'Jew' is throughout a title of honour, which is wrongly usurped by one section of John's opponents. But the ultimate antagonist throughout is Rome. It is only through the policy of Rome that the Jewish opposition has received its temporary power. It is widely recognized that Rome is depicted in the Revelation under several figures: the dragon of 12.3ff., the beast of 13.1ff., and the woman of 17.3ff. The details of these passages cannot be pursued here. Ramsay (*SC*, pp. 94-100) and Caird (p. 171) may well be right in identifying the second beast from the land (Rev. 13.11ff.) with the Commune of the province of Asia. On this assumption we might fairly expect to find illumination on the methods of enforcement of imperial cult from the language of 13.13-17.

3. *The Character and Destination of the Revelation*

a. *The Revelation as Apocalyptic*
The topic of apocalyptic needs to be considered first. I believe that the connection of the Revelation with earlier works of this genre has been overestimated. If apocalyptic, it is apocalyptic with a differ-ence.[33] Previous samples were pseudonymous, and generally imitative and pedestrian. But if John used the machinery of a traditional form, he invested that form with a new dimension, and his work cannot be judged within the limits of a convention. The content is here important, even though the rigid and elaborate structure invites

concentration upon the form. The imagery is used in a pointed and allusive way: the whole differs from much other apocalyptic in the kind of way that allegory is regarded as differing from parable. In extra-Biblical apocalyptic only perhaps the earlier Sibylline Oracles display any comparable concern with the details of geography and history, and the Fourth Book, which alone permits confident judgment on its unity and provenance, was written in Asia shortly before the Revelation (cf. J.B. Lightfoot, *Colossians and Philemon*, p. 96).

Again, detailed literary indebtedness of the Revelation to surviving extra-Biblical apocalypses is unexpectedly difficult to substantiate. It may readily be shown that John shared with them a common stock of imagery, but closer correspondences are too few and too doubtful to be pressed. The list in Charles (pp. lxxxii-lxxxiii) is very short and relates chiefly to 1 Enoch. He finds only two parallels between the seven letters and the Jewish Pseudepigrapha, Rev. 2.7 with *Test. Levi* 18.11 and Rev. 2.17 with *Test. Levi* 8.14. Both of these however are of Old Testament origin, respectively from Gen. 2.9 and Isa. 62.2.

b. *John's Vision and the Old Testament*

We have questioned the extent of the apocalyptic connections of the Revelation. Its relationship with the Old Testament can scarcely be overemphasized. If the point is not continually stressed in this study, it is only because we are here concerned with the historical problem. The Old Testament echoes are probably far more numerous than even the lengthy tabulations in Charles and Swete would suggest. Often our text seems to derive from a meditation combining two or three scriptural passages and applying mingled reminiscences of them all to the present need of a recipient church.[34] Sometimes these groupings may have derived from traditional exegesis,[35] or from existing *catenae* of Messianic *testimonia*.[36] If so, John's application of them is nevertheless luminously pointed and his mind seems to dwell on the context of each.[37]

The influence of the prophets on John's mind is especially strong (cf. Charles, p. lxv). J.W. Bowman draws attention to his repeated claim to this status of prophet for himself, perhaps prophet as opposed to apocalyptist.[38]

There is indeed no cogent reason for doubting the professed character of the book as the record of a vision: the view which explains this form as a literary device of apocalyptic seems to me inadequate.[39] Here however we shall be exclusively concerned with explaining the text in literary and historical terms. The raw materials of ecstatic experience might naturally be drawn from the background, the influences, concerns and responsibilities which pressed upon the person involved. These matters are open to investigation: it would not be wise to dogmatize about the manner of composition of the book. The use of written sources, for example, is neither demanded nor excluded. The open question is how far we may expect to find conscious literary dependence and how far the unconscious reproduction of those influences which pervaded John's mind. We have glanced at the Old Testament aspect: it is remarkable how the Old Testament is never explicitly quoted, but continually echoed and reapplied.

c. *Epistolary Form and Destination*
Deissmann has distinguished the 'real letter' from the literary epistle and places most of the New Testament specimens in the former category (*New Light on the New Testament*, pp. 51-61). This classification, criticized by Ramsay (*SC*, pp. 23-29) in its application to the Pauline correspondence, breaks down completely here. The book as a whole is given epistolary form (Rev. 1.4), and the main sequence of apocalyptic visions is introduced by seven letters of highly formalized parallel structure. They appear quite distinct from the body of the Apocalypse, but prove on analysis to be intimately linked with it.[40] It cannot be supposed that they were ever separately delivered, yet their existence cannot be sufficiently explained as literary convention, for their messages are real and contemporary, and the book containing them was, I believe, conveyed in sequence to the seven churches addressed. And, if literary, they represent a popular literature: doubtless their general sense and many of their allusions were readily understood by all Asian readers, but each is directed with peculiar force to strictly local circumstances.

The point is inseparable from the consideration of the destination of the book. Much ingenuity has been expended on the question why these seven churches were selected in this order. Why not Magnesia and Tralles, which had well-established churches when Ignatius wrote, and which were much greater cities than Thyatira or Philadelphia? Why not Troas, where Paul had found an open door (2 Cor. 2.12; cf. Acts 20.6-12)? The view that the number seven is significant for John as a symbol of universality is true but insufficient. Some of the other suggestions do not stand well under historical criticism.[41]

The work of Sir William Ramsay is instructive here as for much else in the study of the letters.[42] In view of the contrary influence of such notable scholars as W. Bauer and M. Goguel[43] it is well to restate his point. I consider that his arguments for finding in the seven cities the natural centres of communication for an itinerant Christian messenger are decisive, subject only to an inevitable uncertainty in some details of the picture (see *SC*, pp. 171-96). The 'seven churches' were probably recognized already as a group (Rev. 1.4, 11). Ephesus was the messenger's natural place of entry to the mainland of the province of Asia, and the other cities lay in sequence on a circular route round its inner territories. It may readily be supposed that a regular itinerary had been perfected since Pauline times and that the seven focal cities on the route had acquired a special importance as organizational and distributive centres for the church of the area.[44]

The assessment of Ramsay's reconstruction depends largely on the appreciation of geographical factors. In its essentials it corresponds clearly to the facts of communication,[45] and is capable of being worked out rigorously as a highly practical system for the most efficient dissemination of messages to all those cities of proconsular Asia where churches are likely to have existed. Ramsay's attempt to provide routes for secondary messengers operating from the seven cities is highly conjectural, but only because the distribution of churches is unknown to us. He shows in principle how well the scheme was conceived to cover the whole area. Troas was too far north to be efficently reached by the primary messenger: a man from Pergamum might cover it and Cyzicus. Again, Tralles, Magnesia and Miletus could all receive news from a secondary Ephesian messenger long before the original traveller had completed his main circuit. It would be natural, however, that John's supervision of the churches should be exercised over the recognized seven. These he knew intimately, and to them he sends specific and relevant messages.

This point is integral to our plea to view the book historically without a judgment coloured unduly by the supposition that it may be most fruitfully explained as representative of a certain type of apocalyptic, epistolary or dramatic composition. I want to insist on the comparative importance of the detailed historical criticism of background and content in a work which transcends its literary models.

d. *The Place of the Letters in the Revelation*
The intricate structure of the book is another point at issue. It

suggests a deliberate literary skill to which most apocalyptic makes
no pretension. But again we must argue that more of this unity
derives from the situation than is commonly allowed.

It is beyond the scope of this study to discuss the later chapers of
the Revelation in any detail. My present purpose is to clarify in the
light of the previous discussion some points of structure which bear
on interpretation of the letters.

(i) There is in fact a very close relationship between the letters and
other parts of the book.[46] The clearest correspondence is that
between the initial description by which Christ introduces himself to
each church and the attributes ascribed to him in the Patmos vision
(Rev. 1.12-20). These parallels are explicit and verbal, and are found
in all the letters except the Laodicean. A further relationship exists
between the letters and the vision of the heavenly Jerusalem in
Rev. 21–22. That city is set in implicit contrast with the imperfec-
tions of the seven actual earthly cities. The parallels are not in this
case obtrusive or systematic: there are repeated echoes of the same
images, promises developed in a larger context, particular opponents
overcome and disabilities reversed. A third area of relationship
connects the letters with the series of visions which occupy Rev. 4–
20. Here the parallels lend themselves even less to analysis. They are
just echoes of symbols and expressions which appear in the letters or
which suggest that the circumstances of those churches were present
to John's mind. A few of the correspondences are close and illuminating, but in general the reminiscences are elusive and marginal. The
phenomenon is impressive cumulatively rather than in detail.

(ii) The previous paragraph leaves open the question of the nature
and significance of these internal relationships. Both Swete (pp. xlvi-
xlviii) and Charles (p. lxxxviii) tabulate selected parallels as impressive
evidence of the book's unity of diction and authorship. That point is
important, but incidental to our present purpose. The trend of the
evidence cumulatively suggests that this essential unity is to be
established on a wider front, situational as well as verbal. A unity of
historical setting is not easily demonstrated in detail: many local and
contemporary references are probably contained in the later chapters,
but their identification requires caution. The best instances may be
those where a whole context reveals correspondences with a city and
its letter in which verbal and situational parallels reinforce each
other. Allusions to matters like the imperial cult are fairly clear in the
later chapters. The possibility of their offering local material must

also be noted, but used sparingly in the framework of relationship with the letters.

(iii) The explicit parallels between the letters and the Patmos vision raise most acutely the problem of priorities. It will be convenient to distinguish three kinds of priority which need not coincide: (1) priority of order, as encountered by the reader in progress from Rev. 1 to Rev. 22; (2) conceptual priority, as present to the mind of the writer who was familiar with the original situation; (3) interpretative priority, as unravelled by the modern student who does not share knowledge common to the writer and his original readers. Here we observe three points. First, many phrases in the vision of Rev. 1 are of local significance and their presence there anticipates their recurrence in Rev. 2–3. Secondly, conceptual priority in the use of those phrases is seen in the letters, where they are related explicitly to Christ's answer to a local situation in a named city. Thirdly, because this gives the clearest context it will commonly be for us the place of 'interpretative priority'. So I propose to concentrate on interpreting these symbols in the context of the letters rather than in an extensive discussion of Rev. 1.[47]

Two examples will illustrate the application of these principles. A Thyatiran reading 1.15 would on our view recognize *chalkolibanos* as a local product though the explicit association of the word with his city does not occur before 2.18. The reference in 1.15 to its being heated in a furnace may still be of interpretative value when linked to the primary local context. In contrast, the 'morning star', first mentioned in 2.28, may refer to something understood in Thyatira, but in default of a context there we are driven to interpret it through 22.16. In the case (2) and (3) may diverge.[48]

It must be emphasized that each text must be considered on its own merits, but mere priority of order is not decisive, and the setting in a letter is usually the right starting-point if the evidence permits.

e. *Other Possible Literary Relationships of the Letters*
It is not enough to build a case upon verbal parallels without attempting to evaluate them. One recurring distinction in our study is that between literary and situational relationships. There is for example the undoubted *literary* relationship with the Old Testament, but parallels with the Fourth Book of the Sibyllines are probably to be explained through a *situational* relationship, a nearness of date, place and genre.

This distinction is of value in relating the letters to other New

Testament writings. Charles finds that John uses Matthew, Luke, 1 Thessalonians, 1 and 2 Corinthians, Colossians, Ephesians, and possibly Galatians, 1 Peter and James (pp. lxv-lxvi and lxxxiii-lxxxvi). In many of these cases, however, a literary relationship seems very doubtful. The clear Gospel parallels are almost all with sayings of Jesus, and we cannot be sure that these were not known to John through oral tradition or sources of our Gospels. Many of the contacts with epistles are also debatable: they are often verbal details which may reflect no more than a common stock of current idiom. John's knowledge of some of these writings is probable enough, but the evidence does not warrant pressing the point. The possibility may be strengthened by the observation that his mind sometimes seems to dwell on the context of a passage which he reapplies. Thus Rev. 2.9-10 displays successive parallels with James 2.5 and 1.12; Rev. 3.3-5 corresponds with sayings of Jesus as in Mt. 24.42ff. and 10.32 combined with Lk. 12.8, and the Laodicean letter has remarkable echoes of Paul's letter to nearby Colossae. Both Rev. 3.14 and Col. 1.15, 18 appear to combat a form of speculative heresy known from Colossians to have been prevalent in the Lycus valley. This relationship is accordingly situational as well as probably literary. All these cases suggest that John sometimes meditates on New Testament passages in the manner of his treatment of the Old Testament.

There are other cases where the letters reflect the language of controversies treated elsewhere in the New Testament. The clearest example is the echo of the terms of the Apostolic Decree of Acts 15.20, 29 in Rev. 2.14 and 2.20. The origin of this grouping of prohibitions is in the Balaam narrative of Num. 25.1-2, but it evidently had an important history in New Testament times. So, despite the close verbal similarity with Acts (cf. *baros* in Rev. 2.24 with Acts 15.28), this relationship is not directly or primarily literary, but to be understood as deriving from an event and alluding to a definite decision which shaped the terms of subsequent Christian thinking. The allusion to Balaam in Rev. 2.14 may be linked with the history of a kindred controversy, and this may also be reflected in Jude 11 and 2 Pet. 2.15. The supposition of literary relationship in this case would be most hazardous.

The great importance of the province of Asia in the history of the primitive church is reflected extensively elsewhere in its literature. Its place in the Acts and in the Pauline and other epistles needs no special comment.[49] But something should be said about the earliest extra-Biblical Christian literature. The seven accepted letters of Ignatius, datable to about AD 115,[50] are of great value to our study, for three of them were addressed to three of our seven churches, Ephesus, Smyrna and Philadelphia, and a fourth to Polycarp, bishop of Smyrna. It is not clear whether Ignatius knew the Revelation: the matter will be studied in its place.[51] He may have heard phrases of it from the lips of Polycarp or others, but his relationship to it is essentially situational rather than literary. For this very reason his testimony is the more valuable. His impressions of the churches are independent. Yet his knowledge of them is that of a visitor at best. It may sometimes be very superficial.

The name of Polycarp is associated with a series of early Christian writings which shed some light on his church of Smyrna. Ignatius's epistle to him may well reflect a shared knowledge of Rev. 2.8-11: it offers the best evidence for supposing that Ignatius knew the Revelation. In Polycarp's own letter to the Philippians the same themes recur, though without traceable literary dependence: it is as though the writer had sought them meditatively in other scriptures.[52] The Martyrdom of Polycarp and the later *Acta Pionii* may assimilate their heroes and events to a pattern deriving from Rev. 2.8-11.[53] In these historical documents of the church in Smyrna we may glimpse the Revelation as a formative influence. And the strength of local tradition which it reveals is a constant theme of the culture of the ancient *polis* to which we shall have occasion to return.

The subject of classical literature claims relatively slight attention at this point. Important source-material will be found in a great variety of ancient writings where no question of literary relationship arises. Such correlations as those between Rev. 2.8-11 and the Smyrna orations of Aelius Aristides are the more impressive on that account. They give a remarkable insight into the forms of local pride and culture. The connection is situational.

Philostratus's *Life of Apollonius of Tyana* alone is more problematic. Its parallels with Christian documents lend colour to the widely held view that it is an anti-Christian polemic which presents its hero as a rival to Jesus.[54] The authenticity of the surviving letters ascribed to Apollonius is likewise uncertain (cf. *Vit. Ap.* 1.2). In both works the seer is represented as having visited some of our cities (Ephesus, Smyrna and Sardis) at the very period of the Revelation. There seems to be some genuine and valuable local material, especially in the letters. In other cases Philostratus may be taking pains to achieve local verisimilitude; this will at least indicate the existence of local features which were known to his readership.[55] It seems possible that Philostratus knew the Revelation among other New Testament writings.[56]

4. *Methods and Sources*

a. *Observations on Methods of Interpretation*
The history of the many schools of interpretation of the Revelation has been illuminatingly traced by R.H. Charles in his *Studies in the Apocalypse*. Our present method is of necessity that which he terms 'Contemporary-Historical'. To suggest that this is basic is not to disparage other approaches: it is for us the key to the easiest lock, and a difficult text is best unravelled from its clearest and most easily verified sections. *Difficile per difficilius* is bad method. The problems of methodology are in any case narrowed by our concentration on the historical exegesis of the letters. Here the relevance of this approach to the 'things which are' is undisputed, and the alternatives are either less applicable or less germane to our purpose. The Literary-Critical approach needs attention, but its scope is limited by the admitted and intricate unity of the composition.

The present aim is simply to tabulate, especially in the light of the preceding discussion, a few principles governing the handling of the text.

(1) Relate the words and content of a passage to its Old Testament prototype wherever possible.

(2) Discover what these words and concepts were intended to mean to their original readers.[57]

(3) This involves making the broadest possible study of their ways of thought and cultural background. It is important to have a picture of the character and circumstances of the cities. How much Jewish influence was there? What were the local relations of the Jews and Christians, and of both to the pagan community? What kind of allusions might the readers be expected to understand?

(4) We must recognize the varied manner of allusion to contemporary facts. The reference may be specific and pointed (e.g. 'lukewarmness' at Laodicea) or else an idea is used which might suggest a variety of application (so perhaps the 'white stone' at Pergamum). Some symbols appear to express an aspect of truth in Christ as set in implicit contrast with a false substitute familiar to the people of the

city addressed. In this connection we may expect to find analogues with formative features of local religion.[58] In face of the diversity of material we must discriminate, but cannot lightly treat any possibility as rigid, exclusive or final. We must examine the relationship of different kinds of explanation to determine which are primary, necessary, sufficient, legitimate or possible.

(5) Situational and verbal parallels elsewhere in the Revelation may cautiously be used as confirmatory evidence for explanations related to the local context.

(6) There is at times some measure of identification of church with city. This idea needs cautious handling, but we must recognize the remarkable strength and individuality of environmental influence in ancient city life. The churches are apt to be judged by their varying response to their surroundings.

(7) The subsequent history of some churches is noteworthy, especially where it shows the Revelation as a formative influence. This evidence may on occasion by used retrospectively as an index of the original understanding of the text.

(8) Three pairs of letters, Ephesus and Sardis, Smyrna and Philadelphia, Pergamum and Thyatira, specially lend themselves to comparative study, and many interrelated points of similarity and contrast occur throughout them. These parallels are incidental and situational rather than literary or structural,[59] and often indicate features of importance in the conditions of the contemporary church in Asia generally. It is not to be assumed that similar expressions necessarily reflect precisely similar backgrounds in different cities. Thus we should be wary of using Jezebel's teaching as normative of Nicolaitanism merely because it shares features and tendencies characteristic of that movement at Pergamum.

(9) It is suggested that explanations involving etymologies of words or names be used only where there is evidence or likelihood of the contemporary popular currency of those derivations. Currency, not correctness, is the criterion.

b. *The Presentation of this Study*
A few comments may usefully be added at this stage about the arrangement and viability of this study.

(1) The pattern of individual chapters is varied according to the nature of the material. The explicit references of the Laodicean letter lend themselves to treatment in the framework of an exposition of the

text: the Philadelphian requires a more historical approach.

(2) No attempt is made to study every letter exhaustively. The evidence is often very limited, and it has seemed best to present selectively the materials which have a real contribution to make to the interpretation. This selectivity is especially applied to the case of the long and obscure letter to Thyatira. I have endeavoured however always to treat the text fairly and to note its important difficulties, even though I must leave many conclusions open or tentative. It is integral to my task to deal with the evidence, limited as it often is, rather than to present a one-sided case.

(3) Many of the general principles of the study are summarized in this introduction: the particular conclusions from the argument of each chapter are summarized at its end.

The objection may be raised that the whole thesis of this book proceeds from assumptions about local applicability which may simply not be true. It may be said that a caution in the particular is here combined with an unjustified overconfidence about the legitimacy of the whole undertaking.

In one sense I am not offering anything unusual. It might be regarded as an attempt to find the *Sitz im Leben* of the letters in the church, but to do it through a painstaking, if tentative, search through the available positive and external evidence. The validity of the attempt does not hinge on the acceptance of the whole. If some parts stand, the principle merits consideration. A cumulative case is validated by a sufficiency of evidence; if an excess is offered, and some of it is rejected, the basic case is not thereby overthrown. But the attempt to make a fair study of the material dictates the need to tackle many uncertain aspects, and inconclusive discussions open the way to criticisms.

Such criticism needs, I think, to acknowledge the limitations of the evidence. Of course I should not resort to circumstantial pleading if I could be more specific. But knowledge of the period and locality is a difficult matter, where intricate discussion of the bearing of fragmentary materials is sometimes a necessity. I cannot pretend to know all the answers: there is no place here for drawing far-reaching conclusions from the argument from silence.

c. *Summary of Sources*

(1) Ancient Literature. Some ancient writings have already been mentioned in the discussion of literary relationships. Others warrant a brief appraisal here.

The *Geography* of Strabo, completed under Tiberius, was written by a native of Asia Minor, and gives valuable, if often brief, comment about all the seven cities. The *Natural History* of Pliny the Elder (d. AD 79) is a vast, uncritical compendium of fact and fancy from which a variety of incidental information may be cautiously sifted. His Fifth Book includes an account of the relevant parts of Asia Minor, but this is often little more than an enumeration of geographical names. Pausanias, in the second century, though dealing exclusively with Greece proper, was probably a native of Magnesia-under-Sipylus, and gives some valuable information, especially about nearby Smyrna. Strange insights into Anatolian culture and popular superstition appear in Aelius Aristides[60] and in the *Onirocritica* of Artemidorus of Daldis in Eastern Lydia (both second century AD).

There are sources relevant to individual cities. In early times the strange genius of Heraclitus had been largely moulded by his reaction to the peculiar religious and topographical environment of Ephesus. And in two surviving Greek romances, by Achilles Tatius and Xenophon of Ephesus, the temple and cult of Ephesian Artemis figure prominently.[61] At Smyrna a local pride which claimed Homer issued in a characteristic literature exemplified by the lost local historian Hermogenes (*CIG* 3311), of about the first century AD, and the later epic of Quintus Smyrnaeus. Epictetus was a native of Hierapolis, though he spent his later year elsewhere, and his youth was almost contemporary with the Revelation. Arrian's apparently faithful transcriptions of his teaching offer a few significant touches. And the lost medical works of Demosthenes Philalethes of Laodicea are known to have had great influence, and the knowledge of his school may be reflected in the surviving treatises of Celsus, Scribonius Largus and Galen, the last himself a native of Pergamum.

Other works of Greek and Latin literature are important for the historical framework of the period or for background information. Important historians include some of earlier periods. The account of Croesus in Herodotus became proverbial, and we find allusion to it in every kind of later literature.[62] Other historians used extensively for earlier traditions include Xenophon, Polybius, Livy, Diodorus, Appian, Arrian and Dio Cassius. For the first century AD we are greatly indebted to both the *Annals* and the *Histories* of Tacitus, to the gossipy biographies of Suetonius, and again to Dio Cassius. The composition of Josephus's *Antiquities* stands close in time to the Revelation, and it is an indispensable source of information on

Jewish matters, though its reliability on partisan issues must be open to close scrutiny. Relevant historical materials are sometimes found in Cicero's correspondence, especially in letters written from Laodicea during his governorship of Cilicia, in the speeches of Dio Chrysostom, and in the younger Pliny's Bithynian letters (*Ep.* 10). The *Epigrams* of Martial and the *Silvae* of Statius are closely datable to the contemporary Rome of Domitian. Their picture is supplemented a little later by the lurid colours and allusive vividness of Juvenal.

(2) Inscriptions.

(3) Coinage.

(4) Excavation reports. Extensive work has been done only at Ephesus, Old Smyrna, Pergamum and Sardis.

(5) Accounts by modern travellers.

(6) Personal observation of topographical and other detail, and information collected locally or from persons with local knowledge.

(7) Place-names, ancient and modern: a dangerous field, but occasionally revealing of local or ancient thinking.

(8) Modern books. Monographs on individual sites are few, but perform a service in helping to gather the sources, which may otherwise be extraordinarily scattered.[63] The admirable archaeological guides by G.E. Bean have become available since the bulk of the research underlying this study was completed.[64]

The Revelation has been fortunate in the best of its commentators. Some older works are rich in historical insight, though dated and critically defective. The great commentaries of H.B. Swete, R.H. Charles and I.T. Beckwith deserve special mention for their constant exegetical value, though Charles's literary theories commend themselves to few.[65] The wealth of cultural analogy in Moffatt is suggestive, though its value is often suspect, and its assumptions about provenance, chronology and relationship must be carefully checked. F.J.A. Hort bequeathed a fragmentary commentary on the letters.[66] The lengthy introduction of E.B. Allo is particularly valuable for its detailed survey of previous commentators.[67] And most recently there are the major works of G.B. Caird, J.P.M. Sweet and P. Prigent, among others.

The value and applicability of the classes of primary evidence vary greatly. The most important kinds abound for Ephesus, Pergamum and Sardis, and yet our knowledge of them remains fragmentary and there is no guarantee of finding the answers we need amid the welter of detail. A lengthy study of the antiquities of these cities lies beyond our scope. For Thyatira and Philadelphia the scarcity of material poses different problems, and we are driven to the careful consideration of every hint. The evidence of epigraphy and numismatics is particularly important here. Coinage is often in fact the most illuminating key to local religion, and so to the formative ideas of the society.

d. *An Appraisal of Ramsay's Contribution*
There has already been occasion to refer to the special importance of the work of Sir William Mitchell Ramsay in the field of this study. I cannot leave the subject of sources and authorities without some evaluation of a writer who has exerted so large, though often unacknowledged, an influence.

Closer study of the areas in which Ramsay worked has progressively convinced me that he has often been both praised and abused for inadequate reasons.[68] While the pioneer quality of his work has been recognized, he is often censured for (1) an increasingly apologetic standpoint which vitiated his scholastic standing, and (2) a speculative tendency which was prone to go far beyond the evidence.

I am not concerned to defend him against (1), though it must be observed that the later Ramsay's approach was the product of a slow reversal of the Tübingen presuppositions of the early Ramsay. His convictions were those of a convert, persuaded despite himself by the kind of materials his own earlier researches had supplied (see *The Bearing of Recent Discovery on the Trustworthiness of the New Testament*, pp. 31 and *passim*). But (2), while doubtless often a justified criticism, needs closer examination. There are questions here both of method and of the character of Ramsay's writing. To take the latter first—there are demonstrably many places where he makes suggestions based upon little ostensible evidence, but where his views may nevertheless be substantiated, often from evidence contained elsewhere in his own writings. In other words we must sometimes acquit him of unsupported speculation while acknowledging that he has left much hasty and ill-documented writing. Sometimes he has simply omitted to provide applications to the text of materials documented in his earlier topographical works. A case in point is the water-supply of Laodicea, treated by M.J.S. Rudwick and E.M.B. Green as the subject of an allusion in Rev. 3.15-16.[69] Ramsay never discusses this passage in his work on the seven churches, but facts which go far to justify the later hypothesis are contained in his earlier *Cities and Bishoprics of Phrygia* (I.48f.). He might easily have anticipated their contribution. And there are other cases where a painstaking collection of contemporary material points cumulatively to a conclusion which Ramsay had already upheld on a perfunctorily expressed reasoning which may have concealed a real appreciation of the situation. The nature of our present task is sometimes to document his suggestions.

The charge that his method is speculative is less easily amenable to a generalized assessment. The difficulty of the subject-matter often consists in the fragmentary character of the evidence. This makes a correct use of analogy assume a particular importance, and many conclusions are necessarily tentative. Ramsay's intimate knowledge of the country and the institutions and ways of thought of the people may often equip him to use such methods with unusual insight. His results must here be treated with caution on the merits of the individual case.

A more serious problem concerns the Old Testament background of the Revelation, to which Ramsay does less than justice. If the text is sufficiently explained in these terms, why look further? May not the local allusions be in essence gratuitous and unnecessary speculations? We must consider these objections more closely than Ramsay has done.

The influence of Ramsay is most clearly seen in later books on the same theme. Most of them have valuable and suggestive comments, but their historical material is largely derived from him.[70] There are current in these books numerous demonstrable errors of fact, often where the writers have made mistaken and simplistic inferences from his carefully qualified statements. It would be invidious to particularize: misconceptions of the kind will be corrected where necessary in the body of this book.

Ramsay's indirect influence is often unacknowledged and not easily measured. His historical materials have in great measure passed into the general milieu of British scholarship. In Germany his contribution to the study of the Revelation has been noted in the work of E. Lohmeyer.

Chapter 2

THE PATMOS BACKGROUND

1. *John on Patmos*

Patmos harbour is situated some 40 miles from the mouth of the Maeander (Büyük Menderes), the nearest point of the Asian mainland, and about 65 miles from the site of Ephesus. The island is 8 miles long and 5 wide, and according to Pliny (*NH* 4.12.69) it measures 30 Roman miles in circumference.[1] Its coastline is so deeply indented that its land area is much less than these dimensions suggest. Its northern and southern blocks of volcanic hills are separated by a narrow isthmus, near which the ancient settlement stood on a small spur.[2] The small modern port of Skála lies just south, on the southern shore of the land-locked eastern bay which forms one of the finest natural anchorages in the Aegean. The modern town of Patmos clusters around the eleventh century monastery on the summit of Áyios Elías, the 800 foot eminence above, which dominates the southern half of the island.[3]

The primary source for John's sojourn on Patmos is Rev. 1.9. He there describes himself as 'companion' with his churches 'in tribulation and in the kingdom and patience of Jesus Christ' and says he came to be on the island διὰ τὸν λόγον τοῦ θεοῦ καὶ τὴν μαρτυρίαν Ἰησοῦ.[4] This need not imply a penal sentence: the earliest evidence for the tradition of his exile there is an inference from Clement of Alexandria (*Quis Dives* 42), and later and more explicit references are chiefly from western sources (see Swete, pp. clxxvii-clxxviii). The whole tradition might be no more than a plausible inference from our text. Swete refers to the existence of quarries on the northern part of the island, but I find no record of the actual discovery of ancient mines, whose existence is implied in later versions (see Victorinus on Rev. 10.11, cited by Swete).[5]

The occasion of John's separation from his Asian churches must accordingly be regarded as uncertain,[6] though judicial condemnation to exile remains a very probable inference. Caird (pp. 21-23) suggests very plausibly that it may have been a case of *relegatio ad insulam* by the proconsul of Asia to an island within his jurisdiction, as sanctioned by the ruling preserved in *Dig.* 48.22.6-7.[7]

This possibility raises the question whether Patmos was in fact in the province of Asia. I cannot find that the question has ever been asked, and it is unexpectedly difficult to give a decisive answer. The contexts of Strabo and Pliny offer no administrative groupings, and inscriptions are remarkably scarce and uninformative.[8]

Ptolemy assigns to Asia the coastal islands from Rhodes to Tenedos together with Amorgos, Astypalaea and some others (*Geog.* 5.2.28-32), and marks the Aegean, Icarian and Myrtoan Seas as the province's western limit (5.2.1). In his account of the islands belonging to Achaia (3.15.23-30) he includes most of the Cyclades and some of the Sporades by name. Patmos is not named in either list. The reason for this omission is not clear: perhaps its settlement was a dependency of a larger island-state, and so without political status. Geographically its position is marginal: the issue might depend on the latitude permitted in interpreting Ptolemy's reference to islands which τῇ Ἀσίᾳ παράκεινται (5.2.28). On balance its position favours inclusion in Asia: it is more naturally grouped with the eastern islands and is outflanked by Asian Amorgos to the south-west, though the latter's attachment to Asia receives special mention and might be anomalous. Even this tentative judgment makes no allowance for possible changes of boundary, but as Ptolemy wrote in the second century AD it is likely that his testimony will apply to a situation unchanged since the time of Domitian.

The geographical point is of some moment because an answer might shed light on the wider problems of John's fate in Patmos. Caird's hypothesis might be fitted into a natural sequence of events. If a *delator* laid a charge against John, the proconsul, having wide discretion to assign his own penalties within the limits of his *imperium*, might well have chosen *relegatio* as an available and convenient mode of disposing of the case. And if for a moment we assume the judicial sentence and ask the converse question 'Why Patmos?'—the answer may be that it was in Asia, inhabited but without corporate status, and sufficiently isolated. It would be suitable even for a regular penal settlement; perhaps in fact it was.

And it lay within the governor's unchallenged jurisdiction.

It must be emphasized that this is only inferential. If we could determine whether John was in fact exiled by proconsular sentence, this would be valuable as a possible clue to the nature and method of the Roman action against Christianity. But the tradition ascribes the act to Domitian, and Tertullian, who uses the legal term *relegatur*, locates the event in Rome. And John's release is made consequent upon the death of Domitian and by implication upon the cancellation of his acts (Clem. Alex., Victorinus).

We cannot really take the matter further. Inherent probability favours the most natural explanation of the primary text in its most likely situational context. John knew Asia intimately. The immediate background of Rev. 1.9 is likely to be one of forcible separation from his converts there. The whole scene is intelligible with the greatest economy of hypothesis if it happened within Asian jurisdiction. There is no need to invoke Domitian's personal intervention in the case of an unimportant provincial.[9] John's uncompromising stand may naturally have made him an early victim of private accusation when the church was under increasing pressure from both Jewish and pagan opponents in circumstances already suggested. He may have written the Revelation in the subsequent awareness that the logic of the situation was being worked out in a deliberate imperial policy of persecution.

2. Patmos and the Imagery of the Revelation

We must make a distinction between the writer's experience and that of his readers. His surroundings may have contributed to the psychological raw material of his vision, but allusion to them would not have been meaningful to the churches as were images connected with their own experiences. On our view of the first vision of Rev. 1.9-20 and its relation with the letters we argue that even there the operative *Sitz im Leben* is that of the churches in Asia.

It has often been supposed however that the scenery of the island and the writer's sufferings there made their mark directly and indirectly upon the book. A most interesting attempt was once made by J.T. Bent to connect much of the apocalyptic imagery with John's observation of marine volcanic phenomena following an eruption of Thera (Santorini). It suffers from overstatement.[10] But the notable parallels between the language of disaster here and the Exodus plagues in Egypt may have more than a literary basis.[11] This is not to deny the probable influence of the literary tradition of the Exodus or of the machinery of earlier apocalyptic, but to suggest that John's vivid language is coloured by experiences of himself or his churches, whether in Patmos or in Asia. Sardis had suffered in AD 17 a catastrophe of apocalyptic scale which had, I believe, imprinted itself indelibly on the popular memory,[12] and our limited records suffice to show that other parts of Asia had known major disasters later in the century.

Some phrases in the Revelation point to more specifically marine phenomena (8.8-9; 6.14; 16.3, 20). Some of these show striking parallels with the almost contemporary account of exceptional seismic events in Pliny's *Natural History*.[13] Now Bent connects his hypothesis with an eruption of Thera dated to AD 60 and an early date of the Revelation. This is unnecessary, and there are other possibilities. Pliny testifies to several eruptions and emergent islands there, though his dates are confused (*NH* 2.89.202). It is possible that another eruption took place after Pliny wrote and was seen by John on Patmos, or that such effects as the poisoning and discoloration of the sea reached even the coasts of Asia Minor.

The point cannot be pressed. Perhaps the vivid imagery owes something to John's Patmos experience; perhaps rather he recalls phenomena which had afflicted Asia in the experience of his churches to indicate the greater powers of judgment which God yet held in store.

Ramsay's interesting chapter entitled 'The Education of St. John in Patmos' (*SC*, pp. 82-92) merits a note. Some criticism of it is implicit in the preceding discussion. His discussion depends on the attribution of the Revelation and the Fourth Gospel to the same hand. It is not likely that the psychological impact of the Patmos experience, however traumatic, could explain the required transformation of style and personality in the brief time he postulates.

3. *Preliminary Notes on Revelation 1*

We restrict comment on the first chapter here to a tabulation of some points whose preliminary clarification may help to clear the ground and set the scene for the principal discussion.

(a) The opening words lay no emphasis upon the call and authorization of the prophet (contrast Isa. 6; Jer. 1). His identity and authority are known to readers to whom he needs no introduction. His claim to hear and convey the words of Christ was later contrasted with Montanus's presumption to speak in the first person in the name of God (Epiphan. *Haer.* 48.412 = *PG* XLI.871). The point may reflect a pattern of controversy related to the reception of the Revelation in the church.

(b) The introductory address of Rev. 1.1-8 shows parallels with the vision of Rev. 4 and 5.[14] Beckwith (pp. 256, 426-27) argues that these chapters were written before this introduction, and that the occurrence of the common phrases there is accordingly primary. The point reinforces my plea for flexibility in interpretation through the clearest rather than the earliest context.

(c) This view concurs with the observation of a close relationship between the vision of 1.9-20 and the primary local references of Rev. 2–3. John expressed ecstatic experience in terms which applied Old Testament language to portraying Christ with attributes which met the needs of particular churches. The readers would have seen a relevance to themselves which we can only partially recover through close study. The relationship is again situational as well as part of a close literary unit.[15]

(d) The earliest occurrence of the term κυριακὴ ἡμέρα (1.11) may be set against the imperial institution of 'Sebaste-day', first attested in Egypt in AD 68, and later in a Hadrianic inscription of Pergamum (Deissmann, *LAE*, pp. 358-61).[16] Another case in point here is the traditional title of John, *theológos*, which may ultimately have derived from Rev. 1.2 (cf. Euseb. *HE* 3.18.1), and is paralleled by inscriptions of the imperial cult from Ephesus, Smyrna and Pergamum.[17]

(e) The chapter contains some internal evidence explanatory of the structure and interpretation of the book. Verse 19 in effect divides the whole into three sections: the foregoing vision of ch. 1, the 'things which are' in chs. 2–3, and the 'things which shall be' in chs. 4–22. In v. 12 the vision of Christ begins with seeing the seven candlesticks, explained in v. 20 as the seven churches: this may be John's way of saying that his picture of Christ in the midst indicates Christ's concern for them. Verse 20 itself is worth weighing with passages like 17.9 which offer explanations of symbols. Allegorical interpretations cannot however be applied indiscriminately: sometimes the offered explanations are among the most cryptic difficulties (e.g. 13.18 and 17.10).

4. The Problem of the Angels

We cannot leave Rev. 1 without a look at a particular difficulty in John's use of symbolism to which we are introduced in the same v. 20. What are the 'angels of the churches' to whom the letters are addressed? I have little new to say about this familiar crux, and propose to confine my remarks to a survey of the possibilities and a note of possible areas of cultural background.

A choice is generally offered between (1) heavenly guardians of the churches, and (2) human representatives of them, generally their bishops. Three other principal variants deserve consideration: (3) that the 'angels' are personifications of the churches; (4) that they are literally human 'messengers'; and (5) that the term is used in some complex and elusive way or at differing levels, so that we cannot expect to assign it a lexical equivalent that tells the whole story.

These alternatives are not necessarily rigid or exhaustive: the last may include diverse theories or combinations of theories. The central dilemma involved in any simple reading of the symbolism is highlighted in the clash of (1) and (2). Usage throughout the New Testament and in the Revelation in particular points to the meaning 'angel', but only a human representative might properly be held responsible for the works of the church.[18] The other theories are often advanced in the awareness of the difficulties of understanding the 'angels' simply as representative beings either human or divine.

In the Septuagint ἄγγελος is used in rare instances of a human messenger of God (Mal. 2.7; 3.1; cf. 1.1, where the LXX so renders the name or title 'Malachi' itself). In the New Testament it twice denotes simply an emissary (Lk. 9.52; Jas 2.25).[19] Elsewhere it is always used of a supernatural being. The idea of an angel as the guardian of the nation is found in Dan. 12.1, as guardian of the individual in *Jub.* 35.17 (cf. Mt. 18.10; Acts 12.15). A curious parallel for the comparison of angels and stars occurs in *1 Enoch* 86.1-3; 88.1. In the New Testament angels are most prominent in relation to eschatological events, and so especially in the Revelation, where they have varied functions, including the control of natural forces (7.1; cf. Charles, II.475).

Of the theories proposed we may most easily criticize (2) and (4). The former has been tenaciously held (Plumptre, Zahn, *et al.*). The Malachi passages have been used to justify the supposed application of the term to a synagogue official, and so conjecturally to an official in the church.[20] Christian usage however seems decisive against such an unsupported supposition. The individual could scarcely be held responsible for the character of the church, and there is no unambiguous evidence for the idea of episcopal authority in the churches of the Revelation, though it looms large in Ignatius twenty years later. Hort (p. 19) observes that this interpretation is apparently not earlier than Augustine. The reading τὴν γυναῖκά σου in Rev. 2.20 has been used to support it, but this must be rejected on textual grounds. In any case, the symbolism seems to move on quite a different level from that of ecclesiastical organization.

(4) is at first sight attractive, for 'messenger' is the primary meaning of ἄγγελος, and the book may indeed have been distributed through messengers delegated by each church to tour its district. But the same basic objections apply: usage favours 'angels' and the emissary could not be made representative of the community. Nor could he be readily symbolized by the 'stars' of 1.20.

The difficulties of the 'angel' interpretation are of a different order. It is difficult to think of a human writer being instructed to write the words of Christ to supernatural beings. Again, the angels cannot on this view either be held guilty of the faults of their churches. This is not to say that the rendering 'angel' is wrong, but only that at its face-value it does not explain the symbolism.

(3) probably gives the clearest tangible picture: the ἄγγελοι are simply personifications of the churches themselves. This gives the required sense, but raises problems in the usage of symbolism. The 'stars' and the 'lampstands' of 1.20 are made virtually the same thing.[21] Some writers justify this conception by regarding the 'angel' as the heavenly counterpart of the earthly church (Charles, pp. 34-35; Beckwith, pp. 445-46). Thus (5) is in effect made the rationale of (3). The whole subject shows the difficulty of confining this fluid use of symbols within the logical categories of the modern mind.[22]

It is possible that these 'angels' had some analogue in contemporary life which made this usage less strange than it appears. The idea of mediating powers was congenial, and contributed for instance to such phenomena as the Colossian heresy. At another level Stauffer compares the edicts and messengers of Christ with those of Caesar.[23] Again a pagan expression of the idea of a guardian of the individual reappears in Aelius Aristides, writing of an experience in Smyrna.[24] An interesting but difficult class of inscriptions from the Aegean island of Thera (Santorini) and Therasia is also suggestive. They are evidently sepulchral, usually cut on a *stele* of white marble, and consist simply of the formula ἄγγελος followed by a personal name in the genitive case.[25] H. Achelis argued that they were Christian, citing palaeographical opinion for placing them in the first or second century AD, but his interpretation must be regarded as conjectural.[26]

These tantalizing glimpses point at least to the currency of an unexpected term, perhaps a concept developed under Jewish influence, at a date near the Revelation in places near the borders of Asia.

Chapter 3

EPHESUS

1. *Introductory*

The Ephesian letter is in some respects less easily adaptable to the methods of this study than are most of the others.[1] The existing materials for knowledge are at once far more extensive and yet tantalizingly incomplete, and the task of sifting them correspondingly more difficult. The city was the most cosmopolitan of the seven, and on that ground alone we might expect the element of exclusive local reference to be less marked.

The areas of the city excavated by the Austrians in the hollow between the hills of Coressus and Pion give an exceptionally vivid picture of the urban life of Roman times.[2] Yet it is a strangely misleading impression. Ancient Ephesus was a great seaport focused on its harbour; today the site is stranded several miles from the sea on the edge of a swampy alluvial plain and the former harbour is marked by a reed-bed.

The topographical history of Ephesus is a complex subject which has been extensively treated elsewhere.[3] It will be necessary here only to describe briefly the features of importance to the discussion. There were remarkable changes in the physical geography, and the city itself underwent several changes of site and orientation.

The matter is summarized in Strabo (14.1.21 = p. 640).[4] The original Greek settlement, perhaps dating from about 1100 BC, was established in territory occupied by indigenous peoples, Carians and Leleges, and the tribal structure which persisted indicates a continuing mixture of race and culture in the citizen body (*SC*, pp. 234-35). The earliest site was on the northern slope of Pion (Bean, p. 101). The sea must then have come close to the hill. The ancient temple of the great goddess identified with Artemis stood less than a mile outside the walls (Hdt. 1.26).

Ephesus had become prosperous when Croesus of Lydia (c. 560-546 BC) besieged and captured it before attacking the other cities of Ionia. He treated the sanctuary well and contributed generously to the reconstruction of a greater temple, but he destroyed the old city and transplanted its population to the low ground about the temple.

There the population remained until after the time of Alexander, when Lysimachus fortified a new site about a great new harbour at the northern foot of Coressus, over two miles distant from the Artemisium. He had to resort to a stratagem, according to Strabo, to force the people to leave their homes by the shrine. The Croesus temple had been destroyed, burnt by a madman Herostratus to immortalize his name, reputedly on the very night of Alexander's birth (Plut. *Alex*. 3.3 = 665). It was replaced by the great Hellenistic structure which was regarded as one of the wonders of the world. This stood on the same site as its predecessors, but lay outside the harbour-city.

Ephesus reached the height of its wealth and influence in the Hellenistic and Roman periods. It suffered severely at times from the wars of the Diadochi before coming securely under the rule of the Attalids of Pergamum. When Rome assumed power in 133 BC under the terms of the bequest of Attalus III, this wealthy seaport was open to exploitation by ruthless officials. The hatred for Rome was seen in the response of the Ephesians to Mithridates' command for a massacre of Romans in the province of Asia in 88 BC. Not even the suppliants at the asylum of Artemis were spared. But under the *pax Romana* of the Empire Ephesus was a populous and privileged city. Most of the visible remains date from this period, though the walls and towers which scale the crest of Coressus date from Lysimachus.

Yet throughout this great period the commercial prosperity of Ephesus was under the potential threat of the irrevocable silting of the harbour. Strabo (14.1.24 = p. 641) was aware of the danger, and records that the engineers of Attalus Philadelphus had already worsened the situation by a faulty attempt to deepen the entrance. The city's future was limited, and indeed the evidence, fragmentary as it is, suggests a progressive decline, partially masked by a pretentious religious importance.

2. *The Jewish Element in the Background of the Letter*

The first question here concerns the sufficiency of the Old Testament as an explanation of the background of the letter. The clearest instance of such background is found in the pivotal v. 7.[5] The mention of the 'tree of life' takes us back to Gen. 2.9 (cf. Gen. 3.22, 24 and Ezek. 31.8). The concept had a history in Jewish tradition (cf. *Test. Levi* 18.11; *1 Enoch* 24.4; 25.4-5).[6] Otherwise the letter owes comparatively little to the language of the Old Testament. Much of it is written in a relatively direct style of assessment and exhortation. Of its other symbols, the stars and lampstands belong to the structural machinery of the book, the latter recalling the seven-branched Menorah of Exod. 25.31ff. (cf. Heb. 9.2), and the threat that the church shall be moved from its place (v. 5) is not easily explained in Old Testament terms. The righteous 'hatred' of v. 6 finds some parallel in Ps. 139.20-21, but the correspondence cannot be pressed.

This brief survey indicates the limitations of this type of explanation. Other aspects must be understood in local terms. The 'false apostles' and Nicolaitans, and the loss of 'first love' are evidently particular problems affecting the local church. The focal passage is v. 7: there alone the scriptural basis is clear. But it may still be asked why the symbol of the tree was applied to Ephesus. There are strong reasons for seeing in other cases a special suitability of the concluding promise to the needs of the church. Was there a similar appropriateness here? And in v. 5 here *kinēsō*, however understood, is suggestive when applied to the church in a city notorious for its repeated changes of site.

The relationships of this letter with other New Testament writings and with other parts of the Revelation need not detain us. Only the latter can be clearly demonstrated. Apart from the structural parallels there are situational correspondences which are better reviewed in their context.

A more immediate question is that of the position of Jews in Ephesus, and of their relations with the church there. Can the possible references to Jewish tradition in the letter be seen in the context of Jewish influence in the church and city?

There can be no doubt of the great strength of Judaism in Ephesus, though the implications of the fact for the church are much more problematical. There is abundant testimony to the large number of Jews in Asia,[7] and Ephesus was its greatest commercial city. There is moreover strong, though debated, evidence that a Jewish community had possessed its citizenship since Seleucid times. This point merits close consideration for its bearing on the status of Judaism in the city. It is often denied on *a priori* grounds that such citizenship was possible in a pagan city,[8] a position which conflicts with the ostensible statements of Josephus and the claim attributed to Paul of Tarsus (Acts 21.29).

This difficult question cannot be pursued at length here. It may be argued without hesitation that there was in Ephesus a Jewish community with special and guaranteed privileges. And I believe that these privileges included that of citizenship. It may be conceded that this was an exceptional situation, for the religious structure of civic life ordinarily precluded Jewish participation. But when a monarch imposed a constitution on a city he had power to include a tribe or other division whose religious bond was Judaism. There is some evidence that deliberate Seleucid policy favoured this: the denial derives from the study of the more abundant Egyptian materials, but Ptolemaic arrangements are not necessarily normative for Asia. The matter may be regarded as settled in principle if we may accept L. Robert's understanding of the new synagogue inscriptions of Sardis.[9]

In the case of Ephesus it will suffice for the present to cite the relevant authorities with due qualification. The Jews in Ephesus and throughout the rest of Ionia, we are told, 'bear the same name as the indigenous citizens' (τοῖς αὐθιγένεσι πολίταις ὁμωνυμοῦσιν) by gift of the Diadochi (Jos. *contra Ap.* 2.4.39), an expression whose studied vagueness invites suspicion. In an important passage in the Antiquities (12.3.2.125-26), the agitation of the Ionians against the Jews seems to presuppose that a Jewish community already possessed the citizenship and that the fact was resented by their opponents. This at least seems the most natural reading of the case.[10]

Several other passages show a history of particularly bitter hostility between Jew and Gentile in Ephesus. Josephus cites decrees of Lentulus (49 BC) and of Dolabella (43 BC),[11] and an undated decree of the city in *Antiq.* 14.10.25.263-64 is especially interesting. A Jewish petition is granted, τοῦ πράγματος Ῥωμαίοις ἀνήκοντος, and therefore none shall be molested or fined for keeping the Sabbath. There has clearly been a campaign exploiting the possibility of offence against Jewish scruples, and the guarantee is conceded with patent reluctance, and only under Roman pressure. This incident recalls the sharp pagan reaction to the intervention of a Jewish spokesman in Ephesus in Acts 19. The whole pattern of conflict may be seen as a reflection of the reality of Jewish citizenship.

Our case might be strengthened if we could recover some details of the relevant tribal structure as constituted by Antiochus. Ramsay's attempt to do this was a conjecture based on inadequate evidence (*SC*, pp. 234–36). The more recent materials published by D. Knibbe correct and supplement details of the picture without offering any light on the pattern of Jewish participation.[12]

There is then some ground for a cautious acceptance of the evidence of Josephus that the Jewish population of Ephesus included a body of citizens with long-established rights, who looked to Rome for the maintenance of their privileges. There was also a particular bitterness between Jew and Gentile, a factor of importance in understanding the environment of the future church.

The first arrival of the gospel in Ephesus is unrecorded. According to Acts 2.9 Jews resident in Asia were present in Jerusalem on the day of Pentecost. And we are told of 'disciples' in Ephesus before Paul's arrival, though they are represented as imperfectly instructed.[13]

The subsequent importance of Ephesus as an apostolic centre is evident from the documents. As the most strategic cosmopolitan city of Asia it may have become temporarily the headquarters of the whole church after the fall of Jerusalem.[14]

Our purpose here is to raise questions relating to the environment of this outstanding church which bear on the interpretation of the text. Who were then the 'false apostles' (v. 2), who, like the Nicolaitans (v. 6), had been rejected by the Ephesian church? The issue may well turn upon the question whether the main thrust of opposition in Ephesus was Judaistic or libertarian. Nicolaitanism was certainly a movement of the latter kind: discussion of its precise character will be deferred to the chapter on Pergamum, where allusion to it is set in a more informative context. The question remains open whether the 'false apostles' represented a similar or a different, perhaps even opposite, tendency.

We cannot determine how far the church was composed of converts from the powerful Jewish community. According to Acts its presence had provided the initial opening for Paul (19.8), but he had quickly withdrawn from the synagogue (19.9). The writer is at pains to emphasize the impact of the gospel upon both Jews and Gentiles in Asia (19.10, 17), and the sharp division between the communities is reflected in the riot in the theatre (19.23ff.). Perhaps the cosmopolitan character of the city and its existing racial and religious tensions permitted a greater measure of fragmentation of its society than was normal in the closely-knit *polis*.[15] The very size and influence of the apostolic church in Ephesus may have rendered it less vulnerable to the pressures which afflicted the other churches, and its comparative security may have been a factor in its strategic importance. Severance from the synagogue may not have been so recent or so critical an experience as at Smyrna or Philadelphia: the pressures of imperial cult or pagan society, while certainly powerful, may not have been so insistent as upon the weaker and divided churches of Pergamum or Thyatira.

It is likely that Domitian's reign marked a deterioration in the standing of the Ephesian church. That emperor enforced his worship with a rigour hitherto unknown, and a pretentious temple to him was actually established in Ephesus.[16] He appears also to have extended the boundaries of the temple of Artemis, an act whose significance we must consider below.[17] The hints of increasing danger from the pagan opposition will readily explain the activity of Nicolaitans. They also suggest that the 'false apostles' are likely to have been men of similar tendency.

Several possible explanations of these 'apostles' have been suggested: (1) that they were travelling evangelists, who are so called in *Didache* 11.3ff., where instructions are given for receiving and testing them (Moffatt, p. 349; Beckwith, p. 449); (2) that they were Judaizers, like those to whom Paul applies the term ψευδαπόστολοι in 2 Cor. 11.13 (Spitta, p. 251; noted as possible by Hort, p. 21); (3) that they represented a Pauline party, which John condemned as libertarian (the Tübingen view, mentioned but not accepted by Charles, p. 50, and Hort, p. 21); (4) that they were Nicolaitans or similar to them (Bousset, *Die Offenbarung Johannes*, p. 204; Charles, p. 50).

Of these alternatives (3) seems to depend on premises open to extensive objection. There are insufficient grounds for a dogmatic discrimination among the others. In the case of (1) the rejection of the 'apostles' may have been simply on the score of personal character or venality of motive. But the difficulties of the times may well have attracted to Ephesus either Judaistic or antinomian teachers, both of whom might offer the church a tempting rationale for a *modus vivendi* in the face of persecution. If so, I incline to think the libertarian alternative the more likely, for two reasons: (a) verse 6 is then naturally explained as resuming the commendation of v. 2; (b) the background already proposed suggests that the inducement towards making terms with pagan society was the stronger here.[18]

This judgment of probability cannot bear the weight of any superstructure of hypothesis. We cannot justify use of these 'false apostles' in discussing Nicolaitanism, nor in arguing the presence of Gnostic teaching.

The expression 'first love' merits some comment at this stage. Some have supposed this to refer to love of God or Christ, as in Jer. 2.2ff. (Trench, *Commentary on the Epistles to the Seven Churches in Asia*, 3rd edn [1867], p. 79). Most subsequent commentators have preferred to understand it of brotherly love, and relate the reproof in v. 4 to a spirit of censoriousness and division consequent upon the division over false teachers in the church (Charles, p. 51; Hort, p. 22).[19] Thus Beckwith argues that the virtues praised in vv. 2-3 presuppose a continuing love of Christ (p. 450). But it is not clear that the two aspects can be separated. If there were in fact divisions in the church they may have been exacerbated by the differing pressures affecting its Jewish and Gentile members.

The situation was complex and it is not easy to evaluate the Jewish factor in it. The power of paganism in this city was certainly great, and it is not at all unlikely that scriptural language should be applied to encourage those under attack from that quarter. The break from the synagogue, on the other hand, may have been more complete and of longer standing than elsewhere. We cannot easily prejudge the question whether the focal words of v. 7 are to be set against a Jewish background of the recipients. To a closer consideration of that passage we must now turn.

3. *The Tree of Life*

The concept of the 'tree of life' derived originally from Gen. 2.9 and 3.22 and had a long history in Jewish tradition. There are brief references to it in Prov. 3.18; 11.30; 13.12; 15.4 and the idea of unfading trees offering food and healing is elaborated in Ezek. 47.12. Later apocalyptic is much more explicit. In paradise the original condition of unfallen man will be restored. A tree which gives believers the wonderful food of immortality will be transplanted into the holy place, the temple of the Lord (*1 Enoch* 25.5; cf. 24.4). Eating the fruit of the tree of life will then be the reward of the blessed (*Test. Levi* 18.11). The ideas of paradise and the heavenly city tend to merge (*2 Bar.* 4; *Test. Dan* 5.12; cf. Schneider in *TDNT* V. 40), a feature to note in our study of the patterns of thought underlying the Revelation.

There is no reason to doubt that John was familiar with these traditions or that his view of the Old Testament was coloured by traditional interpretations. It is not so clear that he expected recognition of this background by his readers. The trend of evidence elsewhere suggests that the relationship between the Revelation and the earlier Jewish apocalyptic has been somewhat overplayed. Here it is relevant and possible as a partial explanation, but not a sufficient one. John is deeply concerned with the specific needs of his readers. In other cases we find a pointed appropriateness in the promises to the conquerors. We may expect the same here. Our search is for a legitimate explanation, if not necessarily a complete or even primary one.

In his note on Rev. 2.7 F.J.A. Hort wrote: 'It seems at least possible that here, as elsewhere, there is an allusion of contrast to familiar heathen objects. The παράδεισος τοῦ Θεοῦ may conceivably stand over against the vast sacred τέμενος of the temple of Artemis at Ephesus. Whether the Tree of Life had any analogue we cannot tell' (p. 25). E.H. Plumptre (p. 2n.) makes a similar point about the *theologoi* of Artemis and the traditional title of John: 'The name therefore may have been at first the embodiment of the thought that the Evangelist occupied in the service of the true God that position which they occupied in that of the Ephesian goddess, that he was the witness of the Truth, of which her worship was a counterfeit'.

It is the purpose of this study to suggest a development of these lines of thought in relation to the 'tree of life'. I aim to show that this Old Testament idea was chosen and applied to the case of Ephesus because it was peculiarly applicable, because in fact it had an analogue in the Artemis cult.

There is some indication that the 'tree of life' was associated with the cross of Christ in the mind of John. δένδρον, not ξύλον, was apparently the normal and idiomatic word for 'tree' in New Testament times. ξύλον ordinarily had some more specialized connotation. The evidence is collected by J. Schneider in *TDNT* V. 37. He says the meaning 'living wood' is rare, quoting isolated instances from Herodotus, Xenophon, Euripides, Callimachus and the papyri. Most of these seem to refer in context to trees either as sources of fruit and other products, or to trees as cult objects, in either case a connotation which may be relevant here.[20] In the Septuagint, however, ξύλον is common as 'tree'. and δένδρον surprisingly rare. ξύλον is used both of fruit and of forest trees, and of trees as cult-centres. Both words alike represent the Hebrew עץ.[21]

The usual meaning of ξύλον in earlier Greek is 'dead wood', 'timber'. It is noteworthy how often it is applied to an instrument of punishment. It is used of the pillory (Ar. *Nubes* 592; *Lysistr.* 680), of stocks for the feet (Hdt. 9.37; cf. Acts 16.24), of a combination of the two with five holes for head, arms and legs (πεντεσύριγγον ξύλον, Ar. *Eq.* 1049), of a stake for impaling, and of the cross of crucifixion.

In the New Testament the AV renders ξύλον as 'tree' only ten times, whereas δένδρον is used twenty-six times. To the ten we should add the preferred reading of Rev. 22.19.[22] Of these eleven, the sense of the proverbial expression of Lk. 23.31 is properly 'wood'.[23] Apart from this all the uses of the word may be classified under two headings: (a) as occurring in the phrase 'tree of life' (five times, all in the Revelation: 2.7; 22.2 *bis*, 14, 19 *v.l.*); (b) in explicit allusion to the cross of Christ, twice in Petrine sermons in Acts 5.30 and 10.39, in Paul's sermon at Pisidian Antioch (Acts 13.29), in Gal. 3.13, and 1 Pet. 2.24.

The latter five are precisely the passages where the AV alludes to the cross as the 'tree'. The thought of Deut. 21.22-23 underlies all five, and Gal. 3.13 refers directly to it. Conversely we find that ξύλον is used freely in the New Testament for 'wood', and can also mean 'cross', 'stave' (Mt. 26.47; etc.) and 'stocks' (Acts 16.24), but is never used for 'tree' except in explicit reference to the 'tree of life'.[24]

The New Testament writers evidently then adopt ξύλον from the Septuagintal usage in Gen. 2 and 3 and Deut. 21, but only in particular senses, using only δένδρον as a normal and neutral word elsewhere.[25] The phrase τὸ ξύλον τῆς ζωῆς may yet have had an unexpected flavour for the Gentile Christian reader in Asia, especially when viewed in the light of the use made of Deut. 21.22-23 in the apostolic preaching. If not as explicit and shocking a collocation as 'gallows of life', it may still have conveyed disturbing nuances. In Ephesus, I venture to suggest, it had a particular local analogue.

Schneider cites R. Roberts[26] for the interesting view that the 'tree of life' is actually equated with the cross. Roberts writes: 'May it not be that the word was used in this special sense by the early Christians, and that John is thinking of the Cross when he speaks of the "tree of life"? The phrase itself has a previous history in Jewish literature: but may it not have received this new content in its Christian use? Ramsay has shown that there is a studied concentration of meaning into all the symbolism of these letters, and it is not impossible that here ξύλον may contain an allusion to the Cross. If it is objected that this view puts the Cross in the Paradise of God, the answer is that it is precisely there that the writer of Rev sees it.' Roberts refers to Rev. 5.6 (the Lamb standing in the midst 'as it had been slain') and to Rev. 13.8 ('the Lamb slain from the foundation of the world').

The word σταυρός never occurs in the Apocalypse, but E.M.B. Green has recently shown the prominence of the theme of the sacrificial death of Christ throughout the book.[27] His 'salvation', including salvation from sin, as seen for example in the context of Rev. 7.10, is contrasted with the 'salvation' of the imperial cult. In Rev. 22 the tree of life is placed in the New Jerusalem. Here the verdict of Eden is reversed. The disobedience of Adam had denied him access to the tree of life and inaugurated the curse which here is finally extinguished: 'there shall be no more curse' (Rev. 22.3, citing Zech. 14.11 LXX). It is natural to connect these words with Gen. 3, but the very close resemblance between the symbols applied to the heavenly city and to the seven churches suggests that in many particulars Rev. 21–22 is the consummation of Rev. 2–3. In that city there shall be no more the curse of sin for which the cross was the tree of life, the means of salvation. The shortcomings of the cities are there remedied, and the potentialities of their churches realized. John saw no temple in it, 'for the Lord the Almighty God and the Lamb are its temple' (Rev. 21.22). The emphasis on the titles of God and the Lamb contrasts with those of emperor and goddess. If such words suggested to the Jewish reader that the sacrificial system of the earthly Jerusalem was superseded in the heavenly city, might it not equally have suggested to the Asian Gentile that the power of pagan temples was finally abolished there? Under Domitian the temple in Jerusalem had long since suffered destruction, but the double influence of the Artemis temple and of the imperial cult was a contemporary fact in the life of the church in Ephesus. Domitian had built a great new temple for emperor worship.

To the shrine of Artemis we must now turn. There are apparent analogies here with the 'tree of life', the 'paradise of God' and other concepts relevant to the Apocalypse.

Two passages in the literary sources describe the foundation of the holy place of Artemis as a tree-shrine. Callimachus (*Hymn to Artemis* 237-39) speaks of an image set up beneath an oak-trunk:[28]

σοὶ καὶ Ἀμαζονίδες πολέμου ἐπιθυμήιειραι
ἕν ποτε παρραλίῃ Ἐφέσῳ βρέτας ἱδρύσαντο
φηγῷ ὑπὸ πρέμνῳ, τέλεσεν δέ τοι ἱερὸν Ἱππώ.

Dionysius Periegetes speaks in very similar terms, but of an elm:

ἐσίδοιο
παρραλίην Ἔφεσον, μεγάλην πόλιν Ἰοχεαίρης,
ἔνθα θεῇ ποτε νηὸν Ἀμαζονίδες τετύκοντο
πρέμνῳ ἔνι πτελέης, περιώσιον ἀνδράσι θαῦμα (826-29).

The fact of a primitive tree-shrine occupying the site of the later temples is of importance. The excavations of J.T. Wood did not penetrate to the lowest levels of the Artemisium, but D.G. Hogarth reached the basic soil beneath a great depth of accumulated silt, and found remains which he identified with those of this tree-shrine. The history of the subsequent temples and their rebuildings is much confused in the literary authorities, but they testify clearly to the fact of successive structures of increasing magnificence erected upon the same spot, and this general picture has been confirmed by excavation.

The literary references are late, and their poetic language cannot be pressed, but they are valuable as evidence of the persistence of the idea of the sacred tree into the Hellenistic and Roman periods. The rigid conservatism of the cult makes this natural enough. Yet the tradition was apparently very ancient. Perhaps the recurrence of παρράλιος points to the memory of a time before the Cayster silt had left the site far from the sea. There was a βρέτας beneath the tree, and this word is used almost exclusively of a wooden image.[29] Callimachus continues:

κεῖνο δέ τοι μετέπειτα περὶ βρέτας εὐρὺ θέμειλον
δωμήθη   (248-49)

This implies that the tree and the image beneath it, perhaps easily confused in the tradition, were the central feature of the original structure, and their site therefore the central feature of the later succession of temples, in whose time the memory of the tree persisted.[30]

A tree recurs in varied contexts as an emblem of the city or its goddess. The date-palm was the characteristic symbol of Artemis on the coinage of the Anatolian periods of the city, when her indigenous aspect as a nature and fertility goddess was expressed more openly. The British Museum Catalogue lists no fewer than fifty-six coins of

the pre-Roman period on which the tree appears, usually in association with the bee and the stag. They form an almost continuous
series from about 400 BC to the mid-third century, interrupted only
by the temporary Hellenizing of the Lysimachus era, and recur on
the city coinage contemporary with the earlier *cistophori*.[31] On one
of the *cistophori* themselves a stag standing before a central tree
appears as an emblem, corresponding to a bee, a star, a quiver, the
cult-statue, or the head of Hellenic Artemis on the other items of the
series.

On the imperial coinage of Ephesus the tree recurs in interesting
types with legendary or allegorical motifs. Androclus is seen slaying a
boar, an evident allusion to the foundation-legend recorded by
Athenaeus (*Deipn.* 8.59), while behind the hero stands the palm-tree
(*BMC*, Eph. No. 232, of Antinous, under Hadrian, etc.). Another
characteristic type, that of the goddess Nike writing on a round shield
attached to the date-palm, is a more widespread conventional
representation, though much favoured here.[32] Yet other issues show
the huntress Artemis standing beneath the palm (No. 299, of
Elagabalus, etc.).

Ramsay argued in general terms that the Jewish expression 'tree of
life' must be explained with relation to the meaning which Asian
readers might take from the phrase. He suggests the tree was full of
meaning as a symbol 'because to them the tree had always been the
seat of Divine life and the intermediary between Divine and human
nature' (*SC*, p. 248).[33] He notes the occurrence of the palm-tree on
Ephesian coinage (p. 222), but does not attempt further to account
for the usage of Rev. 2.7.

The numismatic evidence suffices to show that the tree, like the
bee and the stag, was distinctively associated with Artemis Ephesia.
Anatolian deities were often identified with cult-objects of stone or
wood: Aphrodite of Paphos, Artemis of Perga and Cybele of Pessinus
are obvious examples. The difficulty for the rigidly logical modern
Western mind is the ease of transition between idea and symbol, and
between different symbols. Thus the grotesque outline of the Ephesian
cult-image has been likened to the silhouette of the bee (*SC*, p. 222).
We may often expect to find a confused and syncretistic expression of
recurring ideas. It is incidentally true of the Apocalypse, which
partakes in some measure of its cultural environment, that it uses the
language of symbol in a manner at once allusive and elusive.

In the Artemis cult, we may suggest, the tree with its image was

closely identified with the presence of the goddess within her *naos*.
This was surrounded by the wider *peribolos* of her *hieron*, enclosing
the *temenos* of which Hort spoke.

Some reference to the character and history of the cult is significant
for our purpose. The Ephesian priesthood evidently knew the great
fertility of the queen-bee, whereas Vergil spoke of *reges* (*Georg.* 4.21,
68). They may also have thought of her as the leader of the migrating
swarm. The goddess was both virgin and mother, virgin in the old
Anatolian sense of being unrestricted to a consort. In this context we
may note that the original site of her shrine was not in the plain
about the sacred tree. It had been moved there in early times from
Ortygia,[34] a grove probably situated in a mountain glen beneath
Solmissus (Tac. *Ann.* 3.61; cf. Athen. *Deipn.* 1.57; Strab. 14.1.20 =
p. 640). The Ephesians claimed, according to Tacitus, that the tree
by which the goddess was born, an olive, survived there in the reign
of Tiberius. The place continued sacred, and was still in Strabo's day
the scene of an annual festival. Its temples still contained ancient
wooden images.[35]

The preceding paragraphs have touched on a variety of points
which are relevant to the understanding of the Artemis cult and of
the city: the interaction of permanence and change in the life of both,
the virgin mother, a goddess of fertility and migration, a cult whose
conservatism imprints its stamp upon changing times.

We must return to the site of the tree-shrine which underlay the
later Artemisia. Hogarth found its lowest levels resting directly upon
the basic soil without a trace of a more primitive occupation:[36] its
beginnings were early, but definite. This accords well with the
tradition of a migration from Ortygia.[37] The siting of the sanctuary
on the marshy plain is not easily explained: it is not surprising that
J.T. Wood took six years to locate it.[38] Pliny (*NH* 36.21.95) says it
was built there for protection from earthquake. Perhaps it was
originally by the shore when the sea still came close to the hill of
Ayasoluk. Perhaps the reason for its transference from Ortygia was
simply the fact of the growing population of the neighbouring Ionian
colony, and the site was then chosen for its springs and its proximity
to a defensible hill.[39]

Whatever the original reason for the choice, the successive shrines
were raised upon the same spot. In a place afflicted by remarkable
changes in the normally permanent environment of land and sea, one
locality in the plain remained fixed as the focus of its intense religious
interest.

4. *The Asylum of Artemis*

Pausanias (7.2.8) speaks of the Amazons and local tribes at the coming of the Ionians as resident about the *hieron* ἱκεσίας ἕνεκα. The fame of the temple as a place of refuge persists throughout its history. The safety which it afforded the suppliant was σωτηρία: the goddess was Σώτειρα (*BMInscrs* 483B). The *Etymologicum Magnum* even offers a grotesque etymology of the name 'Ephesus' on these lines, that the goddess ἐφεῖναι σωτηρίαν to the Amazons who fled to her altar. Suidas tells of the early Ephesian tyrant Pythagoras, who feared to violate the asylum and besieged his victims there. When Mithridates VI in 88 BC ordered the massacre of the Romans in Asia, even the suppliants at the altar were slaughtered, in defiance of a right of refuge hitherto universally respected (Appian 12.23; cf. *SC*, p. 227).

The most important literary authorities on the subject are Strabo (14.1.23 = p. 641) and Tacitus (*Ann.* 3.60-63). Strabo affirms the antiquity of the asylum, and its continuance to his own day, although its bounds had often been changed. Alexander had fixed its radius at one stade, Mithridates at a bow-shot from the angle of the roof, which was a little more than a stade. Antony doubled this distance, and in so doing included a part of the city within the refuge. Strabo's concluding words comment on the evil results engendered by this extension, which must have been a recent memory at the time of his writing: ἐφάνη δὲ τοῦτο βλαβερὸν καὶ ἐπὶ τοῖς κακούργοις ποιοῦν τὴν πόλιν, ὥστ' ἠκύρωσεν ὁ Σεβαστὸς Καῖσαρ. Augustus apparently abrogated only the extension; it seems reasonable to connect his action with the construction of the *peribolos* wall whose discovery and inscriptions assisted J.T. Wood in the finding of the Artemisium.[40] This wall can be firmly dated to 6/5 BC despite the attempt to erase the proconsul's name from the inscriptions.

Tacitus gives an account of the Ephesian embassy to Tiberius when the emperor was seeking to abolish the proliferation of asylums, which had become a dangerous abuse. He exempted this temple, which was one of the few which could prove their ancient right to the privilege (cf. Suet. *Tib.* 37).

The fact of this asylum continued into the last days of the Artemisium, perhaps becoming seen increasingly as in conscious opposition to the growing power of the rival faith. Of later writers Achilles Tatius has much to say of it, though the setting of his narrative is 'extraordinarily vague' and its dramatic date quite uncertain (S. Gaselee, *LCL*, p. 378n.). Perhaps for that very reason the choice of the temple at Ephesus for the climax of the story is noteworthy, for above all else it was popularly known as a place of asylum, and that is just the part it is required to play. Aelius Aristides (42.775 = 308.522), writing under Marcus Aurelius, refers to the temple as a 'refuge of necessity'. A coin as late as Philip the Younger shows the cult-statue between two stags and bears the legend Ἐφεσίων Ἄρτεμις ἄσυλος (*BMC*, Eph., No. 345).

The intervention of the Julio-Claudian emperors had not eradicated the corrupting influence of the asylum upon the city: the bitterest outburst against it is associated with the very time of Domitian, in the Epistles attributed to Apollonius of Tyana.

A mutilated inscription testifies to the fresh extension of the holy place of Artemis under an emperor whose name is lost, but may be restored as Domitian.[41] A fragmentary and much restored text of the second century clarifies the picture a little more. It reads: τὸ τέμενος τῆς Ἀ[ρτέμιδος ἄσυλον] πᾶν, ὅσον ἔσω π[εριβόλου. ὃς δ’ ἄν] παραβαίνηι, αὐτὸς αὑτὸν αἰτιάσεται (*SIG³* 989—*BMInscrs* 520). The operative words have been restored, Ἀρτέμιδος and περιβόλου by Hicks, ἄσυλον by Dittenberger. If this reconstruction is correct, the text may describe a situation already obtaining under Domitian. By his time, if not since Augustus, the whole *temenos* may have been a refuge for criminals. Even if the reconstruction is wrong, the word τέμενος is related to a sufficient context to suggest the sense.

The picture implied is one of a sacred enclosure unchangeably centred upon the spot originally marked by the sacred tree, but varying in extent at different times and sometimes overlapping the bounds of the great commercial city centred on its harbour two miles distant.

This is the context of the words of Strabo which conclude his account of the asylum. Antony's extension of its bounds had then brought a part of the city within its limits. The consequence was that the quarter nearest the Artemisium gave the criminal a sanctuary beyond the reach of the law. It became the headquarters of organized crime, and Augustus was forced to take action to obviate the abuse.

Our other authorities are unequivocal about the evil effects. Centuries earlier, Heraclitus, himself belonging to a priestly family of the temple, had denounced it (Frag. 130). And when Domitian's action reactivated the trouble, almost at the very date of the Revelation, Apollonius writes, in a letter addressed Ἐφεσίων τοῖς ἐν

Ἀρτέμιδι (No. 65): μεμπτοὶ δὲ σύνοικοι τῇ θεῷ νύκτας τε καὶ ἡμέρας, ἢ οὐκ ἂν ὁ κλέπτης τε καὶ λῃστὴς καὶ ἀνδραποδιστὴς καὶ πᾶς, εἴ τις ἄδικος ἢ ἱερόσυλος, ἦν ὁρμώμενος αὐτόθεν· τὸ γὰρ ἱερὸν τῶν ἀποστερούντων μυχός ἐστιν.

Again, in another letter to the same (no. 66), expressing his desire to sojourn at the shrine of the goddess, he asks for a place where he will not contract the need of purificatory rites, though he remain always within.

5. *The Paradise of God*

The dependence of Rev. 2.7 on Genesis is clear. Indeed the reading ἐν μέσῳ τοῦ παραδείσου presumably arose under the influence of the LXX of Gen. 2.9, and expresses a thought implicit in the concept and recurring later in the Revelation. Here I wish to consider the passage afresh in the light of the foregoing discussion, drawing together its separate strands.

Παράδεισος was originally a Persian word, denoting an enclosed garden, especially a royal park. It is interesting to note its peculiar frequency in proconsular Asia, which had once been long under Persian rule. It first occurs in Xenophon, but also in inscriptions.[42] In a document of Itane in Crete a public garden, or 'paradise', is dedicated as a *temenos* of the royal gods Ptolemy and Berenice (*SIG*[3] 463.8-10). Here these two terms are actually equated in a pagan setting. J. Jeremias notes the raising of the word παράδεισος into the religious sphere in the Jewish world (*TDNT* V. 766).

The royal garden was planted with fruit-trees, laid out regularly, and often stocked with animals of the chase. Xenophon (*Oec.* 4.20ff.) tells how Lysander visited the 'paradise' of Cyrus the Younger at Sardis and complimented him on its beauty and regularity: the whole thing was so accurately measured and εὐγώνιος. The same writer describes elsewhere (*Anab.* 5.3.6-13) his attempt to reproduce the holy place of Artemis Ephesia in his Peloponnesian estate. He built a miniature temple with its *xoanon* beside a stream named Selinus like that of Ephesus. There was a grove of trees, 'all that had edible fruit in their seasons',[43] and wild beasts of the chase. We are reminded once more of the asylum coin depicting the sacred stags of Artemis on either side of the central cult-image. The idea of the royal park in which the king walked passes easily into that of a sacred enclosure in whose innermost heart the deity was present.[44] The regular lay-out of the garden may be compared with the squareness of a *temenos* mentioned in an inscription of Smyrna (*SIG*³ 996.30; of c. 1st century AD), and that inscription uses an unusual collocation of words which coincides remarkably with the passage in Rev. 21.16-18 describing the dimensions of the New Jerusalem.[45]

It would be rash to dogmatize about the associations which might have been present to John's mind, but many things throughout the Revelation may be illuminated by the assumption that local conditions and needs carried his thoughts back to the familiar Old Testament scriptures, influencing his choice and directing his application of them. The cities of Asia obtrude analogies with the transient glories of Israel and are seen transfigured in the vision of the eternal city. We may venture to see a series of partial parallels implicit in the background of the passage: the tree of life in the garden of Eden, the tree-shrine in the asylum of the goddess, and the cross, as Roberts placed it, in the paradise of God. In each we find the presence of the deity. But in the New Jerusalem shall be no temple and no curse, but the glory of God and the tree of life 'in the midst of the street of it' (Rev. 22.2).

For the Christian in Domitianic Ephesus these thoughts would, I suggest, have come to a focus in a contemporary reality. The words of the epistle contrasted with a shocking parody which the pagan cult of the city offered. At the heart of its changing fortunes was the theocratic power of the Artemis temple, marked by the fixed point of the ancient tree-shrine which was the place of 'salvation' for the suppliant, surrounded by an asylum enclosed by a boundary wall. But this 'salvation' for the criminal corrupted the city. The Ephesian who had to live with this problem understood the promise of a city-sanctuary pervaded by the glory of God. Of that city it was said: 'There shall in no wise enter into it anything that defileth, neither whatsoever worketh abomination, or maketh a lie' (Rev. 21.27).

In Rev. 2.4 and 5 there is a reiterated insistence on the theme of repentance.[46] That was the need of the church which had lost its 'first love'. The salvation of the cross was for the repentant sinner, in marked contrast with that of Artemis, which gave the criminal immunity to continue his crimes.

Some of the later references to the same symbols fit naturally into this pattern and derive point and force from it. The description of the heavenly setting of the tree of life in Rev. 22.2 is presented in terms very similar to Xenophon's account of his replica of the Ephesian shrine. The topographical motif constantly recurs. 'In the midst' is the Lamb or the throne or the tree.[47] 'Temple' in the Revelation is always *naos*, the inner sanctuary and dwelling-place of God. Yet we have repeatedly the concept of an outer enclosure, not only in 2.7, but in such passages as 11.1-2, and I suggest that we have this paralleled in the enclosing walls of the New Jerusalem. On the preferable reading of 22.19 we may see a warning lest God should take away a man's part from the place of his inner presence *and* from the city. The thought is in fact broadly and deeply rooted both in the Biblical and the pagan worlds. The description of unbelievers as οἱ ἔξω is frequent elsewhere in the New Testament (Mark 4.11; 1 Cor. 5.12ff.; Col. 4.5; 1 Thess. 4.12; contrast Rev. 3.12). And the concept of 'fleeing for refuge within the veil' appears in Heb. 6.18-19; similar terminology is used alike in the Septuagint of the Old Testament cities of refuge and in pagan writings of temple-sanctuaries, including that of Ephesus. Again, in Rev. 21.27 only those shall enter the city whose names are found written in the Lamb's book of life, a symbol taken from the Sardis letter, but suggesting here as there the citizen-roll. Grants of citizenship were permanently inscribed in the inner shrine, at Ephesus on the stones of the Artemisium.[48]

Amid such ideas we may see the Ephesian Christian as finding a picture of refuge in the presence of the Christ who died on the tree, a 'salvation' which he might appropriate only there, and an adoption into the citizenship of the kingdom for the repentant sinner and outsider.

These references are not always rigid or exclusive in their application, but they serve to illustrate a specifically Asian strand in the background, apart from the Jewish. While drawing on much that related to the common culture of the province, John focuses attention on some points which evidently had a rich and almost esoteric significance for the churches in individual cities.

6. *Ephesus as the City of Change*

Ramsay characterized Ephesus as the 'City of Change'. The theme may be traced through the history of the city from Heraclitus onwards. Its fortunes had hinged upon the fluctuations of site and influence between the commerce of the harbour and the temple. The elaborate provisions decreed at the time of the Salutaris bequest in AD 104 illustrate the power of the Artemis cult within a few years of the Revelation (*BMInscrs* 481). In his Prolegomena Hicks suggests (p. 83) that this bequest marked a reaction against Christianity. Perhaps this was provoked by a measure of repentance and renewed vigour in the church which had received the Apocalyptic letter. Yet in AD 161 it became necessary to overhaul the practices of the cult, whose fortunes were closely identified by its devotees with those of the city. The words of the decree of that date (*BMInscrs* 482 = *CIG* 2954a = *LBW* 137) show an increasing consciousness among the citizens that the commercial greatness of Ephesus was doomed as the valley silted and that some saw a future for the place only in the power of the goddess.

Ramsay argued that the use of κινέω in Rev. 2.5 was not a threat of destruction but strictly of movement, recalling the repeated changes made in the site of the city. The precise application may be open to some doubt. He regarded the threat as one of further change, the moving of the site once more to a place where city and church must once again make a fresh start (*SC*, p. 244). The warning should perhaps be understood rather differently: the danger was that the great harbour-city and its vigorous church would be moved back under the deadening power of the temple. If the battle against the Cayster silt were finally lost and the city were severed from its maritime commerce, the old Anatolian theocracy would rapidly reassert itself. The signs could be read by the far-sighted. It was a solemn warning of prospective realities. Unless a deeper renewal and repentance in the church led to a transformation of the community and broke the drift of events, it had to fear a reversion to the temple dominance of Lydian and Persian times as the population progressively drifted back towards the Artemisium.

The chronology of the city's decline is not entirely clear. In the first century Ephesus was at the height of its greatness, but the trends must already have been apparent, for Strabo speaks of an unsuccessful attempt to halt the progressive silting of the harbour as early as the time of Attalus Philadelphus (14.1.24 = p. 641). Yet extensive building schemes continued in the Antonine period, when we must suppose that the problem of the city's future had become obvious and acute.

Ramsay comments further that, whereas usually the transience of human life contrasts with the immutable permanence of nature, in Ephesus we seem to see the normal case reversed, that human choices have been decisive amid a changing scene (cf. Rev. 6.14).

This point may be defended on the basis that it corresponds to the moral view of history which was current in antiquity and that the moral lesson was not lost upon the Ephesian church. As we pass from the beginning of the book to its close, the fixed point of the tree in a fluctuating landscape is replaced by the tree of life and the enclosing walls of the eternal city pervaded by the presence of Christ. The conservatism of a dead orthodoxy is contrasted with the need to meet the challenge of changing circumstances, the deadening influence of the Artemisium with the eternal glory of the 'Lamb slain from the foundation of the world' (13.8).

We suppose that the original readers, familiar with some aspects of the Ephesian background, would have appreciated the force of the letter with a directness impossible for us, and thus have been prepared for local reference in the other letters. For the modern reader this epistle makes a less suitable introduction. He can see the demonstrable influence of the Old Testament on the writer's thought, and rightly stresses this background as primary. He may be disposed to scepticism towards other backgrounds. Too strong an emphasis on local relevance where the available evidence is circumstantial rather than compelling may look like special pleading in favour of a prejudged case. I offer the present hypothesis with a due recognition of its necessarily circumstantial character in the case of Ephesus. Yet I abide by it, and suggest that the underlying thought is illustrated throughout the Revelation. Some of the same concerns and concepts are further reflected in Ignatius's epistle to the Ephesians. The parallels are in some cases close and striking, though apparently independent. In Rev. 2.2 the church in Ephesus was commended for its orthodoxy and its proving of those who falsely claimed to be apostles. According to Ignatius (*Ephes.* 6.2) 'among you no heresy dwells' (and cf. 7.1; 9.1; 10.3). He sees the energy and devotion of this church, but not the seeds of decline which a closer knowledge might have revealed. Charles draws attention to the parallel between the phrase 'that we may be his *naoi*' (Ign. *Ephes.* 15.3) and the similar thought of Rev. 21.3, but rejects literary dependence as an explanation (p. xcviii). Perhaps the Ephesian background supplied a natural contrast which underlies both.[49] It is reasonable to suppose that Ignatius would have known, even as an outsider, those features of the city which were notorious.[50]

7. *Conclusions Summarized*

1. In this chapter the importance and status of the Jewish community in Ephesus has been examined. It seems likely that a body of Jews had possessed the citizenship since Seleucid times, and that this was a factor in the racial bitterness which persisted in the city.

2. The Old Testament background of the letter has been considered. This is very clear and important in the case of the 'tree of life' (v. 7), an idea prominent in Jewish tradition. Even there it is not a sufficient explanation, for the church had probably long been separated from the strong synagogue community and the question arises why this particular form of promise was chosen.

3. John may have seen in the revival of paganism and imperial cult at Ephesus under Domitian a crisis portending systematic persecution of the church in Asia.

4. The problem of the identification of the 'false apostles' is related to known aspects of the history and environment of the Ephesian church. We cannot say dogmatically whether they were Judaistic or libertarian teachers, both of whom might have had an attractive answer to the difficulties of a persecuted church, or whether they were itinerant evangelists rejected for their character rather than the content of their message. The circumstances incline me to believe that here the pagan pressures and the plausibility of the antinomian answer may have been the stronger. This will accord with the reference to Nicolaitans.

5. The Ephesian letter, like others, has a strongly Asian background which indicates that the writer must have known the city intimately. The case for this is extensive and cumulative, and better illustrated from the whole series of epistles than from any one exclusively. It is suggested that this factor is seen also in later parts of the Revelation, though particular allusions in the later chapters are often partial and elusive.

6. It is suggested that the phrase 'tree of life' may have carried the connotation of the cross of Christ to the original readers of Rev. 2.7.

7. The 'tree' and the 'paradise' may have had pointed local analogues in the tree and the *temenos*/asylum of Artemis which gave them a special meaningfulness for the Ephesian Christian. The cross was the place of refuge for the repentant sinner in contrast with the tree which marked the asylum for the unrepentant criminal.

8. The theme of movement and change is important in the history

of Ephesus. I suggest that the threat of Rev. 2.5 may be applied to the prospect of a removal to the site, and beneath the power of, the Artemisium.

9. These suggestions may be tentatively applied to the attempt to clarify the later chapters of the Revelation, especially the New Jerusalem passage, where the faithful have access to the tree of life within the holy city. The same setting may shed light on the Ephesian church of the Ignatian epistle.

Chapter 4

SMYRNA

1. *Introductory*

In Smyrna the element of local historical tradition was peculiarly strong. The city was noted even among the states of proconsular Asia as 'a paradise of municipal vanity'. It claimed to be the birthplace of Homer. It had a notable local historian of about the first century AD. The epitaph of this Hermogenes lists his works, which included a history of the city in two books, essays on the wisdom and on the birthplace of Homer, and a chronological table of Romans and Smyrnaeans (*CIG* 3311 = *IGRR* IV. 1445).[1] In the second century the orations of Aelius Aristides appealed to motifs of early civic history under every variety of metaphor and allusion. In the third Philostratus draws upon the same themes for local colour in his tale of Apollonius of Tyana. The pretentious claims and historical pride of the city are likewise reflected in its coinage and implicit in the public life expressed in innumerable inscriptions.[2]

C.J. Cadoux in his comprehensive work *Ancient Smyrna* acknowledges the help he found in Ramsay's *Seven Churches*, while regarding as fanciful many of the connections Ramsay drew with the local background and his remarks about the civic patriotism of the Smyrnaean Christians (p. 320n.).[3] The difficulty may be acknowledged, but is not I think serious in the context of such a city. For the sentiment of local pride among Christians we may compare Acts 21.39 and perhaps Acts 16.12, on the assumption that the writer had a special interest in Philippi (cf. Ramsay, *SPTR*, pp. 206-209). For the recurring theme of earthly and heavenly citizenship we note Phil. 1.27; 3.20; Eph. 2.19; Heb. 11.13-19; *Ep. to Diognetus* 5. In documents of Smyrna itself the same sentiment appears in *Mart. Polycarpi* 17.1 and in *Mart. Pionii* 6, 20, 30. In view of the evidently liberal policy of Smyrna in granting its citizenship,[4] there is no reason to doubt that converts to Christianity included many citizens, or that they continued to share the characteristic attitude of a citizen to his *polis*.[5]

Two facets of Smyrna's character were its sufferings and its beauty. A few words about each will serve both to illustrate its strength of local tradition and to introduce the following sections.

a. Sufferings

A preliminary question concerns the popular etymology of the name Smyrna. Its identity with the usual Greek word for 'myrrh' has frequently attracted attention (Cadoux, p. 31; W. Michaelis, *TWNT* VII. 457). There is of course no ground for thinking this a true derivation of the name,[6] but there is evidence to support the belief that the coincidence was seen as significant in antiquity. Plutarch (*Sertorius* 1.3 = p. 568) refers to two places with names identical with those of fragrant plants, Ios ('violet') and Smyrna, with the note that Homer was said to have been born at the one and to have died at the other. Plutarch's allusion to those who collected such coincidences is expressed in terms which imply that they thought them significant.

The strange etymologies in the later lexicographers are also likely to reflect thinking previously current (cf. Bürchner in *PW*). The *Etymologicum Magnum*, for instance, connects σμύρνα, μύρον, and μύρω, and refers also to the city name under the same entry (721.32ff.; cf. 595.24, 29; 588.18). Suidas connects σμύρνα symbolically with the tomb (or the sufferings: τάφος, *v.l.* πάθος) of Christ. His words are closely based upon Theodoret's comments on Ps. 45.8 (LXX 44.8), and Gaisford (*ad loc.*) refers also to Theodoret's other allegorical explanations of the word in Cant. 4.6 and 14. There is reason to think that the early Christians placed an allegorical interpretation on those passages in the New Testament where myrrh is mentioned, and that this stemmed from a significance attached to it by the writers. This point must be discussed further in the next section: for the present I suggest merely that the name Smyrna was fitting and expressive to the ancient mind for a city which seemed to exemplify characteristics which myrrh symbolized.

A variety of myths located in the district reiterates these themes. Myrrh itself was explained aetiologically by the myth of Smyrna, or Myrrha, the mother of Adonis (Ov. *Metam.* 10.298-502). Despite the oriental provenance of the story, some authorities connected it with the name of this city (Cadoux, pp. 29-30). The local story of Niobe became a universal type of mourning.[7] This is already true of the treatment of the myth in the Iliad (24.602-17; cf. H.J. Rose in *OCD*, p. 609). And much later Nemesianus links the legends of Niobe and of Smyrna as two well-worn themes (*Cyneget.* 15-16, 26-29).

Other myths describe the misfortunes of the relatives of Niobe. Her father was Tantalus, already in Homer a type of the sinner suffering eternal torment (*Od.* 11.582-92). Her sister-in-law was Aëdon, transformed into a nightingale to lament her son (*Od.* 19.518-23). Her brother was Pelops, who was restored to life after being served up at a feast of the gods (Ov. *Metam.* 4.401-10; Apollod. Epit. 2.3ff.).

Again, the strength of local tradition in the district is notable. Pausanias, for instance, bases his local details partly on personal knowledge (2.22.3; 9.11.7), partly on oral tradition (7.5.1, 2). In this context it is understandable that local forms of these myths suggested and perpetuated the picture of a city of suffering, a concept symbolized by its very name. And the symbolism of myrrh may be pressed a little further. As it had been used in death and burial, in the expectation of an after-life, so Christ himself had died and lived again. The themes of suffering, death and resurrection pervade every verse of our letter.

b. *Beauty*

The second notable characteristic of Smyrna was its beauty. It would be superfluous to repeat the comprehensive collection of allusions to the point in Cadoux (pp. 171-73) or in Ramsay (*SC*, pp. 254-58). The claim was made publicly on the coinage: Σμυρναίων πρώτων ᾿Ασίας ... κάλλει καὶ μεγέθι [*sic*] (*BMC Ionia*, Sm., Nos. 405, 413-14; all of Caracalla). The beauty of the city is the constant theme of the orator Aelius Aristides and it inspires exhortations attributed to Apollonius of Tyana. The numerous incidental allusions in pagan literature are paralleled by others in early Christian writings (e.g. *Vita Polycarpi* 30, in Lightfoot, *Apostolic Fathers* III.462).

The ancient sense of beauty extolled the buildings and their arrangement rather than the natural scenery.[8] It is as a harmonious architectural whole that Aristides likens the city to a flower and to a statue (15.374 = 231.404). Ramsay has laid great emphasis upon his similes, especially on that of a crown (*SC*, pp. 256-59; Ael. Arist. 22.443 = 273.478; cf. 21.437 = 296.471), arguing from the manner of the allusions that this was a familiar emblem of the beauty of Smyrna, and observing that Philostratus characteristically places a locally significant idea in the mouth of Apollonius (*Vit. Ap. Ty.* 4.7). The concept of a crown or wreath is in fact extraordinarily prominent in materials relating to Smyrna. Variations of the motif occur on every pre-Imperial coin listed in *BMC* (Nos. 1-119), and sometimes three times on the same coin (Nos. 35-46). Similar emblems are almost obsessively common throughout the abundant and otherwise more varied types of the Empire.

The familiar symbol of a crown may have originated in the physical appearance of the city rising symmetrically to its 'crown' of battlements. This is implicit in Aristides and explicit in Ramsay. But once adopted, the idea was developed in various aspects of city life. Many such were not peculiar to Smyrna, though some are unusually well exemplified there.[9] The emblem suggested diverse connotations, of athletic victory, festivity, public honour or office, kingship or royal visitation. Apollonius is represented as eliciting new meaning from a familiar concept: it is reasonable to think that the Revelation also alludes to a local emblem, while enriching and transforming its existing wealth of symbolism.

This opening section will serve to illustrate the relevance of the language under consideration. The stricture of Cadoux mentioned at the outset should not deter us from examining the characteristic themes of local patriotism. Cadoux himself stresses 'John's local knowledge (p. 318).

2. *The First and the Last*

Smyrna is represented today by İzmir, the third city of Turkey and the largest in Asia Minor until overtaken by the recent growth of Ankara. As seen from the ancient acropolis, Mount Pagus (Kadifekale), it spreads many miles round the head of its land-locked gulf. The heart of modern İzmir occupies the very site of the Hellenistic and Roman city, rising from the shore up the northern and western slopes of Pagus at the south-eastern apex of the gulf. Originally, however, Smyrna had lain two miles north of this, at Bayraklı by the north-eastern end of the gulf and close beneath the foothills of Sipylus.

The history of this Old Smyrna, originally an Aeolian colony, and later occupied by Ionians from Colophon, is familiar in outline from Herodotus (1.16, 149-50; cf. Strab. 14.1.4 = p. 634; Paus. 7.5.1). The lengthy account in Cadoux (pp. 57-82) may be supplemented by the evidence provided by the Anglo-Turkish excavations at Bayraklı, which have illustrated both the early prosperity of the old city and the completeness of its subsequent destruction.[10] It had evidently defied the power of Lydia for many years, surviving an assault by

Gyges (Hdt. 1.15) before falling to Alyattes, the father of Croesus (Hdt. 1.16). Excavation has suggested that the date of this crucial event was not later than the end of the seventh century BC (*AS* 1 [1951], p. 16).

Ramsay found in Rev. 2.8 a reference to the condition of Smyrna between this destruction and the refoundation as a *polis* about 290 BC (*SC*, pp. 251-52, 269). His view is based on an interesting passage in Strabo: Λυδῶν δὲ κατασπασάντων τὴν Σμύρναν, περὶ τετρακόσια ἔτη διετέλεσεν οἰκουμένη κωμηδόν· εἶτα ἀνέγειρεν αὐτὴν Ἀντίγονος, καὶ μετὰ ταῦτα Λυσίμαχος (14.1.37 = p. 646). The implication is that during the interval Smyrna lost its status as a city, but preserved its identity and tradition while outwardly reduced to an Anatolian-type aggregate of villages.

The titles of Christ in Rev. 2.8 correspond closely to those in his words in the Patmos vision (1.17-18). 'The first and the last' is a divine title from Isa. 44.6 and 48.12 (cf. also Rev. 22.13 and see Charles, p. 31). The latter point is notable because the Smyrna letter seems otherwise less indebted to the Old Testament than any other. Its central theme of life after death is not a prominent subject in the Old Testament, though it became increasingly an interest of the apocalyptists.[11]

In the present case the scriptural background does not exclude reference to the contemporary situation of the church (so Swete, p. 31). If Ramsay is right, there is also a reminder of the actual physical renewal of the city under Antigonus and Lysimachus.

This view needs careful consideration. I should question Ramsay's objection to the rendering 'was dead and lived again' (RV); he is perhaps being unnecessarily pedantic and the essential interpretation does not hinge upon this particular verbal point.[12] That interpretation is sometimes assumed too easily, sometimes in a modified form (Souter in 1-vol. *HDB*; Caird, p. 34), and often dismissed (Cadoux, p. 320n.), but rarely discussed. The unstated doubts might be provisionally formulated under four headings. (1) On grounds of literary analysis: if Charles is correct, the introductory titles were simply derived from 1.17-18 and appended here as an editorial addition which formed no part of the original letter. (2) It may be argued that Ramsay's evidence is inadequate or his methods unsound, and that he is therefore in danger of imposing a fanciful background on the text. (3) Criticism of this interpretation of the history of Smyrna. There is, for instance, more evidence for the existence of a settlement between 600 and 290 BC than he mentions. (4) Some other background might be preferred.

On (1), where Charles suggests that the choice of titles is verbally accommodated to Rev. 2.10d, it must be emphasized that the unity of the letter comprises both phrases and was rooted in the *Sitz im Leben* to which both were addressed. Later commentators have in any case not followed Charles in his view.

On the other three counts some historical study may assist in elucidating the matter. The case is that historical tradition in Smyrna did in fact follow the lines that Ramsay suggested. And the shape of the ancient tradition is the important thing here, not the critical appraisal of the events.

Strabo's evidence may be taken to mean that the reduction of Smyrna to village status was a deliberate act of policy. Smyrna received more drastic treatment than Ephesus, treatment evidently aimed at destroying its Hellenic identity (*SC*, p. 252), and its dramatic fall evidently made a deep impact on Greek feeling.[13] It nevertheless continued to exist through the village period.[14]

Other literary sources attest aspects of the destruction and refoundation. Pausanias (7.5.1-3) distinguishes the 'ancient city' from the existing Smyrna, whose foundation he ascribes to Alexander. The Nemeses had appeared to the conqueror while he slept by their shrine on Pagus, commanding him to found a city there and ἄγειν εἰς αὐτὴν Σμυρναίους ἀναστατήσαντα ἐκ τῆς προτέρας (7.5.2).[15] Perhaps Alexander had actually conceived the project which his successors effected, and local sentiment would readily claim the great Alexander as founder.[16] The legend was certainly current in Roman Imperial times, as it is depicted on coinage (from *BMC*, No. 346, of M. Aurelius), and is mentioned also by Aristides (21.431f. = 265.464).[17]

Aristides' *Palinodia de Smyrna Instaurata* (21, Dindorf) was delivered on the occasion of the city's restoration after earthquake in AD 178. It alludes tantalizingly to the then familiar historical traditions of the city in a fulsome panegyric of her current imperial benefactors, Marcus Aurelius and Commodus. The point of the address turns largely upon the parallels between the city's past and present fortunes. She had had two notable founders, Theseus and Alexander, but now two yet greater (21.431 = 264.463). Destruction might be final for men or for other cities, but this was not true of Smyrna (430 = 264.462-3). Alexander's sleep was but a προοίμιον κατοικίσεως, but these benefactors had restored the city before the messenger started out to ask their help (431 = 265.464). Aristides refers to the state of Athens after the loss of her empire, but declines to enumerate her interim sufferings: a pointed parallel with Smyrna is implied. Local sentiment was prone to dwell upon the splendid rebirth of the city rather than the sufferings of its 'dark age'. The concept of renewed life pervades the speech.[18] In a final simile Aristides compares Smyrna with the phoenix: the successive reincarnations of the bird are likened to the successive refoundations of the city of Theseus and Alexander (436 = 268.470).[19]

The comparison is the more interesting as the phoenix is used by Christian writers as early as Clement of Rome (1 Clem 25) as a type of the resurrection of Jesus. There are also striking, but evidently quite unconscious, parallels with the Revelation.[20]

Ramsay's treatment of the evidence for the existence of Smyrna between 600 and 290 BC is open to criticism,[21] but the essential point is established that the city suffered sudden eclipse coupled with a modest and perhaps tenuous continuance. The history of the site can now be more clearly documented from excavation: 'A cut 90m. long across the northern part of the site has . . . brought to light fifth century occupation, thus filling a gap in the history of the site' (*AS* 2 [1952], p. 23).[22] The sudden numismatic wealth of Phocaea (77 items of early electrum in *BMC*) follows the fall of its rival.[23] Only two electrum coins are doubtfully attributed to Old Smyrna: then a long gap is broken only by one tetradrachm, belonging in style to the early fourth century (Head, *Historia Numorum*, p. 592). On the other hand, Cadoux (p. 92) notes the absence of Smyrna from the Athenian tribute-lists. Politically, for three centuries, in Cadoux's own words, it was 'off the map' (p. 87).

It seems inherently likely that local tradition would tend to tidy and dramatize this history. This may have been achieved by the historian Hermogenes. His work may underlie a view of Smyrna's past familiar to John as later to Aristides.

There is other evidence that the early church illustrated the resurrection from symbols available to it in the current culture. Such was the phoenix, whose legend was repeatedly told in classical writers.[24] The fabulous bird appears in Jewish apocalyptic by about the first century AD.[25] Its use in 1 Clement is rather puzzling, for it seems a very imperfect expression of the Christian idea. Lightfoot discusses the point (pp. 94-97 *ad loc.*), noting the emphasis on the uniqueness of the bird, to which Clement applies the adjective μονογενής.

We have seen that Aristides compares Smyrna with the phoenix; thus the same simile is used in a parallel way of Christ and of the city. And most accounts of the phoenix, including that of Clement, emphasize the use of myrrh in its burial and reincarnation.

We must examine the symbolism attached to myrrh a little further. It had been used in Egypt, the source of the phoenix legend, for the most elaborate form of embalming (Hdt. 2.86), a practice inseparable from the expectation of a future life in which the body would be needed. In the Old Testament it was valued as a perfume (Ps. 45.8; Prov. 7.17; Cant. 3.6) and was especially important as an ingredient of the holy anointing oil (Exod. 30.23). In classical literature are references to its burning as incense in pagan worship (Eur. *Ion* 1175; etc.), its use in medicine (Hdt. 7.181; Cels. 6.2-8) and commonly as a perfume, especially at festive occasions (Athen. *Deipn.* 2.66C; 3.101C; Verg. *Aen.* 12.100; Ov. *Metam.* 3.555; 5.53; Plin. *NH* 13.2.8-18).

In the New Testament the word σμύρνα occurs only twice (Mt. 2.11 and John 19.39) and a derivative form once (Mk 15.23). Commentators note the enormous quantity of myrrh and aloes brought by Nicodemus for the burial of Jesus.[26] Use of these spices evidently accorded with normal Jewish practice (cf. John 11.44), except that their quantity in this case represented a costly act of devotion to Jesus, resembling that of Mary (John 12.2-11). Jesus there applied the lesson of her gift to his forthcoming burial (John 12.7; cf. Mk 14.8; Mt. 26.12). The Gospel tradition, both Synoptic and Johannine, seems to insist that these acts had a significance which merited their special inclusion. Perhaps the point was that myrrh to the Jewish mind represented the preservation of the body, and this was regarded as a prerequisite of resurrection. Mary and Nicodemus had performed acts more significant than they understood.[27]

Again, the gifts of the Magi (Mt. 2.11) may clearly be related to Isa. 60 (esp. v. 6) and to Ps. 72.10. But myrrh is an addition to the gifts mentioned in Isa. 60.6. Now the allegorical interpretation of Mt. 2.11 is attested early,[28] and it seems reasonable to suppose that the Evangelist himself saw symbolic meaning in the inclusion of myrrh, especially as this item is not connected with fulfilment of the prophecy. He writes in the light of the resurrection.

In Rev. 2.8 the conjunction of the name Smyrna with the following titles might well have awakened the associations of the word and name in readers whose city is represented in its own tradition as having undergone an analogous experience. It is likely that they would have known the Gospel tradition in some of the several areas which linked myrrh with the resurrection of Jesus. The parallel with the sufferings of Christ had a message of encouragement for the suffering Smyrnaean Christian who meditated deeply on these scriptures in their bearing on his situation.[29] We may compare the thought of Rom. 6 or of Heb. 2.18. In contrast with the temporary nature of the suffering, Christ is the First and the Last, and the reality of his victory over death is the guarantee of the same victory for his followers. These themes are developed in the following verses.

The suggested background may be further illustrated from the writings of Ignatius and Polycarp. The latter may have been a young man in the church which first received the present letter. He evidently came much under its influence. In his own epistle to the Philippians, a meditation upon numerous texts of scripture, he never quotes the Revelation, though his mind dwells constantly upon the present themes, suffering and the confident hope of resurrection (1.2; 2.1-2; 5.2; 7.1; 8.1; 9.2; 12.2). His epistle reads like the work of a man who had studied in all the scriptures the topics imprinted on his life by our passage.[30]

Ignatius's epistle to Polycarp is also relevant. A personally shared knowledge of our text might well underlie his exhortations to the younger man (*ad Polyc.* 2.3; cf. 1.3; 3.1 and Lightfoot, *Ignatius*, I.443). There are further remarkable parallels in the letter of the church in Smyrna to the church in Philomelium about Polycarp's martyrdom (e.g. *Mart. Polyc.* 17.1; 19.3). Close analogy is drawn between the death of Polycarp and that of Christ (6, 14), and the whole may be seen as presenting a representative fulfilment of Rev. 2.8-11.

3. *The Background of the Church in Smyrna*

The question of the racial and cultural background of this city is of particular significance in view of the problematic reference to Jewish opposition from the 'synagogue of Satan' (2.9; cf. 3.9).

The considerable evidence for the early settlement of Jews in Asia includes little which can be related explicitly to Smyrna.[31] But the indications are that it was likely to have had a considerable Jewish population by New Testament times, and probably much earlier. There are Jewish inscriptions of later periods, and they reveal some unusual and significant details.[32] There is also the testimony contained in the accounts of the martyrdoms of Polycarp and Pionius to the unusually virulent bitterness of the local Jewish community against the Christians.

It is possible that there were Jews who were citizens of Smyrna, as of other Ionian cities.[33] Such a body was particularly unpopular in a Greek city, and the Jews in turn hated their pagan environment. Their vindictiveness against Smyrna may be reflected in the earlier Sibylline Oracles (3.344, 365; 5.122-23, 306-307). Then there is the problematic phrase οἱ ποτὲ Ἰουδαῖοι in a Hadrianic inscription. Mommsen and Ramsay both held that this referred to a Jewish national community no longer recognized in law as a nation since AD 70 (*CIG* 3148.30 = *CIJ* 742; see *SC*, pp. 272 and 444n.).[34]

Christianity may first have reached Smyrna through some Jew of Asia present in Jerusalem on the day of Pentecost (Acts 2.9). It is very possible that there was already a church in the city when Paul came to reside in Ephesus, though the evidence cited from the Pionian Life of Polycarp is debatable.[35] Even if this document as a whole is not authentic and reliable, there is no internal reason to doubt the possibility that this account might be based on an early tradition. The words *nos autem nondum cognoveramus*[36] in the Latin rendering of Polycarp, *Phil.* 11.3, might be held to conflict with it, but such an interpretation would clash also with Acts 19.10, 26, at least if we suppose Polycarp to refer to Phil. 1.3-11 and date that epistle as late as Paul's Roman imprisonment. Polycarp's words, however, may imply no more that that the church in Philippi was older than that in Smyrna (cf. Cadoux, p. 311n.). In any case there were probably some Christians resident in Smyrna from an early date, and the city must have been a primary objective in the evangelism of Asia during Paul's Ephesian residence (Acts 19.10). We can thus be confident that a church became established there in the period c. 52-55, if not earlier. There is no record of its early history, but we may suppose that many Jews were converted,[37] and that the resulting bitterness in the Jewish community was intensified if an influx of Jewish refugees arrived after 70.[38]

The simplest explanation of 'those who say they are Jews and are not' (Rev. 2.9) is that which identifies them with the Jewish community in Smyrna *per se*, which preserved its identity and claimed to constitute exclusively the people of God. They might thus correspond to οἱ ποτὲ Ἰουδαῖοι of the following generation, if we accept the most plausible interpretation of that phrase.[39] Our passage is closely comparable with the Philadelphian letter, and its thought may be understood from such parallels as Rom. 2.28, Gal. 6.15, Phil. 3.23, or the controversy over the term 'children of Abraham' in John 8.33ff. The writer has his own usage of the term 'Jew'. He insists that the true people of God is a spiritual nation, not an ethnic group.[40] The Christians were now the true Jews; those who maintained a racial separation had rejected the Christ, according to John, and were of Satan.[41]

It is remarkable that a writer so Jewish in background could speak in such terms. Probably, in Smyrna, the unbelieving Jews had become active in instigating persecution of the church or denouncing to the authorities those Jews who were also Christians. The situation under Domitian will explain the peculiar power they had. *Delatores* were rife: perhaps here the transition from Σατανᾶ (v. 9) to διάβολος (v. 10) is intended to stress the literal meaning of the Greek term.[42] The reasons for this continued hostility of the Jews, intensified yet further after the Bar Kochba rebellion, are given by Lightfoot (*Ignatius*, I.469). The most striking instance actually relates to Smyrna: the Jews gathered fuel on the Sabbath for the burning of Polycarp (*Mart. Polyc.* 13, 21), as a century later their enmity sharpened the local execution of the Decian edict of persecution (*Mart. Pion.* 4; Cadoux, pp. 378-79).

It is understandable in this context that the letter to Smyrna is the least Jewish of the seven despite the presence of a considerable Jewish community in the city. Charles in fact does not list any Old Testament parallel at all, though he finds two interesting links with other parts of the New Testament: Rev. 2.9 with 2 Cor. 6.10 and James 2.5; Rev. 2.10 ('the crown of life') with James 1.12 (p. lxxxiv). We may however refer the words 'the first and the last' (Rev. 2.8b = 1.17b) to Isa. 44.6 and 48.12, and the 'ten days' of Rev. 2.10 to Dan. 1.12 (cf. Rev. 1.14-15; Swete, p. cxli).

For a writer so deeply imbued with the Old Testament these echoes are notably slight. The last is interesting: it seems to me questionable whether this was conscious reference to Daniel at all, and whether the recipients could have been expected to interpret the 'ten days' from its occurrence there. Many commentators appear to assume that the original readers appreciated what might seem a somewhat erudite parallel (Swete, p. 32; etc.).

The list of New Testament parallels, however, might be extended, and the fact accords with the extensive quotation from the New Testament in a work so early as Polycarp's *Philippians*. These features all testify indirectly to the cleavage between Jew and Christian in Smyrna and tell against the explanation of our letter from Jewish sources outside the canonical scriptures.

The second main topic in this section, the sufferings of the church in Smyrna, is closely linked with the preceding. The context indicates that the Jews were agents of the persecution. It has often been observed that the poverty of the Christians may have been at least partly due to the despoliation of their property by mobs, whether Jewish or pagan. There may have been other contributory causes, the fact that converts were oftener made among the poorer classes (1 Cor. 1.26; James 2.5), and that devoted Christians on occasion reduced themselves to penury by the liberality of their own giving (2 Cor. 2.8; cf. Swete, p. 32), or that it was difficult for an uncompromising Christian to make a living in a pagan city (Caird, p. 35). Jewish hostility was at least likely to have been a factor: their rejection of the Christians placed the latter outside the protection and toleration which the Jews themselves enjoyed.

Ramsay (*SC*, pp. 273-74) pointed out that it was wrong to infer from v. 10 that imprisonment was the most severe penalty to which a Christian was liable, for it was not strictly used as a criminal punishment at all. A. Berger in *OCD* mentions three functions of imprisonment: (1) as a coercive measure by magistrates against recalcitrance (*coercitio*); (2) detention pending trial (*custodia reorum*); (3) to await execution.[43]

In the present context the sense that 'prison' conveyed was probably that of a temporary, interim period of suffering in anticipation of martyrdom.

The following words involve some textual and exegetical uncertainties. An understanding of their setting turns especially on the choice between the readings ἕξετε (‎ℵ and most other MSS) and ἔχητε (A, etc). Swete (p. 32) accepts the latter and regards ἕξετε as a correction made in the interests of the sense. Beckwith (p. 455), however, accounts for the reverse change by arguing that an original ἕξετε was assimilated to the preceding subjunctive πειρασθῆτε, and this appears on balance the more likely. Swete argues that it was part of Satan's purpose to prolong the suffering of the church to 'ten days', whereas many commentators interpret this period as denoting a short or limited time.[44]

The 'ten days' have in fact lent themselves to much debate. The echo of Dan. 1 seems to me insufficient as an explanation. John constantly appeals to a background which his readers knew. It is important to ask what this phrase was intended to convey to them. It is not clear that we have a satisfactory answer.

There are certain indications to support a conjecture that a similar phrase was significant in Smyrna. The possibility should not be pressed too far.[45]

One readily accessible but unnoticed parallel may usefully be cited. In April 1964 I copied in the Agora in Smyrna the words of a dedication reading: ... Ἰούλιον Μενεκλέα Διόφαντον Ἀσιάρχην ἐνδόξως φιλοτειμησάμενον ἑξῆς ἡμερῶν πέντε τοῖς ὀξέσιν ἡ γλυκυτάτη πατρίς. The verb ἐτ(ε)ίμησε must be supplied. The meaning and background of τοῖς ὀξέσιν were obscure.

I have subsequently found this inscription published in L. Robert, *Hellenica*, V. 81-82, and have thus confirmed the accuracy of my transcription.[46] Robert explains this and a parallel from Thyatira (*IGRR* IV. 1230) in the light of some words from an inscription of Sagalassus in Pisidia honouring an imperial high priest: ἡμερῶν δ΄ ὁλοκλήρων ὀξέσι σιδήροις (see Robert in *RA* 5th ser. 30 [1929], pp. 31-32). The context was gladiatorial: 'La nouvelle inscription de Smyrne apporte un nouvel exemple de cette locution abrégée, dans un contexte intéressant; cet asiarque a donné un "munus", pendant cinq jours, avec des armes affilées. Cinq jours, cela témoigne d'une large libéralité'. A point of interest here is that the phrase ἡμερῶν δέκα in Rev. 2.10 has precisely the syntactical form of the corresponding phrases in the Smyrnaean and Sagalassian inscriptions. I then translate the present inscription: 'To Julius Menecles Diophantus, Asiarch, who has gloriously and zealously presented (a show of combat) with sharpened (weapons) five days successively, his dearest city (pays honour)'. We have thus at least the attestation of this form of expression at Smyrna. And if Robert is right there is reason to think that John's words may have recalled to the Christian the language of the arena. An appearance at some great festival there might well await those who were 'faithful unto death'.[47]

Smyrna had been an important centre of the imperial cult since its reception of the neocorate in AD 26. The communal rejection of the Christians by the national Jewish community would accordingly place them in particular danger in the situation we have postulated as obtaining in the last years of Domitian.

The 'ten days' should probably be seen as a limited, intermediate period of suffering, expected to terminate in judgment and death,— but this for the Christian was victory and life, assured by the precedent of Christ's resurrection (cf. 1 Cor. 15.20).

4. *The Crown of Life*

In the final words of v. 10 the concepts of 'faithfulness' and the 'crown' are closely linked. Both are likely to have seemed significant in the historical tradition of Smyrna.

Some commentators have drawn attention to the traditional fidelity of Smyrna to Rome (Charles, p. 55; Swete, pp. lxi and 30; Barclay, pp. 34f.; Blaiklock, *Cities*, p. 100), without always committing themselves to Ramsay's application of it.[48]

Smyrna's characteristic boast of 'faithfulness' originated before the advent of Roman power to the Aegean. An early Hellenistic decree declares her permanent loyalty to Seleucus II and her sufferings in his cause.[49] This faithful endurance, however, and the honours and inviolability conferred upon the city by Seleucus did not prevent a rapid change of allegiance to the rising star of Attalus I Soter (241-197 BC).[50] Smyrna quickly established her claim with him, for we read of his favourable reception of her ambassadors, 'because the Smyrnaeans had most of all men kept faith with him' (Polyb. 5.77.6, 218 BC; cf. Cadoux, p. 128n.). In 197 BC, still as the ally of Pergamum, Smyrna refused to submit to intimidation by Antiochus III, and appealed to Flamininus for Roman help (App. *Bell. Syr.* 2; Liv. 33.38; Cadoux, p. 135). Thus at the coming of Rome Smyrna already possessed a reputation for fidelity to allies, chosen no doubt with skill.

These might seem to us irrelevant matters of distant history, but their importance in ancient feeling may be plainly seen in Tacitus's account of the Smyrnaean case before Tiberius in applying for an imperial temple in AD 26 (*Ann.* 4.56). After recounting the antiquity of their city the Smyrnaeans passed to the thing they relied most upon, their services to Rome. They had sent naval forces to help the Romans even in their warfare in Italy. They had been the first ever to establish a temple to the city of Rome, in 195 BC, a time when her preeminence was not yet apparent, for Carthage yet stood and there were still powerful kings in Asia to be reckoned with. And such was their love for the Romans that when it was reported in their assembly that the army of Sulla was endangered by the severity of the winter and inadequate clothing, those present spontaneously stripped off the garments they were wearing to send them to the legions.

Livy repeatedly mentions the active fidelity of Smyrna to Rome in the years following 195 BC (35 *passim*). Roman recognition of the fact continued. Cicero wrote: *Smyrnam, ... quae est fidelissimorum antiquissimorumque sociorum* (*Philipp.* 11.2.5).

On the side of Smyrna we note the comparative table of Romans and Smyrnaeans by the local historian Hermogenes (*CIG* 3311). The clearest statement is again in Aristides, in his letter pleading for imperial help for the restoration of the city after the earthquake of AD 178. His words are closely reminiscent of those of the Smyrnaean ambassadors in Tacitus.[51]

This selection of evidence will suffice to illustrate the point of Ramsay's discussions (*SC*, pp. 253-54, 275-77). He did not closely document his own case, and he was probably aware of more evidence than he mentions. The words of Tacitus and of Aristides, in particular, show how this 'fidelity' was a commonplace of patriotic speeches.

A note on ἄχρι θανάτου may help to clarify the context. In usage ἄχρι and μέχρι alike, but not ἕως, appear to imply 'up to and including'.[52] The thought then is that the time of interim suffering is likely to terminate in actual death, not the mere threat of it, but that death for the Christian is the prelude to life. We may compare a similar phrase in Josephus which has a quasi-official ring: Coponius was sent as first procurator of Judaea μέχρι τοῦ κτείνειν λαβὼν παρὰ Καίσαρος ἐξουσίαν (*BJ* 2.8.1.117). Even if this were less than the full *ius gladii*,[53] there is no doubt that it included life and death powers over the provincials. The corresponding phrase may then have suggested the prospect of a capital sentence pronounced by authority of the proconsul. The pattern fits the later cases of Polycarp and of Pionius. And the only other occurrence of πιστός predicated of men in the seven letters concerns the death of Antipas at Pergamum (Rev. 2.13). That city was preeminently the centre of the imperial cult, and 'the sharp two-edged ῥομφαία' is probably an allusion to the proconsular *ius gladii*.

The 'crown of life' has been much discussed. Trench (pp. 111-13) argued that it meant a royal crown, but usage seems to require that this meaning be restricted to διάδημα (Swete, p. 33; etc.). στέφανος is generally a garland of victory, festivity, honour or worship. Such a distinction is probably to be strictly applied in the Revelation, where διάδημα is used of the kingship of the dragon (12.3), of the beast (13.1) and of Christ (19.12),[54] but στέφανος elsewhere, where other ideas are uppermost.[55] There is certainly no reason for denying στέφανος its most usual sense here. It is 'wreath', not 'diadem', *Kranz*, not *Krone*. The 'crown of thorns' is admittedly στέφανος in the evangelists (Mt. 27.29; Mk 15.17; John 19.2, 5), but that was literally a garland. To the soldiers it meant mock royalty; perhaps to the writers it also implied victory (cf. Tait, p. 212).

στέφανος in the New Testament frequently alludes to the prize of athletic victory and so to the eternal reward of the faithful (1 Cor. 9.25; 2 Tim. 4.8; James 1.12; 1 Pet. 5.4; cf. also 2 Tim. 2.5; Heb. 12.1). It is also used frequently of an object of pride (Phil. 4.1; 1 Thess. 2.19). The former usage became a commonplace of Christian writings (cf. e.g. Herm. *Simil.* 8.2.1, as explained in 8.3.6). Its earliest occurrence in a religious sense seems however to be in *Test. Benj.* 4.1, a precedent for its use in an author of Jewish culture. There is no ground for dogmatism here about possible literary relationship with James 1.12. It is likely that the metaphor was already familiar from its appearance in 1 Cor. The genitive τῆς ζωῆς has been variously interpreted as epexegetic (Swete, p. 33) or as possessive (Charles, p. 59). The latter view, however, is connected by Charles with a supposed parallel in 2 Enoch 14.2 and 3 Baruch 6.1, referring to a nimbus of light surrounding the sun. It is much more natural to think of 'the crown (= prize) which consists in life'. Many commentators, including Charles himself (p. 58), see allusion to the athlete's wreath here, while recognizing the wealth of symbolic meaning attached to the word (Swete, p. 33; Kiddle, p. 28; Beckwith, p. 455; Hort, p. 26). Some emphasize that Smyrna was famous for its games: Swete refers to Paus. 6.14.3.

Several suggestions have been made about the background and significance of the 'crown' in the letter. We have seen that the emblem was pervasively present in Smyrna. There is (1) allusion to the athlete's crown of victory (Swete, *et al.*); (2) allusion to the crown supposedly given to the presiding priest at the Mysteries of Dionysus (Blakesley in *Smith's DB*, criticized by Plumptre, p. 97, and Hort, p. 26); (3) the crown as a symbol of earthly honour, awarded in Asian cities for civil merit or for military or athletic prowess (Kiddle, p. 28;

Barclay, p. 45); (4) allusion to the crowns worn by pagan sacrificing priests, whose victims the Christians would be (Hort; Swete; Ramsay in *HDB* IV. 555); (5) reference to the eponymous priestly magistrates of the city known as *stephanephoroi* (Hort); (6) the festal crown representing the Christian's joy (garlands were worn by guests at pagan feasts as worshippers of the god; Barclay; cf. *SC*, p. 258); (7) allusion to the physical appearance of Smyrna as compared by the orators with a bejewelled statue rising symmetrically from the sea to the 'crown' of Pagus (*SC*, pp. 256-60; Peake, p. 240; Blaiklock, p. 101).

These explanations are not necessarily mutually exclusive, nor always rigidly distinct. Some are open to obvious criticism, either as factually incorrect or as of doubtful relevance or significance.[56] I suggest that (1), (3) and (7) are particularly fruitful. It is important to try to bring the situation into clearer focus through looking at actual texts and practices of Smyrna.

The idea of the crown recurs in the patriotic orations of Aristides. The city is itself described by this title on the occasion of its restoration after earthquake: 'Ionia has had its crown (στέφανος) saved' (22.443 = 273.478). In another speech he writes: 'I think, if the image of any city ever deserved to appear in the heavens, as they say the crown of Ariadne and other representations of rivers and animals are found among the stars and are honoured by the gods, that the emblem of this city ought to win the contest' (15.374 = 231.404). It is characteristic of Aristides' manner to introduce the figure of a crown obliquely in implied contrast with the city's use of that very emblem. Ramsay argued that the passages of Aristides which liken the city to a statue or a flower are closely related. Its appearance is pictured as a statue rising from the pedestal of the sea to the battlements of Pagus (20.424 = 261.456; cf. 15.371 = 229.401; 41.512 = 289.762). The 'crown' is never mentioned in the same immediate context, and there is no direct evidence for its application to Mt Pagus. That is an inference from Aristides' allusive language. It seems very probable nevertheless.[57]

The crown as a mark of civic honour was a very widespread concept, but may be related specifically to a characteristic practice at Smyrna. A long series of inscriptions testifies to the formula (*CIG* 3216-56; cf. 3157, 3299, 3350, 3379). The words ὁ δῆμος are commonly inscribed within a wreath, and a personal name in the accusative case follows. The crown motif may be repeated or varied.

The practice seems to be that mentioned by Cicero as a notorious example of extravagant praise bestowed on a commonplace person.[58] A point which evokes his emphatic sarcasm is the fact that these honours were awarded at Smyrna to a corpse. Boeckh (*ad CIG* 3216) observes that almost all the corresponding inscriptions are sepulchral, and cites no exception. The promise of a 'crown of life' might readily be contrasted with this institution of a city whose highest honour was awarded posthumously. I suggest that the explanation (3) is seen more pointedly as a facet of the case when viewed in the light of this specific local practice.

The words which Philostratus puts into the mouth of Apollonius (*Vit. Ap. Ty.* 4.7) testify to the attempt to moralize about the familiar emblem of the city, ostensibly at the very date of the Revelation: 'He urged [the Smyrnaeans] to take pride rather in themselves than in the beauty of their city, . . . for it was more pleasing for the city to be crowned with men than with porticoes and pictures or even with gold in excess of their needs'. In the same vein he contrasts men, as travelling representatives of their city, with cities whose beauty is merely that of an immobile statue. Here is exactly the same grouping of similes as in Aristides (cf. *SC*, p. 256).

The same concepts recur in the remarkable body of primitive Christian literature centred upon Smyrna and showing the influence of the present passage.[59]

A further facet merits notice. The theme of the imminent Parousia of Christ is explicitly mentioned in every letter of the seven except the present. Its absence in this case invites explanation. The answer may be that the Parousia was expected to terminate the church's interim period of suffering. That would be the occasion when Christ would bestow the crown of life. There was no need to stress it as a warning or threat.

Another ancient custom involving a crown is relevant in this connection. The term *parousia* was widely used for the official visit of a potentate. If we accept Wilcken's explanation of the difficult Flinders Petrie Papyrus 2.39e, we may see there an early reference to enforced contributions to a fund for presenting golden *stephanoi* to officials at their *parousiai*.[60] Deissmann finds in this practice a background for figurative language in the Pauline and Pastoral epistles: 'While the sovereigns of this world expect at their parusia a costly crown for themselves, "at the parusia of our Lord Jesus" the apostle will wear a crown—the "crown of glory" (1 Thess. ii.19) won by his work among the churches, or the "crown of righteousness" which the Lord will give to him and to all them that have loved His appearing (2 Tim. iv. 8)' (*LAE*, p. 369). He cites evidence for the widespread prominence of the concept of the royal visit. *Parousia* in this sense is frequently recorded from Asia Minor in the Roman period. The visits of Hadrian are particularly well attested, as in many places new eras were reckoned from them (*LAE*, pp. 370-72). Deissmann does not mention the present passage, but those which he explains thus are closely similar in thought and expression. Unlike earthly sovereigns, Christ will give, not receive, this crown at his coming.

To sum up: I accept the relevance of more than one background for this passage. I concede the allusion to the picture of the city rising to the 'crown' of Pagus; such similar language was later used by Aristides. The athletic imagery is also clear, and this certainly became later the dominant idea in the consciousness of the church and in the context of persecution. The crown may also have suggested the award to the victor as he entered upon eternal life, in pointed contrast with a local distinction conferred upon the dead. I have mentioned also a further possibility, applying here Deissmann's explanation of such passages as 2 Tim. 4.8 to suggest that Christ, unlike earthly kings who expected to receive a crown at their official visits, would himself give the 'crown of life' to those who had continued faithful to the end.

The final promise to the conqueror here is difficult.[61] In any case it is a Jewish phrase, whether Rabbinic in origin (Charles, p. 59;[62] Swete, p. 33; Anderson Scott, p. 141; Beckwith, p. 455) or Biblical (Hort, p. 27; Peake, p. 240 and note). The expression actually occurs in Plutarch, *Moralia* 942F, though the thought there, which Hort characterized as Neopythagorean, is remote from that of our passage.[63] Hort himself is surely right to connect this usage with three later occurrences of 'the second death' in the Revelation itself (20.6, 14; 21.8). Beckwith, while quoting the Targums for the Rabbinic view, thinks that John needed to explain the term to his readers and therefore did so in these later passages. Hort, rejecting both Rabbinic and pagan backgrounds, sees the source of the imagery in Gen. 19.24 as echoed by Ezek. 38.22 with relation to Gog. This may perhaps be the ultimate source, but it is likely that the phrase was familiar to John from its occurrence in contemporary Judaism. It was also suitable to this context and to the condition of the church, which was thus assured that martyrdom meant entry on a life exempt from death. The expression was fitting in a city which had undergone successive disasters and refoundations. One might speculate that such a phrase may have been used by the hostile local Jews against the Christians they had rejected, threatening them with divine condemnation at a future judgment beyond the physical death of the arena.

5. Conclusions

1. There is good reason to think that the present letter contains allusions to ideas which were current in contemporary thinking in the city of Smyrna, as seen in such writings as the orations of Aelius Aristides and the Life of Apollonius of Tyana.

2. It is suggested that the ancient mind found significance in the coincidence between the name of the city and the word σμύρνα. The symbolism of weeping, burial and resurrection attached to myrrh may have been reflected in the portrayal of a city of suffering.

3. The introductory address of v. 8 may be related to the local tradition of the city's history, which represented it as risen again from oblivion. We must recognize that in fact Smyrna had a more nearly continuous history than Ramsay and his followers have allowed. The point may be extensively illustrated from Aristides.

4. Aristides applies the simile of the phoenix to Smyrna. References to this and to myrrh in the early Christian literature are discussed. It is suggested that the use of these symbols in both contexts facilitated the identification of the fortunes of the city with the death and resurrection of Christ. The words of Rev. 2.8 may have been directed against the beginnings of the Docetism which Ignatius attacked a few years later.

5. Relations of the church with the local Jews have been discussed. It is considered that the background of v. 9 is the bitter opposition of the community as such rather than of a sectarian 'magical' Judaism. The especial antagonism of the Jews of Smyrna is illustrated from later documents of the local church. Further implications of the situation as existing under Domitian have been argued in the Introduction.

6. The separation of the Christian and Jewish communities may help to account for the comparative lack of Jewish allusion in this letter. The reference to the 'second death', a phrase commonly held

to be Rabbinic, perhaps answered a Jewish taunt in Smyrna.

7. The allusion in v. 10 to the proverbial faithfulness of Smyrna is accepted and further illustrated.

8. The 'crown of life' probably had varied connotations for a Smyrnaean reader. Several points of special local significance are noted. John enriched the significances of a familiar symbol. It is further suggested that the words are orientated to the 'coming' of Christ, in implied contrast with the crown presented to a human potentate at his *parousia*.

9. Some tentative discussion of the 'ten days' of tribulation is offered. Possible connections with local history and literature might be suggested, in particular with the interpretation of a local inscription.

10. Attention may be drawn to the relevance of the extensive literary parallels in later documents of the Smyrnaean church. It is beyond the scope of our present task to elaborate. The literature, especially as relating to Polycarp and Pionius, points to the continuing influence of our letter in the local church and illustrates interpretations offered in the present discussion.

Chapter 5

PERGAMUM

1. *Introductory*

The huge granite citadel-hill of Pergamum[1] rises a thousand feet above the plain of the river Caicus (Bakır Çay) and some ten miles inland from the Aegean coast. It dominates an immense expanse of country from the rolling hills of the Mysian hinterland in the north-east to the sea in the west. Its lower slopes are uniformly steep on all sides and the modern road reaches the summit plateau only by describing a long spiral round more than a complete circuit of its flanks. The principal buildings of the great Hellenistic and Roman city occupied this plateau, itself a steeply inclined plane facing south, and overlooking the present town of Bergama in the plain. Many ancient structures spread also about the site of the modern town, and the Asklepion and its associated buildings far beyond it.

The whole area is far too large for obvious suitability for defence in that primitive age when the tiny summit of Sardis was an impregnable citadel, though there is some evidence for early occupation of the hill.[2] Some traditions exist of early times. The Pergamenes claimed as their founder Telephus, a hero of Arcadian origin who guided the Greeks to Troy. Their city had originally been at a site nearer the coast and the land had been sacred to the Cabiri.[3]

Pergamum first emerges clearly into history at the close of the fifth century BC, and then only in an isolated incident, whose interest lies in the light it throws on the unsettled condition of the land under nominal Persian rule (Xen. *Anab.* 7.8.8-22). Local dynasts of the period are represented on the earliest Pergamene coins, dated by style to 420-400 BC.[4] We find the city already the stronghold of a chieftain rendering little more than nominal allegiance to his Persian suzerain, intriguing with Greek powers and engaging freely in local wars and brigandage. This pattern is further seen in the career of Orontes, the satrap of Mysia and Ionia (c. 362-348 BC).[5] His significant connection with Pergamum is attested by an epigraphical fragment which seems to have belonged to an officially displayed history of the later Attalid kingdom (*OGIS* 264a.5-10). He is there said to have transferred the citizens again to the ancient site on the hill.[6] The earlier Attalids evidently saw themselves as his successors as rulers of the integrated entity he had once held. He may have been the first to exploit effectively Pergamum's potential as a dynastic stronghold, its characteristic later role.

Another feature of Pergamum may date from a similar period. Pausanias tells how one Archias introduced the Asklepios cult from Epidaurus (2.26.8).[7]

For about twenty years after the death of Alexander, Pergamum was the stronghold of Heracles, his son by a Persian princess Barsine.[8]

After the death of Antigonus at Ipsus in 301 BC, Lysimachus, king of Thrace, came into possession of his treasures (Diod. Sic. 20.107.3). According to Hansen (p. 15), the Paphlagonian Philetaerus was in the employ of the Macedonian commander who yielded him the treasure at Synnada. Lysimachus in turn entrusted to this Philetaerus the custody of Pergamum and a war-treasure of 9000 talents deposited there (Strab. 13.4.1 = p. 623). Philetaerus probably received this commission very soon after Ipsus (cf. Hansen, p. 16), and his faithful discharge of this duty may therefore have continued for nearly twenty years. Finally, however, incurring the wrath of Lysimachus's wife Arsinoe, he revolted in 282 BC. The words of Strabo, πρὸς τοὺς καιροὺς ἐπολιτεύετο, ὁρῶν ἐπιτηδείους πρὸς νεωτερισμόν, might aptly describe the opportunistic policies of the dynasty he founded. He placed himself under Seleucid protection and continued a further twenty years in secure possession of Pergamum and its treasure 'by a continual policy of promises and services rendered to the power currently ascendant in his neighbourhood' (Strabo).

The successors of Philetaerus were Eumenes I (263-241), Attalus I Soter (241-197), Eumenes II (197-159), Attalus II Philadelphus (159-138), and Attalus III Philometor (138-133).

The achievement of Eumenes I was to break free from the Seleucid dependence[9] and extend a principality which at first probably comprised little more than the central Caicus valley (Hansen, p. 22). He even advanced against Antiochus I and defeated him near Sardis

(Strab. 13.4.2 = p. 624).[10] His position may not have been easily secured, for he was at one point compelled to negotiate with rebellious mercenaries (*OGIS* 266). He never took the title 'king', but he accepted divine honours as *euergetes* from a servile citizenry of Pergamum (*OGIS* 267.34-7; cf. Hansen, p. 24).

Attalus I was the first ruler in Asia to refuse tribute to the plundering Gauls (Liv. 38.16.14). He defeated them in a great battle near the source of the Caicus (*OGIS* 276), and assumed the titles 'king' and 'saviour' in commemoration of the victory.[11] The occasion also provided the impulse for the development of a new school of sculpture first represented in its great monuments, notably the great altar of Zeus Soter. It also doubtless helped to establish the cult of the divine ruler.

Attalus's subsequent conquests from the Seleucids proved evanescent (Hansen, pp. 33-43), but his later involvement with the affairs of Greece led to a brief participation in the First Macedonian War as an ally of Rome (*CAH* VIII.124; Hansen, pp. 46ff.). Rostovtzeff (*CAH* VIII.591f.) argues that the Attalids realized they had no means of fulfilling their ambitions of supremacy in Asia Minor without the intervention of some external power strong enough to undermine both Macedon and Syria. Such a power was Rome, but it was not then apparent that Pergamum itself would eventually succumb to its ally. Attalus was the first to invoke Roman aid (cf. Polyb. 21.20.2-5) while remaining independent of it: his successors rose to an almost imperial splendour as Roman vassals.

It was the ambitious anti-Seleucid policy of Eumenes II which impelled Roman intervention in Asia Minor itself (Liv. 35.15.7-8;[12] cf. 37.33.4). He is represented as the party most strongly opposed to conciliation of Antiochus, even when blockaded in his own territory (Polyb. 21.10.1-11; Liv. 37.18.1-19.6). A few months after that his war policy culminated in the decisive victory of Magnesia in autumn 190, which marked the end of Seleucid authority north of the Taurus. The accounts of the allied embassies after the battle illustrate vividly how, despite the prominent part assigned to Eumenes in it,[13] the disposal of the fruits of victory lay exclusively with the Romans.[14] Eumenes' representations were favourably received by the Senate, and he gained a territory comprising most of Asia Minor north of the Taurus (Liv. 37.54.5-6; Diod. Sic. 29.11).[15]

It was again Eumenes who precipitated the Third Macedonian War between Rome and Perseus (Liv. 42.6.3; 11.1). Yet at that time, despite his benefactions to the Greek states, most of them favoured his enemy, the operative reason probably being that recorded by Livy (42.5.6): *Quia omnia non obiecta Romanis volebant.* Despite also the new unpopularity he had acquired as the protégé of Rome, he subsequently lost Roman favour too. He was suspected of traitorous communication with Perseus, and Roman power was placed at the disposal of his brother Attalus with a view to supplanting him, a design frustrated only by Attalus's refusal to participate.[16] It had become evident that the kingdom itself was at Rome's disposal. Finally the Senate passed, expressly against Eumenes, a decree that no king should be permitted to come to Rome (Polyb. 30.19.6; Liv. Epit. 46).

It is unnecessary to detail the political events of the closing years of the Attalid kingdom.[17] The last act of Attalus III, however problematical in its motivation, was the logical conclusion of the development of events: 'he left the Romans his heirs' (Strab. 13.4.2 = p. 624).[18]

Direct Roman rule was not established without incident. The revolt of Aristonicus made capital of existing social unrest and its suppression entailed a series of campaigns (*CAH* IX.102-105).[19] The final settlement by M'. Aquilius saddled the Romans with new administrative burdens which the senatorial government was ill-equipped to bear. The wealthy inner territory of the Attalid realm was organized as the province of Asia (Strab. 14.1.38 = p. 646; cf. *CAH* IX. 106), an acquisition later regarded as the occasion of the corruption of Rome by greed and luxury (cf. e.g. Plin. *NH* 33.53.148).[20] Many years of subsequent oppression explain the provincials' enthusiastic reception of Mithridates VI as *theos* and *soter* in 88 BC (Diod. Sic. 37.26) and their savage execution of his command for the massacre of Romans (App. *Mithrid.* 4.22; Vell. Pat. 2.18), an event in which Pergamum played a conspicuous part.

The character of the city was much influenced by its central political role. It was also a great religious centre, partly because religion became a major instrument of policy. Ramsay has described the principal cults of Attalid times, Zeus and Athena, the protectors of the city, and the more Anatolian rites of Dionysus and Asklepios, where the Greek names mask the bull-god and the serpent-god (*SC*, pp. 284-87).[21] Many dedications to Zeus Soter and Athena Nicephorus are extant, celebrating Attalid victories.[22] The *cistophori*, the typical silver coins of the kingdom, bore designs representing the *cista mystica* and serpents, respectively the emblems of Dionysus Cathegemon and Asklepios Soter. They were minted in a number of the principal cities and seem to show an attempt to inculcate a sense of national unity expressed through a community of popular religion (cf. *SC*, pp. 286-88). The kings built in Pergamum itself a series of great national temples.[23] The great altar of Zeus Soter stood on a lofty terrace (Zschietzschmann, col. 1257). The temple of Athena (cols. 1258-59) and the huge precinct of the Asklepion (col. 1260) were both elaborate constructions of later Attalid times on the sites of simpler shrines.[24]

Apart from this careful exploitation of existing cults the kings fostered an explicit ruler-cult. The title of Attalus 'Soter' duplicated that of the Zeus he honoured. Eumenes II used not only 'Soter' but also 'Theos' (*OGIS* 302 with 305) and his mother is described as the wife of a god (Attalus I). A complex of buildings near the royal palace has been identified as the *temenos* of this cult. Originally erected under Attalus I, it was enlarged and beautified by Eumenes II, under whom the living king and queen had priests and priestesses.[25] After the Attalid period divine honours were granted in Pergamum to some not of royal blood.[26]

Whatever the subsequent civil status of Pergamum, it evidently continued to be the religious capital of the province of Asia. To the earlier strata of Anatolian and Olympian religion and of ruler-cult was added the worship of the Roman emperor.

2. The Throne of Satan

a. *Political Background and Ruler Cult*

It is sometimes assumed without question by those who have followed Ramsay that Pergamum long continued to be the official capital of Roman Asia.[27] Ramsay's argument for this belief in *SC*, pp. 289ff., is somewhat perfunctory, though his conclusion is integral to his view of the present letter. He had in fact stated his case in greater detail in *HDB* III.750f. V. Chapot, however, had meanwhile maintained that Ephesus was the capital from an early period of Roman rule and that Pergamum was of lesser importance.[28] This view likewise is frequently assumed, and revealed in *obiter dicta*.[29]

In view of the unexpectedly elusive character of the question it will be of value to summarize something of the evidence bearing on the functions of the two cities.

The case of Ephesus is conveniently treated first. Ephesus was a great cosmopolitan centre, and probably the seat of financial administration in the province throughout the period, but this is not tantamount to a proof that it was the official capital. Phrases may be cited which treat it as representative of, or synonymous with, Asia, but these are in popular or informal parlance.[30] Its proud claim to be the proconsul's first landfall in the province (*BMC Ionia*, Eph., No. 342) might even stand in default of the right to make a larger claim. There is in any case the possibility of changes of status at some point hidden from us by the sparseness and chronological uncertainty of our evidence.[31]

The first-century writers, however, seem to award a primacy to Pergamum. The words of Strabo (13.4.2 = p. 623) are almost studiously vague,[32] and it is not clear in what sense we may press Pliny's *longe clarissimum Asiae* (*NH* 5.33.126). Ramsay argues that Pergamum's supremacy in the imperial cult is decisive, and that religious and civic primacy could not be separated (*HDB* III.750-51; *SC*, p. 289). He supposed that as Pergamum had been the recognized capital of the old kingdom it continued so until Hadrian elevated Ephesus in view of its undoubted practical importance. He regards a transference of capital about AD 129, the date of Hadrian's second visit to Asia, as 'practically certain', and actually made this assumption a *terminus ad quem* for the writing of Rev. 2.13 (*HDB* III.751). Here again however his reasons are quite indecisive. He says that Hadrian permitted Ephesus a second neocorate and issued silver coinage of Diana Ephesia, thus according her status as a Roman deity. Hadrian however adopted the unprecedented practice of issuing 'cistophoric' tetradrachms with local religious types from a dozen or more mints during his visit.[33] Mattingly remains doubtful whether even then the central mint was at Ephesus or Pergamum. He prefers the latter possibility (p. clix).

The heart of Ramsay's case is really the neocorate. Three times Pergamum was the first to receive the honour or a repetition of it, and its status in the cult is shown by the coins of the Commune of Asia which represent the emperor being crowned by the province in the first temple there (*SC*, pp. 283ff.). And there are many instructive indications on the coinage of the early years of Roman rule to suggest that Pergamum had a close, though perhaps not exclusive, connection with authority.[34]

Dogmatic conclusions should not be drawn here. Pergamum probably long retained the prestige of having been the original capital. But of the circumstances of any change we are wholly ignorant. In any case the province was unusual in having from the start a developed rivalry between several important cities. The Romans may have recognized this fact in their distribution of civic honours.[35] There is evidence in particular for a prolonged and bitter rivalry between Ephesus, Smyrna and Pergamum (Dio Chrysost. 34.48).[36] The triviality of the argument was extraordinary, as Dio says, 'about the shadow of an ass'. He adds significantly: 'for the real authority and power belong to others'. It may be that then Ephesus had in fact attained a predominance which her rivals persistently refused to acknowledge. But perhaps there was a deliberate ambiguity about the whole thing. Rome ruled and would humour and patronize rivalry about names and titles if she held the substance of power. In any case meetings of the Commune were held in the several neocorate cities (Chapot, pp. 465-66), and the proconsul had to travel among the several judicial centres.

Pergamum's primacy in the imperial cult is certainly important. The early emperors had been slow to sanction a personal cult. Temples to Rome had existed since that at Smyrna in 195 BC. Augustus in 29 BC permitted the erection of temples to Rome and himself at Pergamum and Nicomedia. The cult of the living emperor was for non-Romans (Dio Cass. 51.20.6-7; cf. Suet. *Aug.* 52). It spread rapidly: Augustan inscriptions from other cities of Asia reflect the spontaneous growth of unofficial civic cults.[37] The provincial temple at Pergamum is portrayed on many coins of the city and of the Commune (*BMC Mysia*, Perg., from No. 236, of Augustus). It served as a precedent for the cult in other provinces (Tac. *Ann.* 4.37) and spread under later reigns to be observed by all Roman subjects (Dio Cass. 51.20.7). The competition for the honour of possessing a second provincial temple in AD 26 (Tac. *Ann.* 4.15) testifies further to imperial reluctance on this point. But the institution, once established, could be made into a test of political loyalty, whose machinery could easily be activated by an emperor disposed to do so.

b. *The Reference of Rev. 2.13*
The background of the 'throne of Satan' has been seen in several ways, which are not necessarily mutually exclusive: (1) allusion to Pergamum as a centre of pagan religion generally.[38] (2) It has been further suggested that the acropolis itself looks like a great throne when seen by a traveller approaching from Smyrna. This however is

only a picturesque association which might appeal to a modern visitor without necessarily relating to an ancient reality.[39] (3) Reference has been seen to the throne-like altar of Zeus Soter, so dominant as to typify Satanic heathendom. The obsessive serpent-motif of its sculptures and the title 'Soter', like a blasphemous parody of its Christian use, would alike give point to this identification.[40] (4)The Asklepios cult has a yet stronger claim than the last, and for some of the same reasons. This god was also designated 'Soter', and was closely identified with the serpent. Though he had celebrated shrines elsewhere he was preeminently the *Pergameus deus* (Mart. *Epig.* 9.16; cf. Philostr. *Vit. Ap. Ty.* 4.34; Stat. *Silv.* 3.4.23-24). His cult offered a species of personal 'salvation' which might be set in pointed contrast with that of Christ. (5) Most commentators see the principal or only background in the position of Pergamum as the centre of emperor worship. This was the present threat to the church, and the reminder that Christ has the 'sharp two-edged ῥομφαία'[41] is then set against the proconsul's *ius gladii*. It was on this ground that the Christian faced the actual threat of Roman execution. The strength of this interpretation resides in its recognition of the historical and textual context.

c. *The Context of the Passage*

The 'sword' of v. 12 is taken up in 'the sword of my mouth' in v. 16: both expressions are combined in the Patmos vision (1.16). The idea of a weapon issuing from the mouth is based on Isa. 11.4 and 49.2, but is pointedly modified. We must differ from Charles (p. 26) in emphasizing the organic unity of the present context as applied to the situation of the church. It suggests the authority of the spoken word, in particular the sentence of the judge, and is associated in Rev. 19.13 and 15 with the 'word of God' (cf. Heb. 4.12; Eph. 6.17).

οἶδα ποῦ κατοικεῖς (v. 13). The commentators sometimes stress the use here of a verb denoting permanent residence. This church was set in a post of danger from which it had no right of escape.[42] The letter is unique in its special emphasis: in every other case Christ knows the 'works' of the church, here primarily their situation.[43]

The theme is continued in the context of the allusion to Antipas, 'who was slain among you, where Satan dwelleth'.[44] The sense here is clear, but the syntax so unorthodox that textual corruption is often suspected. Ἀντίπας is usually explained as an indeclinable name in the genitive. It is common in the Revelation for an appositional phrase following this case to be left in the nominative (e.g. 1.5; 3.12; cf. Charles, pp. cxlix-cl).[45]

The word μάρτυς here has been rendered 'witness' by many (e.g. Swete, p. 36; Beckwith, p. 459), but Charles, p. 62, regards this as the earliest occurrence of the technical usage 'martyr', comparing Rev. 17.6. The former view seems preferable, and μου is then objective. The title 'the true witness' is elsewhere given to Christ (Rev. 1.5; 3.14). Antipas is thus identified with his Lord; he has been faithful in testimony to the point of death.

The immediate historical allusion is obscure. The context seems to demand reference to a definite past time of crisis (cf. οὐκ ἠρνήσω) which had placed the whole church under great pressure to deny the faith. Antipas was perhaps the first to suffer death, or a test case of whom the authorities chose to make a public example. It is not even clear whether he was a Pergamene: the words παρ' ὑμῖν might even suggest he was brought from elsewhere to suffer in Satan's headquarters, where the church was committed to an inevitable struggle with his strongest forces.

This tells us nothing yet of the detail of official policy. The Christian was involved inevitably in conflict if he would be true in his testimony to Christ, but the authorities may not have seen the *nomen Christianum* as the point at issue.[46]

d. *Religious Background and Polemical Parallelism*

The peril of the church is surely to be related to the pressure of the imperial cult. The case of Antipas showed the way things were going. The whole religious history of Pergamum is instructive because it shows how the backgound of divine kingship made the place so apt a setting for the development of the forms of emperor worship.[47]

Deissmann (*LAE*, pp. 342ff.) quotes extensive evidence for the growth of what he terms a 'polemical parallelism' between the cults of Christ and of Caesar. A striking example of the use of divine titles for the emperor is extant at Pergamum from within the lifetime of Augustus.[48] Under Nero the practice becomes regular. He is designated ὁ σωτὴρ τῆς οἰκουμένης (*OGIS* 668.3, of Ptolemais; cf. *CAH* X.732) and ὁ τοῦ παντὸς κόσμου κύριος (*SIG*³ 814.32, of Acraephiae in Boeotia.[49] And in an inscription of Cos he is identified with Asklepios (*IGRR* IV. 1053).

It is well known that Domitian required to be addressed as *dominus et deus* (Suet. *Dom.* 13; Mart. *Epig.* 9.56.3), a title corresponding to that applied to Jesus in Thomas's confession (John 20.28). In this kind of subject questions of chronology and dependence are vitally important, but may be difficult to answer from fragmentary evidence. Conclusions must then be cautious. But the actual phenomena are striking. Several technical terms of the imperial worship are closely parallel with expressions used in the Revelation in a Christian sense, and some of the most telling evidence comes from some of the same cities of Asia.

The traditional title *theologos* applied to John (cf. Rev. 1.2) is such a term, its pagan technical use being attested only from Pergamum, Smyrna and Ephesus.[50] Again the κυριακὴ ἡμέρα (Rev. 1.10) corresponds with the 'Sebaste day' first recorded in Egypt in AD 68, and subsequently in a Hadrianic inscription of Pergamum (*LAE*, pp. 358-61). The terms κύριος and σωτηρία are also important. The latter word occurs only three times in the Revelation (7.10; 12.10; 19.1), each time in a very similar context where a great voice proclaims the 'salvation of our God', perhaps in pointed contrast with the imperial salvation and its official liturgy.[51] The word σωτήρ never occurs, but κύριος is frequent and significant in cases which suggest a similar parallelism.[52] Finally, the εὐαγγέλιον proclaimed in Rev. 14.6 may be set against the use of the word in an important decree of Augustus, of which damaged copies are extant from Priene, Dorylaeum, Apamea and Eumenea (*OGIS* 458.40, of c. 9 BC).

We must conclude that the expression 'throne of Satan' refers primarily to the emperor-cult as enforced from Pergamum at a time of critical confrontation for the church. We note the strong hints of the growth of a 'polemical parallelism' between Christ and Caesar. The claims of Caesar are viewed by John as a Satanic parody of those of Christ. And some of the imagery of the later chapters may rightly be seen to refer to Rome as a persecuting power and so to reinforce our picture. That however would merit fuller examination on a wider front.

3. *Balaam and the Nicolaitans*

I have deliberately deferred consideration of the Nicolaitans from the treatment of Ephesus because their character and teaching appears here in a much more explicit context, both verbal and circumstantial.[53] Rev. 2.6 gives no information about them beyond the commendation of the Ephesian church for hating their works. They are mentioned only in these two passages, though the parallels between the Pergamum passage and the teaching of Jezebel at Thyatira (Rev. 2.20ff.) indicate that she represented a similar phenomenon. The value of Irenaeus's references to the Nicolaitans is doubtful. The primary passage (*adv. Haer.* 1.26.3) tells us that they followed Nicolaus, one of the seven deacons of Acts 6.5, but adds nothing which might not have been inferred from the Revelation. In a passing remark in 3.11.7 he treats them as the earliest representatives of the error of Cerinthus and ascribes to them a Gnostic cosmology. That however might be an inference from a tradition connecting John's opponents with the '*gnosis* falsely so called' of 1 Tim. 6.20, to which Irenaeus here appears to refer.[54] These tenets might then have been read back from subsequent developments. The Pergamum and Thyatira passages seem to oppose errors of practice rather than of speculative doctrine, though the phrase 'they have not known the deep things of Satan' (Rev. 2.24) might hint at some kind of Gnostic background for the Jezebel teaching.[55]

The question of Gnosticism is not easily silenced, but this may not be the place to raise it.[56] We must seek to explain Nicolaitanism in terms of the present context. Several preliminary questions need consideration here. (1) What incident in the Old Testament narrative of Balaam is in mind here? (2) What is the point of the emphatic comparison (οὕτως . . . καὶ σύ . . . ὁμοίως) between Balaam and the Nicolaitans? (3) Was this equivalence, or at least some polemical use of the name Balaam, already familiar to the original readers of the Revelation? (4) Is there any connection between 'Balaam' here and any other heretical movement of the New Testament period? In particular is there any relationship with the use of his name in Jude and 2 Peter?

(1) Balaam's advice to Balak is never explicitly recorded, but an inference may be made from the comparison of Num. 31.16 with Num. 25.1-2.[57] It is implied that Balaam was responsible for contriving the sin of Israel with the daughters of Moab. The incident was already elaborated in midrashic tradition by the first century AD (Philo, *Vita Moysis* 1.54.295ff.; Jos. *Antiq.* 4.6.6.126ff.). In Josephus especially we have a long narrative incorporating the account of a conflict between Moses and one Zambrias.[58] It is important at least to realize the importance attached to Balaam in Jewish tradition and the possibility that John expected his readers to recognize allusion to it here.

On (2) we must note the explanation which regards 'Balaam' as etymologically equivalent to the eponymous 'Nicolaus'. This view, first proposed by C.A. Heumann in 1712 (Swete, p. 28, *ad* Rev. 2.6), is often rejected summarily because (a) it assumes an unwarranted subtlety in bilingual playing on words, (b) it reduces the likely allusion to the historical founder of the sect to a merely symbolic name, and (c) the proposed etymology is wrong anyhow. But none of these objections is cogent: the problem might be differently viewed in historical perspective. The inference (b), that no actual Nicolaus existed if his name is treated symbolically, is unjustified. Indeed, supposing his existence, we may see a play on an actual man's name as a suitable basis for a slogan of current controversy. Then it might have a previous history and need not be an arbitrary invention of the writer. And it would be immaterial whether the etymology were philologically correct.[59] It matters only whether it was actually current. It is dangerous to impose on it what may still be no more than a modern fancy, but the controversial use of 'Balaam' is very variously attested and the reference to him here is very pointed. Moreover the emphatic equation of the names might be seen in this light: Balaam and the Nicolaitans are alike in the name and alike in nature. We do not press the point and it is not crucial, though an attractive possibility. In any case the comparison reinforces the impression of allusion to a situation familiar to the readers.

This leads us directly to (3). There are many relevant considerations here. It is surprising to find in the Pergamene letter an apparently stronger element of Jewish tradition than in any other (cf. the 'hidden manna'). Was there a considerable Jewish community in the city?

The evidence suggests that there was actually less Jewish presence in Pergamum than in most of the other cities. It was never primarily a centre of commerce, being badly placed with relation to the great trade-routes. And Attalid policy was less likely to favour their settlement than the Seleucid: there is no evidence that the kings ever granted citizenship to bodies of Jews, and their centralized exploitation of the wealth of their kingdom did not encourage independent enterprise. Under the Romans Pergamum suffered badly from the war against Aristonicus (Magie, pp. 160-62), and was doubtless much despoiled by the rapacity of republican govenors. In 62 BC Flaccus confiscated there an unspecified, but small, amount of Jewish gold (*Pergami non multum*, Cic. *pro Flacco* 28.68), and some of this may have come from subordinate cities of the *conventus*, which included

Thyatira (cf. Plin. *NH* 5.31.114ff.). After that the central position of the city in the imperial cult did not favour the development of Jewish settlement.[60]

Doubtless there were some Jews in Pergamum, and perhaps their number greatly increased after AD 70. But the evident Judaistic language of our text receives no easy explanation in these terms. And the suggestion of a popular etymology of the name 'Balaam' is not easily set in the context of a Semitic-speaking community.[61]

There is however evidence for the use of 'Balaam' in Jewish controversy as a type of false teacher. The readers may indeed have been familiar with this as a commonplace of current tradition. The question remains what its point is here. Does the emphatic equation of v. 15 drive home a recognized identification or shock the reader with an unexpected one into realizing that a party tolerated in the church was subverting its very foundations?

So we reach (4). Can we identify Nicolaitanism through the further consideration of the Balaam analogy? The problem entails some study of the use of 'Balaam' in other Jewish and Christian writings. In *Pirke Aboth* 5.2 he appears as a type of wickedness: he who possesses an evil eye, a boastful soul and a haughty spirit is a disciple of Balaam the wicked and shall inherit Gehenna, whereas the disciple of Abraham shall inherit heaven. The date of this passage is uncertain, but it has been suggested that the reference is to Jesus.[62] The claim to be the true successors of Abraham is a commonplace of Jewish-Christian controversy from New Testament times. Other Jewish passages which single out Balaam for special detestation seem also to treat him as a type of Jesus.[63] Thus Titus, Balaam and Jesus are associated in hell as three representatives of the enemies of Judaism (b. Giṭṭin 56b, 57a).[64] Again, a strange Rabbinic interpretation of Ps. 55.23 is taken to refer to Jesus, who, like Balaam, lived only thirty-three years, less than 'half their days' (b. Sanh. 106b).[65]

The problem is why the Jews saw this apparent equivalence between Balaam and Jesus. The Rabbinic materials are probably all later as they stand, but the New Testament references and the Christian use of Balaam's prophecy in Num. 24.17 as a Messianic proof-text (e.g. Lk. 1.78f.) point to an early controversy involving his name.[66] And this prophecy was present to John's mind in writing the related Thyatiran letter, where a combined reminiscence of Ps. 2.7-9 and Num. 24.17 seems to underlie Rev. 2.26-28. The Jew might taunt the Christian with relying on the testimony of the representative false prophet of Jewish history and tradition, the man who led the nation astray and was the antagonist of Moses and the law. The point of this line of objection to Jesus may then have been that his followers were undermining the law and teaching an antinomianism which gave licence to immorality. Paul was ever conscious that his gospel of faith was open to this perversion (e.g. Rom. 6.1), but he refused to countenance it.

'Balaam' in our text is clearly to be applied in a different way. Christians who recognized the moral claims of the gospel might naturally refuse the opprobrious term for themselves and apply it to the kind of perversion of their faith to which the underlying criticism seemed truly applicable.

Nicolaitanism is presented wholly as a practical error, for διδαχή is here applied to Balaam's practical counsel (cf. Beckwith, p. 460).[67] He taught Balak to cause Israel to stumble by eating things sacrificed to idols and by committing fornication. The association of these sins goes back to Num. 25.1-2. In the New Testament they are again connected in two other very significant passages. In Acts 15.20, 29 abstinence from these sins is made a fundamental condition of a *modus vivendi* for Gentile converts in mixed communities.[68] In Rev. 2.20 Jezebel is represented as inculcating the same sins, but their order is reversed. Possibly in Pergamum idolatry was the greater problem, but in Thyatira immorality, whether literally or as a figure for apostasy. The Pergamene church faced direct pressure to conform to the idolatrous worship of the emperor: Thyatiran Christians found their livelihood depended on belonging to a pagan organization with its attendant immorality. Allowing for these differences of setting we may suppose that the movements in Ephesus, Pergamum and Thyatira were essentially similar. Nicolaitanism had locally gained a partial control in the church, though John regards it as wholly subversive. We cannot tell from these texts whether it possessed a dogmatic system. The indications are (a) that it is to be explained in its situational context, and (b) that it represented an antinomian movement like that which Paul had faced at Corinth, whatever else it may have been otherwise.

What then is implied by φαγεῖν εἰδωλόθυτα in this context? Two aspects of the problem had arisen at Corinth, the consumption of idol-consecrated meat from the public market, and participation in the idolatrous guild-feasts (see 1 Cor. 8.1-13 and 10.20-30). The latter was the particular issue in Thyatira. Here there may be some contrast with the 'manna' of v. 17: the victor is promised heavenly sustenance though his present circumstances entail physical hunger.[69]

The available local evidence does not clarify the choice very much. *Collegia* existed but are not particularly prominent.[70] It is notable however how closely these and other aspects of the city's life are subordinated to the emperor's authority and cult. One inscription (*IGRR* IV. 353), which refers to the guild of *hymnodoi* of Rome and Augustus, lists materials and services provided for a series of festivals. There are interesting parallels with early Christianity and with some of the language of the Apocalypse in particular.[71] This peculiar cultic integration of local life suggests that here the temptation to violate the Apostolic Decree was inseparable from the pressure to conform to emperor worship.[72]

Paul had formerly waged a battle on two fronts against legalism and against antinomianism. I suggest that the ground of this double conflict shifted as the political consequences of the fall of Jerusalem unfolded. I have argued in the Introduction that Christians in Asia faced a dilemma in which their safety was assured only by accommodation either to pagan society or to Judaism. The differing incidence of the complementary threats posed by the Nicolaitans and by the 'synagogues of Satan' may be explained in local terms, as the pressure of the imperial cult activated forces in the pagan or in the Jewish environment of the church. At Pergamum the case seems clear: the cult had its central impact and the influence of Jewish opponents was probably slight.

The root of Nicolaitanism may be found in the misrepresentation of Pauline freedom. Paul had apparently not imposed the terms of the Apostolic Decree on the Gentile churches beyond Galatia: at Corinth he had preferred to refer the question of sacrificial meats to individual judgment and social responsibility. There were those who might take their cue from his refusal to reduce the matter to a categorical prohibition. Under the new pressures a liberal party might claim Pauline precedent for upholding freedom to participate. John replies that their teaching violates the terms of the Decree, to which Paul himself, according to Acts, had assented. He further stigmatizes their teaching as of Balaam, whose name we suppose to have been a current slogan, perhaps against Christianity generally, but rightly applied only to an antinomian perversion of it.

The question of possible connection with the references to Balaam in Jude 11 and 2 Peter 2.15 is fraught with difficulty. The internal evidence for the dating of these epistles is clearly capable of very diverse interpretation. It is desirable to keep the options open.[73]

We cannot in the present limits do more than raise some questions and possibilities here. It is possible for instance that 'Balaam' in these epistles might refer to a recognized movement, perhaps identical with the Nicolaitans. The false teachers of both epistles were evidently antinomians, whatever else they were also. And the allusion to Paul in 2 Peter 3.15-17 fits the supposition that the writer is combatting views which appealed to a corruption of his teaching. But we cannot assume that the opposition in Jude and in 2 Peter necessarily represented the same movement or time. The latter is more explicit, and the postulation of differences between them may well turn on the validity of the argument from silence in Jude. Nor can we press the supposition of the identification of either with Nicolaitanism. It would be hazardous to venture any genealogy of the similarities. At most one might venture that the Balaam-Nicolaitan equivalence, however interpreted, points to a conflict which already had a history and a terminology. Is it conceivable that a technical use of 'Balaam' derived from its occurrence in an earlier document, and that that document could have been Jude or even 2 Peter?[74]

Finally we must consider in the light of this discussion the question of Gnosticism raised at the outset. There is some evidence that the false teachers of both Jude and 2 Peter held some speculative philosophy, but the data do not admit of any positive identification. It might be argued that they were no more than straightforward antinomian libertines who were ready to use such current philosophical arguments as came to hand to justify their position. Cosmological speculation was already rife in Pauline churches, to judge from Col. 1.15-17 (cf. 2 Pet. 3.5). But even in the comparatively explicit language of 2 Peter the primary concern is with the moral influence of the opposition.

The case for believing that the Nicolaitans were an essentially Gnostic sect has been stated by Harnack (*Journal of Religion* 3 [1923], pp. 413-22), but some of his assumptions are unwarranted. He assumes that Jezebel's teaching was normative, and so he makes the Thyatiran letter the primary source for the Gnostic content of Nicolaitan doctrine. He argues that John's repugnance towards them may have been due to their being Satan-worshippers or radical dualists. All this is surely a wrong basis of argument. It is based on the interpretation of the Thyatiran passage in the light of secondary evidence. The statements of Irenaeus and others may only relate to later developments of Nicolaitan apologetic.[75]

We conclude that Nicolaitanism was an antinomian movement whose antecedents can be traced in the misrepresentation of Pauline liberty, and whose incidence may be connected with the special pressures of emperor worship and pagan society. The important 'Balaam' simile may point to a relationship with similar movements facing the church elsewhere, but the nature of such relationship is a matter of speculation in default of explicit data. There may have been a Gnostic element in Nicolaitanism, but in our primary texts it is a practical error and not Gnosticism *qua* Gnosticism. In the context of Pauline teaching it might claim his precedent, but the growth of speculative philosophy and the recession of apostolic authority might lend moral indifferentism a changing rationale.

We note that the whole church, in the person of its 'angel', is called to repent of having Nicolaitans in its midst (ἔχειν is twice used in 2.14-15). The 'coming' of Christ is here apparently a visitation in judgment, conditional upon the whole church's failure to repent, but directed explicitly against the Nicolaitans.[76] No such general call to repentance is issued to the Thyatiran church, though the corrupt teaching seems to have had a deeper hold there. Perhaps at Pergamum the error was quite simply felt to be more amenable to the guidance and discipline of the church.[77]

Christ's answer is summed up in v. 16. The second allusion to his sword of judgment is put in more absolute terms, closer to the Old Testament prototype. He holds the true and ultimate authority.

4. *The Manna and the White Stone*

The syntactical peculiarity of the first clause of the promise to the conqueror (v. 17b) need not detain us, for it has no interpretative importance.[78] The manna and the white stone, however, both present problems. The first seems clearly rooted in Jewish tradition, but its point here is more debatable; the second has attracted great diversity of interpretation and the difficulty is a matter of discrimination among alternatives.

a. *Manna*
The allusion is ultimately traceable to Exod. 16.32-34, where the

Lord commanded a sample of manna to be preserved as a memorial for future generations. Tradition was quick to explain its subsequent disappearance. It was taken to have been originally kept in the ark of the covenant (cf. Heb. 9.4),[79] and on the destruction of Solomon's temple Jeremiah, according to 2 Macc. 2.4-7, was warned to take the tabernacle, the ark and its contents to Sinai and there hide them underground. There they would remain until the coming of the Messiah, when Jeremiah would reappear and deposit them in the new Messianic temple in Jerusalem. A variant in *2 Baruch* 6.7-10, ascribing their concealment to an angel, is almost contemporary with the Revelation. Neither of these passages mentions manna, but its inclusion in this tradition is inferred from Heb. 9.4 and explicit in the Rabbinic sources (so Yoma 52b).

Charles (p. 65) distinguishes sharply another line of tradition about manna, according to which it was the food of angels (cf. Ps. 78.25), and would again descend from heaven in the Messianic kingdom as the food of the saints. This also appears in the contemporary *2 Baruch* (29.8) and in *Or. Sib.* 7.148-49, probably of the second century AD. Charles sees in this concept a continuation of the Balaam analogy: as the ancient Israel, when tempted by Balaam, was fed by a material manna, the true Israel of the future, after overcoming temptation by his spiritual successors, would be fed by a spiritual manna. Part of this victory in the case of the Pergamene church would consist in their abstinence from forbidden meats. Charles therefore excludes the tradition deriving from Exod. 16 on the ground of the relevance of the other to the local situation.

Most other commentators do not rigidly separate the two possibilities. The word κεκρυμμένου seems a clear allusion to the first.[80] And a long tradition of allegorical interpretation of the manna goes back to Philo,[81] and is represented in teaching attributed to Jesus in John 6.49-58.

Several problems are raised. Is the promise only eschatological, or is it intended to give the church strength in its present dilemma? Is it to be closely connected with the 'white stone'? Have these symbols a life-setting in the problems of the Pergamene church?

Most of the commentators tend to reject such relevance in favour of a purely eschatological understanding of this, as of the other promises. But even such a view gains point from the setting of the present: the heavenly feast will belong to those who now abstain from the imperial *eidolothuta*.[82]

b. *The White Stone*

The use of ψῆφος is likely to limit the alternatives, but it need not be assumed that any one solution is definitively or exclusively correct. The primary meaning 'pebble' and the derivative sense 'vote' are both very freely applied, but other uses are more specialized and require definition from their context.[83]

Charles (p. 66) and Swete (p. 40) make the general objection to the suggested interpretations that all of them postulate a stone either not inscribed or not necessarily white. This might be conclusive against any of them if presented in rigid isolation, but this symbol is likely to be suggestive rather than rigidly allusive. There may be no single analogue for all the terms of the image and its development: it is quite in John's manner to combine diverse reminiscences. The value of examining the background here is to simplify and restate the problem by selection and exclusion.[84] Some of the possibilities cannot be separated from the view taken of the 'new name'. Is this a new name of Christ, as in Rev. 3.12, or of the individual Christian?

I tabulate the more important suggestions under seven comprehensive headings:

(i)   A 'jewel' in Old Testament or Jewish tradition.
(ii)   The judicial *calculus Minervae*, the casting vote of acquittal.
(iii) A token of admission, membership or recognition.
(iv)   An amulet with a divine name.
(v)   A token of gladiatorial discharge.
(vi)   Allusion to a process of initiation into the service of Asklepios.
(vii) Simply as a writing material whose form or colour was significant.[85]

(i) At least three different suggestions have been made under this heading. The only important one is that which sees allusion in the present association of symbols to the Rabbinic tradition that jewels fell from heaven with the manna.[86] Its merit is simply that it explains the collocation of the manna with the stone. But the point of the allusion is not apparent. It is merely the least unsatisfactory of the attempts to find a Jewish background. And it depends on the assumption that the readers, probably largely Gentiles here, would recognize unaided an allusion to a specialized use of ψῆφος.

This approach needed to be considered first as we may rightly expect a primary background in the Jewish material. Here it does not help. Earlier views of this type were maintained by commentators who were unwilling to allow a heathen reference. Apart from that prejudice it seems doubtful whether the suggestions of Stuart or Trench would have been proposed.[87]

(ii) The 'white ψῆφος' has often been thought to denote acquittal. It was ancient practice for jurors to signify guilt or innocence by casting black or white pebbles into an urn (Ov. *Metam*. 15.41-42; cf. Plut. *Alcib*. 22.2 = p. 202D and *Mor*. p. 186F). At the legendary trial of Orestes before the Areopagus at Athens, Athena as presiding judge had resolved a deadlock by casting her vote for the accused (Aesch. *Eumen*. 737-56).[88]

This view, which goes back to Andreas, has had wide currency, but is often criticized as an imperfect and incomplete analogy which does not explain the 'new name' and is inappropriate to the conqueror (Trench, p. 132; Stuart, p. 470).

There are however some considerations more favourable to this view, if we may allow the legitimacy of seeing it merely as a facet of the case, one suggestive, if incomplete, line of meditation for the Christian in Pergamum. (1) The future 'conqueror' was precisely the person who might have to prove his steadfastness in the face of judicial condemnation. The words would convey to him the assurance of Christ's power as true judge to override the false verdict of the human court. (2) Grimm and Thayer point out a connection of νικᾶν with ψῆφος in forensic language. A successful litigant is described as νικήσας (Theophr. *Char*. 17.8) and the 'prevailing' vote is νικητήριος ψῆφος (Heliodorus, *Aethiop*. 3.3 *fin*.). We may add νικᾷ δ' Ὀρέστης (Aesch. *Eumen*. 744) from the *locus classicus* of the proverbial acquittal. (3) The use of ψῆφος to mean 'vote' is probably the commonest, even where the context is not explicit. The question here might turn on whether local or contemporary circumstance supplied a clear implicit setting for the reader to choose between the two natural senses of 'pebble'/*tessera* and 'vote'.[89] (4) A curious non-judicial instance of the proverbial 'vote of Athena' occurs in Philostratus's account of a sophist of Pergamum. In view of this writer's propensity for cultivating local colour the possibility is raised that his rather forced expression reflected a popular association of Pergamum. And there are other indications of strong cultural and religious links between Pergamum and Athens, especially in the matters of the cult of Athena.[90] (5) The interpretation accords well with the background of 2.16 in Isa. 11.4 and 49.2, as contrasted with the proconsul's *ius gladii*.

(iii) The *tessera* ('token') had many uses as a token of admission or recognition. Reference to a wide variety of practices had been seen here, and several suggestions must be grouped under this heading.

There was the *tessera hospitalis*. The two parties in a contract of friendship broke a *tessera* and each retained a severed half. They or their descendants might later recognize their pledge of relationship by possessing complementary halves (Plaut. *Poen.* 958, 1047-49, 1052; cf. *Inscr. Orelli* 1079, of AD 321). The wide divergence of date and provenance of the attestations suggests that the practice was widespread, though there is no evidence that the token was white or inscribed, or for its particular local currency. The idea of a personal relationship pledged by a secret sign is however very apposite here.[91]

W. Barclay cites a view that *tesserae* were given to 'clients' to identify them as entitled to the liberality of their patrons under the Roman social system of *salutatio*. I have not found ancient authority for such tokens, and the clearest account of the practice of patronage (Juv. *Sat.* 1.95-134) implies that the donor knew his clients personally.[92]

Bousset (p. 214), Charles (p. 66) and others refer to the action of the emperor Titus in casting among the people wooden tokens which entitled the bearer to free entertainment (Dio Cass. Epit. 66.25.5). This is an isolated attestation, though comparable acts of bounty are commonly recorded of other emperors.[93]

The best ground for inferring possible allusion to a ticket of admission to a feast is contained in a second-century inscription of Pergamum describing the conditions and fees for admission to an unidentified association.[94] The right of entrance and membership was evidently a restricted and expensively bought distinction. There would probably have been a token of membership.

The *tessera militaris* was used for the secret conveyance of information through the responsible *tesserarius* (Sil. Ital. *Pun.* 15.475; Liv. 39.30.4). There was a tendency to use the name of a patron deity as password and inspiration to battle.[95]

Another custom is mentioned of granting victors at the games *tesserae* which qualified them for rewards at the public expense. This suggestion appears to derive from a comment of Arethas cited by Swete (p. 40).[96]

Many writers have seen allusion to one or more of the numerous usages of this kind.[97] Some are attractive, but at most they offer only a partial analogy. We must look elsewhere for a fuller understanding of the background.

(iv) The view which sees the 'white stone' as analogous with a pagan amulet inscribed with the secret name of a pagan god has been one of the most popular, gaining strong support from Charles (pp. 66-67), Moffatt (p. 358) and Beckwith (p. 461). *BAGD* cite a parallel in Artemidorus, *Onirocr.* 5.26 = p. 258, which refers to a plate of bronze inscribed with the name of Sarapis and hung around the neck. Many other examples may be found in the literature of ancient magic.[98]

On this interpretation the written name will be that of God or of Christ, as in Rev. 3.12 (cf. 14.1; 19.12). The point is then in allusion to ancient ideas of the power of divine names. To know the name of a deity was to possess a claim upon his help: here the power of Christ to save and protect is exalted over that of his pagan rivals.

This interpretation gives a sense apt to the need of a church threatened by the power of a hostile religious system. But as usually presented it stands or falls by the view taken of the 'new name'.[99] We must resume this point at (vi) below.

(v) Another attractive reading of the evidence merits some prior consideration. Allusion has been seen to yet another kind of *tessera*, one supposedly given to a gladiator at his discharge from the arena, exempting him from the obligation to risk his life again there. Many of the tokens involved survive (*CIL* I.717-76; etc.). They take the form of elongated rectangular tablets of bone bearing the name of a man, the letters 'SP', and the day and year, often incised in sequence on the four faces. Most examples belong to the first century BC or AD and come from Rome.

The interpretation of many types of *tessera* is very difficult. The present type had been usually understood in the light of the words of Horace:

> *Prima dicte mihi, summa dicende Camena,*
> *Spectatum satis et donatum iam rude quaeris,*
> *Maecenas, iterum antiquo me includere ludo?* (*Epistles* 1.1.1-3)

The gladiatorial allusion is clear, for the performer was given his wooden practice-sword (*rudis*) at his discharge (cf. Cic. *Philipp.* 2.29.74; Ov. *Trist.* 4.8.34). It was inferred that 'SP' on the *tesserae* was short for *spectatus*, which may commonly signify 'proved' or 'tested', and that here the word was a technical term for 'discharged'. The persons mentioned were apparently of servile or other lowly origin, and an inscription (*CIL* VI.631, of the second cent. AD) lists the names of many gladiators, two of which have the letters 'SP' appended.

The objections of Ramsay in *SC*, pp. 302-303, when taken with his little-noticed subsequent article 'The White Stone and the "Gladiatorial" Tessera', *ExpT* 16 (1904-5), pp. 558-61, are decisive. (a) The letters in all cases probably stand for *spectavit* (or *spectat*), not *spectatus*. Ramsay's earlier opinion here, supported by *tesserae* of doubtful authenticity (*CIL* I. susp. b, c, p. 200), was confirmed by the studies of M. Rostewzew (*Römische Bleitesserae*, pp. 2-3). It was further suggested that a sample from Arles should be restored *spectat num(en)* (*CIL* XII.5695.1 = 1.776a). If this is correct, the whole concept of a 'gladiatorial' *tessera* is seen to be based on a misunderstanding.[100] (b) The analogy on this view fails in any case at its essential part, for there is no hint to explain how the inscription could have been a 'new name'.[101]

(vi) The categorical rejection of this theory does not exclude the possibility that a different understanding of the same evidence may be more promising. Ramsay (*SC*, pp. 312-15) refers to an obscure passage in Aelius Aristides' *Hymn to Asklepios* (6.69 = 40.72). The orator attributes his rhetorical success before the imperial family to the encouragement of the σύνθημα he had with him. This was evidently a secret symbol which signified his relationship with the god. Ramsay connects this token conjecturally with the bestowal of the new name Theodorus upon Aristides (26.518 = 334.592). Rostowzew's suggested interpretation of the 'gladiatorial' *tesserae* might then substantiate the connection. Aristides had a vision of the god in a dream and received a token bearing his 'new name' as a mark of his initiation in the service of the god. The underlying practice of *incubatio* was largely a superstition of the uneducated and this would sufficiently account for the mistaken association with gladiators, who were drawn from similar social classes, and also for the paucity of reference in cultured literature (cf. however Ar. *Plutus* 653-747). The Roman examples were sometimes dated on the first of January (*CIL* I.739, 741, etc.), a day said to have been a festival of Asklepios.[102] None of the known specimens is from Pergamum, but the importance of the Asklepios cult there and the fact that the Aristides parallels are located there lends a strong circumstantial appeal to the theory.

This idea is attractive. It probably offers the most complete analogue for our passage and sets it in sharp contrast with a practice likely to have been current in Pergamum. The conqueror is strengthened in the service of his Lord by the pledge of a new relationship.

Some critical comments are however necessary. (a) The evidence for the postulated custom remains circumstantial and inferential. There is abundant material bearing on the appearance of the god in a dream and his conferring of new names,[103] but the link between these aspects and the surviving *tesserae* turns wholly on the acceptance of Rostowzew's inference. (b) A different incident, partially cited by Hort (p. 29), is recorded, where Aristides, after the death of a slave Philumene, received a written oracle bearing his name with additional names signifying 'salvation' and the statement that Philumene had given her life in his stead (27.540 = 353.627). This testifies at least to the currency of similar motifs with a different background of thought. (c) H. Mattingly has more recently maintained that *CIL* XII.5695.1 should be restored *spectat num(mos)*, and that the *tesserae* under discussion were accordingly 'tabs attached to bags of silver denarii, to show that they had been tested for genuineness'.[104] The viability of Ramsay's view would then hinge still more on the strength of the circumstantial evidence for their connection with Asklepios. (d) A close examination of the names on the *tesserae* collected in *CIL* shows that most are of servile types, actually followed in two instances by *s(ervus)* (*CIL* I.736, 743) and usually by the *nomen* of the master in the genitive case. This suits Ramsay's remarks about the social status of the persons, but does not suit the analogy. The whole point was that a new name was supposedly inscribed on the token. But there is scarcely one with religious meaning,[105] and nothing analogous with 'Theodorus'. This does not disprove the connection, for the usages at Rome and at Pergamum might have been different. But it does undermine the foundation of a case which rested on the supposition that the usages were similar.

We must then doubt Ramsay's analogy with this class of *tesserae*, while acknowledging that their true use is uncertain. There may indeed have been some analogue in the Asklepios cult, and perhaps Aristides' σύνθημα is relevant.

(vii) Ramsay also suggested (*SC*, pp. 304-305) that a principal significance of the 'white stone' was simply its suitability as a material for bearing the inscribed name. The symbolic importance of different kinds of writing surface was a commonplace of antiquity.[106] The theme is constantly stressed in many of the varieties of token or amulet we have already discussed. It was also peculiarly prominent at Pergamum. The action of Ptolemy V in forbidding the export of papyrus from Egypt threatened the growth of the library at Pergamum and impelled Eumenes II to substitute the 'parchment' which takes its name from that of the city.[107] Ramsay (*HDB* III.751) sees a contrast between the 'white stone' and the perishable material which Pergamum boasted.

On first visiting Pergamum I was struck with the fact that the Acropolis and its buildings are of a coarse, very dark brown granite, which contributes much to the stern and inhospitable atmosphere of the fortress. The numerous inscriptions *in situ* on the lower terraces are cut on blocks of white marble whose colour and texture form a strange contrast with the natural stone. They have clearly been transported up the mountain for their explicit purpose.[108]

These observations again touch aspects of contemporary symbolism, though they are plainly inadequate as a complete explanation. ψῆφος is not the most suitable word to denote stone as a material. Nor should we follow Trench (pp. 130-31) and Ramsay (*SC*, p. 305) in drawing too close an analogy with the symbolism of the colour white elsewhere in the Revelation.

c. *The New Name*

The principal issue here has already been noticed. There need not necessarily be a rigidly exclusive choice between the main alternatives. Ramsay is probably right in observing that to the Anatolian mind the divine and human aspect might easily pass into each other (*SC*, p. 307).

In view of the veiled opposition to the state religion which characterizes the letter we might readily accept an analogy between the 'new name' as of Christ and the title 'Augustus' (*SC*, p. 310). The inscriptions of this city are rich in elaborate proclamations of the divine titulature of emperors. This background would accord well with the context of the letter and with some of the possibilities already discussed. Charles (p. 67) insists upon it and compares Rev. 3.12.

The balance of probability however inclines me to think that a new name for the individual is primarily meant. The analogy of Rev. 3.12 is not necessarily determinative, for John uses similar symbols differently in different settings. That name is promised to all victors, but this name is the peculiar possession of each individual (cf. Beckwith, p. 462). Rev. 19.12 does not offer a satisfactory parallel, for the secret name of Christ there is known to none but himself. Again, the more promising analogues of the 'white stone' seem on balance to be those which stress the individual nature of its blessing. The new name symbolizes the individual's entry into a new life, status or personality. The idea was familiar in the ancient world, when names were significant and linked with character.[109] The thought may then be compared with that of 2 Cor. 5.17. The interpretation also rests upon Old Testament parallels in Isa. 62.2 and 65.15.

The principal difficulty in this view has been noted by Charles (p. 67n.): the conqueror is promised a new character—but he has already shown by his faithfulness that he possesses this. The eschatological nature of the promise may however stand if we take this to allude to a perfecting of a new and transformed relationship with Christ (cf. 1 Cor. 13.9-12).

d. *Conclusion*

It is well to emphasize again John's elusive way of using symbolism. It is certainly possible that the present group of promises contained explicit allusion to a local custom. But here the composite grouping of concepts seems very likely to reflect the pattern of the original situation, for several partial analogues are relevant and suggestive. The value of the discussion is to permit discrimination within the field of choice. The alternatives may be considered both on their individual merits and on their coherence and compatibility. The connection of the 'manna' with the 'white stone' is a particular issue here. They might be taken as connected in meaning, or as set against parallel features of the local background. Probably both are eschatological, but expressed in terms meaningful to the suffering Pergamene church.

The most relevant concepts seem to be those of initiation, recognition and personal relationship. Among the detailed analogues those of particular value seem to be tokens of admission and the *tessera hospitalis* as a pledge of relationship, the vote of acquittal, and the symbolism of writing materials. The popular amulet theory is more problematical. Its usual combination with the idea of divine names is highly characteristic of ancient thinking, but not very apposite here. The *tesserae* inscribed 'SP' pose interesting questions, but should after all be excluded from consideration, for their association with gladiatorial discharge is mistaken and that with the Asklepios cult dubious. There remains evidence, particularly in Aristides, that visions of the god were linked both with possession of a commemorative token and with the assumption of a new name. Though many features of the practice are not clear, it is reasonable to think there may have been some implicit contrast with the institutions of the *Pergameus deus*.

5. *Conclusions*

1. A preliminary survey of the history of the city helps to explain several features of its later character. The religious policy of its kings fostered ruler-worship, and the city's importance as the first centre of the imperial cult may be seen against this background.

2. Ramsay's argument that Pergamum was the capital of Asia needs examination and qualification. The explanation of the 'throne of Satan' as referring to its primacy in the imperial cult and of the sword as referring to proconsular authority may however be accepted. There may be incidental allusion to the other great shrines of the city, especially the throne-altar of Zeus Soter and the worship of Asklepios Soter, both associated with the serpent, the Biblical emblem of Satan. Here the church was committed to residence in the headquarters of its adversary.

3. The context supports this interpretation. In v. 16 the sword is associated with the authority of the spoken word, in particular the sentence of the judge. Antipas may have been remembered as a first victim or as a test case, and there had apparently been a definite past time of crisis.

4. Much evidence can be cited from proconsular Asia for the growth of a 'polemical parallelism' between the institutions of Christ and of Caesar, and this helps to explain the symbolism.

5. The problem of Nicolaitanism is treated here in its primary context. Later references to the sect are suspect either as mere inferences from the Revelation, or as coloured by later developments. The problem here centres upon the significance of the comparison with Balaam. It is surprising to find allusion to Jewish tradition in a city where the evidence for Jewish settlement is so slight. Balaam's name or a play upon it may already have been current in Christian-Jewish controversy. Christians rejected the application of this reproachful name to themselves, but might use it of an antinomian perversion of their gospel.

6. We cannot be dogmatic about the broader affinities of Nicolaitan-

ism, beyond the fact that it represented an accommodation with pagan society and imperial cult. Attempts to establish its identity with the similar movement at Thyatira or with other New Testament controversies are not conclusive. Nor can Harnack's case for the Gnostic content of Nicolaitanism be established. It may simply have used arguments drawn from the misrepresentation of Pauline freedom.

7. The 'hidden manna' is again rooted in Jewish tradition. The clearer line of this tradition is that ultimately derived from Exod. 16.32-34. There may be a background in the pressures of emperor-cult, and a full understanding of its significance in any case may involve the question of its relationship with the 'white stone'.

8. The 'white stone' is discussed at length. Several partial analogues are noted. A critical study of the background helps to define the area of choice.

9. The 'new name' is here better understood as the name given to the individual than as a title of Christ. The usage is different here from that of Rev. 3.12. This preference is then a factor in the choice of analogues for the 'white stone'.

Chapter 6

THYATIRA

1. *Introductory*

The longest and most difficult of the seven letters is addressed to the least known, least important and least remarkable of the cities. The letter was not, I think, obscure to the church in Thyatira; the problem lies in our remoteness from the contemporary facts. The epistle is much concerned with matters of everyday life, which are transient and rarely accessible to historical study, least of all from a standpoint distant in time and place. The scantiness of our usual materials makes the difficulty the more acute. Thyatira is very rarely mentioned in ancient literature, and its site is covered by the modern town of Akhisar, which betrays few outward signs of its past and whose presence has prevented excavation. The primary sources consist mainly of inscriptions, supplemented by coinage, but neither is particularly rich, and their evidence is often tantalizingly incomplete.[1] Our study will accordingly need to be topical and selective, though most of the problems of the text will be considered in their place.

The character of the site has been described by Ramsay (*SC*, pp. 316-19). All the other six cities are visually remarkable. Thyatira alone lies on almost level ground in the centre of a broad vale bordered by gently rising hills. Its river is another and a lesser Lycus (Gurduk Çay), a tributary of a northern tributary of the Hermus (Gediz Nehri). The basin is separated from that of the Caicus, Pergamum's river, only by a gentle watershed, crossed without difficulty by the modern railway. An extensive area of sandy plain south-east and south-west of Thyatira offers no obstacle to an enemy approaching from Sardis or from Magnesia ad Sipylum (Manisa).

Thyatira is first known to us as a Seleucid colony, whose foundation is ascribed to Selcucus Nicator at the time of his war with Lysimachus (Steph. Byz. on Thyat.).[2] An older settlement had almost certainly existed, for the name is native Lydian.[3] The statement of Stephanus that Pelopia and Semiramis were older names is not to be accepted, though these and Euhippia were evidently *cognomina* of the city.[4] The original settlement was probably an Anatolian *kōmopolis* centred upon the shrine of the goddess known from later sources as Artemis Boreitene.

The siting of the Seleucid colony implies that Lysimachus then controlled the Caicus valley through his deputy Philetaerus (*SC*, p. 317). It remained a Seleucid outpost against the subsequent rise of an independent Pergamene state until it changed hands and assumed its characteristic role as the Attalid outpost. Pergamum may first have gained control in 262 BC, when Eumenes I at his accession defeated Antiochus I near Sardis (Strab. 13.4.2 = p. 624). Thyatira's position required it to be a frontier garrison, but its vulnerability made it liable to suffer reconquest with every fluctuation in the balance of power (cf. *SC*, pp. 317-19). Most of the scattered literary references to its early fortunes represent it as the victim of a conquering army.[5]

The city's definite adhesion to the Pergamene realm after 190 BC is attested in its rare *cistophori*, probably to be assigned to 188, if not earlier (Head, *BMC Lydia*, p. cxxi; Robert, *Villes d'Asie Mineure*, p. 34).[6] Even after that it suffered the ravages of Prusias, it fell to the pretender Aristonicus at the outset of his revolt in 133 (Strab. 14.1.38 = p. 646), and was the site of Fimbria's camp at the coming of his rival Sulla (Plut. *Sulla* 25.1 = p. 467).[7] Throughout this early history the city was compelled by circumstances to play a part for which it was not well fitted. The coming of the stable conditions of the *pax Romana* eventually favoured its growth. Its open position at the confluence of easy routes then made it an ideal manufacturing and marketing centre. Its coinage, which had ceased after the *cistophori*, was resumed under Augustus (*BMC Lydia*, p. cxxi). The increasing abundance of later inscriptions suggests that Thyatira, still of limited importance at the time of the Revelation, reached a peak of prosperity in the second and third centuries (cf. *SC*, pp. 323-24). The words of Rev. 2.19 were addressed to a growing church in a growing city.

In the very mixed character of later Thyatira its military origins were an important factor. The city's most obvious peculiarity was then its unusually large number of influential trade-guilds. Associations of this kind were an ancient feature of community life in Asia, especially in Lydia (cf. Hdt. 1.93). In many cities of the area, including Thyatira, Philadelphia and Hierapolis, they seem to replace the more usual civic tribal structure. They might in fact have appeared as *collegia* of the type which the Romans tried to suppress elsewhere, but which owed their continuance here to their established antiquity and their deep integration into community life.[8] Their prominence at Thyatira, however, is quite exceptional. I shall argue that this great development was orientated towards the provision of the auxiliary services of a garrison city, though its commercial possibilities were only realized after the original stimulus had disappeared. I suggest that the growth of Thyatira is closely related to some important aspects of the military and economic policy of the Attalid kings.

Many commentators on the Revelation have seen a close relevance in the trade-guilds to the background of our letter.[9] The nature of that relevance is open to question. The interpretation of the letter in fact turns much upon our understanding of its application to the actual facts of life in Thyatira. The method of our inquiry is here especially useful, even if conclusions must be provisional.

Something may be said here of the general part the guilds played in the city.[10] The clothiers, for example, commemorate their erection of a triple gate, colonnades and workmen's houses (*CIG* 3480 = *IGRR* IV. 1209). Most of the inscriptions are not closely datable. Most are likely to be later, but there is every indication that the activities they record were characteristic of the whole early Imperial period. Thyatira possessed, moreover, a variety of other *collegia* which were not primarily trade associations. There were (as often in other cities) οἱ πραγματευόμενοι Ῥωμαῖοι (*IGRR* IV. 1235, probably of the 1st cent. AD), and an unusual group οἱ ἀκμασταί (apparently 'men in the prime of life', *IGRR* IV. 1234). Even more curious were the bodies of youths of the three gymnasia which voted and inscribed honours in due form to their sports heroes at the local games (*IGRR* IV. 1217, 1246, 1264, 1266-69). The frequency of the practice suggests that such actions were regarded as integral to the education of the young in the current conception of citizenship. There were also otherwise unknown village communities within the city territory which erected honorific statues.[11] This coexistence of trade and village organizations is another pointer to early Lydian origins.

Three notable features of these guilds are (1) their religious basis,

(2) their apparent localization, and (3) their persistence.

(1) The local religion will claim some further scrutiny below. The god Apollo Tyrimnaeus was evidently conceived as, *inter alia*, patron of the guilds, and their feasts were essentially religious occasions, which took place in the temple (cf. *SC*, p. 146).

Modern conditions may be held to throw unexpected light on (2) and (3). The widespread evidence for the localization of ancient guild communities[12] is strangely paralleled here in the layout of the modern town, where the central bazaar is divided by narrow streets into a series of blocks, several of them occupied each by a separate trade, conspicuous among them being vendors of dyed fabrics and bronzesmiths, the latter selling goods made in the interior of the same premises.

These facts in themselves are interesting and illustrative, but their significance must not be overemphasized.[13] There is however abundant attestation of the remarkable historical continuity of localized institutions in Asia Minor, especially where their origin was religious.[14] This city appears to have changed in character least of the seven; it will not be surprising to find that it preserves in detail features of its ancient counterpart. This is not to say that actual guilds exist in the modern city or that the modern craftsmen necessarily preserve skills of the ancient. It would be dangerous to approach the ancient town through the modern, but there is occasion tentatively to correlate the two.

The subject of trade leads directly to the only New Testament reference to Thyatira outside the Revelation. At the riverside at Philippi Lydia, a seller of purple (*porphuropōlis*) of Thyatira became the first recorded Christian convert in Macedonia (Acts 16.14). This term is not known otherwise from Thyatira, but the guild of βαφεῖς is mentioned at least seven times in the inscriptions, far more than any other.[15] The art of dyeing was very anciently practised in Lydia and Caria (Hom. *Il.* 4.141-42); it was even said to have been invented at Sardis (Plin. *NH* 7.56.195). Clerc points out that the dye used was obtained from the madder root, the so-called 'Turkey red', for this was still employed in Akhisar in his own time (p. 94; cf. *SC*, pp. 325-26).[16] Strabo, moreover, testifies incidentally to the ancient use of 'the roots' at Hierapolis (13.4.14 = p. 629), where the waters were specially adapted to dyeing.[17]

In the absence of other evidence the little known of Lydia is instructive. She was a 'God-fearer' (Acts 16.14). As Philippi had no synagogue (cf. Acts 16.13),[18] it seems more likely that she first encountered the Jewish faith in her own city.[19] The direct evidence for Judaism at Thyatira is confined to the problematic 'Sambatheum' inscription (*CIG* 3509), and we know nothing of the coming of Christianity to it. We might guess that it was evangelized by persons unknown during Paul's residence at Ephesus (c. 52-55; cf. Acts 19.10). Lydia may have been an influential representative of the βαφεῖς at Philippi, but nothing is subsequently recorded of her, and it is unknown whether she returned to Thyatira or played any part in its evangelization.[20] Her presence in Philippi, however, reflects the continuing connection of the Thyatiran colonists with their Macedonian homeland.

Any further notion of the origin and status of a Jewish community in Thyatira must be based on inference from the probabilities of Seleucid and Attalid policy. There is no evidence and no great likelihood of a Seleucid *katoikia* of Jews here.[21] Of the Attalids little can be said. Their policy was more centralized, and less directed to the development of city-life (see e.g. Rostovtzeff in *CAH* VIII.606, 615). I can find no evidence that they favoured Jews in their cities, nor do the unsettled conditions of early Thyatira seem congenial for extensive Jewish settlement. If the small, but unspecified, amount of Jewish temple-gold confiscated by Flaccus at Pergamum in 62 BC represents the total contribution of the *conventus*, we may infer that the amount of temple-tax collected in the subordinate centre of Thyatira was negligible. It is likely that Jews came as resident aliens when the Roman peace made the city an increasingly important commercial centre. If they lacked the organized status and privileges they sometimes enjoyed elsewhere, they had perforce to come to terms with a mixed pagan society in which they had no part. The situation may have favoured their exploitation of syncretistic cults.[22]

Apart from the question of Judaism, the city seems to have been racially very mixed, and the syncretism of its religion may be traced to this factor (*SC*, pp. 320-21). The local god was formally designated 'Helius Pythius Tyrimnaeus Apollo' (*CIG* 3500; *BCH* 11 [1887], p. 101, No. 24; etc.), a title reflecting a composite conception of his nature, probably at once Lydian, Macedonian and Hellenic. Macedonian and native elements in the population were together from the outset: here too Lydia and Mysia met. The diversity in the imperial period may have been even greater. There are traces both of Persian and Egyptian settlers in the district.[23] Greek-Latin bilingual inscriptions occur with perhaps unusual frequency, and include many private documents.[24]

Syncretism in religion was the natural ancient way of uniting disparate elements. That civic harmony was the ideal we may perhaps infer from a coin, of Alexander Severus or later, which depicts the turreted city-goddess on the obverse and a figure named Homonoia on the reverse (*BMC Lydia*, Thyat. No. 56). Such a type is frequent on alliance coins; here it seems to denote the internal harmony of the parts.

2. *Chalkolibanos*

The word χαλκολίβανος (or χαλκολίβανον),[25] rendered 'fine brass' in the AV of Rev. 1.15 and 2.18, is otherwise unknown. It is evident from the inadequacy of early attempts to explain it that its true significance had already been lost.[26] Suidas defines it as 'a kind of *electrum* more precious than gold'. *Electrum*, however, is itself an ambiguous term.

In modern times Trench (pp. 38-39) argued that the word was a Greek-Hebrew hybrid containing the root לבן ('to make white').[27] Hort (p. 17), feeling a contradiction between the apparent requirements of philology and sense, took up Suidas, assuming that amber, as a fragrant gum, might be called 'brass-like frankincense', and that this term was then used indiscriminately as a synonym for ἤλεκτρον, even where the word denoted not amber but a metal. He then concurs with the consensus of more recent commentators that the present contexts and the Old Testament passages underlying them alike require us to understand *chalkolibanos* as a metal (so Charles, p. 29; Swete, p. 17; Moffatt, pp. 344-45; Beckwith, pp. 438-39).

I suggest that an acceptable solution must take account of several factors. (1) The underlying Old Testament passages, in particular Dan. 10.6, require us to understand a shining metal, and a similar sense is surely required for *chalkolibanos*. This is confirmed by the allusion to the refining fire (Rev. 1.15).[28] (2) We must suppose that the word was intended to be intelligible to the original readers. It is reasonable to think that the change from the phrase in Dan. 10.6 was deliberate. It has often been suggested that our term was familiar to the important local guild of bronze-workers (*SC*, p. 329; Kiddle, p. 37; Caird, p. 43). (3) In this connection it will be well to raise the nature of the relationship of 1.15 and 2.18 within a closely-wrought whole. I maintain that this is only sufficiently explained if we consider Dan. 10 to have been closely linked in John's mind with the circumstances of the local church. His point may then best be seen in the context of the Thyatiran letter.[29] (4) Any attempted derivation must meet the philological requirements. We here anticipate some later discussion by noting the neglected possibility that the word might be a 'copulative compound', a formation regular, if relatively rare, in the Greek language. Whatever *chalkolibanos* is, we may expect it to be a high-quality metal alloy of the copper, bronze or brass type. An alloy might naturally be given a name compounded of those of its component metals, χαλκός and a hypothetical -λίβανος. The difficulty in the order of compounding would thus be overcome, the two elements being parallel as in ἰατρόμαντις or γλυκύπικρος. I shall argue on independent grounds that *chalkolibanos* may have been an alloy whose composition can be identified. It will then be possible to suggest both a meaning and an opposite etymology for λίβανος.

I begin with some simple lexical definitions. The word χαλκός (Latin *aes*) may be applied indiscriminately to copper, bronze and perhaps brass, but commonly to bronze, the alloy of copper with a little tin.[30] Pure copper is too soft to make good tools or weapons. The early discovery of the versatile properties of the alloy was a landmark in human prehistory, and bronze continued vital despite the scarcity of tin in the Mediterranean world.

Brass is the alloy of copper with zinc. It was known in antiquity, but perhaps never common before Roman times. It was then used for coinage by Julius Caesar (H. Mattingly, *Roman Coins*, 2nd edn, p. 28), and under Augustus it became the regular alloy used for imperial *dupondii* and *sestertii* (Mattingly, p. 121). There can thus be no doubt that brass was common then, or that it was capable of being produced by a regular method, for the proportions of zinc in the abundant surviving coins are considerable, if variable (E.R. Caley, *Orichalcum*, p. 1). This alloy was named ὀρείχαλκος (Latin *orichalcum*, later and erroneously *aurichalcum*), though it was probably often loosely called χαλκός by non-technical writers, rather as 'brass' is often used for 'bronze' by older English writers, including the AV translators.

Despite these facts it is often denied that the ancients knew, or could have known, zinc. There are technical difficulties in the isolation of zinc in metallic form, and it has been supposed that brass was made by using zinc compounds without ever producing the actual metal. The method is described by R.J. Forbes in his *Metallurgy in Antiquity*, pp. 275-76. He denies emphatically that the ancients could ever have made metallic zinc commercially.[31]

There is no reason to doubt that brass was usually made as Forbes has said, but there are two decisive arguments against his denial of the alternative. (1) Ancient objects of metallic zinc are extant. Only one specimen may be considered certain and of rigorously authenticated date and provenance. It is from the Agora excavations at Athens, and not later than the second century BC. But one such example is decisive.[32] (2) One crucial passage is extant in ancient literature where zinc appears to be named. This describes a metallurgical process applied to a 'stone' found at Andeira in the Troad, and it explains that the metal produced, ψευδάργυρος, when added to χαλκός, forms ὀρείχαλκος. Two terms of the equation are known: the unknown item can hardly be other than zinc, which, as a white metal, might aptly be termed 'false silver' (Strab. 13.1.56 = p. 610).

Now we have observed that the Thyatiran guild of χαλκεῖς is attested in an inscription (*IGRR* IV. 1259). The frequent coin-types both of Hephaestus and of Athena helmeted (*BMC Lydia*, Thyat. Nos. 24, 30-32, 50, 82) reflect the city's association with both war and crafts (cf. *SC*, p. 326). And bronze-working has apparently continued as a speciality into modern times.

What was the origin of this industrial development in Thyatira? Where did the raw materials come from? Can it all be explained in geographical and economic terms?

There is no evidence for the present or former occurrence of copper ores in the immediate neighbourhood.[33] There are only lignite mines in the mountains behind Soma and Kırkağaç, almost midway between Pergamum and Thyatira. The nearest recorded copper mines were at Cisthene (Strab. 13.1.51 = pp. 606-607) and in the neighbourhood of Andeira (Strab. 13.1.56 = p. 610). Both these places were near Adramyttium.[34] In his account of Andeira Strabo further mentions that 'false-silver' was also made around Mt Tmolus. We may infer the former existence of further ores there. Thyatira lies between Adramyttium and Tmolus.

The location of a metal industry in Thyatira is probably to be explained from its early military importance. Xenophon, in the course of a vivid account of Agesilaus's war preparations at Ephesus in 396 BC, records the contributions of a number of crafts strikingly reminiscent of those listed among the Thyatiran guilds, and including χαλκεῖς and χαλκοτύποι (Xen. *Hell.* 3.4.17; as in *IGRR* IV. 1259). Thyatira, as a garrison city, was naturally also an arsenal, organized for military preparedness.[35] Its political masters evidently adapted the indigenous guild-structure to their purpose. The circumstances lead us to see this as the work of the Attalids, concerned with the security of Pergamum, and developing their territory as a whole with close central supervision of its strategic and economic resources.[36] Rostovtzeff has shown that the principal natural resources of this territory, in particular its war materials, timber, pitch, horses, and mines of copper and silver, were located in the Troad.[37] Its vulnerable point, however, was its south-eastern border, where Thyatira guarded the approach. The establishment of a direct road from Adramyttium to Pergamum ensured an integrated speed of internal communication between the two strategic areas through the capital. There is thus a ready explanation of the Thyatiran industries, and a strong presumption that its ores were derived from the Andeira district.

We must turn next to the problem passage in Strabo.[38] He writes: ἔστι δὲ λίθος περὶ τὰ Ἄνδειρα ὃς καιόμενος σίδηρος γίνεται· εἶτα μετὰ γῆς τινος καμινευθεὶς ἀποστάζει ψευδάργυρον, ἢ προσλαβοῦσα χαλκὸν τὸ καλούμενον γίνεται κρᾶμα, ὅ τινες ὀρείχαλκον καλοῦσι. (There is a stone near Andeira which when calcined becomes iron; then, when heated in a furnace with a certain earth, it distils 'false silver'. When this receives the addition of copper it becomes the so-called alloy which some call 'orichalcum'). The passage is almost repeated by Stephanus of Byzantium (on Andeira), who indicates that he is quoting from Theopompus and Strabo. Theopompus then is evidently Strabo's source, and the information may have become confused in transmission. Perhaps neither writer understood the process, and their original informant may have been studiously vague in the interest of secrecy.

Forbes criticizes Strabo severely. The reference to iron is absurd, and the whole 'technical nonsense' (p. 286). He refers to Isidorus's definition of *aurichalcum* as evidence of the grotesque misconceptions possible even later. That writer evidently thought that the ore calamine was a kind of drug for purifying copper into brass (*Etym.* 16.20.3). Forbes accordingly dismisses the alternative involving metallic zinc.

But Strabo's account, however garbled, represents an intelligible reality. Forbes does not discuss the explanation already offered by Leaf (pp. 287-89 *ad loc.*), who describes the passage as 'an unmistakable account of the production of metallic zinc, and its use with copper to make brass'. He writes, following *EBr*: 'The process of reduction of the ore involves two stages. The ore has first to be roasted or calcined, in order to remove all volatile components as completely as possible, because these, if allowed to remain, would carry away a large portion of the zinc vapour during the distillation. The ore is thus converted into zinc oxide. The oxide is then mixed with carbon, placed in closed crucibles, and distilled through a tube opening outside, from which it comes in a liquid form.' Leaf shows that iron is likely to have been one of the principal impurities removed by the first stage: this accounts for the mention of it, even if Theopompus or his informant misunderstood the point. γῆ τις would be carbon, probably in the form of lignite, found in the Troad, and near Kırkağaç, only about fifteen miles from Thyatira by the Pergamum road. ἀποστάζει is highly significant, for it implies the production of the 'false-silver' in drops, and that is precisely the way zinc would form in a closed vessel (so Caley, p. 24). Strabo could scarcely have hit by accident upon these several technical details if his description had no underlying substance.

Leaf, Michell and Caley among modern writers concur in accepting the basic intelligibility of Strabo's account. None of them has related the process to a wider context; it is expounded as an isolated curiosity. Strabo need not imply that 'false-silver' or brass were necessarily produced at Andeira, only that that was the source of the ores. Thyatira is a known centre of such metal-work. Its ores almost certainly came from the area of Adramyttium and the Troad. Reference to the 'furnace' in 1.15 hints at local familiarity with the refining process. Perhaps local lignite was used.

Some points must be noted about the origin and production of ὀρείχαλκος, as recorded in other ancient authorities. There is a persistent tradition of decline from former standards of workmanship in metals and of the early existence of a precious form of ὀρείχαλκος, perhaps derived from the Pontus district, a famous early centre of metallurgy.[39] The only known Greek objects of brass or zinc bronze have been found in the Black Sea area (Caley, p. 30). Statues of the material were made from the mines of Chalcedon (Ps.-Arist. *De Mirab. Auscult.* 58 = 834b), and the Attalids were interested in the

Pontic trade and accordingly maintained good relations with the cities of the Straits.[40] Here are pointers to the route by which sophisticated techniques might have reached the Attalid kingdom from an ancient centre of metallurgy.[41]

Perhaps those techniques were in fact less extraordinary than we suppose, though it is unwise to discount the possible capabilities of early Asianic civilization: the decline of its primitive flowering is a well attested phenomenon.[42] We may in any case accept that zinc was known in the likely source of Thyatira's metal, whether or not that knowledge represented the remnant of a more ancient skill. The continued practice of unusual skills was likely to have been an esoteric matter, whose details were the guarded prerogative of the craftsmen of a temple or guild. These factors will readily account for the ignorance of later, non-technical writers and lexicographers.[43]

I suggest then that an alloy of copper with metallic zinc was made in Thyatira, the zinc being obtained by distillation. This was a finer and purer brass than the rough and variable coinage-alloy. It may have derived from older skills preserved by the craftsmen of the guild. The product, I suggest, was known there as χαλκολίβανος, which I conjecture to be a 'copulative compound', literally rendered 'copper-zinc',[44] λίβανος being an unrecorded word, perhaps peculiar to the trade, for a metal obtained by distillation, and so derived from the verb λείβω.[45]

If then the context is of local industry, it seems likely that the local patron-god Apollo Tyrimnaeus is in John's mind. Kiddle renews the old suggestion that this god was represented by a bronze statue in the town (p. 37). Caird (p. 43) refers to the coins where he is depicted grasping the emperor's hand, and suggests that the picture of Christ in the letter was put forward in deliberate opposition to this combination of local and imperial religion. There is no evidence about the statue, but the approach is probably correct.

John's mind is dwelling on Ps. 2.7-9 in this letter: the promise to the conqueror is closely based on that passage. And the phrase 'son of God' is found only here in the Revelation:[46] it reflects Ps. 2.7. The designation may be set against opposing religious claims or against a syncretistic attempt to equate the person of Christ with deities recognized by the city. We are again reminded of the coins celebrating the deification of Domitian's infant son at his death in 83, coins which show the child seated on a globe surrounded by seven stars.[46] The recurrence of motifs so reminiscent of the Revelation (e.g. 1.16,

20; 2.1) again prompts the thought that the pretensions of the imperial cult were seen as a Satanic parody of the realities in Christ. The Thyatiran Christians were subject to organized paganism, but the realities of the case were those of Ps. 2, where the Lord was master of oppressive earthly powers. In the 'Son of God' the church had her true champion, irresistibly arrayed in armour flashing like the refined metal from the furnaces of the city. He was the true patron of their work. His keen eyes discerned the good from the bad. He rejected the badness of Jezebel's teaching.

3. *Jezebel*

After warmly commending the loving service and expanding works of the Thyatiran church, Christ condemns their undiscerning toleration of a false prophetess. There are problems here: the text, the identity of 'Jezebel', and the background of these words, which are crucial for the interpretation of the whole passage following.

The textual question may be summarily treated. Two uncial manuscripts (A and 046 = Q, of the 10th century) and many cursives and versions insert σοῦ after τὴν γυναῖκα. The decisive weight of textual authority however appears against this (ℵ, C, etc.), and the addition is readily explained by dittography.[48]

The importance of the variant is simply that it has been made the basis of a proposed identification of Jezebel as the wife of the 'angel', that is, of the 'bishop', of the church.[49] This view has long been canvassed without ever commanding wide acceptance, though Zahn argues for it (*Kommentar* I.286ff.). I consider that the manuscript evidence is fatal to it and the interpretation of the 'angel' beside the point here.

There is no ground for the definitive identification of 'Jezebel'.[50] The probable explanation is simply that she was an unknown woman who had undue influence in the local church and met the problem of Christian membership of the trade-guilds with permissive antinomian or Gnostic teaching. Of the attempts at a more precise identification the most important is that advanced independently by Blakesley and by Schürer, that she was the Sibyl Sambathe, who had a shrine 'before the city' (*CIG* 3509).[51]

This view deserves consideration. Schürer was tentative in his advocacy of it, but it has often been rejected summarily on the ground that the Sibylline priestess could not have been a member of the church or within its jurisdiction (Charles, p. 70; Beckwith, p. 466; etc.), though Ramsay (*SC*, p. 337), Peake (pp. 246-47n.) and Swete (pp. 42-43) give careful and sympathetic thought to it. And a more radical doubt is implied by V.A. Tcherikover's doubt (*CPJ* III.46) whether the inscription refers to a shrine of the Sibyl at all rather than simply to a Jewish synagogue.[52]

Some complex ramifications are involved in the assessment of the possibilities. It is very likely that there is much confusion between the derivatives of Σαμβάθη and of σάββατον, and the widespread occurrence of 'Sambathion' as an apparently pagan personal name in Egypt is an unsolved problem.[53] And it may be just the writer's point that the original Jezebel was a heathen whose ways had been accepted and who had corrupted the chosen people. It is quite conceivable that in this racially mixed city the church was threatened by some monstrous syncretism of Christian, Jewish and pagan elements through a priestess who combined 'magical Judaism' or Gnostic views with a professed adherence to Christianity.

On my first visit to Thyatira I was shown a mosque (the Ulu Cami = 'Grand Mosque') preserving traces of previous Christian and perhaps pagan antecedents, and apparently associated with the name of Lydia.[54] The name Lydia might well have replaced that of an old deity whose shrine stood here on a site then 'before the city'. This continuity of sacred sites is a familiar phenomenon in Anatolia. It is possible that this might have been the site of the hypothetical 'Sambatheum', but more probable that it was that of the city-goddess Artemis Boreitene, who apparently shared a common precinct with Apollo Tyrimnaeus, a union reflected in the marriage of their representative priest and priestess (*IGRR* IV. 1225 = *BCH* 11 [1887], p. 478, No. 57).[55] The god is more prominent on the public evidence of coins and inscriptions, though probably the native conception made him the subordinate consort of the goddess. He was described as πρόπολις, a title taken to imply that his temple was again 'before the city'.[56]

This argument is necessarily a very condensed version of an evaluation of many circumstantial data. There is much illustration to be found of the general character of the local religion, but its bearing on the Sambathe issue is doubtful. An evidently religious site challenges identification, but the facts counsel caution. Sambathe is not the only, nor the most probable, conjecture.

The epitaph which mentions the Sambatheum gives a precise

description of the location of the tomb: Φάβιος Ζώσιμος κατα-
σκευάσας σορὸν ἔθετο ἐπὶ τόπου καθαροῦ ὄντος πρὸ τῆς πόλεως
πρὸς τῷ Σαμβαθείῳ ἐν τῷ Χαλδαίου περιβόλῳ παρὰ τὴν δημοσίαν
ὁδὸν ἑαυτῷ ἐφ᾽ ᾧ τεθῇ καὶ τῇ γλυκυτάτῃ αὐτοῦ γυναικί . . . (*CIG*
3509) (Fabius Zosimus set this sarcophagus in place on an unoccupied
site before the city near the Sambatheum in the precinct of the
Chaldean beside the public street, for himself to be laid there and for
his dearest wife . . .). The date is Trajanic, or at latest Hadrianic,[57]
so we may reasonably assume that a building then familiar already
existed at the date of the Revelation. Unfortunately the inscription
was not found *in situ*, but the coffin was re-used as a water-container
in a house in the town (Boeckh *ad loc.*). Only the recurring, and here
explicit, 'before the city' might possibly help.

The character of this Sambathe is obscure. The evidence has been
clearly stated by Schürer (pp. 49-52). The list of Sibyls in the
Prologue of our extant Jewish Sibyllines is plainly drawn from the
same source as that in Lactantius (*Div. Inst.* 1.6.8-12), who ascribes
his information to Varro. This writer is then probably also the source
for the name Sambethe [*sic*], which is not mentioned by Lactantius.
The Sibylline prologue describes this Sibyl as Chaldean or Persian.
Pausanias (10.12.9) calls here Sabbe, and makes her the Hebrew
Sibyl, though some called her Babylonian or Egyptian. This clearly
derives from a different source: the name Sabbe however is agreed to
be a hypocoristic variant of Sambathe (Schürer, p. 52; Tcherikover,
CPJ III.47f.). Again, Suidas calls her the Chaldean Sibyl, also known
by some as Hebrew or Persian. The ethnic 'Chaldean' coincides with
the '*peribolos* of the Chaldean'[58] in our inscription.

Four of the ten Sibyls of the Varro tradition are explicitly located
in cities of proconsular Asia (Erythrae, Marpessus, Samos and
Phrygian Ancyra), and some earlier parts of the Jewish Sibyllines
(especially Book 4) have an Asian provenance a few years earlier than
the Revelation. If a Jewish sectarian writer assumes the identity of a
Sibyl, it implies some aptness in the role. And Pausanias, who
ascribes a Hebrew origin to Sabbe, was the most likely to have had
local information. There is in fact some circumstantial probability
that the Sambatheum involved a syncretistic cult with a distinctively
Jewish element. But even this is open to doubt, and if in fact true, we
cannot firmly identify the place or assume Schürer's equation of
Sambathe with Jezebel.

The choice of the name 'Jezebel' in 2.20 is likely to be pointedly apt, as was that of 'Balaam'. The ground of condemnation of the original Jezebel was that she had brought idolatry into Israel (1 Kings 16.31-33; 21.25-26). The same is true of the Thyatiran Jezebel: she taught her followers 'to eat things sacrificed to idols'. The syncretism exemplified in the city is in point here, but the particular problem seems to have been the guild-feasts, as the occasions when the Christian may have been particularly pressed by the need to conform to his environment.

Something of the actual teaching and influence of Jezebel may be learned from the letter. She called herself a prophetess (2.20), and led the servant of Christ astray to commit fornication and to eat things sacrificed to idols. The association of these prohibitions goes back, as we have seen, to Num. 25.1-2, apparently the incident occasioned by Balaam's evil counsel. In contemporary pagan society the problem of the *eidōlothuta* arose either when meat sold in the public market had already been consecrated to an idol or at the feasts of such bodies as trade-guilds.

The relationship of this passage both with Acts 15 and with Rev. 2.14 needs some brief consideration. The words οὐ βάλλω ἐφ' ὑμᾶς ἄλλο βάρος (2.24) are closely reminiscent of Acts 15.28, and Charles infers that John had the Apostolic Decree in mind (p. 74). There are curious problems here. I suppose that the Decree was only directly applied by Paul to the Gentile churches already existing, notably those of South Galatia. Paul does not, for instance, appeal to it when dealing with the problems at Corinth. Why then is it echoed in these letters to Asian churches which were also presumably founded during Paul's later Gentile ministry? The answer seems to be that its principles needed reassertion in the local situations and that its agreed apostolic authority was recognized by the parties in the churches. There may be some point in the reversal of order: the teaching of Jezebel was not necessarily the same in emphasis as that of the Nicolaitans. The order here suggests that what the church tolerated was primarily immorality, whether literal or as a figure for apostasy, and that licence for it was the primary object of the prophetess (so Charles, p. 71).[59]

Further data for an estimate of Jezebel may be inferred from the subsequent verses. Verse 21 may imply that a definite warning had already been given her: the reference would have been understood by Thyatiran readers (cf. Beckwith, p. 467). Verse 22 again involves problems of interpretation and background, according to the view taken of κλίνην. This has been variously explained as a bed of pain or a funeral bier, or ironically of a dining-couch, with the implication that this was the emblem of her sin. The first suggestion has been adopted by most commentators. Charles explains it thus from Hebrew idiom, and this view is consonant with the fate threatened against her 'children'.[60] Hort (p. 30) suggested a 'funeral-bier'; but this is not supported by the context, and the Biblical parallels with βάλλω require the other sense. Ramsay (*SC*, pp. 351-52) strongly maintained here a reference to the dining-couch at the guild-feasts.[61] It seems likely enough that there are allusions which escape us here through our ignorance of the inner life of the guilds, but the primary meaning is probably 'sick-bed'.[62]

It would be instructive to know the position of women in the guilds. Ramsay (*SC*, p. 353n.) refers to an inscription (*BCH* 28 [1904], pp. 23-24, No. 2), then newly published, where a leading citizen gave a dinner for all the male and female community, the men dining in one temple and the women in another. But this evidence from Panamara, near Stratonicea in Caria, is an uncertain foundation for arguing Thyatiran practice.[63] We know that Lydia at Philippi was a businesswoman who dealt in the products of a guild prominent in her native Thyatira. After her conversion she may have faced problems of membership and participation in the guild.[64] 'Jezebel' may herself have had a business interest to protect.

τοὺς μοιχεύοντας may be understood figuratively of those in the church who had been led astray by Jezebel into idolatry, though incidental reference to its immoral character is not excluded. Repentance is still open to this class, in contrast with 'her children' who have committed themselves wholly to her ways. They will be killed ἐν θανάτῳ. This expression is not tautologous, but derives from the LXX rendering of דבר ('pestilence'; see Ezek. 33.27 LXX and Rev. 6.8; cf. Jer. 21.7).[65]

A problem here is that the judgment upon the children seems more severe than that upon Jezebel herself. There may be reference to the killing of the sons of Ahab (2 Kings 10.7), though that is not in context presented as a judgment upon his wife. Beckwith (pp. 467-68) finds a parallel rather in the death of the child of David and Bathsheba, where this was conceived as the punishment of the erring parents, comparing v. 23 with 2 Sam. 12.14. Perhaps the 'pestilence' is to be linked with the 'sick-bed' of Jezebel, with emphasis upon the fatal results of the disease. Perhaps again, in view of the following words, 'and all the churches shall know', the meaning is that the severe penalty will be a solemn warning to others. The Lord would not be deceived by plausible self-justification; his judgment would discern the motives of the heart. The words ὁ ἐραυνῶν νεφροὺς καὶ καρδίας are closely based upon Jer. 17.10 (cf. Jer. 11.20; Ps. 7.9), νεφρός being used only here in the New Testament. 'The kidneys were regarded by the Hebrews as the seat of the emotions and affections (Jer. xii.2), and the heart of the thoughts' (Charles, p. 73).

Some important, though problematic, evidence is contained in v. 24. Two explanations of 'the deep things of Satan' are widely held: (1) that the phrase is an ironical retort to the claims of Jezebel's followers to esoteric knowledge of 'the deep things of God' (Swete, pp. 45-46; etc); (2) that the opposition actually boasted of a knowledge of 'the deep things of Satan', saying that the spiritual man should experience all evil to demonstrate his superiority over it (Hort, p. 31; Moffatt, p. 362; Beckwith, pp. 468-69). In either case the question arises whether there is any connection with the use of similar phraseology by later Gnostic sects. Exegetically I think there is not much between the alternatives, and many commentators are content to leave the issue open (so Charles, pp. 73-74; Caird, pp. 44-45). Beckwith argues for (2) as being the natural sense of the language if the whole phrase is to be attributed to the opposition. This however is not decisive, for ὡς λέγουσιν may possibly go with the following words (Hort), or it may imply only 'to use their kind of language'. In either case there is evident allusion to something the original readers understood, and it is easier to suppose the opposition got their acceptance in the church if their stated claim was to know 'the deep things of God'.

The background then is important in studying this crucial verse. Three questions may be raised about the whole matter of Jezebel's teaching. (1) Is the present phrase to be related closely to 1 Cor. 2.10 (τὰ βάθη τοῦ Θεοῦ; cf. Rom. 11.33; Eph. 3.18)? In fact, are the problems of Thyatira to be related closely to the antinomianism combatted earlier in Corinth? (2) Can we assume that this teaching was Nicolaitanism, as at Pergamum, and if so is it here in a significantly different setting? (3) Ought we rather to connect the teaching with later developments of Gnosticism?

A generalized answer to these problems is that these possibilities and other similar phenomena probably represent diverse phases and developments of a widespread tendency. I should provisionally accept the common assumption that Jezebel's teaching was Nicolaitanism, but in rather a different setting. At Pergamum the Christian's *life* was directly threatened by the pervasiveness of the imperial cult, here his *livelihood* by the issues involved in membership of the guilds. The teaching of a woman in the church provided him with an answer to his pressing problems. It met what were easily represented as the plain necessities of commercial life. It may have been a shock to hear this popular teacher equated with Jezebel. The church may well have denounced and shunned the grosser forms of syncretized paganism in the city while harbouring teaching which, in John's view, imperilled those whom it led into the very same evils.

Presumably Jezebel argued that a Christian might join a guild and participate in its feasts without thereby compromising his faith. He was initiated into a superior wisdom. He knew the idol was nothing and he could not be defiled by that which did not exist. Pauline phrases insisting on the Christian's liberty from the law might be pressed into service: our letter replies in the terms of the Apostolic Decree to which Paul, according to Acts, had assented. This was just such a *modus vivendi* as was required, but Jezebel's version contravened its accepted principles. The local situation favoured the accommodation of incompatible beliefs and practices: the letter insists on individual devotion to a Lord who searches the hearts of men and demands a consistency of life. The love and faith commended in the church might easily be corrupted by compromise with pagan society: the guilds themselves were devoted to good works.

Most of the commentators have recognized the relevance of guild-membership to our text (Charles, pp. 70-71; Ramsay, *SC*, esp. pp. 346-49; Kiddle, p. 39). Beckwith supposes that the exhortation here is merely to hold fast to standards of Christian purity and fidelity within them (pp. 464-65). But I think the point is that membership necessarily involved contradiction of the Apostolic Decree and the needed repentance must necessarily involve repudiation of the guilds. Here, as at Ephesus and Pergamum, the Christian's hardest pressure came from the inducements to conform to paganism rather than Judaism. There are certainly parallels with Paul's war on two fronts, against libertinism and legalism, but under the new tensions induced by Domitianic policy the issues were being fought on rather different ground. On the question of Gnosticism we must suspend judgment in view of the uncertain data.

4. *The End of the Letter*

The concluding promise of this letter is probably the most difficult of the seven. I will begin with some observations about its form before considering the problems of its content. (1) In this and the three following the order of the concluding formulae is transposed.[66] (2) Only in this case is the final promise made dependent on a double condition, ὁ τηρῶν in effect defining the usual term ὁ νικῶν. In context the victory consisted in keeping to the end the works of Christ rather than those of Jezebel (cf. Swete, p. 47). (3) Only in two cases, here and at Pergamum, are two apparently distinct promises made to the victor, each separately introduced by the word δώσω.[67]

The first promise (vv. 26b-27) is taken from Ps. 2.8-9. The central problem here is the interpretation of the word ποιμανεῖ, which follows the LXX of Ps. 2.9. The passage as a whole, however, is rather a free rendering adapted to the writer's point than strictly a quotation from any known version. The substitution of ἐξουσία for the LXX κληρονομία is perhaps noteworthy, for the Christian in Thyatira might have seemed in a condition of powerlessness.[68]

ποιμανεῖ is a more difficult matter. Charles (pp. 75-76) formulates two questions here. (1) Has John simply borrowed this rendering from the Septuagint? (2) What meaning does he attach to the word?

Charles argues that as it is John's habit to translate independently from the Hebrew there is no need to infer that he is simply borrowing from the Septuagint, while it may be allowed that that version supplied him with a Greek vocabulary. The question of such dependence does not in fact seem clear, and the meaning of ποιμανεῖ must probably be settled from its present context. The Massoretic text of Ps. 2.9 gives the meaning 'break': the Septuagint, using a different vocalization of the original, derived it from a verb meaning 'tend', 'pasture', and so 'rule'. This verb רעה however also means 'devastate', 'destroy', as in Mic. 5.6 and Jer. 6.3. ποιμαίνειν is used as the regular translation of this verb even where it gives a sense otherwise unparalleled in Greek.[69]

On (2), therefore, our choice lies between (a) 'rule' (so most versions and commentators), and (b) 'destroy' or 'break' (Charles; Lohmeyer, p. 29). ποιμαίνειν is used in this primary sense in Rev. 7.17, but its parallelism with συντρίβεται here and with πατάξῃ in 19.15 might be held to suggest that in those passages and in 12.5 it should be rendered 'destroy'.[70] But in the final analysis the sense of the context seems against this interpretation. The promise is of power over those to whom the Thyatiran church is now in helpless subjection. The 'rod of iron' then corresponds to the 'sword' at Pergamum as an emblem of authority. This symbol however has explicit precedent in Ps. 2.9.[71]

The allusion to the familiar picture of the potter smashing the rejected vessel is also taken from Ps. 2.9. The idea is developed in Jer. 18.1-11. Its use here is apt in view of the known existence of a guild of potters in Thyatira.[72]

The concluding words of the verse, 'as I also have received from my Father', clearly recall Ps. 2.7. This expression must be compared with the title 'Son of God' (v. 18). For other instances of the subordination of the Son to the Father in the Revelation we may refer to Beckwith (p. 314; cf. John 10.18). Again we must note the possibility that the emphasis on the person and attributes of Christ in this letter is set against the background of contrast with the local deity.

The second promise, that of the 'morning star', has never been satisfactorily explained. The following points may help to clarify the issues.

(1) Most commentators find, *inter alia*, a reference to Christ himself.[73] Certainly in Rev. 22.16 he is 'the bright and morning star'. But we still have to explain the point and background of so describing him here. In the absence of an explicit context, we must suppose it referred to something the first readers understood. But perhaps they did not immediately take it to refer to Christ: perhaps that is a further identification first made in 22.16.

(2) A star and a sceptre are mentioned together as emblems of Messianic authority in the prophecy of Balaam in Num. 24.17 (so Hendriksen, p. 73; cf. Mt. 2.2). If the opposition at Thyatira is to be taken as an expression of Nicolaitanism, equated at Pergamum with the teaching of Balaam, it is the more interesting that we have here a likely reminiscence of words attributed to Balaam. If his name had become an accepted type of antinomianism there would be the more point in citing his words as unwilling testimony to the sovereignty of Christ.[74] This suggestion fits the supposition that the terms of Num. 24 were familiar slogans in a current controversy: the 'morning-star' allusion needed no explanation. And why should the star of Balaam have been identified explicitly with the morning star, unless at least there are further facets in the history of the concept?

(3) The implied reference to the sovereignty of Christ has been

worked out against the background of the existing world order. The planet Venus had been seen as an emblem of authority since Babylonian times, and the claim of the Caesars to be descended from the goddess enabled them to appropriate the idea as *das Zeichen der Weltherrschaft* (Lohmeyer, p. 30; cf. Lohse, p. 28).[75] The church in Thyatira may already have been facing a syncretistic alliance of imperial and local religion, though the surviving evidence is of later date (*BMC Lydia*, Thyat. No. 94, of Caracalla, onwards). This kind of contrast with world powers would help to explain how the language of Num. 24.17 had been brought into the arena of the church's current conflict.

(4) Some appeal to Dan. 12.3 and regard the star as emblematic of the immortality of the righteous.[76] Moffatt accordingly takes the 'morning star' of the 'dawn' of salvation or eternal life.

Other suggestions seem in general to have less claim to acceptance.[77] The exploration of Jewish literature, of the later chapters of the Revelation and of local circumstances will each furnish materials for conjecture, but none which offers a secure background for the thought of the passage. There was certainly a Messianic interpretation of Num. 24.17 which was apparently current in sectarian Judaism: the star there however denotes the leader and lawgiver of the sect, and is not identified with the morning star.[78]

We must conclude, in default of more clearly verifiable data, that the precise point of this promise is lost and any attempt to assign it a firm *Sitz im Leben* is necessarily speculative. It seems likely that John's mind passed from Ps. 2.7-9 to reminiscence of Num. 24.17, in both of which a rod or sceptre was the emblem of authority in passages taken Messianically. The connection in the latter of sceptre with star then leads him to the 'morning star', a concept which then needed no explanation. He sees Christ as the true embodiment of the qualities of that star, and makes the identification explicit in Rev. 22.16. The obscurity of the expression here lies precisely in its allusiveness. It is because it needed no amplification that we are given no context.

5. Relations with the Later Chapters

The search for light on this chapter from the later chapters of the Revelation is a particularly elusive matter. We may tentatively suggest the relevance of Rev. 13.17, in the account of the second beast, where no man may buy or sell unless he bears the *charagma* of the beast. These words seem likely to have referred to an existing problem, and Thyatira was the place where the alliance of a pagan system with the imperial cult was liable to involve the Christian in commercial ruin. Ramsay (*SC*, p. 105) supposed that a trade-boycott may have been enacted by the Commune of Asia, and that this was one of the means by which it assisted the enforcement of persecution, the methods of the campaign being inferred from Rev. 13.13-17 and 19.20 (cf. *SC*, pp. 98-103).

A constant difficulty is that of isolating such references where they are often subtly blended. The harlot 'Babylon the great' is identified with Rome (17.18), but the portrayal of her is reminiscent of the language used of Jezebel.[79] The horseman of Rev. 19.11-16 who is to rule with a rod of iron may be set against the horseman-god of the city (cf. also 12.5). Again, those who received the mark of the beast in their right hands are distinguished from others who bore it on their foreheads (13.16; cf. 14.9 and 20.4). The symbolism is suggestive of craftsmen who were branded as apostate by their membership of the guilds. The usage would accord with the use of symbols in contemporary conventions of numismatic representation, the 'right hand' standing for their working lives as opposed to their professed status.[80]

6. *Conclusions Summarized*

1. Discussion of the political, economic, and geographical background of Thyatira leads to a conjectural identification of *chalkolibanos* as a refined alloy of copper or bronze with metallic zinc, the resulting product being finer than the *orichalcum* commonly used for imperial coinage. An etymology is suggested for the word which, while itself hypothetical, would provide a natural answer to the philological objections against earlier attempts. The background study confirms and gives content to the supposition that *chalkolibanos* was a trade term whose meaning was familiar in Thyatira.

2. Several characteristics of this rather unremarkable city can be traced. It is here argued that the great development of its trade guilds may be connected with its early history as a garrison city and that they exemplify the localization and continuity which seem to characterize other aspects of its life. Its religion and organization point to a quest for a syncretistic reconciliation of diverse elements in its population.

3. Little evidence exists on the subject of the origin or status of Judaism in Thyatira: the 'Sambatheum' inscription bears disputed testimony to the possible influence of a syncretistic 'magical' Judaism there by the time of the Revelation.

4. While recognizing the difficulty of much of this letter we accept that many of its phrases are to be related to practices involved in the local trade-guilds.

5. The identity of 'Jezebel' is unknown. We must presume she was an influential member of the church. No specific alternative can be substantiated, though the identification with the supposed 'Sambathe' merits consideration.

6. The character of Jezebel's teaching may be seen against the background of the Apostolic Decree of Acts 15. The emphasis here seems to be on the tendency to immorality, whether literal or figuratively of apostasy. The temptation to immorality and idolatry here is likely to have been connected particularly with the practices of the trade-guilds. Jezebel probably taught that a Christian should participate in them for the sake of his livelihood and represented moral scruples as a denial of Christian liberty: it is shown that this *modus vivendi* denies rather the agreed principles of Acts 15 on Christian conduct in pagan society. The situation may be aptly compared with the antinomianism of the Nicolaitans at Pergamum, but it is an open question whether Jezebel's teaching was actual Nicolaitanism or, for that matter, an actual manifestation of Gnosticism. It was at least a doctrine of similar antinomian tendency, perhaps prompted by a slightly different situation.

7. The promises of vv. 26-27 are discussed with reference to their background in Ps. 2.8-9. We may follow Ramsay here in seeing allusion to the weakness of the church at the mercy of organized pagan society.

8. None of the explanations offered for the 'morning star' seems cogent or sufficient. The absolute character of the promise suggested that it needed no explanation to its original readers. The difficulty is in our ignorance of some contemporary fact or situation. There is reminiscence of Num. 24.17. Perhaps this saying was pressed into service in current controversy, in which the name of Balaam may have been a current slogan. The expression might symbolize sovereignty, immortality or priority, and the writer later represents Christ as himself embodying the qualities of the true morning star.

Chapter 7

SARDIS

1. *Introductory*

'Sardis was one of the great cities of primitive history: in the Greek view it was long the greatest of all cities.' So Ramsay begins his account (*SC*, p. 354). This was a city strangely dominated by its illustrious and proverbial past. It is just the point which its own delegates to Tiberius in AD 26 are represented as making the basis of their claims (Tac. *Ann.* 4.55.7-8).

The extensive irregular triangle of the middle Hermus basin, a fertile plain broken broken by minor hill ranges, is dominated by the long ridge of Tmolus (Boz Dağ), rising over 7000 feet at the southern margin of the vale. The acropolis of Sardis on a spur above the plain commanded the whole district. The beginnings of the city remain obscure. Recent excavations have been throwing great light on its early importance, without so far penetrating to the beginning of the settlement.[1]

The geological character of the acropolis is remarkable. Ramsay (*SC*, pp. 354-56, 360-62) has well described some of its features. The tiny summit plateau, 1500 feet above the plain, is surrounded by precipices except at one point where it is joined to the mass of Tmolus by a narrow saddle, and even this approach is steep and difficult. The rock of this acropolis is 'a coarse and friable conglomerate' (p. 360). To call it 'rock' at all, however, conveys a misleading impression. The whole mountain is composed of an immense thickness of an earthen material which crumbles at a touch, yet forms almost vertical cliff-faces.[2] The erosion of these precipices has produced a theatrical landscape of extraordinary strangeness. The main hill is flanked by isolated earthen pinnacles, each several hundred feet high, and capped each with a solitary tree or fragment of masonry. It appears that the roots and stones have formed a resistant apex, yet it is scarcely conceivable that erosional features of such size could have formed in geological time so short as to be related to the life-span even of a succession of trees.[3] There is however other evidence of erosion on a remarkable scale. It has certainly affected the extent of the summit-site, for at its least exposed side the late Byzantine fortifications are in places overhanging an abyss. Ramsay (*SC*, p. 355) was doubtless right to emphasize the smallness of primitive cities, but the present summit is a mere fragment. Most of the original Sardis has surely fallen over the edge.[4]

The plural form of the name Σάρδεις is an indication that the lower city developed early.[5] The tiny citadel was the royal stronghold and wartime refuge of citizens who ordinarily lived below (cf. *SC*, p. 356). The later city occupied an extensive area of the Hermus plain and the Pactolus valley, respectively north and west of the acropolis.[6] North of the Hermus is a tract of undulating hills which separate it from the sacred Gygaean lake (Hom. *Il.* 2.865; 20.390-91), later called Lake Coloe (Strab. 13.4.5 = p. 626), the modern Marmara Gölü. The hills near its shore are profusely scattered with tumuli, some of enormous size.[7] This was the burial ground of the kings of early Lydia, and the largest mound is probably that ascribed to Alyattes (Hdt. 1.93). Serious investigation of this necropolis has only recently begun.[8]

At the western foot of the citadel the Pactolus, a small tributary flowing northward from Tmolus to the Hermus, separates it from a 'Necropolis' mountain to the west. The latter, though never mentioned by Ramsay, forms an important part of the city area, and the hundreds of cave-tombs scattered about its crumbling precipices have been important in recent investigation.[9] Like the tumuli of Bin Tepe, they appear to date exclusively from the Lydian period, though they were occasionally occupied later as refuges in time of emergency.

The visible ruins of Sardis are extensive but fragmentary. The two gigantic unfluted columns yet standing of the Hellenistic temple of Artemis are the principal landmark of the Pactolus valley. But the heart of the Roman city occupied a terrace north of the Acropolis, and here may be seen the complex which includes the gymnasium and the recently excavated synagogue.[10]

Sardis was prominent in early Greek tradition. In legend Midas of Phrygia rid himself of the Golden Touch by washing it off in the springs of Pactolus, which then assumed the gift and turned its sands to gold (Ov. *Metam.* 11.136-45, cf. 85-88). The existence of gold-dust in the stream is attested as fact by Herodotus (1.93; 5.101) and Strabo (13.4.5 = pp. 625f.), though the latter says the supply was exhausted before his own day. There must certainly have been gold in the neighbourhood, for the wealth of early Sardis is abundantly recorded, and the tradition that the oldest coinage, of electrum, a gold-silver alloy, was minted there under King Gyges is confirmed by the provenance and attribution of surviving specimens (cf. Hdt. 1.94 with *BMC Lydia*, pp. xviii-xxii and 1-8).[11] The golden sands of Pactolus became proverbial and were the subject of varied literary allusion in every period of antiquity.

The traditions of the early political history of Sardis are rather confused.[12] A 'Heraclid' dynasty was supplanted soon after 700 BC by Gyges, the first of the Mermnad line. Possibly the change marked a shift of racial ascendancy from Maeonian to native Lydian.[13] Perhaps also the decline of Phrygia opened the way to Lydian hegemony in Western Anatolia.

The fabulous wealth of Lydia was thought to date from the time of Gyges.[14] He was also the first king in the area to become known to the Assyrians, and his name appears in the form 'Gugu' on cuneiform inscriptions.[15] It is widely accepted that he was the historical prototype of Ezekiel's 'Gog' and that his name thus became in Jewish tradition a type of the forces of evil in the last days.

The historical Gyges was finally surprised and slain by the raiding Cimmerians: excavations have revealed a burning of the lower city in the mid seventh century (Mitten, p. 44). A huge mound in the Bin Tepe complex, provisionally identified as his tomb from the description in Hipponax (frag. 15, Bergk), was investigated in 1963, and proved to be an enlargement of an inner tomb of superb but unfinished masonry, the blocks bearing a monogram tentatively interpreted as *gugu* in Lydian script.[16]

There are two special reasons for devoting so much space to Gyges. (1) The drama of his rise and fall made him a proverbial figure and lent itself to the kind of moralizing later applied to his descendant Croesus. (2) There may have been some connection with Jewish tradition about Gog, who reappears in Rev. 20.8.

The traditions of this wealthy and aggressive dynasty may be traced from Herodotus through Alyattes to a climax in his son Croesus. Much of the familiar Herodotean account of Croesus may safely be pronounced unhistorical. This has not prevented its exerting an immense influence on the moral feeling of antiquity.[17] The most significant part of the narrative concerns Croesus's attempt to forestall the rise of Cyrus of Persia. He sent messengers to test the wisdom of the oracles, and gave his implicit trust to that of Delphi, which answered him correctly (1.47-49). On consulting it about war with Persia, he was encouraged with the response that if he crossed the Halys, then his frontier, he would destroy a great empire (1.53). He accordingly found pretext for war, disregarded wiser counsel, and attacked and captured Pteria (1.71-76). On the arrival of Cyrus an indecisive battle was fought. Croesus, having the smaller army, withdrew to Sardis, dismissed for the winter season his powerful allies from Egypt, Babylon and Sparta, and summoned them to reassemble in five months. Meanwhile he disbanded all but his Lydian troops, 'never expecting that after so close-fought a campaign Cyrus would venture against Sardis' (1.77). Cyrus however followed unobserved: αὐτὸς ἄγγελος Κροίσῳ ἐληλύθεε (1.79). Croesus, caught off guard, led his formidable Lydian cavalry desperately into battle, but the horses were thrown into confusion at the sight and smell of the camels which Cyrus had posted in front of his army (1.79-80). Croesus then summoned his allies and prepared to endure a siege in his precipitous stronghold. But on the fourteenth day Sardis fell. An enemy succeeded in climbing to an unguarded point, 'where no guard was stationed, for there was no fear that it would ever be captured at that place, for the acropolis is sheer and impregnable there' (1.84). Cyrus took Croesus alive and set him on a pyre to be burnt to death. In his extremity Croesus remembered the warnings of the wise Athenian Solon and cried aloud his name. On hearing the story Cyrus reflected on the uncertainty of human life and repented of his purpose to kill his prisoner. The fire could not now be quenched, but Apollo sent a providential rainstorm which saved Croesus, who thus survived to become an adviser at the court of his conqueror and to complain against the misleading advice of the oracle. The empire he had destroyed was his own (1.86-91).

The freedom of moralistic and anecdotal invention here is evident. The intended burning of Croesus must be rejected because fire was sacred to the Persians and not to be polluted by contact with death. Sir J.G. Frazer has drawn attention to the existence of a different version of Croesus' fate: according to Bacchylides (3.23-62) he mounted the pyre himself with his family rather than suffer slavery at the sack of Sardis.[18] Frazer argues from contemporary religious parallels that this self-immolation was thought to assure immortality by the purging away of the mortal (*Adonis*, pp. 91ff.).[19] In the difficult subject of the local religion of Sardis there are at least clear hints of a preoccupation with death and renewed life, a fact to note when discussing Rev. 3.1. Perhaps what the Greeks saw as *nemesis* was to the victim apotheosis. The actual fate of Croesus must remain uncertain. It is perhaps likely that he attempted apotheosis by fire, and possible that he was actually reprieved from this by the action of his conqueror.

Even at dates later than the Revelation 'to capture the acropolis of Sardis' was proverbially 'to do the impossible'.[20] The surviving accounts give different rationalizations of the extraordinary physical difficulty of the achievement, but agree in postulating a lack of vigilance in the defenders.[21] Ramsay's dramatic portrayal of the impact on the Greek world of this sudden collapse of the impregnable city (*SC*, pp. 357-59) is true to the huge surviving mass of ancient anecdote and allusion.[22] It had the immediate effect of bringing Persia to the shores of the Aegean, and so changed the pattern of Greek history. The case for seeing historical allusion in the letter to Sardis is related to an appreciation of the formative and proverbial character of the event. It is impracticable to reproduce the literary evidence in the present study: there is far too much of it.[23]

Sardis was never again after 546 BC the capital of an independent state. It became immediately the seat of the Persian governor (Hdt. 5.31), but its strength did not exempt it from surprise and capture on later occasions. As soon as Cyrus departed his first satrap was surprised and besieged in the acropolis by a Lydian revolt (Hdt. 1.154). In 499 BC the Ionians audaciously raided and burnt the lower city (Hdt. 5.100). Xerxes made Sardis the base from which he invaded Greece (Hdt. 7.37, 41), and returned there defeated (8.117; 9.3). At the approach of Alexander, however, the Sardians hastened out to surrender their city without resistance (Arr. *Anab.* 1.17.3; cf. 3.16.5). Alexander ascended the undefended citadel and was greatly impressed by its immense strength (1.17.5; 334 BC). Nevertheless the place was again captured by Antiochus III in 214 BC through the negligence of the defenders.[24]

Sardis was Antiochus's base in his final struggle with Rome (Liv. 37.18.6). After Magnesia however he abandoned it without a defence and withdrew to Apamea (Liv. 37.44.5-7). Sardis was merely the scene of the settlement when he surrendered Asia beyond the

Taurus (Liv. 37.45.3ff.). After that it lost all political importance under the rule of Pergamum and of Rome.

Sardis, like neighbouring Philadelphia, suffered a catastrophic earthquake in AD 17. Pliny describes it as the greatest disaster in human memory (*NH* 2.86.200). Tacitus names Sardis as having been the place most severely hit.[25] Excavation has illustrated extensively the renewal of public buildings after the disaster. There is no reference to the matter in the Sardian letter, though it must certainly have remained long in local memory. It is remarkable that it also passed into Christian tradition, for Orosius mistakenly identified it with the events at the time of the crucifixion.[26] Its impact was evidently such that it seemed an event of almost apocalyptic scale. The literary allusions suggest that something unusually catastrophic happened at Sardis. The language of Tacitus and Orosius, in particular, taken with the visible character and known history of the acropolis, prompt the conjecture that this was nothing less than the sudden collapse of a great part of the mountain and the consequent disappearance of much of the very site of the original fortress-city.[27] In any case it is likely that some of the imagery of the Revelation may be related to local memory of the catastrophe (e.g. 6.14-16; 8.8; 11.13; 16.18-20).

Only nine years after the disaster Sardis competed with ten other Asian cities for the honour of obtaining an imperial temple. Although its delegates rested their claim exclusively upon the greatness of its ancient history there is no reason to doubt its rapid recovery. It assumed the title 'Caesarea' (*BMC Lydia*, Sard. No. 110, of Caligula), but this appears to have fallen quickly into disuse as the memory of Tiberius's generous relief faded.[28] The city long retained a considerable commercial prosperity derived from its advantageous position on the roads from Smyrna and Pergamum to the interior. The days of its royal and military splendour were certainly gone and its civic pretensions unreal, but Ramsay's portrait of it as a city in decay (*SC*, p. 368) is not justified.

2. *Jews and Pagans in Sardis*

a. *Jews*

The earliest reference to Sardian Judaism may perhaps be contained in the Old Testament itself. Obadiah 20 mentions a place of Jewish exile named Sepharad. The probability that this is identical with

Çparda, the Persian name for a district adjoining Ionia (J.A. Bewer, *Obadiah*, p. 45; A.H. Sayce, *HDB* IV. 437), and that in turn with Sardis, the great western capital of the Persian Empire, is confirmed by the discovery at Sardis of an early Lydian-Aramaic bilingual inscription on which the consonants ספרד appear as the Aramaic form of the name of Sardis.[29] The date and significance of this inscription remain open to question. It was erected in the tenth year of a king Artaxerxes, but it is not clear which of the three kings of that name is meant. Torrey prefers Artaxerxes I Longimanus (465-424 BC).

Three views have been held of the significance of the discovery: (1) that the occurrence of Aramaic at Sardis is simply due to its use as an official language under the Persian Empire. (2) It is suggested that its use implies the presence of a considerable Aramaic-speaking population, possibly of Jews, at the time. (3) Torrey has founded upon this evidence a supposition that Aramaic was widely spoken in Asia Minor in the Christian era among Jews and as the regular language of the primitive church.[30]

Of these suggestions (3) must be rejected. The supposed use of an esoteric language within a closed community cannot indeed be easily disproved, but the hypothesis is tenuously founded, and we cannot readily explain the rapid expansion of the Asian church within such a framework. There is no later evidence for the widespread use of Aramaic in Anatolia, and the weight of evidence suggests a rapid decline even of the native languages before the advance of Greek.[31]

The decision between (1) and (2) is not so easy. Here I will simply make three observations to which further studies point. (a) The Taurus was at many periods a linguistic barrier, and the occurrence of Semitic languages in Western Anatolia is apt to be anomalous and subject to special explanation. (b) The assumption that the Persian government used Aramaic officially is at least an open question in its application to Western Anatolia, where the indigenous people were not of Semitic speech. (c) Official use of Aramaic will not in any case explain the Sardis bilingual, which is a *private* sepulchral document with an appended warning of divine vengeance upon profaners of the tomb. The first text is the Lydian: the Aramaic is evidently a translation of it and is presumably intended to convey the warning to potential offenders who spoke that language.[32]

We may then suggest that the Sardian bilingual constitutes prima facie evidence for the existence of an Aramaic-speaking settlement there in the fifth or fourth century BC, though we cannot make firm statements about the status of the language in Asia Minor generally.

The language problem is apposite to our study for various reasons. (1) The hypothesis that Aramaic was widely spoken at Sardis at such a date is consonant with other indications that the city was a principal, and perhaps very early, centre of the Jewish Diaspora.[33] (2) Some study of antecedent historical probability is relevant to the treatment of Torrey's theory of the Aramaic composition of the Revelation. (3) The possible evidence for early Jewish settlement suggests why such names as Sepharad and Gog gained currency in Jewish tradition.

Commercial expansion may have induced some voluntary dispersion of Jews even before the kings of Assyria and Babylonia initiated compulsory transplantation of populations.[34] It seems inherently probable that the character of Sardis as a western metropolis and a great centre of trade made it exceptionally attractive to Jewish settlement. Under Artaxerxes I, perhaps the very king mentioned in the bilingual, Jewish interests seem to have been represented officially at the Persian court by Ezra (Ezr. 7.11ff.), and their commercial communities may have had royal sanction or support. Josephus says that Antiochus III established 2000 Jewish families from Mesopotamia in Phrygia and Lydia (*Antiq.* 12.3.4.149), and Sardis was the capital of Lydia. And this was probably not an unprecedented act, but represented a policy of establishing bodies of potentially loyal colonists in Graeco-Asiatic centres (see *SC*, pp. 131-33, 143-44, 146-48). Two important passages in Josephus (*Antiq.* 14.10.17.235; 14.10.24.259) purport to quote documents of the Roman period concerning Jewish privileges in the city. Both are problematic, but there is no reason to doubt the genuineness of their main content, while allowing that Josephus's representation of their texts merits careful scrutiny, especially in its implication that there were Jews who held the citizenship of Sardis.

The possibility of such Jewish citizenship in a Greek city has long been a subject of controversy. It may be conceded that normally it was not possible except through apostasy. But there are indications that occasionally a body of Jews was corporately enfranchised when a constitution was forcibly imposed on a city by one of the earlier Seleucids.[35] Sardis is one of the handful of cities where this exceptional arrangement is likely to have applied, and the new inscriptions from the synagogue there may be considered decisive.

Even in the synagogue the persons concerned use Greek names, and appear to claim as citizens the title Σαρδιανοί, some even being city councillors.[36]

The recent discoveries made in the synagogue-complex in fact give a remarkable picture of Sardian Judaism, though such evidence from a rather later period must be treated with caution and in the awareness of the provisional nature of its current interpretation. It is remarkable that the building is not only of exceptional size, but is situated in a focal position and forms part of the gymnasium-complex (Mitten, pp. 63-64).[37] The evidence for the acceptance of a Jewish community in a pagan society seems to be unique, and contrasts sharply with the indications of racial and religious tensions in Rome, Alexandria or Ephesus. Another feature of the synagogue is the re-use of sculptured Lydian religious reliefs in the structure (Mitten, pp. 51-55). Numerous details tend to confirm and illustrate an impression that Jews and Christians in this city had long sought a *modus vivendi* by accommodation to their pagan surroundings.[38] This is the most natural explanation of the acceptance and affluence of the synagogue community, and the relationship may have been established very early.

A further relationship, that of the church and synagogue, is an important question on which it is difficult to pronounce confident judgment. We cannot tell how far the earliest Christians of Sardis were converts from Judaism, but we infer from Rev. 3.4 that the majority had 'soiled their garments', apparently by some accommodation to their environment.

Despite the unquestioned importance of Sardis as a centre of the Diaspora, the evidence for its position in Jewish tradition is problematic. The probable original identifications of Sepharad and of Gog were both lost, though the names persisted. The placing of the former in Spain goes back to the Targum of Jonathan, and though Gog recurs in the Pseudepigrapha (*Or. Sib.* 3.319, 512; *Jub.* 8.25), the only precise geographical reference (*Or. Sib.* 3.319) assigns him to Ethiopia. The Sibyllines are in fact of limited value here, for the oracles concerned are all of very doubtful provenance and date.[39]

Other aspects are more promising. The proverbial history of Croesus was certainly familiar to Jews in the first century.[40] And the problematic Lud or Ludim of Gen. 10.13, 22 and 1 Chron. 1.11, 17 (LXX Λούδ, Λουδιείμ) are identified with the Lydians by Josephus (*Antiq.* 1.6.4.114) and by the LXX translators of the prophets.[41] This may have no more basis than the similarity of names but the alliances of Lud with Tyre and Egypt are correctly applied to Lydia and its seems possible that an accurate Jewish tradition is here preserved.

b. *The Pagan Religious Background*
The subject of the pagan cults of Sardis is extremely obscure. Its religion, like that of other Asian cities, operated at two levels. The public image largely represented on coinage identified the local deities with Hellenic counterparts, but the underlying Anatolian cult, which had a much deeper influence upon the people, is almost hidden from us. The principal goddess, commonly known as Artemis, sometimes with the epithet Coloene from her shrine at Lake Coloe (Strab. 13.4.5 = p. 626), was the native Cybele or Cybebe.[42] The recurring themes of Sardian coinage confirm that in some aspects she resembled rather Demeter and her daughter Core/Persephone, especially as death-goddess.[43] The huge Hellenistic temple in the Pactolus glen was dedicated to her. Many coins also depict her Anatolian cult-image, a draped figure of human outline but without human features.[44] Some present the familiar story of the rape of Persephone (*BMC Lydia*, Sard. No. 131, of Trajan, etc.), but in many cases this has been modified with Anatolian conceptions.[45] The goddess was also protectress of the city, and so represented with a turreted headdress (Nos. 49-52, of Attalid times, etc.).[46] Her usual attributes are ears and stalks of corn, a poppy flower or head, two long lighted torches, and coiled serpents: she is shown travelling in a car drawn by two winged serpents.

The most frequent male deities on the coinage are Zeus Lydios, portrayed with eagle and sceptre, Heracles and Dionysus. The Phrygian Men is less common. In all these identities may be mingled aspects of the subordinate consort of the goddess. There may also be some association with the native complexes of myths of Attis (cf. Paus. 7.17.9-12; Ov. *Fast.* 4.221-44) and of the local heroes Tylus and Masnes.

Coins and other sources alike indicate the existence of a rich native cult-mythology portrayed in enigmatic religious scenes and disguised under Hellenized assimilations. A valuable article by G.M.A. Hanfmann, 'Lydiaka', in *Harvard Studies in Classical Philology* 63 (1958), pp. 65-88, attempts to interpret some of it in the light of its probable continuity with Hittite religious ideas. There is abundant illustration

in this material of the preoccupation of the local religious consciousness with the problems of death and immortality.

The Attis-Cybele cycle of cult-myth was an expression of the
nature religion of Anatolia. Hanfmann argues (p. 66) that the early
sixth-century BC Minotaur relief found at Sardis is a Hellenized
adaptation of the *taurobolium*, a rite by which the worshipper,
originally the king, was rejuvenated with the life-force of a bull slain
over him and in whose blood he bathed. This has long been seen as
an immortality ritual; here too is probably the idea behind the story
that Midas of Phrygia committed suicide by drinking bull's blood
(Strab. 1.3.21 = p. 61).[47] Such practices were associated with the
cult of Attis, who represented the decline and revival of the year.
Cybele and Attis were the guardians of the grave, and the after-life
was originally seen as a reunion with the Earth-Mother. The serpents
associated with the goddess were seen to emerge from the earth and
possessed the power of rejuvenation by sloughing their skins.[48]

A characteristic local expression of these ideas appears in the myth
of Tylus and Masnes, recounted with variations in Pliny (*NH*
25.5.14, following the lost *Lydiaca* of Xanthus) and in Nonnus
(*Dionys.* 25.451-552) and illustrated on Sardian coinage (No. 179, of
Alexander Severus). The hero Tylus was killed by the bite of a
serpent which was then itself slain by the giant Damasen (= Masnes
of the coin). The serpent's mate revived it with a magic herb of
immortality.[49] The surviving hero, seeing this, obtained the plant
and similarly revived Tylus. The two heroes were perhaps doublets
of one original character: they were sons of Earth, ancestors of
Lydian royalty, and both were identified with Heracles (Hanfmann,
pp. 71-72).

The recurring Heracles figure at Sardis is important. Sir J.G.
Frazer has connected it closely with the Heracles-Sandon of Tarsus,
who was annually burnt in effigy,[50] deriving both from a common
Hittite source. The point of the identification seems to relate to
Heracles' fiery death on Mount Oeta (cf. Soph. *Trach.* 1191ff.). Now
several cases are recorded of the self-immolation of Eastern monarchs
in time of extremity, as at once an ultimate sacrifice and as the means
of immortality. Frazer suggested that the burning of Croesus was an
attempted apotheosis of this kind. The elusive resurrection-concept
pervading the myths comes here to focus in a personality, the
circumstances of whose fall made an indelible impression upon
succeeding generations. We are familiar with its impact upon the

Greek moralists, but to the local mind moulded by the concepts of Anatolian religion it may have appeared in a different light. If John alluded to the familiar tale of the surprise and fall of Croesus he may also have had in mind his vain attempt to achieve immortality, and have seen some analogy between this and the condition of a church whose public reputation for spiritual vitality was belied by reality. In time of crisis its real unreadiness would be exposed.

Similar themes might be illustrated extensively. Several coins show Pelops, a Lydian hero restored to life in the myth (*BMC*, Nos. 132, 168, 175). Other instances have been discussed in my original thesis. There is for instance a complex of versions of a myth which apparently purport to explain the origin of the royal cemetery on the shore of the sacred lake,[51] and this in turn finds curious parallels in Rev. 19.17–20.15, a passage which contains many other echoes of the Sardian letter and its background.[52]

The pursuit of such tentative and circumstantial connections could issue in unwarranted speculation, but there are reasons for thinking that images drawn from Sardis lent themselves to apocalyptic treatment and are deeply woven into the structure of the book. A striking example is contained in Rev. 6.12-17. Much of the language of this passage is taken from the Old Testament prophets (esp. 6.15, 16 from Isa. 2.10, 19 and Hos. 10.8), but it is combined and adapted to paint a picture of unpreparedness which would have been very forceful to a Sardian reader. The cave-tombs in the crumbling faces of the mountain Necropolis provided a treacherous refuge in extreme emergency. In Rev. 6 the potentates and multitudes hiding in the caves beg the mountains to fall and entomb them rather than face the Lamb at his Parousia.[53]

3. *The Text of the Letter*

The first problem to consider is the relation of the present text to previous Biblical literature. The tabulation of the evidence by Charles and Swete gives a surprising, and probably inadequate, idea of this primary source material. Both agree on the Old Testament background of the phrase 'I will not erase his name from the book of life', and refer to Exod. 32.32-33 (Charles, p. lxxviii; Swete, p. cxli). Charles connects them also with Ps. 69.29 (LXX 68.29) and regards them as translated from the MT under influence of the LXX rendering. Swete cites Isa. 4.3 and compares other passages in both the Old Testament and the Revelation.

Apart from this phrase neither commentator finds any Old Testament or apocalyptic echo in the letter, but Charles lists considerable New Testament parallels, and postulates explicit dependence on Matthew.[54] We cannot in fact dogmatize about the last point, for the words might derive from a Matthean source, or from an independent tradition. In any case it is remarkable that the stern warnings of this letter are almost unique in Rev. 2 and 3 in being parallel with words ascribed to Jesus in the Gospel tradition.[55]

These Biblical references do not actually exhaust the matter. There is some similarity between the content of Rev. 3.2 and Ezek. 34.4, but nothing to prove dependence. There may however be a significant connection with the prophecy of Obadiah against Edom, whose capital Sela (Petra) was, like Sardis, a rock-city of supposed impregnability. Obad. 3-5, in particular, contains parallels both of language and setting, and we have seen that Sepharad in Obad. 20 may actually be Sardis. Apart from this there is no hint that John's exhortation takes its rise, as elsewhere, from a meditation on the Old Testament. The solemn directness of appeal is couched almost in the words ascribed to Jesus.

The Sardian letter is much more clearly related to certain other passages in the Revelation itself. The seven spirits and the seven stars are respectively paralleled in 1.4 and 1.20, where the seven stars are explained as the angels of the seven churches. There is also a striking comparability of content with the Ephesian letter. (1) The introductory words are closely parallel, and both speak of Christ as the one who has or holds the seven stars. (2) Both churches are censured for their fall from an earlier standard and are called to repentance on that account (note the identical sequence μνημόνευε ... μετανόησον in 2.5 and 3.3). (3) Both letters are explicit in promising the victor ζωή under appropriate figures.

It seems quite wrong to attach any structural significance to these parallels. The two churches merely had some similar characteristics and were subject to somewhat comparable environmental influences.[56] There was a great difference in the extent of the decline: at Ephesus an incipient danger threatened a successful and generally faithful body; at Sardis the deterioration had reduced the church's apparent life to an outward sham.

The parallels with other parts of the Revelation are less easily analysed. Some have already been noted. Where actual textual parallels are lacking there are sometimes symbols reminiscent of

Sardis, especially in accounts of ultimate judgment. There is little contact with the vision of the heavenly city except in the repeated allusion to its citizen-register, 'the book of life' (20.12, 15; 21.27; possibly 22.19).

The first problem in the present text is the meaning of the 'seven spirits of God' (v. 1). The phrase is elsewhere known only in the Revelation, in 1.4, where Charles (p. 78) considers it a 'manifest interpolation', in 4.5 and in 5.6. In each case it is combined with the seven stars, and in 1.4 with Christ himself; in 4.5 it is equated with seven torches of fire, and in 5.6 with seven eyes. When these passages are thus compared it seems clear that a passage in Zechariah (4.2-10) underlies the idea expressed in them all. There seven lamps (Zech. 4.2) and seven eyes (4.10) are successively related to the activity of the Spirit of the Lord (4.6). Only Rev. 5.6 is verbally based upon Zechariah: Beckwith observes (pp. 426-27) that here a phrase is used at the outset in anticipation of its place in the vision of Rev. 4 and 5 — the first occurrence is not necessarily primary.

The most important of the suggested explanations of the phrase are: (1) from a polytheistic background, identifying the seven spirits with planetary deities equated with the archangels (Bousset, pp. 184-87). John, however, is emphatic against angel-worship (Rev. 19.10), and in 1.4 these spirits are associated with Christ in a context implying a divine designation. (2) Charles notes this difficulty in rejecting 1.4, and argues from Jewish sources that angels are intended (pp. 12-13). (3) Some understand the spirits from later Jewish interpretation of Isa. 11.2 to denote the 'sevenfold'[57] operation of the Spirit. (4) Swete, accepting a reference to the Holy Spirit, thought the 'spirits' were seven because the churches in which they operated were seven. (5) Beckwith (pp. 424-27), also seeing allusion to the Spirit, explains the number 'seven' from Zech. 4.10.

The last seems clearly the best of these suggestions, for it relates to a background which illumines all the occurrences of the phrase, and which was evidently in John's mind. He might well see a fitness in applying the images of Zechariah to the manifold activity of a Spirit who could meet the needs of the seven diverse communities, and that number would readily symbolize the universality of his work, the point in Swete's suggestion. There is no reason to think John intended allusion to Isa. 11.2-3. We take the phrase to be suggestive imagery rather than theological exposition. The plurality of spirits is not to be made the occasion of unintended difficulty.

Why however is this portrayal of Christ applied to Sardis? A key factor in the answer seems to be the evident relationship with the Ephesian letter. The difference between the two addresses, and the allusion to the 'seven spirits' in particular, may have been calculated to emphasize the power of the Spirit to meet every need, even to revive those at the point of death (cf. *SC*, pp. 372-74). Sardis moreover had been in the past, as Ephesus in the present, the natural centre and commercial metropolis of the area which included the seven cities. So both might be aptly reminded that Christ had all the seven stars in his keeping.

For the use of ὄνομα ('a name that you live', v. 1b) commentators often cite Hdt. 7.138.[58] The evident meaning is that the church had an outward 'form of religion', but not 'the power thereof' (2 Tim. 3.5). It is remarkable that ὄνομα occurs four times in this brief letter. This unusual usage may be set against the different, but equally strange, use in v. 4. Here it means 'reputation', there 'individual'. Perhaps the thought of names written in the 'book of life' underlies the use of the figure in both cases.

Later writers have often followed Ramsay (*SC*, pp. 375-77) in seeing here a reference to the dramatic traditional history of the city and its decline from its former prestige (so Moffatt, p. 364; Peake, p. 249; and cf. Charles, p. 78). But Ramsay's picturesque language needs qualification. Sardis was no longer a seat of power, and its function as a fortress had been superseded, but it retained a considerable importance evidenced by the scale of its reconstruction after the earthquake. The basic point stands. And the historical allusion of the following phrases is so plain that we are justified in seeing a similar background throughout the context. There may also be a valid background in the local preoccupation with the themes of death and renewed life. The 'life' offered by Christ to the victor (v. 5) is then set in implicit contrast with a sham current in the city. Possibly we should see specific reference to the fate of Croesus, seen by the Anatolian mind as an apotheosis, but to the Christian a monumentally tragic example of false reputation and self-deception.

'Be watchful, and strengthen the things which remain ... ; for I have not found your works perfect before God' (Rev. 3.2). The commentators call attention to several verbal points here. (1) γίνου is to be rendered 'show thyself' rather than 'become' (Hort, p. 32; Beckwith, p. 473). (2) τὰ λοιπά is best taken in the traditional way to mean 'that which survives', an exceptional usage found elsewhere in the Revelation (8.13; 9.20; 11.13), corresponding to Latin *reliqua* rather than to its normal equivalent *cetera*.[59] (3) The tense of ἔμελλον is explained as epistolary, and its number as a *constructio ad sensum* (Charles, p. 79; etc.).[60] (4) There is a manuscript variant involving the presence of an article before ἔργα.[61] The anarthrous reading is the more difficult, it is attested early, and the insertion of τά by dittography (cf. v. 2) is readily understandable. Charles (p. 80) and Beckwith (p. 474), who accept τά, both do so on the ground that is makes easier sense in context; but for that very reason it seems less likely to be original. With σοῦ ἔργα the sense must be 'I have not found any works of thine carried out fully' (so RV; Hort, p. 33; Moffatt, p. 364). There is no reason to find a problem in reconciling this wholesale condemnation of the church with the commendation of individuals in v. 4. (5) We may note the emphatic ἐνώπιον τοῦ Θεοῦ μου.[62] The implication is that their works might pass human scrutiny, but not that of God.

Almost all the commentators have recognized local allusion in this and the following verse to the two famous occasions when the citadel of Sardis had fallen through lack of vigilance. It is unnecessary to cite authorities here: the point had been frequently observed before Ramsay. It may however be desirable to emphasize that such allusion to relatively ancient history was not only possible, it was habitually made. In the case of Sardis and Croesus the present usage can be specifically and abundantly paralleled.[63]

There may well be in the Revelation reference to local memories of the great earthquake imagery with other concepts and language closely related to the letter and its situation. Such are Rev. 6.14-17; 8.8; 11.13; 16.18-20. Mountains are overthrown (6.14, 16; 8.8; 16.20); parts of the great city are destroyed (11.13; 16.19); in one verse (11.13) the exceptional uses of ὄνομα and λοιπός are repeated together. It seems especially true of this letter that a potentially valuable key to understanding its whole background is to take its text in conjunction with these related passages.

'Remember therefore how thou hast received and heard, and be vigilant and repent: if then thou dost not watch, I will come as a thief, and thou shalt not know what hour I will come upon thee' (v. 3).

The changes of tense are noteworthy. εἴληφας is here probably to be taken aoristically (Hort, p. 33; Moffatt, p. 364; Beckwith, p. 474; cf. Rev. 5.7. Contrast however Swete, p. 50). The words of the verse are closely comparable with the admonition to Ephesus (2.5). A call to repentance is included in all the letters except those to Smyrna and Philadelphia: only however at Ephesus and Sardis is it consequent upon a call to remembrance. In the case of Sardis the fine beginning is less emphasized and the need of vigilance reiterated.

The precise meaning hinges on the sense given to πῶς. It is natural to take this strictly of the manner of the church's reception of the gospel; Beckwith, however, in view of the command τήρει, prefers to render πῶς as equivalent to 'what' and to see reference to the *matter* of the gospel received.[64] In any case, the absolute use of τηρεῖν is unusual, although a suitable object is readily supplied (cf. however Philo, *de Leg. Alleg.* 3.84). The general purport is clear, and there is no hint here of outward persecution or inner heresy. The distinctive character of the church's faith had rather been so far lost in accommodation to society that it aroused no opposition. Spiritual poverty and complacency were thus leading the church into moral error (cf. v. 4). Belief in the imminent Parousia of Christ had evidently also waned (cf. Moffatt, p. 364; Kiddle, p. 46). The words ἥξω ὡς κλέπτης must refer primarily to this eschatological coming (Charles, p. 81; Beckwith, p. 474), as in other New Testament passages where the same simile is used (Mt. 24.42-44; Lk. 12.39-40; 1 Thess. 5.2, 4; Rev. 16.15).

The phrase ποίαν ὥραν is peculiar. The case may be due to attraction to an objective sense after γνῷς, but we may compare John 4.52 and Acts 20.16 (Hort, p. 33; Charles, p. 81). The sense of ποῖος, however, here equivalent to τίς, is paralleled by the language of Mt. 24.42-43 and Lk. 12.39, which contain the words of Christ on which the present verse is based. Both Rev. 3.3 and 16.15 are drawn from sayings corresponding with these Synoptic passages, but we cannot dogmatize about their supposed Matthean origin.

The relationship of 16.15 with the Sardian letter calls for special comment. Its extreme abruptness in that context has led some (Charles, p. 88; Moffatt, p. 448) to insert it between 3.3a and 3b, where it would certainly be apt, and where it would enable a series of 'ἰδού-sayings' to be discerned in the last four epistles (2.22; 3.3, 9, 20).

The objections to this idea seem to be decisive. (1) There is no textual warrant, and it is difficult to see why the verse should have been interpolated in a context where it seems so harsh. (2) The reading ἔρχεται (א original hand) for the unprefaced ἔρχομαι in 16.15 looks like an early attempt to smooth the relationship of the verse to its original, but difficult, context. (3) Moffatt's 'ἰδού-sayings' are not in any case parallel or uniformly related to the structure of their letters. (4) The whole context of 16.15 as it stands has, I suggest, the circumstances of Sardis in mind: it is one of the stronger pointers in corroboration of our argument for a *Sitz im Leben* of the later chapters in the life of the churches. And Beckwith notes John's manner of abruptly interjecting short sayings, sometimes without prefatory words, but apt as a comment on their context (cf. 13.9-10; 18.20; 20.6). Here the blind movement of earthly forces towards an unforeseen climax elicits a final cry of warning in the words of Christ. Here are to be enacted the eschatological events against which the Sardian church was admonished to watch. The imagery of the whole passage suggests a last pointed appeal here to the careless Christians of that city.

The reminiscence in 3.3b of the coming of Cyrus 'like a thief' requires no further comment.

In v. 4 the writer turns from the unworthy majority to commend the few in the church who had resisted the influence of their environment. Again the word ὄνομα is used in an unusual, though different, sense. The meaning here is 'individuals': possibly the choice of word is influenced by the thought of the following verse.

Some commentators have seen reference here to the reputation of Sardis for immorality (Charles, p. 78; cf. Hdt. 1.93; Aesch. *Pers.* 45). The bad character and factional hatred endemic among the citizens is repeatedly censured in the ostensibly contemporary Letters of Apollonius of Tyana (38-41, 56, 75, 76). There are varied and remarkable references in the documents of the indigenous religions of Lydia and Phrygia to matters like the chastisement with disease of those who came morally unclean to perform their vows.[65] The primary meaning here is allusion to the contamination of Christian witness by accommodation to the surrounding life (Beckwith, p. 475. Cf. Rev. 7.14).[66]

The significance of the 'white raiment' promised to the few in Sardis is open to diverse interpretation. It has been observed that this promise is exceptional as an eschatological declaration which is not introduced by the formula ὁ νικῶν (Bousset, p. 224. Cf. however Rev. 2.10). The possible suggestions about the background of the phrase are not necessarily mutually exclusive. (1) Sardis, like Laodicea, had long been a famous centre of the clothing industry, especially for rich dyed fabrics. The significance of the symbol here however seems different from that in 3.18, and its reference to local industry less clear.[67] (2) W. Michaelis, on λευκός (*TDNT* IV. 241-50), emphasizes that heavenly clothing was seen as a divine gift and signifies the heavenly glory of those adjudged righteous. So Swete finds that in scripture white apparel denotes festivity (Eccl. 9.8), victory (2 Macc. 11.8), purity (Rev. 7.9-10) and the heavenly state (Dan. 7.9), and sees these associations as meeting in the present phrase (p. 51). (3) Some older writers compare the parable of the wedding-garment (Mt. 22.11-13) and see here some specific reference to imputed righteousness or to baptismal robes (Trench, p. 167; Tait, p. 314),[68] or to the spiritual body of the faithful in the resurrection (cf. 2 Cor. 5.1-4; so Kepler, p. 67; cf. Swete). No allusion of this kind however seems necessary or likely. (4) Ramsay argued that the Roman triumph was present here to the writer's mind. Roman citizens wore a pure white toga at holidays and religious ceremonies, but especially at a triumph (*SC*, p. 386; cf. Juv. *Sat.* 10.45). Paul certainly uses the metaphor of the Roman triumph in Col. 2.15 and develops it in 2 Cor. 2.14-16. On this view the aspect of victory would be especially prominent: Sardis was notoriously a city of defeat and unfulfilled promise, from which the royal pomp of former times had departed, but where the few should walk with Christ in the triumphal procession of his final victory.[69] It is remarkable that Tertullian understands Rev. 7.14 in this way.[70]

The point of using the verb περιπατεῖν here has been variously explained. Swete (p. 51) saw allusion to Jesus' peripatetic ministry in Galilee rather than to Enoch, who 'walked with God' (Gen. 5.22). The word is however readily enlisted in support of the picture of the white-clad attendants of the conqueror walking in his triumphal procession.[71] Ramsay's view on the point is certainly attractive.

ἄξιος in a good sense is elsewhere in the book predicated only of God and of Christ (4.11; 5.9; contrast 16.6). Similar usages are however found elsewhere in the New Testament.[72]

The words to the victor begin by repeating the promise of white clothing in more general terms. The question has been raised whether ὁ νικῶν is to be taken as referring to a class of persons distinct from the anticipatory ὀλίγα ὀνόματα (Beckwith, p. 475). The answer turns in part upon consideration of the originality and meaning of οὕτως. This reading is strongly attested by the earliest authorities: the alternative οὗτος (P, Q, ℵ corrector, and many cursives) may be a very early variant, but could easily have arisen from dictation, being easier and a phonetic equivalent.[73]

Three explanations of οὕτως have been offered: (1) inferential, as possibly in 3.16 (Hort, p. 33); (2) to mean 'likewise' (= ὁμοίως or ὡσαύτως), the simplest solution, but a usage not easily paralleled (Swete, p. 51; cf. perhaps Rev. 11.5); (3) to mean 'thus' (as being a conqueror, in his capacity as conqueror).[74]

These usages were perhaps not differentiated in John's mind. In any case the best analogy seems to be with 3.16, where again he repeats inferentially an idea already stated. Unless we insist upon (2) there is no need to make the word οὕτως a reason for postulating a separate class of persons here. It is unnecessary to press the words too far: the few whose garments are undefiled are alone ready for the Lord's coming; they are potentially also those who will then walk in his triumph as victors.[75]

'I will not erase his name from the book of life' (v. 5). These words are based on Exod. 32.32, where Moses pleads for God's forgiveness of the people's sin or else to be blotted himself out of the book which God had written. The character of this 'book' is much elaborated in the Pseudepigrapha from concepts contained in other Old Testament passages. There was a register of actual Israelite citizens (Ps. 69.28; Isa. 4.3), and this served as a model for allusion to a citizen-roll of the heavenly kingdom (Dan. 12.1-2; Phil. 4.3; cf. Lk. 10.20; Heb. 12.23). There were references also to other books, as that of judgment (Dan. 7.10) and of remembrance (Mal. 3.16), and to patterns of God's plans (Exod. 25.9, 40; cf. Dan. 10.21). The evidence for the development of these ideas in later literature is tabulated by Charles.[76] Some of them occur in the Revelation (5.1ff.; 20.12).

The idea of a citizen-register was equally familiar in the Greek world. There are numerous epigraphic references to the registrars and record-officers of the cities of Asia Minor, though their titles vary widely.[77] Sardis itself, as the western capital of the Persian and Seleucid empires, housed the royal archives relating to an extensive area.[78]

Moffatt (p. 365) cites several instances in classical literature of the erasure of names from the civic registers. Of special interest here is the regular Athenian practice of deleting the names of condemned persons before their execution. ἐξαλείφειν was the technical term for such degradation.[79]

The idea of such a register of the citizens of the heavenly kingdom occurs elsewhere in early Christianity outside the New Testament.[80]

It is natural to suppose that the old Jewish conception was easily extended in a world where contemporary civic practice was so similar. There may be reminiscence of this city's ancient possession of the royal archives. In the present context there is probably allusion to some contemporary threat to the faithful few in the church. Moffatt refers here again to the phraseology of the curse of the Minim: 'May the Nazarenes and the Minim suddenly perish, and may they be blotted out of the book of Life [*sic*] and not enrolled along with the righteous'. I have argued in the Introduction that the adoption of this formula in the synagogue is a relevant factor in a complex situation underlying the *Sitz im Leben* of the Revelation. In Sardis we suppose that the bulk of the church had found a *modus vivendi*, perhaps within the synagogue on Jewish terms. The Nicolaitan compromise is not mentioned here: perhaps the church enjoyed a reputation for spiritual vitality in rejecting this, but at the cost of acquiescence in the opposite compromise. The potential victors are the faithful few against whom are directed the explicit synagogue threats of deletion from the book of life. Those who are thus threatened with both physical and spiritual death receive assurance that Christ will not treat them as their enemies desire.

This line of interpretation is attractive here, but necessarily depends on our very scanty materials for the relations of pagan, Jewish and Christian communities. We hear from the Apollonius literature of bitter factional strife in Sardis; we know that the Jews were unusually influential there, and probably well placed to invoke even the secular authorities against a minority of Christians who resolutely refused an accommodation to their terms. At the least they could delete their names from the synagogue-register when the Christian's precarious entitlement to safety lay in acceptance there.

The concluding words of the verse are again closely reminiscent of words of Jesus in the Gospel tradition. The form of the saying might be seen as a combination of Mt. 10.32 with Lk. 12.8, which concludes ἔμπροσθεν τῶν ἀγγέλων τοῦ Θεοῦ. We cannot however infer with certainty here a knowledge of either Gospel or indeed of Q. The most significant difference from the Synoptic versions is the substitution of τὸ ὄνομα αὐτοῦ for ἐν αὐτῷ. This however naturally sustains the repeated emphasis on ὄνομα in our passage.[81] The background of these words is not clear, though they will fit very well with the suggestions already made. The implication is that the bulk of the Sardian church had been ashamed of the name of Christ and would not confess it before men. The 'few' were alone like the Philadelphian church, which had not denied his name (Rev 3.8). In each case the issue is confession of the 'name'.[82] The problem could well have been the same in both cases,—and about Philadelphia we are rather better informed. Perhaps in both it involved the pressure to participate in a form of Jewish worship which denied that 'name'.

4. *Conclusions*

1. Sardis was a city whose history and legend had become proverbial. The reasonableness of discerning allusion to it in the letter may be illustrated from innumerable ancient literary parallels. Possible reflections of it are also contained in Jewish tradition.

2. Herodotus's account of Croesus in particular is a remarkable example of the ancient proclivity for finding moralistic anecdote in the interpretation of historical events. The extraordinary impact which his sudden reverse had on the Greek world was remembered centuries later. It was a classic story of pride before a fall, of misplaced trust in riches, and of lack of vigilance. Perhaps too, Croesus, like other Oriental monarchs with whom he has been associated in tradition, attempted apotheosis by fire. This idea was contrary to the Hellenic understanding of the event, but may have been familiar to Christians who lived in a city whose religion dealt in such ideas of death and renewed life.

3. A correct understanding of the topography of Sardis and of its history helps to illustrate further how its reputation for strength was belied by events. The evidence also suggests that the earthquake of AD 17 was a disaster of almost unparalleled magnitude. Several passages in the Revelation which are otherwise suggestive of the background of Sardis may also reflect local memory of these seismic phenomena.

4. Ramsay's picture of Sardis as a city in decay in New Testament times is overdrawn. Its political and military importance had disappeared, but it recovered from disaster, competed for the honour of a neocorate, and continued to have some commercial prominence.

5. The influence of Judaism at Sardis is noted. The Lydian-Aramaic bilingual is probably to be understood as testifying to the early existence of an Aramaic-speaking community in the city. It is an open question whether that community contained Jews, though there are other indications that a strong Jewish presence was established there unusually early. The argument that there was

actually a large Jewish citizen-body in Sardis, often rejected summarily, is corroborated by recent epigraphic evidence from the great synagogue. The Jews may have strengthened their position through a long-standing accommodation to surrounding pagan culture. There is no evidence known of specifically anti-Semitic tensions, as in other cities.

6. A discussion of the obscure subject of Sardian pagan religion offers further examples of preoccupation with the themes of death and resurrection, though the Anatolian conceptions are apt to be disguised under approximations to superficially similar Greek myths.

7. The literary relationships of the present letter are peculiar. The Old Testament background is less prominent, but there are remarkable references to words attributed to Jesus in the Synoptic tradition. There are striking parallels with the Ephesian letter and situational links with the later chapters of the Revelation.

8. The difficult allusion to the 'seven spirits of God' may best be explained in connection with parallels elsewhere in the Revelation, which suggest that Zech. 4.2-10 underlies them all. This will give the simplest explanation of the number 'seven' and imply the manifold activity of the Spirit in meeting the need of every church, even that of Sardis.

9. Verses 2-3 are explained as containing pointed allusions to the history of the city. We cannot however follow Charles in inserting 16.15 here. That verse must be explained in its present context, where it is abrupt, but in a way consonant with John's manner and with a Sardian background of thought there also.

10. The 'white raiment' is not necessarily to be explained by analogy with Rev 3.18. Ramsay's comparison with the Roman triumph is attractive. The pomp of victory had long since departed from Sardis. The majority of the church were unprepared for the Parousia of their king. But when he came the waiting few should walk with him in his triumphal procession.

11. The 'victor' cannot be rigidly distinguished from the 'few' of the previous verse. The 'book of life' recalls the citizen-registers common to the Jewish and Hellenistic worlds, an image apt in an ancient centre of the royal archives. It is suggested that here a majority in the church had gained acceptance in the synagogue at the cost of implicit denial of the 'name' of Christ. The faithful few had perhaps faced deletion from the synagogue-register, a matter of serious import under Domitian, but were assured that their names

should never be deleted from the heavenly book. On this view they were resisting a temptation like that which the 'synagogue of Satan' had imposed on the churches of Smyrna and Philadelphia. The peculiar reiteration of ὄνομα in the letter will suit the emphasis on the book or register.

Chapter 8

PHILADELPHIA

1. *Introductory*

The site of Philadelphia is covered by the modern town of Alaşehir, situated less than thirty miles ESE of Sardis. Its situation may best be observed from the central summit of the three-peaked hill at the southern limit of the town. Like Sardis and Laodicea, the place stands at the southern edge of a level river-basin. Its river, the Cogamis (Alaşehir Çayı),[1] stands in a relation with the main stream of the Hermus (Gediz Nehri) closely resembling that of the Lycus with the Maeander. In each case the tributary continues inland the easterly trend of the main basin and provides a better route to the interior. The main road SE from Philadelphia climbs some 2000 feet over the eastern spurs of Messogis before descending to the Lycus-Maeander confluence, forming part of the vital route from Pergamum through Thyatira and Sardis to Laodicea, and so to the east. The low hill which was the acropolis of Philadelphia forms the outermost spur of the long range of Tmolus which encloses the whole basin on the south. The city reached down the concave slope to the plain, its modern counterpart having grown somewhat beyond the compact square of the Byzantine walls. Beyond the river the northern hills rise more gently, but to a height sufficient to conceal any view of the Catacecaumene, the 'burnt land' of the Lydo-Mysian frontier (Strab. 12.8.18 = p. 579; 13.4.11 = p. 628). The proximity of this volcanic region however played a crucial part in the early history of Philadelphia.

Literary references to early Philadelphia are even fewer than those to Thyatira, and epigraphical and numismatic materials are scantier.[2] It was an Attalid foundation, named from Attalus Philadelphus and perhaps established by him, though the last point, frequently repeated by modern writers, appears to rest only on the late authority of Stephanus of Byzantium (on Φιλαδέλφεια), where it might be only an inference from the name. One might have supposed that recognition of the importance of the site would have followed more closely upon Attalid annexation of the area in 189 BC. There are indications that we should not exclude the possibility of a foundation within the lifetime of Eumenes II, during which his brother's loyalty had already won him his cognomen.[3]

There are also some hints in favour of supposing that a pre-Attalid settlement had stood on the site.[4] A.H.M. Jones (*Cities*, p. 54) has argued that the organization of Philadelphia by trade-guilds proves that this, like Thyatira, originated as a Lydian town, a view criticized by D. Magie (*Roman Rule*, II.982n.) as an insecurely founded inference from evidence of the Imperial period. Jones may nevertheless be right, for the continuity of such patterns of community life is a feature of Anatolia. The site, never yet excavated, has been seen as typical of the positions chosen for Pergamene foundations (*HG*, p. 86), but this is consistent with the possibility that its acropolis was occupied earlier.[5] Ostensibly, however, it was the most recently established of the seven cities.[6]

Ramsay characterizes Philadelphia as 'the Missionary City', explaining the purpose of its foundation as an attempt to educate the peoples of newly annexed Lydia and Phrygia in Greek culture and loyalty to a Hellenized monarchy, while also guarding an important route (*SC*, pp. 391-92). He may be underestimating its military importance.[7] His conception was further connected with the city's position as the gate to Phrygia, it being at the head of two other important routes running east and north-east into that land. The first forms part of that which he calls the 'horse-road', the most direct but a hilly way from Ephesus up the Cayster basin to the pass above the Cogamis valley, where it reached the great route from Philadelphia to Laodicea, and thence south of the Banaz Ova towards Eumenea and Pisidian Antioch (*CB*, II.579-81). The second corresponded closely to the line of the modern railway from Alaşehir to Uşak, going by Blaundus and Clanudda to Acmonia (*CB* II.588-91). Philadelphia was admirably placed to serve as a centre for the development of the area along these roads. Its Hellenizing mission is further inferred from the Hellenic character of its coinage (*SC*, pp. 392-94), as contrasted with the underlying Anatolian religious character evidenced by epigraphy (*SC*, pp. 394-95).[8]

This view is overstated, but its general probability is consistent with the historical and geographical facts and with the methods of Attalid policy. The 'open door' of Rev. 3.8 may reasonably be compared with Paul's usage of the phrase in 2 Cor. 2.12 and 1 Cor. 16.9 (cf. Acts 14.27).

Some other features of the city must be briefly noted. Its name may be held to commemorate the proverbial loyalty of the brothers Eumenes and Attalus, whichever of them actually founded it. Polybius alludes to the remarkable devotion of the four brothers to their mother Apollonis (22.20). He puts into the mouth of Philip V of Macedon a speech in which he upholds their example to his own sons (23.11.6-7; cf. Livy 40.8.14, here closely following Polybius). Among numerous references to united action of the brothers[9] two incidents are of special interest. When a false rumour of Eumenes' assassination in Greece had reached Pergamum and Attalus accepted it *celerius quam dignum concordia fraterna erat* and assumed the kingship, Eumenes on his return forgave him and Attalus resumed his secondary position (Liv. 42.16.7-9; Diod. Sic. 29.34.2; 172 BC). In 168/67 Attalus was representing his brother at Rome when Eumenes was under suspicion of correspondence with the enemy Perseus. He almost succumbed to pressure to challenge or supplant his brother with Roman help, but, reminded that the kingdom *fraterna stare concordia*, he finally refused (Liv. 45.19-20, following Polyb. 30.1-3; cf. Diod. Sic. 31.7.2). Thereafter he resisted constant Roman efforts to turn him against Eumenes (Polyb. 31.1; 32.1), and finally succeeded him upon his death.

The motivation of this 'brotherly love' may have been political and prudential. It is however characteristic of ancient feeling that it should yet be remembered, commemorated and become a formative influence. Eumenea, a foundation of Attalus Philadelphus (Steph. Byz.; cf. *CB*, II.353n.), was named from the elder brother and as late as the third century AD celebrated games called *Philadelphia* in honour of their fraternal affection (*BMC Phrygia*, p. lxii, of Gallienus; cf. *CB*, II.366).[10] The same thing was celebrated at Philadelphia in the long persistence of such coin-types as of twins suckled by a wolf (*BMC Lydia*, Philad., Nos. 77, 78, of Septimius Severus) or of two identical young men who represent it on an alliance coin (see *SC*, p. 393).

Another feature of the city was the remarkable fertility of its territory, its volcanic soil being particularly suitable for vines.[11] This fertility was however the consequence of the city's proximity to the Catacecaumene, the volcanic 'Burnt Land' of the Lydo-Phrygian frontier, and it was itself peculiarly liable to earthquake.

The history of the city is unknown until an unprecedented disaster brought its name to the notice of our literary authorities.

2. First Century Philadelphia

The great earthquake of AD 17 evidently had so profound an effect upon Philadelphia that the context of the apocalyptic letter must be closely related to it. The disaster made a remarkable impact on the contemporary world as the greatest in human memory (Plin. *NH* 2.86.200), and also passed in a distorted form into much later Christian tradition (Oros. 7.4.13, 18). Tacitus (*Ann.* 2.47.3-4) names Sardis as having been the worst hit, but Philadelphia was prominent among those whose tribute was remitted for five years. These cities were the two nearest to the volcanic district. Other writers refer to the disaster and to the emperor's generosity in relief (Dio Cass. 57.17.8; Strab. 13.4.8 = p. 628; Vell. Pat. 2.126.4): even Suetonius concedes unwilling approval to Tiberius here.[12]

The two most remarkable passages, however, both written within a few years of the great earthquake, are both concerned exclusively with Philadelphia, and constitute the earliest important literary testimony about it. Strabo writes: 'The Catacecaumene too, which is occupied by Lydians and Mysians, received its name for some such reasons [volcanic disturbances]. And Philadelphia, the city near it, has not even its walls secure, but they are daily shaken and split in some degree. The people continually pay attention to earth-tremors and plan their buildings with this factor in mind' (ἀρχιτεκτονοῦντες πρὸς αὐτά, Strab. 12.8.18 = p. 579). The second passage is even more instructive: 'Beyond the Lydians are the Mysians and the city of Philadelphia, full of earthquakes (σεισμῶν πλήρης), for the walls never cease being cracked, and different parts of the city are constantly suffering damage. That is why the actual town has few inhabitants, but the majority live as farmers in the countryside, as they have fertile land. But one is surprised even at the few, that they are so fond of the place when they have such insecure dwellings. And one would be even more amazed at those who founded it' (13.4.10 = p. 628). The writer goes on to describe the neighbouring Catacecaumene, observing that no tree except the vine grew there.

Many features here can be paralleled in the capricious onset of modern earthquakes. If Sardis suffered catastrophically in the original shock, Philadelphia, probably closer to the epicentre, suffered many lesser tremors, perhaps for years afterwards.[13] After an earthquake people seek protection in the open air. In Philadelphia this had become almost a way of life when Strabo completed his work. The city was probably slow to recover, and its fears may have been renewed by later shocks in the area, notably that which destroyed Laodicea in AD 60. There is probably a reference to the conditions of life in Philadelphia in the promise to the conqueror: 'he shall no more go outside' (Rev. 3.12).[14]

Numismatic evidence for the effect of the catastrophe upon Philadelphia is less striking than Ramsay's account implies (*SC*, pp. 397, 407). It is true that no coins were struck under Tiberius, but the city's clearly datable series does not begin until Caligula, and its undoubtedly earlier, but undated, issues have been variously attributed to periods from the Attalid to the Augustan. In fact there is little positive evidence on the point from the coins of any of the cities affected.[15] Only perhaps in Sardis is an illuminating detail preserved which may reflect the effect of the disaster on the only place whose coinage otherwise forms a fairly continuous series.[16]

The gratitude of the victims to the emperor is however very variously attested, and sometimes reflected in their subsequent coinage. A huge pedestal found at Puteoli bears a dedicatory inscription to Tiberius surrounded by the names of Asian cities, the list, though mutilated, corresponding nearly to that of the earthquake victims in Tacitus (*CIL* X.1624; Tac. *Ann.* 2.47.3-4). The name 'Philadelphea' [*sic*] is fully preserved. Later coins and inscriptions of some of these cities show that they assumed an imperial name or cognomen about this time, or honoured Germanicus with a posthumous cult. Both points apply to Philadelphia. It takes the name 'Neocaesarea' (*BMC Lydia*, Philad., No. 55, of Caligula: no. 56, of Claudius) and one of its magistrates is described as priest of Germanicus (Nos. 51, 52, of Caligula).[17]

The concept of Philadelphia as a new city with a new name to honour the divine emperor whose patronage had restored its fortunes has again been related to Rev. 3.12. The difference between the response in Philadelphia and in Laodicea to the offer of imperial aid is also striking. Both were the occasion of ancient comment.[18]

There is no evidence later than Claudius for the use of the name Neocaesarea. Under Vespasian however the city took the imperial epithet 'Flavia' (*BMC*, Nos. 60, 61, of Vesp.; No. 62, of Dom.).[19] It was a great honour for a city to be permitted to assume such titles, and they bound it closely to the imperial service (*SC*, p. 410; cf. pp. 397-98, 409-10).

Even at the close of the century Philadelphia is likely to have recovered little, though it is not recorded whether it suffered from later earthquakes in the area.[20] The title 'Flavia' may point to another instalment of imperial aid after another such disaster: Suetonius notes Vespasian's generosity in this respect (Suet. *Vesp.* 17).

The fertility of the district may meanwhile have been a key factor in reconstruction. Rostovtzeff has cited abundant evidence that Asia Minor was intermittently subject to shortage of corn and even famine. Much of its corn-supply was needed for the eastern armies, while Rome had the monopoly of the produce of Egypt.[21]

In AD 92 Domitian issued an edict requiring at least half the vineyards in the provinces to be cut down and no new ones planted (Suet. *Dom.* 7.2; 14.2; Philostr. *Vit. Ap. Ty.* 6.42; *Vit. Soph.* 1.21 = p. 520; dated by Eusebius, *Chron.*), an act bitterly unpopular in Asia and not rigorously enforced everywhere.[22] This measure has been much discussed. S. Reinach regarded it as a drastic means of protecting the vine-growers of Italy, but Rostovtzeff seems right in treating it as an attempt to encourage corn-production at the expense of vines (p. 201; cf. Suet. *Dom.* 7.2; Stat. *Silv.* 4.3.11-12, of c. AD 95).[23] There is significant evidence of famine in Asia Minor at the time. Emergency action was taken by the imperial legate of Galatia at Pisidian Antioch to control prices and prevent storing and exploitation.[24] This shortage may have been local, and Rostovtzeff may be overconfident in asserting that the inscription proves that the vivid picture in Rev. 6.6 refers to a widespread famine in Asia Minor. This passage, however, is strikingly illustrated by the inscription, and we may accept that it actually refers to the decree of Domitian as well. Whatever the precise import of Rev. 6.6, it seems to reflect intelligible hardships of the time, famine prices and a remedy which threatened the vines and perhaps the olive-groves of the province.[25] There is interesting light here on the likely dating of the Revelation.[26]

How did the crisis affect Philadelphia? Perhaps no city in Asia was so heavily dependent on viticulture (Strab. 13.4.11 = p. 628; cf. the coinage *passim*). Dionysus was the principal deity and vines are extensively grown in the neighbourhood even today. Corn was also produced (cf. the coin types of Demeter), but this was probably not enough even for local needs in times of bad harvest, when even the richest areas lived under threat of famine (Rostovtzeff, II.147-49, 599-600n.). The economy of the city was probably precarious in any case after its sufferings. If the local harvest failed, the payment of famine-prices and transport costs to bring corn from outside may have been beyond the slender resources of the place. Its one regular source for the necessary revenue was its wine-production. To such a city the edict of Domitian would have been the last straw. Already the widespread overproduction of wine may have reduced the price disastrously for the Philadelphian economy. The compulsory cutting down of vineyards removed the last resource. Volcanic soil, ideal for vines, was not in any case necessarily suitable for corn (cf. Verg. *Georg.* 1.54).[27]

This background receives some possible support from the scanty epigraphical materials. Rostovtzeff has noted the crucial responsibility carried by the *sitōnēs* and *agoranomoi* in Eastern cities in times of shortage (I.146). Both offices are strikingly prominent in some instructive inscriptions of Philadelphia, unfortunately not datable. One *agoranomos* had served with distinction ἐν δυσχρήστῳ καιρῷ (*IGRR* IV. 1640 = *CIG* 3418 = *LBW* 650).[28] Another had been generous in πέψις, apparently a distribution of cooked food to the people (*IGRR* IV. 1637 = *CIG* 3419 = *LBW* 647). This usage of the word and of the cognate verb πέσσω in *IGRR* IV. 1638 seems to be unparalleled. Perhaps this was an exclusively local institution, a regular 'liturgy' by which a rich man undertook to provide rations for the poor. Was the food a cheap substitute for corn? Does the practice show the need to organize services to neet a chronic shortage? If so, this might best suit an early Imperial date, when we know that Philadelphia was weak and troubled.[29]

The imperial titles which had bound the place to the service of the emperor must have seemed hollow after AD 92.[30] The impetus to recovery derived from the earlier benefactions had long since been dissipated without solving long-term problems. Hopes in the Flavian dynasty had finally been dashed by the action of the imperial patron himself. For most of the century the state had probably reverted largely to the older Lydian pattern of agricultural villages 'outside' the city. When we read Rev. 3.7-13 in the light of the apparent contemporary reference of Rev. 6.6, we may infer a *Sitz im Leben* closely consequent upon the final disillusionment. The character of

Christ stands in implied contrast with that of the imperial god. He will never betray a church which has continued to confess his name when weak and rejected (cf. 3.8). His name will permanently characterize them and be a pledge of their relationship with God (cf. 3.12).

I can find no external evidence for the existence of a Jewish community in Philadelphia during this period, though a few years later Ignatius had to combat a Judaizing schism in the church there (Ign. *Philad.* 6.1; 8.2). The only direct reference is later, probably of the third century: an inscription found at Deliler, about ten miles east of Philadelphia, mentions a 'synagogue of the Hebrews' (Keil and von Premerstein, *Dritte Reise*, p. 32, No. 42).[31]

The presence of Judaistic influence is however attested by the reference to the 'synagogue of Satan' (Rev. 3.9), as by Ignatius. The parallel with Smyrna (Rev. 2.9) is likely to reflect a similarity of background. These are the two cities where we have independent information about the pressures, though the interpretation of the Ignatian evidence here is problematic.

We may ask why Jewish influence should have operated so strongly in an economically weak city. Possibly Philadelphia offered opportunities for exploitation by the less scrupulous by the sale of necessities at extortionate prices. The strong language of Rev. 3.9 would be the more intelligible if some such opportunism of the writer's opponents had given them an unpopular hold on the city. And neighbouring Sardis was a great centre of the Diaspora.

3. *The Text of the Letter*

It seems clear from the foregoing section that the present letter is strikingly apposite in its allusion to contemporary circumstance. In closer consideration of the text we must look first at the Old Testament background of its language.

The clearest examples of direct reference to the Old Testament here are at 3.7, taken from Isa. 22.22, and in 3.9, taken from Isa. 60.14 (cf. Ps. 86.9; Isa. 45.14; 49.23).[32] Two shorter phrases paralleled in the Old Testament are ἐγὼ ἠγάπησά σε (3.9, from Isa. 43.4), and τὸ ὄνομα τῆς πόλεως (3.12, from Ezek. 48.35; see Charles, p. lxxviii; Swete, p. cxlii). Charles finds no connection with the Pseudepigrapha, though he elsewhere parallels the 'new name' at Pergamum (2.17) with *Test. Levi* 8.4 (p. lxxxii). The similar words in Rev. 3.12 may better be referred to Isa. 62.2 (cf. Isa. 65.15).

These verbal reminiscences are far from exhausting the Old Testament influence on this letter. I think the writer was meditating closely upon the contexts of at least two of the passages he cites (Isa. 60.10-22; Ezek 48.30-35; and perhaps also Isa. 22.22-25). In the first case there are points of contact both with Rev. 3.7-13 and with Rev. 21.22-26.[33] The writer is apparently applying Isa. 60 creatively to the situation of the church in Philadelphia. The further relation between our letter and Rev. 21 is anticipated in the reference to the 'new Jerusalem' in 3.12. Moreover, the description of the heavenly city in Rev. 21 is largely drawn from Ezek. 47 and 48 (so esp. Rev. 21.12ff. from Ezek. 48.30-35). We have seen that this passage in Ezekiel is verbally paralleled in Rev. 3.12. I suggest that its use in the Revelation is connected with John's sense of its applicability to local circumstances in Philadelphia.

Christ is here first described as ὁ ἅγιος ὁ ἀληθινός (v. 7). Charles gives Jewish precedents both for this asyndetic use of two divine designations and for 'holy' as a title of God (p. 85). ἀληθινός in classical usage is strictly 'genuine' as opposed to 'unreal', and this sense is distinguished from ἀληθής, meaning 'faithful to one's word'. It is very doubtful whether any such distinction may be maintained here.[34] Hort (p. 34), followed by Charles (p. 86), sees in the Revelation the Old Testament conception of truth expressed in Ps. 146.6 (LXX 145.6): τὸν φυλάσσοντα ἀλήθειαν εἰς τὸν αἰῶνα (cf. Rev. 3.14; 6.10; 19.11). This faithfulness of Christ may then be set against the suggested background of disillusion with imperial patronage. This tells against the view of Moffatt (pp. 365-66), Beckwith (p. 478), and Kiddle (p. 49), all of whom stress the sense 'genuine' and interpret the phrase as an assertion of Christ's Messianic authenticity against the objections of the hostile Jews of v. 9. The latter possibility cannot readily be excluded, for Judaic opposition to Christian claims is an evident factor in the situation.[35]

The latter words of the verse are quoted from the account of Eliakim who controlled entry to the king's house (Isa. 22.22). Their use here is often seen against the hostile Judaism in the city. So Moffatt writes (p. 366): 'Christ alone, the heavenly κλειδοῦχος, has the right to excommunicate' (cf. Beckwith, p. 479). Such an assurance would be profoundly relevant to Christians faced with expulsion from the synagogue. Hort (p. 34) writes: 'His opening is doubtless primarily the admission of Gentiles despite Jewish resistance. His shutting is the exclusion of unbelieving Israel despite their parentage and privileges.'

The allusion to the 'open door' is more problematical. It has usually been taken to denote an opportunity for effective missionary effort, as in 1 Cor. 16.9; 2 Cor. 2.12; Col. 4.3 (so Trench, pp. 180-81; Charles, p. 87; Swete, p. 54; Ramsay, *SC*, p. 404; Hort, p. 35). This view has been criticized by Beckwith, whose arguments rest largely on the strongly eschatological tone of the letter. He regards the 'open door' as denoting admission to a place or state, comparing Rev. 3.20; 4.1; Acts 14.27 and John 10.7, 9, and arguing that the expression must be taken with the previous verse to signify one of the acts of opening and shutting there taken to belong to the eschatological kingdom. He explains ἣν οὐδεὶς δύναται κλεῖσαι αὐτήν against the admitted background of Jewish hostility, in the sense 'shutting Gentiles out of the Messianic kingdom' (p. 480).

The two views are not necessarily to be treated as exclusive alternatives. What did the phrase mean to the original recipients? I concede that it conveyed an assurance that their present unjust rejection would be redressed in the future kingdom. But I think it also had a more immediate application as a stimulus to evangelism. There are three reasons in favour of this. (1) Charles (pp. 86-87) and Swete (p. 54) seem to be correct in taking ἰδού . . . αὐτήν as a parenthesis on the assessment of the works of the church. On this reading the words are most easily understood to refer to the present opportunity. (2) The adaptation of the expression does not necessarily demand a repetition of its eschatological application there. Indeed, it is in John's manner to use a derived concept pointedly in a new setting. Here the attributes of Christ may be seen as made relevant to the present situation. The missionary interpretation, then, is at least not excluded on this ground. (3) There is some reason to think the Philadelphian church actually took the phrase so. This depends on circumstantial historical argument to be considered in the next section.[36]

Moffatt (p. 366) refers to Ignatius, *Philad.* 9.1, where Christ is himself described as θύρα τοῦ πατρός (cf. 1 Clem. 48.2, 3). The recurrence of reference to a door is interesting, whether or not Ignatius knew the present passage. But in any case the thought is different, for here the identification with Christ is not made. We may in fact accept the viability of the missionary view while recognizing that Ramsay has overstated his point. It may be further illustrated from the work of Sir William Calder on developments traceable to the influence of this church.

The closing words of v. 8 resume the evaluation of the church's condition. It had *only* little strength: this is surely the implication of μικράν. The church was rejected and vulnerable even within a weak and impoverished community.[37] 'And yet (καί here adversative: see Charles, p. 87) you have kept my word and have not denied my name.' It is recognized that this commendation refers to the contemporary problem of the church, and the context suggests that the trial was brought upon it by its Jewish enemies.

There is an apparent difficulty in placing the church's confession of Christ's name in a Jewish setting at so late a date. Torrey actually argues from this to the necessity of an early (Neronian) date for the Revelation,[38] and Ramsay sees the difficulty in Spitta's idea that Jews could have been the agents of open persecution (*CRE*, p. 300; cf. Spitta, *Die Offenbarung von Johannes*, p. 477). The answer to these problems may lie precisely in the historical background we have argued in the Introduction. There was the inducement for the Christian to seek sanctuary in the synagogue, where in turn he might meet rejection. The existence of the problem even later in this very church may be inferred from Ignatius.[39]

The opening words of v. 9, ἰδοὺ διδῶ ἐκ τῆς συναγωγῆς τοῦ Σατανᾶ, are difficult. διδῶ has been variously treated:[40] (1) literally, 'I give men of the synagogue (as your converts)' (Beckwith, p. 481; Hort, p. 35); (2) Hebraically, to mean 'I (will) make', like the following ποιήσω (Charles, p. 88);[41] (3) removed by emendation.[42]

On any view the construction of the whole sentence is awkward, and there is no justification for emendation. The syntactical oddities of the sentence may all be paralleled in the Revelation.[43] The harshness of style is in John's manner, and the text, however strange, is to be explained as it stands. The sense seems fairly clear despite its manner of expression. Probably (2) should be preferred to (1). This is confirmed by the following ποιήσω, even though Torrey sees difficulty in the sequence of incongruous verbs as synonyms.

The interpretation of these opening words has some bearing on the problems of the following promises. That from Isa. 60.14 spoke in its original context of Gentile submission to the people of God (cf. Isa. 45.14 and Hort, p. 35). Here its terms imply that the present specific hardships of the Philadelphian church shall be redressed. The honourable title of 'Jew' has been usurped by the church's opponents. When these 'false Jews' submit in the day of fulfilment, the roles will be reversed. Whether this promise was understood by the readers to refer to the immediate earthly future, or, more probably, to the last times, the choice of this scripture was related to their present rejection. And an eschatological understanding of the promise accords with the context (esp. v. 10) and with the more probable rendering of διδῶ. Then the unbelieving Jews shall know that the church is the object of Christ's love. The words ἐγὼ ἠγάπησά σε are also taken from a passage expressing the love of God for his redeemed, who are precious above other nations (Isa. 43.3-4).

The problems of v. 10 have been listed and discussed in a valuable article by Schuyler Brown:[44] (1) What precisely does Christ promise the church in Philadelphia? (2) Is this promise exclusively for the Philadelphians, or is it of general application to all Christians? (3) Is the 'hour of trial' a local, particular persecution or an eschatological event? (4) Is it to be identified with any of the other future happenings described in the Revelation? (5) What is the meaning of πειράσαι? (6) Who are 'the inhabitants of the earth'?

The most easily answered question is (6). The phrase occurs elsewhere at Rev. 6.10; 8.13; 11.10 *bis*; 13.8, 14 *bis*; 17.8, and always alludes to the enemies of the church.[45] Brown then argues that πειρασμός cannot here be local or allude to any persecution of Christians, but that here alone in the New Testament it must denote eschatological tribulation for all men, a usage explained from Dan. 12.10a, where the θλῖψις which sanctifies the elect drives the sinner deeper into sin. The words τηρήσω ἐκ are to be understood from John 17.15: God's people shall receive special protection in the trial rather than exemption from it (ἀπό; cf. also 2 Pet. 2.9). This nature of the trial also precludes its identification with any of those in the later visions of the book. He accordingly rejects Charles's view (p. 89) that this verse must be understood from the sealing of the faithful in Rev. 7. The 'hour of trial' must be used generally of universal tribulations preceding the Lord's return.

Brown's general case seems soundly based, and sufficiently disposes of Charles's idea that 3.10 was a redactional addition in the light of Rev. 7. This is the only hint of a world-wide tribulation in the seven letters, and it is too generalized to permit of this kind of identification. We may however comment: (1) Rev. 7 itself contains certain features which suggest a relevance to the circumstances of Philadelphia.[46] (2) Much depends on the strict rendering of τηρήσω ἐκ (as opposed to ἀπό, Prov. 7.5 LXX). The Johannine parallel may not be decisive here. (3) It does not necessarily follow that the promises of victory, here or elsewhere, are only generic in content (Brown, p. 311). We shall argue that some phrases of the letter were locally applied and were influential on the subsequent history of the Philadelphian church. If the church then believed it was living in the last times it made no distinction between immediate and eschatological fulfilment.

Several verbal points in v. 10 deserve mention, though they are incidental to its main problems. (1) ἐτήρησας, here as in v. 8, and like οὐκ ἠρνήσω there, emphasizes the actual steadfastness of the church under past difficulty. The tense is best rendered by a perfect (so AV, RSV and NEB against RV), for the difficulty and the faithfulness alike continue into the present. ἐτήρησας also anticipates the promise beginning τηρήσω. (2) The compressed expression τὸν λόγον τῆς ὑπομονῆς μου is difficult. The word-order requires us to take μου with ὑπομονῆς.[47] There is then the question whether μου should be taken subjectively (Charles, p. 89; Swete, p. 56; Hort, p. 35) or objectively, as referring to the endurance of Christ as their example or to that which he requires of them. There is a similar ambiguity in 2 Thess. 3.5, but Rev. 13.10 and 14.12 are clear parallels for the former view.[48] (3) It is not certain whether μελλούσης should be pressed to imply imminence or whether it is here merely an auxiliary of future time, as probably in 3.16.[49] As the periphrasis was increasingly replacing the future participle and infinitive it seems better not to make too much of μέλλω here. The imminence of the trial is not in question, but the emphasis is upon the swiftness of Christ to the rescue.

Verse 11, then, is to be taken closely with the preceding words. Christ's coming is here a comfort, as in 22.7, 20, not a threat (2.5, 16; 3.3).[50] The picture here is the familiar one of the athlete's crown of victory (cf. esp. 2 Tim. 4.8). Swete (p. 57) comments on the warning: 'The vacant room left by the lapse of a Church may be filled with the rise of another', referring to Rom. 11.17-24 (the wild olive) and Mt. 25.28 (the talent taken from the unprofitable servant). The use of the athletic metaphor was appropriate in Philadelphia, on whose inscriptions games and festivals are specially prominent.[51] Here the language derives point from the precariousness of life in a community so liable to ruin from natural disaster or economic change. So too enemies of the Christians might seek to disqualify them, but the victory was theirs by right if they only maintained their witness and were not now tempted to turn aside from the rigours of their appointed course.

The promise to the victor (v. 12) stresses his future stability and security. The metaphorical use of στῦλος is paralleled in 1 Tim. 3.15 and Gal. 2.9, where again it refers to persons.[52] The 'pillar' here however is that which stands firm (cf. Jer. 1.18) rather than that which supports (Isa. 22.23, a passage already cited in the letter, and Isa. 56.5). There is no occasion to find difficulty in the reference to the 'temple of my God' as contrasted with the New Jerusalem which had no temple (see Charles, p. 91).

The background of this metaphor and its sequel needs some discussion. At the outset we note that ἐπ' αὐτόν might refer to στῦλον, or more probably to the previous αὐτόν (= ὁ νικῶν). As the victor is identified with the pillar, the difference may not prove important except as it affects the metaphorical picture, whether in fact any ancient practice of inscribing names on pillars is relevant to the writer's point. In view of his allusive manner the possibility should not be excluded on this verbal point, and the commentators have offered several suggestions. (1) Reference is seen to the pillars Jachin and Boaz which Solomon set before his temple (1 Kings 7.21; 2 Chron. 3.15, 17). A.M. Farrer writes: 'The two ideas, "I will fix him in a sure place" and "I will honour him with my name' are drawn together by the recollection that the twin pillars in Solomon's temple had "personal" names'.[53] (2) The victor himself receives the names on his forehead, an allusion to the writing on the forehead of Aaron (Exod. 28.36-38).[54] (3) It has often been suggested that there is reference to a local custom by which the provincial priest of the imperial cult at the close of his year erected in the temple precinct his statue, and inscribed upon it his name, and that of his father and home and his year of office. Despite the distinguished support for this view I find no evidence that this precise custom existed, and the terms in which it is repeated by successive commentators are necessarily excluded as anachronistic by the fact that Philadelphia did not receive the neocorate until about AD 213.[55] (4) There is probably the thought of the city's sufferings from earthquake, especially in view of the contrast with the background of the words ἔξω οὐ μὴ ἐξέλθῃ ἔτι. Reference to the pillar then speaks of ultimate security assured in God for those who held fast through temporary weakness.[56]

These possible backgrounds are not necessarily mutually exclusive. I should favour Exod. 28.36-38 as the primary Old Testament source, here amalgamated with related ideas and applied to the need of the church.

The interpretation and background of the sequence of 'names' requires some further comment. The reiteration of the words τοῦ Θεοῦ μου is remarkable (cf. also 3.2). Beckwith (p. 486) points out in this an emphasis on the certainty of the Lord's promise. The idea of the 'new name' seems to be based on reminiscence of Isa. 62.2 and Ezek. 48.35, both from passages influential as a whole upon the composition of this letter.[57] There is a valuable discussion of the individual names in Swete, pp. 57-58. He notes that the name of God was put upon every Israelite (Num. 6.27; cf. Deut. 28.10; Isa. 43.7; 63.9; Dan. 9.18-19; James 2.7). The new Jerusalem was to be the successor of the old Jerusalem now already in the past.[58] Citizenship of this city was already the potential privilege of Christians (Gal. 4.26; Heb. 12.22; cf. Phil. 3.20).

The main issues here concern the heavenly Jerusalem. It seems clear that the mention of this city is to be related to the vision of Rev. 21-22, especially to Rev. 21.2.[59] This 'new Jerusalem' has an Old Testament background, especially in Ezek. 48. There is also good reason to accept Ramsay's idea that 'the city of my God' would recall the names assumed by Philadelphia in honour of her imperial benefactors.[60] The faithfulness of Christ stood in pointed contrast with the bitterness of disillusionment with that other patronage. Perhaps too the picture of the symmetrical beauty of the heavenly city as developed in Rev. 21 contrasted as sharply with the continued poverty and the wrecked and neglected buildings of the existing city. None of the frequent elaborations of the idea in the Jewish Pseudepigrapha sufficiently explains the creative and allusive use made of apocalyptic imagery here.[61] And the security of the heavenly city stood against the sense of the precariousness of life.[62]

The further consideration of the concluding words of the verse is inseparable from some account of the evidence for the subsequent history of the Philadelphian church. The descent from heaven of the new Jerusalem was a Montanist expectation, and there is reason to connect the origins of that movement with this church. The evidence has in fact been plausibly presented by Sir W.M. Calder to show that our letter had a remarkable sequel as a formative influence on those who came to expect a very literal and material fulfilment of its prophecies. The very possibility of this outcome indicates that it was felt to speak with peculiar relevance and authority to the church's condition. There is thus valuable light to be shed on the original understanding of the text.[63]

4. The Evidence of the Later Philadelphian Church

In this section two principal topics will be discussed: (1) the bearing of later writings, in particular the relation of Ignatius's epistle to the Philadelphians with our text; (2) Sir William Calder's case for the connection of this city with the origins of Montanism.

Ignatius's letters to Philadelphia and to Smyrna differ from others of the group in the fact that he had personally visited the churches before writing to them.[64] It is not however clear whether he knew the seven Apocalyptic letters. It is an attractive supposition that there might be literary relationship between Ign. *Philad.* 6.1 and Rev. 3.12, but this is not conclusive. Writing of those, both circumcised and uncircumcised, who do not speak of Christ, Ignatius says: οὗτοι ἐμοὶ στῆλαί εἰσιν καὶ τάφοι νεκρῶν, ἐφ' οἷς γέγραπται μόνον ὀνόματα ἀνθρώπων. The latter clause contrasts pointedly with our text, and in a place where he has just been dealing with the Judaistic opposition in this very church. Is he contrasting them with a picture of the church familar to his readers, with a sarcastic play on the incongruity of στῦλοι and στῆλαι?[65]

Ignatius might in any case have heard memorable phrases from our letter while in Philadelphia even if his own epistle were essentially a quite independent composition. And his portrayal of the church makes it look rather perplexingly different from that commended in the Revelation. There is deep disunity within it (2.1; 3.1, 2, 3; 6.2; 7.2; 8.1, 2): a schismatic group is summoned to submit anew to the authority of the bishop (3.2). There is Ignatius's characteristic stress upon ecclesiastical authority, but the threat to be feared is less explicitly the Docetism he combats elsewhere than a Judaizing opposition (esp. 6.1) coupled with a conflict, of debated significance, about the scriptural basis for faith (8.2). Lightfoot terms it a Judaic Docetism, like that elsewhere, but here attacked from its Judaic rather than its Docetic side (*Ignatius*, II.242). The brief mention of the virtues of the church (Pref.; 11.1) is largely overshadowed by this intense preoccupation with its problems.

A measure of the difficulty may be explained by Ignatius's difference in standpoint, purpose and emphasis, and by the development in the church's position. A public dispute was obvious to a visitor, the years of spiritual endurance were not. John had known the deeper qualities of the church, and the Apocalyptic letter may have hardened further the determination not to deny the name of Christ.

Now it is remarkable that in both cases the bitterest opposition is Jewish. In both cases the circumstances merit close study. Jewish revival and Jewish proselytization of Christians at this period are phenomena which require some explanation. We have proposed that behind Rev. 3.9 is a situation which illumines the relations of local church and synagogue under Domitian. Ignatius, *Philad.* 6.1,[66] refers to 'hearing Judaism from the uncircumcised': apparently Gentile proselytes to Judaism were themselves active in proselytizing Christians. If acceptance in the synagogue offered a status of exemption from the liability to imperial cult, this was a standing inducement to the weaker Christian. Even after Domitian, hostile Jewish informants might still activate the standing machinery of persecution.

Here we turn to the problematic passage in Ignatius, *Philad.* 8.2: ἐπεὶ ἤκουσά τινων λεγόντων, ὅτι ἐὰν μὴ ἐν τοῖς ἀρχείοις [67] εὕρω ἐν τῷ εὐαγγελίῳ οὐ πιστεύω· καὶ λέγοντός μου αὐτοῖς ὅτι γέγραπται, ἀπεκρίθησάν μοι ὅτι πρόκειται. ἐμοὶ δὲ ἀρχεῖά ἐστιν Ἰησοῦς Χριστός, τὰ ἄθικτα ἀρχεῖα ὁ σταυρὸς αὐτοῦ καὶ ὁ θάνατος καὶ ἡ ἀνάστασις αὐτοῦ καὶ ἡ πίστις ἡ δι' αὐτοῦ.

This is not the place for a full discussion of the passage. The main immediate questions concern the words of Ignatius's opponents. (1) What do they mean by ἀρχεῖα? (2) What do they mean by εὐαγγέλιον? (3) How is the sentence to be construed?

We should probably follow Lightfoot in taking the ἀρχεῖα to be the Old Testament (*Ignatius*, II, p. 271).[68] The εὐαγγέλιον may be the written Gospel. The most satisfactory rendering then seems to be that of Lightfoot: 'Unless I find it (the point at issue) in the archives, I do not believe it (because it appears) in the Gospel'.[69] In any case the issue seems to be one of authority: the attack was directed against the validity of the new preaching or new writings. The church was being challenged to prove its case from the Old Testament, and its claim to be able to do so was itself in dispute. There were now left no eyewitnesses of the Gospel events. The records assumed a new importance in opposing the consequent Docetism. The church could then be deeply troubled by an attack on them and by the insistence that Christians use only the acknowledged Scriptures. The situation was readily usable as a Jewish rationale to induce the wavering Christians to return to the fold of the synagogue. We may suppose that the fashion of Christian apologetic by elaborately allegorical Messianic interpretation of the Old Testament (cf. e.g. Barnabas 5-

16) was at once stimulated and challenged by this development. In Philadelphia this problem of authority may have been early and acute, well calculated to induce doubt in some already weakening under the standing threat of persecution. Ignatius writes as though the controversy were new to him, and his critics were evidently not silenced by a standard answer.

Was the Revelation itself one of the Christian documents under attack? Ignatius alludes to the part played by prophets, here evidently Christian prophets, in the gospel proclamation (5.2), and this book was Christian prophecy *par excellence*. The Apocalyptic letter, with its emphasis on steadfastness, might naturally become the charter of the rigorists in the Philadelphian church. The place certainly became a centre of Christian prophecy, for Ammia, a shadowy figure of evident contemporary importance, is emphatically assigned to it (Euseb. *HE* 5.17.3-4). She is classed with the prophets of the apostolic age, and the orthodox repudiate the claim of the Montanist prophetesses to be her successors. She marks the watershed at the source of the great controversy which split the Phrygian church later in the second century. Montanism was rigorous and ecstatic, and laid great emphasis on the revelations received by its prophetesses. Calder argued that it originated in Philadelphia under the influence of our epistle.[70]

Calder draws attention to an exceptional class of early Christian epitaphs of the later third century and perhaps in some cases of the first two decades of the fourth. Most of the examples derive from the district round the headwaters of the river Tembris (Porsuk Çayı) in north-west Phrygia.[71] They are unique in their use of the formula Χριστιανοὶ Χριστιανοῖς, publicly displayed, and coupled with the exceptionally early use of other Christian titles and symbols (pp. 317-18). They have been much discussed. Their uniquely bold Christian profession is to be explained as an expression of Montanism, a view first proposed but later abandoned by Ramsay (see *CB*, II.491) and generally accepted by subsequent writers.[72]

Calder's most distinctive contribution is his topographical study of the origin of Montanism, which leads him to connect the Tembris monuments with a movement arising out of Philadelphian Christianity. The tendencies exemplified in Montanism were doubtless widely present in the church, but why should the schism have been precipitated in Phrygia and its documents show so peculiar a geographical distribution?[73]

Calder suggested that a Montanist type of Christianity entered southern Phrygia from a point on a great road, came into conflict with a more accommodating type from the Lycus valley, and was driven northward from its earlier centre to a remote and backward area of north-west Phrygia. This explains why the literary authorities place Montanism in central Phrygia in the second century and the inscriptions in the north in the third (pp. 323-24). Where then did it originate? An anonymous writer quoted by Eusebius, *HE* 5.16.7, says that Montanus first appeared at 'Ardabau', a village ἐν τῇ κατὰ τὴν Φρυγίαν Μυσίᾳ. The village name is evidently corrupt, and the district might perhaps be anywhere from Philadelphia to Dorylaeum in the north. The early location of Montanism around Pepuza must however support the former: the places mentioned in the second-century stage of the controversy are all around the great routes running eastward from Philadelphia into Phrygia.[74]

Calder observes that Montanism drew its inspiration from the Apocalypse, and argues that its likely district of origin should lead us to expect some connection with the Philadelphian letter (p. 326). He finds some obvious links. The 'door' set before the church is interpreted as the route of evangelistic enterprise leading into Phrygia. The Montanists proved in extreme danger their worthiness of the commendation 'Thou hast not denied my name'. The announcement to the Philadelphians of a great tribulation and of the New Jerusalem was adopted and became a central feature of Montanist teaching. The heavenly city was to descend to earth at Pepuza, about seventy miles eastward (p. 327). The Montanist controversy might be significantly, if partially, understood as a clash between conflicting schools of missionary expansion representing the respective influences of Philadelphia and Laodicea (p. 328).

This is plainly not the whole truth of the matter, but is probably correct as far as it goes, and the sub-apostolic records of the Philadelphian church will substantiate other elements in the relationship.[75] Again, in the letter of the Smyrnaeans to the church in Philomelium, Polycarp, the ideal martyr, is contrasted with the renegade 'Phrygian' Quintus [76] and by implication with the eleven fellow-martyrs, all of them from Philadelphia. His martyrdom was 'according to the Gospel' (*Mart. Polyc.* 1), but the writers do not commend 'those who surrender themselves, for the Gospel does not teach thus' (4). It is still a testimony to the unflinching stand of the Philadelphian church that a whole batch of martyrs should have been brought from this small city alone.

The argument so far is largely a recapitulation of Calder. An obvious criticism is that his presentation of the case is closely tied to the assumed correctness of the 'missionary' interpretation of the 'open door' of Rev. 3.8. I am inclined to accept this on the analogy of Pauline usage and as plausible in the total context of the Philadelphian church. Even so, the case for the connection of Philadelphia with the origins of Montanism need not depend on this point. Conversely, the independent evidence for the connection affords some support for thinking the words were then understood as an exhortation to evangelism.

Calder's case is strengthened by further epigraphic evidence contained in later publications.[77] Some of these meet the problem of the gap in time and place between the literary and epigraphic references to Montanism, a questionable part of the original hypothesis. Most significant among them are two inscriptions published by Calder himself from the Pepuza district and a remarkable, but much later, document from Mendechora, a village near Philadelphia.[78]

We shall conclude the section with some general observations enlarging upon certain relevant aspects of the Montanist controversy: (1) its geographical and historical origins; (2) its character; and especially (3) its relationship with the Revelation.

Under the first heading little more need be said. The vexed question of the chronology of the movement is not here important,[79] for we are concerned with its pre-history. The point is not a simple supposition that Montanism as such arose out of Philadelphian Christianity, but rather that it gave explicit expression to tendencies and formulated answers to problems which existed in that milieu. The Montanists may have claimed to be the true successors of the rejected Philadelphian church. Certainly they laid great stress upon the Revelation. Their claims need not be accepted without qualification. There were, however, as Calder says (p. 334), 'Phrygians before Montanus'.

The evidence for the geographical distribution of early Montanism may now be enlarged, and the further materials confirm the original hypothesis.[80] It is significant that the movement flourished in areas where such bold confession might prove unusually dangerous. Mendechora, like the Tembris district, may have been included formerly in an imperial estate.[81]

A final geographical point concerns a difficult passage in Epiphanius,

Haer. 51.33, in which he refutes the attack of the Alogi on the Revelation. The reason why they could object that no church existed in Thyatira was simply that it had gone over to Montanism. This corroborates the evidence of the outlying open-profession epitaph found near that city (Calder, No. 13).

Most of the literary authorities for Montanism are the secondary writings of opponents, or likely to be unrepresentative for other reasons.[82] A special importance therefore attaches to the fragments attributed to Montanus and his prophetesses, which are collected in Bonwetsch, pp. 197-200. Some brief comment on them may help to clarify our principal concern, the relation of the movement with the Revelation. It is significant that the orthodox objections to the new prophets were originally directed not against their matter but their ecstatic manner.[83] Montanus speaks in the person of God, as the passive vehicle of revelation (frags. 1, 3-5). At the heart of the controversy was a problem of inspiration. The Montanists were in effect providing additional scriptures, a situation which implies some existing degree of recognition of the authority of the apostolic writings.[84] The ground of this controversy takes us back to that of Ignatius, *Philad.* 8.2, and to the emphasis that the martyrdom of Polycarp, in implied contrast with those of his Philadelphian fellow-sufferers, was 'according to the gospel'. Again, a very early reference to the Revelation is contained in the letter of an unnamed anti-Montanist to Avircius Marcellus of Hieropolis (Euseb. *HE* 5.16.3). He hesitates to write lest he seem to be adding τῷ τῆς τοῦ εὐαγγελίου καινῆς διαθήκης λόγῳ (cf. Rev. 22.18; Selwyn, *The Christian Prophets*, p. 17). The Montanists did precisely that. In maintaining the continuance of prophetic revelation they were providing one answer to the attack exemplified in the Philadelphian church of Ignatius upon the authority of the original documents in a setting remote from the first generation of eye-witnesses.

Montanism, however, shows much more specific allusion to the formative influence of the Revelation. The penalty clause of the open-profession epitaphs sometimes reads τὸν Θεὸν σὺ ἀναγνοὺς μὴ ἀδικήσεις, a formula apparently based on Rev. 6.6, which we have already connected closely with Philadelphia.[85] Further details of the same type might be accumulated.[86]

A central idea is the expected descent of the the New Jerusalem from heaven. There is a clear relationship on this point between the Philadelphian letter and Rev. 21–22, where the concept is developed in terms often reminiscent of the circumstances of Philadelphia. When it comes down the σκηνή of God will be with men and he will camp with them and they shall be his people (21.3). The square enclosure of the walls is described: the twelve gates have the names of the twelve apostles (21.12-16). The gates are not closed by day, and there is no night there (21.25). Most of the details here are closely comparable with Old Testament prototypes in Ezek. 48 and Isa. 60. This fact does not exclude local reference. Indeed the Montanists developed the whole concept into a literal prophecy to which they expected a localized fulfilment. The site of their headquarters at Pepuza has never been precisely determined.[87]

A final point concerns the topography of Philadelphia itself. The square enclosure and chess-board street pattern of modern Alaşehir, so untypical of Turkish towns, invite some explanation. I cannot find that this peculiarity, though plainly seen in the panoramic view from the acropolis and illustrated in photographs, has ever previously aroused comment. The original date of the lay-out is not clear and could perhaps not be determined without excavation. Possibly the influence of the epistle on the later Christian city is seen in some attempt to rebuild the town in a form which approached an ideal of symmetry inspired by the promise which linked the church with the promise of the New Jerusalem.

5. *Summary and Conclusions*

1. The problematic early history of Philadelphia is reexamined, and some assumptions are questioned. The evidence does not permit certainty about the existence of a pre-Attalid settlement or about the date of the actual Attalid foundation. Strategic factors may have dictated the early garrisoning of the site soon after Magnesia.

2. The proverbial 'brotherly love' of Eumenes and Attalus is briefly discussed and shown as a formative feature of the local tradition of a city which prided itself on a corresponding loyalty.

3. Ramsay's argument that Philadelphia was intended to be a 'missionary city' is questioned. His suppositions about the intentions of its founders are dubious inferences from later evidence. There may be some truth in the idea: the interpretation of the 'open door' of v. 8 as denoting evangelistic opportunity, on the analogy of passages like 1 Cor 16.9, may well be correct. It is supported both on exegetical grounds and because the sequel suggests that the local church actually took it that way.

4. The likely consequences of the earthquake disaster of AD 17 in the subsequent life of the city are reexamined. The practice of living outside the city probably continued long. Philadelphia may have reverted to being an Anatolian κωμόπολις dependent on a precarious agricultural economy. The volcanic soil was unusually suitable for vines, but too little wheat was grown, and the city may have suffered during periodic famines. It is argued that Rev. 6.6 refers to Domitian's edict against vines in AD 92, a measure which may have been intended as a drastic means of increasing corn production, but which hit Philadelphia with exceptional severity because of its dependence on viticulture. The act violated a code observed even by a conquering enemy: it was unprecedented in a patron. The character of Christ (v. 7) may be set against disillusionment with the imperial god. The final promise of strength and stability is addressed to the church in a city of repeated earthquakes where living 'outside' had become a way of life.

5. There is no early record of the presence of a community of Jews in Philadelphia. The phrase 'synagogue of Satan', however, as at Smyrna, is taken to refer to such a body of ethnic Jews who rejected the claim of Christians to be the spiritual Israel. Jews were certainly active in the city a few years later, when Ignatius wrote, and were then proselytizing even Gentile Christians. The phenomenon is explained by the position of power given to Jewish communities by the pressures of the Jewish tax upon Christians.

6. The Old Testament background of the text is examined. It is suggested that the writer applied to the local situation ideas from various relevant passages on which he was meditating.

7. The words of v. 7, derived from Isa. 22.22, present Christ as holding power of admission and excommunication in the heavenly kingdom. This reinforces the suggestions made about the background of local Jewish opposition which appeared to hold that power. It does not exclude the possibility that θύρα is used in v. 8 with a different, evangelistic, connotation.

8. The problems of v. 10 are discussed, and Schuyler Brown's recent elucidation of them broadly accepted, but the expectation of a universal trial does not detract from the particularity of the words in Philadelphia. The promises of victory were here addressed to a church facing the prospect of disaster, and its response reflects its application of the text to itself.

9. The background of the allusion to a 'pillar' in v. 12 is not wholly

clear. Verbally the passage is best taken to mean that the names are written on the conqueror rather than the pillar, and the Old Testament background may then be Exod. 28.36-38. The inscribed columns before Solomon's temple may also be in mind: probably two or three distinct concepts are amalgamated. The stability of the pillar may be set against the recent difficulties of church and city.

10. The historical circumstances confirm the likelihood that 'the name of the city of my God' would recall the fact that Philadelphia had taken new names and titles from the family of the imperial god. The 'New Jerusalem' as a city of ideal symmetry may be set against the conditions of life in the contemporary city.

11. The evidence of the later church is particularly relevant in this case, as the influence of the letter gives possible insight into the original interpretation of it. The epistle of Ignatius to this church is important for a different reason. Its relationship with the Revelation is essentially situational rather than literary, but it gives a very different picture of the church. The differences may be partly due to his standpoint as a visitor who had encountered a public dispute and partly to developments later than the Revelation in the controversy over authority.

12. In the difficult passage in Ignatius, *Philad.* 8.2, we follow Lightfoot in understanding the ἀρχεῖα to be the Old Testament. In any case, the issue is one of authority, and it appears that Jewish opposition, now possessing an acknowledged canon of scripture, was attacking the Christian documents. The church was being challenged to prove its case from the Old Testament, and its claim to be able to do so was itself in dispute. This situation may be seen as a development of the opposition from the 'synagogue of Satan'. The attack on the basis of Christian belief reinforced the pressures which had been operative under Domitian and were always liable to be reactivated. It helps to explain the unexpected power which hostile Jews held over the church and accords with the growth of doubts represented by the Docetism which Ignatius opposes here and elsewhere.

13. Philadelphia was a notable centre of early Christian prophecy. In the controversies over authority the Revelation itself may have been under attack and its message have become a particular comfort and charter for those who applied it to themselves. It thus became a formative factor in the later history of the church and a stimulus to a vigorous and defiant temper in the face of official rejection. This

accords with the circumstantial probability of Calder's case for the connection of Montanism with the district. A closer examination of the character of Montanism and its historical and geographical antecedents brings out further points of relationship with the Revelation, especially with passages related to Philadelphia. The Montanist claim to provide inspired teaching additional to the apostolic writings may have been an extreme answer to a challenge to those writings. Their expectation of the descent of the New Jerusalem near Pepuza is a concept derived from the Revelation and related to Philadelphia.

Chapter 9

LAODICEA

1. *Introductory: The Cities of the Lycus*

The traveller from Philadelphia first sees the Lycus valley from the neighbourhood of Buldan. He stands over the north-western apex of a large triangular basin, above the point where the main stream of the Maeander (Büyük Menderes) emerges from its upper gorges and flows along the western margin of the valley, meeting its tributary the Lycus a few miles southward. The southern skyline is dominated by the great massifs of Salbacus (Baba Dağ) and Cadmus (Honaz Dağı), both exceeding 8,000 feet in height. The northern range is comparatively ill-defined, but its lowest escarpment is marked by a long white scar, conspicuous even at this distance of 15 miles, which indicates the site of Hierapolis at modern Pamukkale.

The Lycus valley has always been important as offering the easiest route from the Aegean coast to the Anatolian plateau. The commercial importance successively of Miletus and Ephesus channelled traffic from the east along the lower Maeander valley, but above its junction with the Lycus the rugged terrain offers no route up the main stream. The south-easterly trend of the Lycus basin however provides a natural inland continuation up a long gentle ascent to the Çardak watershed at 2,800 feet, and thence by Lake Anava (Acı Göl) to Apamea (Dinar).[1]

The character of Laodicea, which became the greatest city of this valley, is to be seen against the character and history of the district as a whole. The valley falls geographically into two parts. The lower is a broad plain, bordered on the south by a tract of alluvial hills from which the high peaks rise abruptly, and on the north by the Hierapolis ledge. The upper part to the east is narrower and has a steeper gradient. The two sections are separated by a belt of low hills forming a step some three miles wide across the valley and interrupting the easy passage of the river, which traverses them by a narrow gorge.

In early times the principal city of the whole district was apparently Colossae, situated where the river leaves the upper basin by the narrow cleft. Early references indicate its importance as a stage in travel between Sardis and the East.[2] It is a natural site for early settlement, combining the advantages of a defensible hill at the sudden narrowing of the route with a supply of pure water.[3]

Herodotus mentions one other *polis* in the valley, Cydrara, at the frontier of Phrygia and Lydia, where the road to Caria branched off that to Sardis, which had to cross the Maeander. This may have been the same as the later Hydrela, a city whose name is known from Livy 37.56, Strabo 14.1.46 = p. 650, and Pliny, *NH* 5.29.105, and from a few coins. The site is unknown, but Ramsay infers that its territory occupied the north bank of the lower Lycus and that the later Hierapolis grew on the territory of the older state and then achieved political independence of it.[4] Cydrara/Hydrela presumably lay between Hierapolis and the Maeander and marked the earliest position of a focal road-junction. Laodicea owed its importance to its situation at the crossroads in a later age.

The Lycus valley was acknowledged to be debatable ground between Phrygia, Lydia and Caria. Colossae alone is consistently assigned to Phrygia, though the whole district was administered in Roman times as part of the Cibyratic *conventus* (assize-district) of Phrygia (Plin. *NH* 5.29.105).[5] Differences of ethnology may have been reflected in religious variations within the valley (cf. *CB*, I.6-9). Ancient ἱεραὶ κῶμαι leave little trace in literature, but must have been important centres of local life, especially in an area of such remarkable physical phenomena. Hierapolis must have originated as the religious centre of the Hydrelitae. It achieved civic status under Eumenes II (*OGIS* 308; cf. Magie, p. 308). Its earliest coins are doubtfully dated to the 2nd century BC, and until Augustus they bear the legend 'Hieropolis' ('the city of the *hieron*').[6]

The religious centre south of the Lycus was at the temple of Men Karou, probably located at modern Gereli, near Sarayköy.[7] Strabo describes its position as lying in the territory of the city of Attuda, and connects it with the later establishment of a famous medical school associated with Laodicea (Strab. 12.8.20 = p. 580; cf. *BMC Caria*, Attuda No. 18). Attuda itself, like its neighbour Trapezopolis, was in difficult country in the hills towards Salbacus: the temple-village probably became as important a centre as the *polis* (*CB* I.167). Silver coinage from Attuda is known, and dated by Head to the Pergamene period. The city was too isolated from the roads to be important later, and it was supplanted by Laodicea, a Seleucid foundation on territory probably subject previously to the sanctuary (*CB* I.169).

The new city was probably established by Antiochus II (261-246 BC) and named after his first wife Laodice, whom he divorced in 253.[8] It was on the site of an older place called successively Diospolis and Rhoas (Pliny), of which nothing is known. Such colonies were intended to strengthen the Seleucid hold on the land and were peopled with those likely to be loyal. The original population may have been largely Syrian (*CB* I.33), but a body of Jewish citizens was probably included. Laodicea stood on a low flattened eminence a kilometre square at the outer edge of the hills south of the Lycus, immediately opposite Hierapolis at a distance of 6 miles. Its site is strong but not impressive: there are higher hills close behind.

It is likely that the establishment of the new city deflected the Maeander route south of the Lycus. That now left the Sardis highway at Colossae and ran straight through Laodicea to Men Karou. Hydrela ceased to command the junction (*CB* I.160-61).

Little is known of the early history of Laodicea. Pergamene rule must have influenced it greatly. The Attalids apparently founded Tripolis to balance its Seleucid proclivities. This was strictly a city of Lydia, but geographically it belongs to the Lycus basin, though separated from the other cities by the Maeander, on whose right bank it stood (*CB* I.192-94). It commanded the river-crossing near modern Yenice. Meanwhile Attalus II's activities in Pamphylia and his foundation of the seaport Attalia (modern Antalya; Strab. 14.4.1 = p. 667) increased the importance of the route which ran southward from the Lycus valley through the narrow gap between Salbacus and Cadmus, by Themisonium and Cibyra to Pamphylia. This road naturally met the others at Laodicea, beneath the entrance to the gap. Laodicea thus became the crossroads where the route from Ephesus to the East crossed that from Pergamum and Sardis to the south coast. Both the Attalids and the Romans paid special attention to the building and upkeep of such principal highways.[9] Laodicea flourished at the expense of both Tripolis and Colossae, though the considerable coinage of the former suggests that it retained some importance in the Roman period. Laodicea appears as a judicial and administrative centre in the correspondence of Cicero at the time of his proconsulship of Cilicia, to which the Cibyratic *conventus* was temporarily attached.[10]

In the New Testament three of the cities of the Lycus valley are mentioned. Laodicea, Hierapolis and Colossae.[11] In Col. 4.13 Laodicea and Hierapolis are mentioned together as possessing churches in the letter addressed to the third city. The beginnings of Christianity in the district are fairly clear in outline. The prohibition of the Spirit against preaching in Asia (Acts 16.6) had evidently restricted Paul's earlier travel in the province to a transit of its northern borders. He is said to have reached Ephesus overland by traversing τὰ ἀνωτερικὰ μέρη (Acts 19.1), which may refer to the upland road through Tralla to the Cayster valley (*CRE*, p. 94; cf. map in *HDB*, Extra Vol., following p. 400). During Paul's stay in Ephesus we may presume that Epaphras took the gospel to the Lycus valley, primarily to Laodicea (Col. 1.6, 7). Paul's words in Col. 2.1 are most naturally taken to mean that at the date of writing he had visited neither Laodicea nor Colossae in person. I regard this epistle as written from the Roman imprisonment, and Paul's intended visit to Colossae (Philem. 22), if ever accomplished, as subsequent to a hypothetical release. The 'epistle from Laodicea' (Col. 4.16) seems most likely to be our Ephesians.[12] Paul's intervention at Colossae, in a church he had not founded, was evidently exceptional; the other letter was perhaps a circular to the churches of Asia, delivered first at Laodicea, the natural centre of the Lycus district. Unless we identify the letter of Col. 4.16 with Philemon, which seems quite unsuitable, it is natural to suppose from Col. 4.9 that Onesimus, and therefore the household of Philemon, belonged to Colossae, not Laodicea. Lightfoot has suggested however from Col. 4.17 that Archippus, presumably the son of Philemon (Philem. 2), held responsibility in the church in Laodicea. The two cities were only ten miles apart, and Col. 4 suggests habitual communication between them.[13]

We have already a pattern characteristic of early Christianity in the Lycus valley, of closely related churches in the trio of cities to the apparent exclusion of their neighbours. The prominence of Laodicea and of Hierapolis is easily explained. They had become the great cities of the district, the former as the centre of its trade and manufacture, the latter as combining the importance of a religious and medical centre with a thriving woollen industry like that of

Laodicea. Colossae is a different matter. It had certainly declined, though in the first century it may have retained a modest importance from the sale of its fine wool (Strab. 12.8.16 = p. 578).[14] Its coinage is scanty, mostly Imperial (but cf. *BMC Phrygia*, p. xlix). It was increasingly overshadowed by Laodicea, and may never have fully recovered from the severe earthquake of AD 60. It later became quite insignificant, and when replaced by Chonae (Honaz) at a more defensible site three miles distant its very name was forgotten (*CB* I.213-14).[15]

The valley itself has some remarkable scenic phenomena consequent upon its volcanic character. It has suffered much from earthquakes. The land is well-watered, but its streams are remarkable to a varying extent both for their heat and for their calcareous deposits. The temperatures of some are close to boiling point: the waters of Hierapolis, though less hot than some, have formed spectacular petrified cascades almost unique in the world. The problems of earthquake and water-supply were prominent themes in the life of the district, and, coupled with the need of defence in troubled times, have exercised decisive influence on the subsequent movements of population.

2. *The Jewish Background*

a. *The Jews in the Cities*

It seems likely that Laodicea had a large Jewish population, and very possible that they included an important citizen body. The evidence however is mostly indirect and inferential.

We have seen that Antiochus III is reputed to have settled 2,000 Jewish families from Mesopotamia in Lydia and Phrygia (Jos. *Antiq.* 12.3.4.149). Lightfoot points out that Laodicea, a Seleucid foundation on the borders of the two, was a natural centre for the immigration (*Colossians and Philemon*, p. 20). In 62 BC the proconsul Flaccus confiscated large amounts of Jewish gold bound for Jerusalem, among them the sum of over twenty pounds weight at Laodicea (Cic. *pro Flacco* 28.68). The places mentioned were all capitals of *conventus*, and the sums collected may represent the totals of temple-tax from their respective districts. It has been calculated that the amount from Laodicea would imply a population of 7,500 adult Jewish freemen in the district.[16] As the wealth of the area evidently grew greatly during the following century the Jews may be presumed to have increased correspondingly in numbers and affluence.

Epigraphical evidence to this effect from Laodicea is almost wholly lacking, but this may testify only to the Hellenization of the Jewish community.[17] A Jew with a Greek name is not easily identified unless the context refers to some aspect of his religion.

Talmud references are cited by Lightfoot (*Colossians and Philemon*, pp. 21-22) to suggest that the Jews of Laodicea were the epitome of the ease and laxity of the Diaspora: 'Thy father fled to Asia; flee thou to Laodicea' (Baba Mezi'a 84a),[18] and 'the wines and the baths of Phrygia have separated the ten tribes from Israel' (Shabbath 147b).[19] To these we may perhaps add Shabbath 119a, which tells of lavish hospitality at a table of gold provided by a man of an unspecified Laodicea.[20]

None of these materials tells us anything of the political status of the undoubted Jewish community. We have to infer the likelihood that they formed a citizen-body from the analogy of Seleucid policy elsewhere and from their evident strength and integration in the city. There is however no record of such racial and religious tension as often accompanied the presence of such Jewish citizen communities elsewhere.

In the case of Hierapolis the evidence is more direct, though some of its implications are difficult to interpret. Several undoubtedly Jewish epitaphs are preserved whose form is closely adapted to cultural features of the surrounding society.[21] Their number has been augmented by recent discoveries.[22] Fines for unauthorized burial could be made payable to 'the *katoikia* of the Jews settled in Hierapolis' (Judeich, No. 212 = *CIJ* 775) or to 'the *laos* of the Jews' (Judeich, No. 69 = *CIJ* 776). The use of the word *katoikia* points to the presence of a community with defined privileges, perhaps including that of citizenship (see Ramsay, *Expos.* 6th ser., 5 [1902], 95ff.).[23]

The evidence is at least clear about the fundamental fact of Jewish presence and privilege: its difficulties of application are evidently occasioned by the very integration of the community into pagan society. The attempt to identify individual Jews is often hazardous.[24]

If these things were true of Hierapolis, they may have been more emphatically true of Laodicea. In constitution the cities differed, Hierapolis being composed of trade and village communities, probably preserving the old Lydian pattern, whereas Laodicea was organized by tribes, some of whose names are known, but not their number.[25] The Jews of Laodicea may have become so integrated with their affluent society that they were indistinguishable within it, perhaps even leaders in its commercial expansion as its most vigorous and united class.

The Jewish background of the valley bears not only upon the Apocalypse directly, but on the Colossian heresy, which Lightfoot saw long ago as compounded partly of a Jewish deviation akin to Essenism (*Colossians and Philemon*, pp. 73ff. and esp. pp. 94ff.). There is no independent evidence whether there were Jews at Colossae, and comparison of Col. 4.12 with 4.11 suggests that the evangelist Epaphras was himself a Gentile. Laodicea, as the principal centre of the district, may have been the source of the cosmological speculation affecting the Colossian church, and the identification of its Jews with Gentile society may naturally have fostered an accommodation to pagan thought-forms.[26] Lightfoot regarded the fourth book of the Sibylline Oracles as representative of a heterodox Judaism in Asia (pp. 96-97): its date is about AD 80, and it refers to contemporary circumstances of Laodicea (4.107ff.).

These hints lead us naturally to the problems of the Jewish literary background of the present letter. There is for instance a significant parallel between Rev. 3.14 and Col. 1.15ff. The nature of the relationship must be considered. It seems likely that the literary parallel reflects a relationship of situation, and that both passages are rooted in the need to answer local tendencies of speculative thought in which the influence of Judaism and its adaptation to sectarian and syncretistic forms were a contributory factor.

b. *The Old Testament and Hebraic Background*

The literary relationships of the Laodicean letter are peculiar in several respects. Some of them are clearly tabulated by R.H. Charles. He finds only three Old Testament parallels: Rev. 3.17 with Hos. 12.8; Rev. 3.19 with Prov. 3.11-12; Rev. 3.20 with Cant. 5.2; all echoes of the Hebrew text rather than of the Greek versions. This list does not exhaust the matter, for it takes no account of the most important Hebraic passage in v. 14. He finds no parallels with the Pseudepigrapha. He considered it highly probable that John was acquainted with the Colossian epistle, observing three verbal parallels in the present brief letter, as many as with the whole Old Testament.[27] Yet he finds 'no resemblances between the diction and thought of the other six letters and the Pauline epistles' (p. 95). We may add from the evidence of his own analysis (pp. lxxxiv-lxxxvi) that Colossian parallels scarcely exist elsewhere in the Revelation.[28]

Again, this letter stands comparatively apart from other parts of the Revelation itself. It is unique in that the introductory words of Christ are not drawn from the Patmos vision of Rev. 1.13ff. Nor are there the usual obvious parallels with the the final vision of the heavenly Jerusalem. And even the imagery here is largely distinct from that which finds recurring echoes elsewhere in the book. There are several points of contact with the other letters, but the underlying thought and background are subtly different or sharply contrasting.[29] And whereas the other six letters fall by subject and character into three convenient pairs, this has no clear affinity among them.

The crucial passage, then, is in 3.14: 'These things says the Amen, the witness faithful and true, the beginning of the creation of God'. This is not precisely an echo of any Old Testament passage, though apparently related to Isa. 65.16. Commentators have generally accepted this background, though R.H. Charles was doubtful, and L.H. Silberman, *JBL* 82 (1963), pp. 213-15, offers a radically different solution based upon a midrash on Prov. 8.22 in Bereshith Rabbah 1.1, rendering the unique title Ἀμήν as 'Master Workman' and presenting Christ as the Father's adviser in creation.[30] Another line of thought is prompted by J. Finegan, *Light from the Ancient Past*, 2nd edn, pp. 294, 587, who draws attention to a passage in the Qumran Manual of Discipline where an acrostic with esoteric meaning is based on the letters אמן. John's use of the title 'Amen' might then be placed against some usage current among Jewish nonconformists.[31] The word is taken up from its Biblical context in answer, and Christ is equated with the 'God of Amen' of Isa. 65.16. In that passage, as Kiddle observes (p. 57), the exalted monotheism of the God of creation made moral claims on the undivided loyalty of his people. The Septuagint renders the title τὸν Θεὸν τὸν ἀληθινόν, and our passage in turn uses ἀληθινός characteristically, implying that Christ is true, and will fulfil his word (cf. Charles, pp. 85ff., on Rev. 3.7), and so applying to him language used only of God in the Old Testament.[32]

The most striking Biblical parallel of this Hebraic passage, however, is not in the Old Testament at all, but in Col. 1.15ff. We may accept the strong probability that the Colossian epistle was familiar both to John and to the church in Laodicea (cf. Swete, p. 59). But the strong and explicit parallel of content and context is surely more than verbal: it is called forth in reply to similar tendencies of thought persisting in the district (so Lightfoot, pp. 41-42). The use of ἀρχή both in Col. 1.18 and Rev. 3.14 rests upon Prov. 8.22,[33] but in both places we argue that the application to Christ as the preeminent 'uncreated principle of creation' is set against a similar tendency in the local *Sitz im Leben*. I should hesitate to offer any identification of a definite movement, but some of its facets can be traced in both the literary and historical materials: the merging of the uniqueness of Christ into a hierarchy of mediating powers, a syncretism of nonconformist Judaism with speculative philosophy and esoteric *gnosis*. And this was a district where an influential Judaism had demonstrably accommodated itself to the standards of surrounding society.

It seems then that this most Jewish part of the letter was also relevant in its message to the church. The analogy of the Colossian epistle again testifies to the infiltration of Jewish sectarianism into the church. Yet the general tenor of this letter is little concerned with combatting heresy. It is directed against a moral and spiritual complacency and enforces its lesson with a series of vivid and distinctive images which owe little to the literary background we have discussed. The ideas χλιαρός, ἐμέσαι, κολλύριον have no obvious Old Testament or Jewish antecedents. We shall argue that they were all very relevant to aspects of life in Laodicea. And even the most interesting literary parallels are to be found in a rather later work, in Arrian's apparently faithful transcriptions of the words of Epictetus. Epictetus was a native of the Lycus valley.

The Jewish explanation of this letter is limited in application. The message was relevant to the situation of the church, and the relevance was apparently enforced by pointed allusion to local circumstance. In the following sections we shall examine this background.

3. *The Laodicean Lukewarmness (Rev 3.15, 16)*

Earlier commentators often looked for some kind of local allusion in these verses, and offered various moralistic speculations which cannot reasonably be sustained.[34] Ramsay does not discuss the passage at all in *SC*, a remarkable omission, especially as in *CB* he had earlier discussed aspects of the water-supply of the district from which later writers have drawn significant inferences. The extraordinary phenomena of the waters of Hierapolis have captivated attention in this connection, and have often diverted notice from Laodicea itself. Thus H.B. Swete (p. 60) sees reference to these hot waters as cooling in their course over the plateau opposite Laodicea.[35]

The petrifying qualities of the streams at Hierapolis are accurately described by Strabo (13.4.4 = pp. 629f.) and by Vitruvius (8.3.10). Modern travellers have been impressed by the almost unique scenic wonders of the great cliff below. Hot, sparkling waters rise from deep pools on the city-plateau, which they cross in narrow raised channels built of their own deposit of calcium carbonate, and spill over the escarpment edge in white cascades through stepped pools of snowy incrustation.[36] The cliff is in full view of Laodicea, six miles away. It is some 300 feet high and extends nearly a mile. Its ever-changing reflections of light and colour are unspeakably beautiful, especially when viewed against the backdrop of the snowy peak of Cadmus. The waters are said to be 95°F. Springs as hot, or hotter, are found elsewhere in the district, though they do not elsewhere find such visually spectacular expression.[37]

A paper of special importance for the interpretation of our passage is M.J.S. Rudwick and E.M.B. Green, 'The Laodicean Lukewarmness', *ExpT* 69 (1957-58), pp. 176-78, to be considered with the comments of P. Wood in *ExpT* 73 (1961-62), pp. 263-64. Rudwick and Green point out the difficulties in the accepted interpretation that ζεστός, χλιαρός, and ψυχρός are to be applied absolutely to persons, as denoting spiritual fervour.[38] They show (1) that such usage is almost unparalleled,[39] and (2) that 'cold' and 'hot' seem to be presented as indifferently desirable alternatives. If coldness is commended it can hardly mean apathy.

The problem is not new. Trench (pp. 200-203) felt it acutely, and like other older commentators devoted great space to the attempt to explain why 'cold' might be preferred to 'lukewarm'.[40] Rudwick and Green argue that the water-supply of Laodicea was warm, and suggest tentatively that a contrast was implied with the hot medicinal waters of Hierapolis and the cold pure waters of Colossae. So the church was judged for its ineffectiveness rather than its half-heartedness, for the barrenness of its works rather than its spiritual temperature (p. 178). This exegesis seems to be correct, and in general correctly related to the local circumstances.[41] I hope to be able to supplement the evidence a little further in the light of other authorities, in the hope of clarifying exactly how the words would have struck a Laodicean Christian of the time.

To the ancient testimonies quoted by Rudwick and Green may be added that of Tyconius (late 4th cent.): *NEQUE FRIGIDUS ES NEQUE*

FERVENS. Id est inutilis. UTINAM FRIGIDUS ESSES AUT CALIDUS. Id est, quocumque modo utilissimus.[42]

The plausibility of the suggestion that 'hot' refers to the springs at Hierapolis is self-evident. The allusion might be generalized to include the other hot waters of the district, but exclusive reference to Hierapolis seems likely. The medicinal virtues of its streams are reflected in the local religion (see e.g. *CB* I.104–105, and cf. the numerous representations of Asklepios and Hygieia on coinage). The city's consequent prosperity as a health centre and its obtrusive proximity to Laodicea corroborate this application. Such a view of the precise reference of ζεστός is further strengthened when taken in conjunction with ψυχρός, for cold, pure water is a notable feature of Colossae and doubtless an important factor in its choice as a site of primitive settlement, though notably scarce elsewhere in the district.

The site of Colossae is carefully described by its modern discoverer, W.J. Hamilton (*Researches*, I.509-13), who notes that three clouded streams join above an ancient bridge and fall together into a chasm lined with travertine deposits of the water. Just below the bridge, however, a clear and pure stream falls in a double cascade into the gorge. This is evidently identical with the *ayasma*, or sacred spring, of mediaeval legend (*CRE*, pp. 469-71). Modern accounts have usually been interested in the physical phenomena associated with the other streams: the ancient inhabitants were concerned with necessities, and this stream, apparently perennial, alone met the basic need.[43] So the hot waters of Hierapolis were medicinal, the cold waters of Colossae pure and life-giving. We turn next to Laodicea.

Rudwick and Green emphasize that the site of Laodicea was chosen for its position at an important road-junction. 'It lacked a natural water-supply, for there are no springs on the site, and the Lycus River dries up in summer' (p. 177). The remains of a remarkable aqueduct of stone pipes indicate that the people derived water from a source south of the city, perhaps from the hot mineral springs near Denizli, the modern town five miles distant.[44] This would have cooled only slowly in the pipes, and on arrival the supply would have been tepid and its effect emetic. The writers observe that today the villagers of Eçirli, below Hierapolis, are obliged to stand their drinking water in jars to cool.

Wood in general accepts this view, with comments which I will summarize: (1) that even cold the waters tend to cause vomiting, and are locally used only for irrigation; (2) that the pipes were so constructed to keep the water hot; (3) that Eçirli in fact has a regular supply of cold drinking water from its village fountain; (4) that there is an all-season stream slightly east of Eskihisar, the Turkish hamlet nearest to Laodicea,[45] and (5) that remains of an aqueduct of conventional type lie to the west.

On some of these points further comment may be useful. (1) It is probably true that the waters of the district generally have an emetic tendency, independently of their temperature. I have not seen the source of the aqueduct, nor could it easily be traced since the recent disturbance of the ground for cultivation-terracing,[46] but the deposits which encrust its remains testify unmistakably to its calcium carbonate content. Its badness was primarily due to its impurity rather than its warmth.[47] (2) It is not clear why warm water should have been desirable. It has been alternatively suggested that the source was cold, and that the warmth was due to the exposure of the stone pipes to the sun. There is actually no direct ancient testimony for the inference that the water was tepid. Careful observations and calculations by my friend Dr G.W. Blanchard in August 1966 confirm the essential point. He considers that conditions were very stable in the pipes and that little change of water temperature would have occurred: the remains are most easily consonant with the supposition that water from a warm source was still warm when it reached the city, and in any case the deposition in the pipes proves that the water was not cold.[48] To (3) and (4) we may perhaps add mention of the Gümüş Çay (Asopus), the stream west of Laodicea, which appears clear and cold, and has been observed to flow in some abundance in August. The explanation may be that potability is a relative term, and that habit or necessity may make people less exacting. Strabo testifies to the fact that the waters of Laodicea were petrifying and yet drinkable (13.4.14 = p. 630). Our point is that such waters were hardly palatable. With regard to Eçirli Chandler records that the local landowner of his time 'expressed his regret, that no water fit to drink could be discovered there' (p. 270). (5) I can find no reference to a second aqueduct at Laodicea. To the west I know only of the piers of the bridge which conveyed the road across the Asopus to the Ephesian gate.

Our authorities emphasize both the abundance of water in the district and its bad quality. The Lycus itself is 'turbid with white mud' (E.J. Davis, *Anatolica*, p. 77), its waters 'nauseous and undrinkable' (*CB* I.215n.). Denizli (literally 'sea-like') was apparently settled and so named because of the abundance of its waters, though I am assured that most of these are not very palatable. Chandler records that many of Tamerlane's men were destroyed by drinking a spring which 'stagnated and petrified' at a place 'Tanguzlik', probably a corrupt form of 'Denizli' (p. 267).[49] The precise description by E.J. Davis (p. 101) of the Hierapolis water accords with the remarks of Rudwick and Green about Eçirli, and is probably representative of many streams in the district: 'It is not wholesome, and good drinking water must be brought from a considerable distance; but after the water of the source has been thoroughly exposed to the air it loses its injurious properties, and though not palatable, may be drunk'.

It seems likely that these last words may present accurately the predicament of ancient Laodicea. Perhaps the earlier settlements were small enough to manage with poor water from the local streams, but the growth of a large city necessitated a supplementary supply which had to be brought from a distance. The fullest account of the resulting aqueduct is that given by Hamilton (*Researches*, I.515-16), in whose time the water-towers and distribution-pipes in the city were still more largely preserved. The remarkable form of the duct has attracted special attention, for most of it seems to consist of hollowed stone blocks laid in a double line along the surface of the ground.[50] The thick layers of incrustation within the pipes bear plain and visible testimony to the badness of the water. There is no certain record of the date of construction. Ramsay observes that the remains 'probably are not later, though they may be earlier, than the time of Hiero', a wealthy benefactor of the 1st century BC mentioned by Strabo (12.8.16 = p. 578; *CB* I.48). He gives no reason, but it seems likely that the growth both of the city and of the personal wealth of the citizens created both the need and the opportunity for such a benefactor to devote his resources to a great water undertaking at that period. As Chandler observed (p. 261) that deposit from the duct encrusted the end of the large Hadrianic building (probably a gymnasium, dated by the dedicatory inscription *CB* I.72, No. 1; cf. *ibid.*, p. 47), we must presume that the aqueduct was still in use then. We may conclude that it was a feature of the city at the date of the Apocalypse.

There are many unanswered questions about the Laodicean water-supply. The principal facts are clear: the problems concern details.[51] The church in Laodicea may have seemed notably successful to the outside observer, and was itself blind to its own spiritual ineffectiveness. The point was brought home forcibly through an illustration taken from local life: the affluent society was far from the sources of its life-giving water, and when by its own resources it had sought to remedy the deficiency, the resulting supply was bad, both tepid and emetic. The effect of their conduct upon Christ was like the effect of their own water: no other church was condemned in terms so strong. The hot and cold waters of the city's neighbours were each acceptable in their place. Judgment is passed on the 'works' of the Laodiceans, not on their lack of enthusiasm: the following verses diagnose the symptoms of their spiritual malady.[52]

I conclude with a striking parallel from a very different source in which the words ἐξεμέσαι and κολλύρια are strangely conjoined. In Arrian, *Epict.* 3.21, Epictetus, a native of Hierapolis who betrays little contact with Judaism or Christianity, likens unqualified persons who enter lightly upon lecturing or the mysteries successively to those of a weak stomach who throw up their food and to those who misuse eyesalves.[53] To the latter image we shall return.

4. *Propriis Opibus* (Rev. 3.17)

It has already been noticed that the opening words of v. 17 echo the Massoretic text of Hos. 12.8. It has also been widely recognized that the whole following passage is rich in local allusion.[54] The church was evidently influenced by the material self-sufficiency which characterized the city, and this was reflected in their spiritual complacency. When v. 17 is taken closely with v. 18,[55] it is seen that the sequence of adjectives 'poor and blind and naked' in the diagnosis anticipates a series of corresponding remedies: 'gold', 'white garments' and 'eyesalve'. In the present section I shall consider the wealth and self-sufficiency of Laodicea, and in the next the local industries which were the basis of that wealth and to which allusion is evidently made in the passage.

It has often been observed that Laodicea was a banking centre (*SC*, p. 416; Charles, I.93; etc.). Cicero cashed his bills of exchange there on his arrival in his province of Cilicia in 51 BC (*ad Fam.* 3.5.4; *ad Att.* 5.15.2). Possibly Laodicea acquired this function during this brief period when the Cibyratic *conventus* was attached to Cilicia (56-49 BC),[56] and was then the proconsul's point of entry and the natural place to draw his *vasarium* in the local currency.[57] The amounts already extorted by Roman officials from Asian cities in the

Mithridatic period and later testify to their enormous wealth (see Tarn and Griffith, *Hellenistic Civilization*, 3rd edn, p. 113). Laodicea's advantageous position made it representative of the trade of the east in Horace.[58] Already in the first century BC it had possessed individual citizens of remarkable wealth. There was Hiero, who bequeathed to the city more than 2000 talents and embellished it with many public works. He was followed in the time of Antony by the orator Zeno and his son Polemo (Strab. 12.8.16 = p. 578). Despite the previous smallness of Laodicea and its siege by Mithridates, the geographer tells us, 'The fertility of the country, and the prosperity of some of its citizens, made it great'. Coinage testifies strikingly to the existence of other benefactors. In the time of Augustus two of them were actually portrayed on quasi-autonomous coins.[59] Under Nero or shortly afterwards we find Julius Andronicus *euergetes* (*BMC Phrygia* Laod., Nos. 70-73), just when Laodicea was involved in the problems of reconstruction after earthquake.[60] But the most remarkable instances of the power of individual wealth are found in the members of the Zenonid family, which became the greatest in Asia Minor. The elevation of Polemo to the kingship must have seemed a success story *par excellence*. Some of the family behaved with regal ostentation as private citizens of Laodicea while their relatives received thrones at Roman hands (see *CB* I.42-45 and the discussion on Rev. 3.21 below).[61]

The aspirations and values of society as a whole were reflected in the coinage. A Laodicean coin of Antoninus Pius depicts the infant Plutus seated on the bend of a cornucopia containing corn and fruit (*BMC*, No. 98). Hierapolis, which must have shared a similar prosperity, has a similar type portraying a goddess Euposia holding cornucopiae and a seated infant (*BMC Phrygia* Hierap., Nos. 35-37). We might venture to translate her name as 'Affluence'.[62] Cornucopiae and ears of corn are recurring motifs of Laodicean coinage, often as emblems of the Tyche (e.g. *BMC*, Nos. 252, 259). There is evident reference to an awareness of the advantages of the city's position in types of Hecate *triformis* (Nos. 218, 255) or of the city-goddess enthroned between Phrygia and Caria (no. 228), or between wolf and bear representing the local rivers Lycus and Caprus (Nos. 229, 260). Most such numismatic materials are appreciably later than our period, but the features they present accord with those which characterize the city earlier.

Before discussing the manufactures which contributed to the

wealth of the city we must consider the events which followed the earthquake of Nero's reign. They provided a memorable occasion for local pride and ostentation, and were still topical at the date of the Revelation.

There is evidence that Laodicea had appealed to Rome and received help in reconstruction after earthquake damage on one or more occasions under Augustus (Strab. 12.8.18 = p. 579; Suet. *Tib.* 8; see Magie, pp. 469, 1331f.). It was normal practice to expect and to receive such relief. Tiberius had given generous help to many of the greatest cities of Asia after the terrible earthquake of AD 17, though Laodicea is not mentioned as having suffered at that time.

It seems possible that behind later events lies a history of bad Laodicean relations with Rome, and that the royal status granted to members of a family of her citizens only accentuated her attitude of proud independence.[63] Perhaps this is the background of the remarkable words of Tacitus which describe the disaster he dates in AD 60: *Eodem anno ex inlustribus Asiae urbibus Laodicea tremore terrae prolapsa nullo a nobis remedio propriis opibus revaluit (Ann.* 14.27.1).[64] This was evidently unusual, and the pointedness of Tacitus's remark suggests that the case was notorious. Lightfoot (*Colossians and Philemon.*, p. 44n.) comments: 'In all other cases of earthquake which Tacitus records as happening in these Asiatic cities . . . he mentions the fact of their obtaining relief from the Senate or the Emperor.' Magie (p. 564) seems to infer that Rome was unwilling to help and that 'the inhabitants were forced to rebuild the city at their own expense'. I think this less likely than that the Laodiceans refused the offer. This is the implication of Tacitus's wording and the most natural reading of the case. It is tempting to speculate whether Tacitus might have seen a letter from Laodicea containing the refusal preserved in the Roman archives. Then his phrase *propriis opibus* might well render a Greek original ἐκ τῶν ἰδίων, which recurs with an almost defiant emphasis on Laodicean inscriptions of the years of reconstruction.

A further interesting text is contained in the Fourth Book of the Sibylline Oracles, written about AD 80 in Asia:

τλῆμον Λαοδίκεια, σὲ δὲ στρώσει ποτὲ σεισμὸς
πρηνίξας, στήσῃ δὲ πάλιν πόλις ἱδρυνθεῖσα (4.107-108).

We may compare three other Sibylline passages, 5.317-23; 5.290-91; 7.22-23. These may refer to the same earthquake: if the first does, it constitutes independent testimony that the whole district was involved in the disaster.[65] The special importance of 4.107-108, however, is that it alludes to the reconstruction. Why was this included in the Sibylline catalogue of woes, unless perhaps it had attracted special attention and was intended to authenticate the prophecy in the eyes of these who knew the actual sequel?

The severity of the catastrophe may have had long-term effects on the cities, and these can in part be traced. Hierapolis had probably shared much of the prosperity of Laodicea, and presumably accepted imperial aid, but its coinage, previously rich, ceases abruptly with the beardless Nero, and is scarcely resumed before Trajan.[66] Head in the *BMC* volumes on Phrygia, Lydia and Caria records no coin from any city of the Lycus district except Laodicea throughout the intervening period, and even Laodicea has only two items under Vespasian, but a richer series under Domitian. Colossae, Hydrela, Attuda and Trapezopolis have so few coins of other dates that no conclusions can be drawn from this absence,[67] but the abrupt numismatic poverty of Hierapolis, Laodicea and perhaps Tripolis is sufficiently marked to be suggestive. Laodicea set about the great task of recovery without external help.

The proud generosity of citizens to their community is not at all a Laodicean peculiarity: instances of such benefactions by individuals or guilds have already been cited.[68] The feature of Laodicea is the scale and ostentation of the donations, and the point which they derive from their relation to the reconstruction. And since there are comparatively few published inscriptions from Laodicea, whose site has been much despoiled and less explored, the existence of the following evidence is the more interesting, and its preservation largely due to the massiveness of the structures on which most of it was inscribed.

Apart from the large Hadrianic building, probably a gymnasium, most of the principal edifices whose ruins survive appear to date from the period of earthquake reconstruction.[69] First there is the *stadium amphitheatrum*, with an arena 900 feet long, semicircular at both ends, with continuous seating round the whole circumference (*CB* I.47). Its completion can be precisely dated to the latter part of the year 79, and it bears the proud claim of an individual, Nicostratus, that he erected it ἐκ τῶν ἰδίων, though in fact his death made it necessary for his heir to complete the work.[70]

The same phrase or an equivalent occurs on other inscriptions, some of them datable to this period. The same Nicostratus, styled φιλοκαῖσαρ, set up another dedication 'out of his own resources' in the same year (*IGRR* IV. 846). A similar phrase occurs in the record of the numerous offices and benefactions of one Q. Pomponius Flaccus, whose activity is attributed to the first century of the Empire.[71] Among other services he heated the covered walks and provided piped oil at the baths. It is insisted that he went to great personal expense. The provision of these refinements is characteristic, though they hardly suggest the needs of a period of basic reconstruction.

A final important example can be related to a period shortly before the composition of the Revelation. It may usefully be quoted in full, incorporating Ramsay's restoration of the name of the emperor: Δ[ιὶ] μεγίσ[τῳ] Σ[ω]τῆρι καὶ Αὐτοκράτορι [Δομιτιανῷ erased] Καίσαρι Σεβαστῷ ἀρχιερεῖ μεγίστῳ, δημαρχικῆς ἐξο[υσίας τὸ ?, ὑπάτῳ τὸ ?, αὐτοκράτορι τὸ ?, Τιβ]έρ[ιος Κλαύ]διος, Σεβαστοῦ ἀπελεύθερος, Τρύφων τοὺς πύργους καὶ τὰ περὶ τοὺς πύργους καὶ τὸ τρίπυλον σὺν [παντὶ τῷ κόσμῳ καθιέρωσεν] (*CB* I.74, No. 5 = *CIG* 3949 = *IGRR* IV. 847 = *MAMA* VI.2). Ramsay noted that the length of the erasure and the titulature suited Domitian rather than Nero, and a freedman of Claudius might still be active, especially if this were early in Domitian's reign. The improved transcription in *MAMA* includes a fragment of the last line of a preceding Latin text, and this lends some support to a dating c. 88-90.[72] J.G.C. Anderson observed that the stones of this inscription lay near the site of the Syrian gate of the city, and this may have been the structure referred to.[73] The erection of this great triple gate and towers falls within a generation after the earthquake, and they were the gift of an individual. New gates and fortifications may have marked the culmination of the rebuilding: they enabled the city to exclude whom it would.[74]

I conclude that there is good reason for seeing Rev. 3.17 against the background of the boasted affluence of Laodicea, notoriously exemplified in her refusal of Roman aid and her carrying through a great programme of reconstruction in a spirit of proud independence and ostentatious individual benefaction. The flourishing church was exposed as partaking of the standards of the society in which it lived (cf. *SC*, p. 428). It was spiritually self-sufficient and saw no need of Christ's aid. The following words are more specific: they connect its hidden needs with the assurance of Christ's remedy, and again the language employed derives additional force from its pointed allusion to some of the sources of the city's wealth.

5. *Poor and Blind and Naked* (Rev. 3.17)

There is strong emphasis in σύ, and in the use of the article before the predicate: 'It is thou who art self-satisfied and boastful that art the wretched one *par excellence*' (Charles, I.96).

It is surely the context of a great commercial city which explains the employment of the word ἀγοράσαι (v. 18; cf. Isa. 55.1 LXX and Mt. 25.9-10). The emphasis here is on παρ' ἐμοῦ: Christ is the source of the true remedy, and those who want spiritual goods of true quality must transact their business with him (cf. Charles, I.97). Many commentators have drawn attention to the relevant Laodicean industries, and I shall assume much of their material and enlarge on those aspects where a fuller consideration seems important.

(a) *Gold.* We have already discussed Laodicea as a banking centre. There is emphasis here on the purity of the refined gold Christ offers. Swete, p. 62, refers to the thought of a fiery trial by which the dross must be removed from the church, comparing Ps. 66.10 (LXX 65.10), Zech. 13.9, Isa. 1.25. The idea of cleansing through suffering appears in v. 19.

(b) *Eyesalve.* Many commentators have followed Ramsay (*CB* I.52; *SC*, pp. 419, 429) in relating κολλύριον to the medical school at Laodicea and the 'Phrygian powder' which he connects with it. The school, established in Strabo's time (12.8.20 = p. 580), was apparently in Laodicea, though its parent shrine of Men Karou lay in the territory of Attuda. Its founder, Zeuxis, is named on Laodicean coinage.[75] His school followed Herophilus of Chalcedon, a leading dogmatic physician of the third century BC, who is known to have written on ophthalmology (see L. Edelstein in *OCD*, p. 423).

The connection of 'eyesalve' with this institution at Laodicea is only an inference, derived from two passages, neither of which attributes such a product directly to the city. (1) Pseudo-Aristotle, *Mir. Auscult.* 58 = 834b, describes the mines of the island of Demonesus at Chalcedon. Speaking of malachite (χρυσοκόλλα), the writer refers to the high price commanded by the best quality of this mineral: καὶ γὰρ φάρμακον ὀφθαλμῶν ἐστιν. He comments on the exceptional eyesight of the copper-miners, and concludes οἱ ἰατροὶ τῷ ἄνθει τοῦ χαλκοῦ καὶ τῇ τέφρᾳ τῇ Φρυγίᾳ χρῶνται πρὸς τοὺς ὀφθαλμούς.[76] (2) Galen, in a passage dealing successively with the treatment of the eyes and ears (*de San. Tuend.* 6.12),[77] writes ὀφθαλμοὺς δὲ τονώσεις τῷ διὰ τοῦ Φρυγίου λίθου χρώμενος ξηρῷ κολλυρίῳ...

The common element of the two texts is their ascription to Phrygia of an important eyesalve material. Ramsay observes that Laodicea was the one famous medical centre in Phrygia and that to the Greeks 'Phrygian' sometimes stood for 'Laodicean' (*SC*, p. 419).[78] The evidence, thus baldly stated, does not justify the conclusion so often assumed as fact. There are however some circumstantial pointers which favour the supposition.

The contexts of both the passages cited are helpful here. The first refers to Chalcedon, and the Laodicean physicians are known to have followed a pioneer ophthalmologist from Chalcedon. In the second Galen immediately proceeds to describe a treatment of the ears with an ointment explicitly Laodicean: πρότερον μὲν ἐν Λαοδικείᾳ μόνῃ τῆς Ἀσίας σκευαζομένου καλλίστου, νυνὶ δὲ καὶ κατ' ἄλλας πόλεις. His point may have been to draw attention in this case to a fact which everybody then knew to be true of the eyesalve.

Surviving ancient works on ophthalmic medicine are most impressive.[79] The principal first-century authorities are Celsus and Scribonius Largus. Both give lengthy series of recipes for eyesalves (Cels. 6.6.2-8, 30ff.; Scrib. Larg. *Comp.* 18-37). In one of them, named *rhinion, lapis Phrygius* is mentioned as an ingredient (Cels. 6.6.30): another was sometimes called *tephron* from its ashen colour (Cels. 6.6.7). Although Celsus relies much elsewhere on the Hippocratic Corpus, these passages are evidently drawn from a different source.[80] Both Romans seem to follow a common medical tradition: their prefaces suggest a critical dependence on the dietary theories of Asclepiades and a common acknowledgment of the authority of Herophilus of Chalcedon.[81] Herophilus emphasized the value of medicaments: so Celsus (5.1ff.) describes the individual effects of many drugs which are elsewhere compounded into eyesalves, again in a non-Hippocratic passage.

The scanty authorities suggest a rapid development of ophthalmology from about the Augustan period.[82] Many oculists are mentioned *passim* by the medical writers. Wellmann dates the oculists' stamps frequent in the western Roman provinces to the second century onwards. The titles and uses they record compare closely with the literary accounts of eyesalves (thus *Inscr. Orelli*

4233-34). The facts point to the existence of a widespread movement based on a common tradition of scientific medicine. The evidence of Celsus, in particular, suggests that this movement was ultimately derived from the work of Herophilus of Chalcedon.

The Laodicean school of medicine was Herophilean, its founder was succeeded by Alexander Philalethes, another distinguished pupil of Asclepiades (see Wellmann in *PW* on Alex. No. 99), and Alexander's pupil at Laodicea was the Herophilean Demosthenes. This Demosthenes, also surnamed Philalethes, was renowned as an ophthalmologist, and wrote a standard work on his subject which had great influence and was extant in translation in mediaeval times (see *PW* Dem. No. 11). In his person we have explicit evidence for the connection of Laodicea with a leading figure of first-century ophthalmology. He was the product of a school which presumably continued the specialized interest of its master Herophilus.

Alexander may have lived under Nero. His influence, and that of the Laodicean school, may have been paramount at the date of the Revelation.[83] The position and commercial character of Laodicea would readily foster the marketing of such knowledge. The words of Epictetus (Arr. *Epict.* 3.21.21) allude to a dissemination of *collyria* among those who lacked the knowledge to apply them. We may conjecture that the skilled treatment of patients was sometimes subordinated in Laodicea to the more lucrative business of selling patent medicines.

It is not possible to identify any of the known salves as from Laodicea. In the recorded recipes, however, the same active constituents constantly recur: metallic salts, especially those of copper and zinc, alum, and many herbal drugs. The copper derivatives recall the pseudo-Aristotle passage which mentions the 'Phrygian powder', and similar zinc compounds are used in modern eye ointments.[84] It would be interesting to know how readily a suitable combination of these items was available to Laodicea.[85]

The 'Phrygian stone' again cannot be securely identified, though there is a plausible case for a conjecture which would suit a Laodicean provenance. In scientific contexts the term seems to be used consistently, subject to the semantic vagueness habitual in ancient nomenclature.[86] Pliny, as well as Celsus, associates it with other minerals said to have been used in eyesalves, though he says it was itself useful only for dyeing (*NH* 36.36.145ff.). Forms of alum, notably *schiston* or *scissile*, are mentioned in the relevant passages in these writers, and their medicinal value described in Celsus, 5.2. W.G. Spencer accordingly suggests in *LCL* Celsus, Vol. II, p. xix, that the associated 'Phrygian stone' was a kind of alum. As alum is readily pulverized, this would facilitate identification also with the τέφρα. The waters of Hierapolis are said to be rich in alum (*CB* I.106), this probably being the constituent which made them so remarkably adapted to the dyeing industry (cf. Plin. and Strab. 13.4.14 = p. 630). Pliny further describes the use both of *schiston* and other forms of alum (*alumen*) in ointments for both the eyes and ears (*NH* 35.52.186, 188f.). And, finally, I am assured that local people today find medicinal value in bathing their eyes in the Hierapolis waters, the alum content apparently being the beneficial agent.

We thus find considerable circumstantial reason for connecting the 'eyesalve' motif with Laodicea. The city probably marketed extensively and profitably an ointment developed locally from available materials, whose exact composition may have been kept secret from commercial rivals. The church in Laodicea, the city where they claimed to treat physical myopia, was blind to its spiritual blindness.[87] The words might lend themselves to varied application. There might for instance be a further contrast between this human concoction and the God-given medicinal waters of Hierapolis. The diagnosis was that they needed what only Christ could supply.

It seems unnecessary to attach to the *collyrium* of Christ a specific allegorical meaning, like Swete's 'ἐλεγμός of the Holy Spirit' (pp. 62-63): the emphasis is rather on Christ himself as the true source of spiritual vision (Beckwith, p. 491; cf. Col. 2.2-3).

(c) *White raiment.* In this case the local facts have been more plainly preserved, and it will not be necessary to cast the net so wide. Commentators as early as Trench (p. 207) have seen allusion to the clothing industry of Laodicea and in particular a contrast with the glossy black wool of its sheep. Knowledge of the breed rests primarily upon Strabo (12.8.16 = p. 578): 'The country around Laodicea produces sheep remarkable not only for the softness of their wool, in which they surpass even that of Miletus, but also for its raven-black colour. And they get a splendid revenue from it . . . ' Vitruvius attributes the colour of the Laodicean sheep to the character of the local water and evidently alludes to them in his use of the phrase *coracino colore* (8.3.14). His words suggest a deliberate attempt by breeders to achieve this colour, whatever the merits of the means allegedly used.[88]

The subject of the woollen industry is clearly treated by Ramsay in *CB* I.40-42 (cf. *SC*, pp. 416ff.). The edict of Diocletian on prices, of AD 301, to which he refers, is conveniently accessible in *CIL* III.Suppl., pp. 1910-53. The prominence of Laodicea in the trade of that date is abundantly attested by the innumerable items named from it (pp. 1942-49 *passim*).[89] A guild of ἀπλουργοί is mentioned in a Laodicean inscription of uncertain date (*CIG* 3938 = *CB* I.74, No. 8), and the city was apparently notable for woollen *paenulae* before the date of the Revelation (Plin. *NH* 8.73.190).[90] Most of the categories of clothing mentioned in the sources were not peculiar to Laodicea, and some were adaptations of types originating elsewhere (cf. *CB* I.41), but the local appropriation of so many kinds is a striking testimony to the city's manufacturing and commercial vigour.[91]

I find no record that any of these types was individually described as of black wool, though we may presume that the local material was extensively used.[92]

In considering the background of Rev. 3.17f. we must note that the two associated cities were also celebrated for their woollen industries. The wool of Colossae gave the name *colossinus* to the colour said by Pliny to be that of the cyclamen flower (Strab. 12.8.16 = p. 578; Plin. *NH* 21.27.51).[93] The inscriptions of Hierapolis attest guilds of wool-washers (Judeich, No. 40) and of dyers (Nos. 50, 195), and Strabo (13.4.14 = p. 630) attributes to the waters a notable dyeing industry.

The terms of the text do not suggest an undiscriminating reference to the trade of the three cities so much as emphasis on a peculiarly Laodicean product which had enabled that city to defeat its commercial rivals in a field where they were also celebrated. In view of Pliny's words *lanarum nigrae nullum colorem bibunt* (*NH* 8.73.193), following closely upon his account of the wool of Laodicea, we might suppose that the distinction consisted in this, that Laodicea dispensed with the costs of dyeing for the luxury market by promoting a fashion in black glossy fabrics from the natural fleeces of an animal developed by its own breeders.[94]

A local pagan evaluation of the symbolism of black and white clothing exists in a curious passage of Artemidorus of Daldis (2nd cent. AD). In divination from dreams white garments presage death for the sick and black recovery, for the dead are dressed in white while the survivors mourn in black (*Onirocr.* 2.3 = p. 86). This omen forms part of a considerable paragraph on the disadvantages of white clothing, and the passage later deals with such Laodicean specialities as βίρρος and φαινόλης [*sic*].[95] We cannot draw firm conclusions from this kind of material, but the evidence gives insight into popular superstition on a point where our text stands in sharp contrast.

The use of 'white raiment' in Rev. 3.18 must be related to Dan. 7.9 (cf. Rev. 1.14), but most recent commentators have concurred in seeing local significance in the words.[96] The primary meaning conveyed by the symbol here and elsewhere in the book seems to be righteousness: hence it was the garb of the heavenly kingdom (Rev. 4.4; 19.4). There may be also the thought of the festal garments provided for the coming of a prince in triumph, an aspect more prominent in the slightly different context of Sardis (Rev. 3.4-5; cf. Eccles. 9.8). Trench (p. 211) sees here the righteousness of Christ not only imparted but imputed: the Revelation speaks of white garments as given (6.11; 19.8), and as made white through washing in the blood of the Lamb (7.14).[97] The emphasis is well stated by Kiddle (p. 59): 'The looms of their city could not weave cloth to cover their sins; . . . righteousness was the white raiment which God demanded, . . . and this they must get from Christ'.

So we conclude that in the whole passage local facts are used to present Christ as the source of the remedy for the church's hidden needs of spiritual wealth, vision and holiness.

6. *The Door and the Throne*

Local allusion has not so often been seen in the concluding verses of the letter. Ramsay regarded Rev. 3.19-22 as forming an epilogue to the whole series, and not as part of the Laodicean letter at all (*SC*, pp. 431-33). He gives in effect three reasons: (1) that such an epilogue is needed to conclude the whole group; (2) that it is incomprehensible why faithful Philadelphia and ineffective Laodicea should alone be ranked among those whom Christ loves; (3) that 'all reference to the Laodiceans has ceased. The final promise has no apparent relation to their situation and character' (p. 431).

The first two points may be briefly answered; the third is central to our theme. On (1) it seems sufficient to say that the letter itself equally requires a conclusion parallel in form to those of the other epistles; on (2) that this is in fact 'a touching and unexpected manifestation of love to those who deserve it least' (Charles, p. 99; cf. Peake, p. 253n.). All the churches knew the love of Christ, but it is specially mentioned in encouraging the faithful and in earnest appeal to the complacent.[98]

The third point is the crux of the matter. Ramsay's case for the separation of these verses has not commended itself to other commentators, but others have rarely related their exegesis closely to local circumstances where he declined to make the attempt.[99] There is however reason to think that the message of these verses was relevant to the church in Laodicea. The following paragraphs are an attempt to answer Ramsay's third point from evidence of the kind he has himself provided.

a. *The Background of Rev 3.20.* It is important to look rather more deeply into the historical background than the case might seem at first sight to warrant. A brief sketch of the city's relations with Rome is instructive here. Despite its vulnerable position it initially resisted Mithridates, but later surrendered to him its Roman commander Oppius (App. *Mithr.* 3.20; cf. Chapot, pp. 26n., 37). The Peace of Dardanus (probably 85 BC) is said to have included a clause granting amnesty to cities of Asia which had supported Mithridates (Memnon, frag. 35, cited in Greenidge and Clay, *Sources for Roman History*, p. 150). Sulla's settlement was nevertheless severe, though he granted freedom to certain allied cities. Laodicea, a possible deserving case, is not named among them (App. *Mithr.* 9.61): its position is not however clear, for an inscription of the period acknowledges gratitude to the Roman people for an unspecified benefit (*CIL* I.587 = *CIG* 5881; cf. *CIL* VI.374 and see Chapot, p. 37).[100] In the following years Asia suffered severely from the crippling taxation imposed successively by Sulla and Lucullus and from the rapacity of its governors, and Laodicea figures prominently in the records, despite its apparent claim to Roman favour. Sulla demanded immediate payment of five years' taxation, an exaction which caused great suffering and debt in the cities (App. *Mithr.* 9.62-63). Plutarch gives the amount as 20,000 talents, and records that the people were subjected to the insults of the soldiery billeted upon them, to whom their hosts were compelled to pay a daily sum. They also had to provide dinner (δεῖπνον) for the soldiers and their guests, and clothing and daily subsidies for their officers (Plut. *Sulla* 25.2 = pp. 467-68; cf. Reinach, *Mithridate Eupator*, p. 209). Laodicea, as capital of a *conventus*, and temporarily as point of entry into Cilicia, was inevitably a place occupied by the governor's staff and troops, and consequently suffered the imposition of this abuse of traditional hospitality. It was the scene of a corrupt and scandalous trial influenced by Verres (Cic. *II Verr.* 1.30.76), which again showed Roman administration in its worst light.

Before the Sullan indemnity had been paid, Lucullus levied a 25 per cent tax on crops, and taxes on servants and houses (App. *Mithr.* 12.83 fin.), a severe blow to a city whose early prosperity depended much on the fertility of its soil (Strab. 12.8.16 = p. 578). Then Flaccus confiscated twenty pounds of Jewish gold at Laodicea in 62 BC (Cic. *pro Flacco* 28.68). The results of years of misrule are strikingly reflected in the correspondence of Cicero's Cilician governorship. Writing from Laodicea within three days of his arrival in his province, he refers to the patent wounds inflicted by his predecessor Appius (*ad Att.* 5.15.2; cf. *ad Fam.* 13.56). A few days later he has concluded that the district has been permanently ruined: in Laodicea, Apamea and Synnada they could not pay the capital tax (*ad Att.* 5.16.2). He refers to this again as *acerbissimam exactionem capitum atque ostiorum* (*ad Fam.* 3.8.5). Presumably this was similar to the Lucullan tax.

Cicero himself is determined that he and his staff shall not profit a farthing from his administration,[101] and such is the local feeling that he will not permit acceptance even of those perquisites allowed by the recent *Lex Julia de Repetundis*, or of any enforced hospitality whatever.[102] So he writes: 'Understand that we are declining to accept not only hay or what is usually given under the Julian law, but even firewood, and nobody is accepting anything except four beds and a roof, and in many places not even a roof, and in most cases we remain in a tent' (*ad Att.* 5.16.3). Plutarch comments on the probity of his governorship in similar terms: he received no bribes even from kings, he kept open house to visitors, and freed the provincials from providing δεῖπνα (Plut. *Cic.* 36.2-3 = p. 879).[103]

It would be hazardous to argue from the events of this period to the situation of the Revelation without some indication of the persistence of attitudes engendered by this Roman misrule. Whereas Smyrna boasted a fidelity to Rome rooted in distant history (Tac. *Ann.* 4.56), Laodicea displays a vigorous and self-sufficient independence. Some fragments of local evidence illustrate the idea further.

A decree of the *boule* of Hierapolis, unfortunately not datable (J.G.C. Anderson, *JHS* 17 [1897], p. 411, No. 14), legislates against extortion by *paraphulakes* on duty in its village dependencies. They are to provide for their journeys from their own resources and to

requisition nothing except μόνον ξύλα καὶ ἄχυρα καὶ μον[ήν], terms
which precisely reflect in the local setting those of the Julian law.

Again, under Hadrian, a Roman proconsul and his staff on a visit
to Smyrna billeted themselves upon the best household in the city in
the absence of their host. The latter on his return at night angrily
expelled his powerful visitor from the house. The proconsul was the
future emperor Antoninus: the outraged householder was Polemo
the sophist, of Laodicea (Philostr. *Vit. Soph.* 1.25). We shall note
further the influence of this Laodicean family which became the
most powerful in Asia Minor and its effect on the character of the
city. The present point is that even after the Julian law Roman
officials long retained the power to requisition lodging, and that such
imposition fell upon the richest cities and individuals. Buckler and
Calder observe that the point of a phrase in a late inscription of
Laodicea (*MAMA* VI.15, lines 8-10) is in its allusion to the city's
ancient character as a *Residenzstadt* which had entertained the
proconsuls of Asia.

The interpretation of Rev. 3.20 must yet be considered more
closely. Here we may note that this background contrasts with
Christ's refusal to force an entry. His coming is not a threat, but a
precious promise for the individual who will invite him, and the
δεῖπνον of which he speaks is not extorted with insult, but 'the
symbol of an enduring friendship' (Rudwick and Green, p. 178n.).[104]

This line of thought does not exhaust the possible local background of the verse. Rudwick and Green say: 'The source of the
imagery is again probably local. The city was set foursquare on one of
the most important road junctions in Asia Minor, and each of the
four city gates opened on to a busy trade route. The inhabitants must
have been very familiar with the belated traveller who "stood at the
door and knocked" for admission.' Specific reference to the city gate
seems possible in view of the very recently built monumental triple
gateway and fortifications which apparently completed the reconstruction and equipped the citizens to deny entrance to whom they
would. Known officials include νυκτοστράτηγοι and παραφύλακες.
The wealth in the banks was not to be accessible to the visits of
potential thieves.

These suggestions are not necessarily mutually exclusive, for the
concept of a closed door may have aroused varied connotations in the
mind of a Christian in Laodicea. Deep feelings of a people are often
shown on their sepulchral monuments, and tombs in Phrygia were

regarded as the houses of the dead, and regularly bore the representation of a door. It is characteristic that the form of descecration
feared was the intrusion of an unauthorized corpse into the grave: the
outsider who gained admission evidently deprived the owner of his
exclusive possession and privilege in the after-life.[105] The eschatological aspect of our passage stands in contrast with this thinking:
Christ's blessing is not exclusive; he will even share his throne.

b. *The Background of Rev 3.21.* There is a possible connection of
background between Rev. 3.20 and 3.21. Events of 40 BC must have
had far-reaching implications for Laodicea. In that year Labienus
Parthicus invaded Asia, and 'no city closed its gates till he reached
Laodicea-on-the-Lycus, which the orator Zeno and his son Polemo,
soon to be famous, held against him' (Tarn and Charlesworth in
CAH X.47). This statement appears to rest on Strabo 14.2.24 =
p. 660.[106] The result of this resolute action was that Polemo received
a throne, and Strabo elsewhere stresses his benefactions to his native
city as among the causes which made her great (12.8.16 = p. 578).
Polemo's elevation in fact followed closely on his defence of Laodicea.
Antony made him ruler of a part of Cilicia in 39 BC (App. *Bell. Civ.*
5.75) and in 36 BC he was already king of Pontus (Dio Cass. 49.25.4;
Plutarch, *Antony* 38.3 = p. 933).

Lightfoot (*Colossians and Philemon*, p. 6) writes: 'More to our
purpose, as illustrating the boasted wealth and prosperity of the city,
which appeared as a reproach and a stumbling block in an apostle's
eyes, are the facts that one of its citizens, Polemo, became a king and
a father of kings . . . ' He did not however apply this observation to
Rev. 3.21.

Much of the evidence for the subsequent history of the Zenonids is
summarized in *CB* I.42-46, which includes a conjectural genealogical
table on p. 46 (cf. also *CRE*, p. 27). Polemo obtained a distant link
with the imperial family through his marriage with Pythodoris, the
granddaughter of Antony. At least one of their sons became a king,
Zeno of Armenia (Strab. 12.3.29 = p. 556 with *IGRR* IV. 1407); their
daughter Tryphaena married Cotys, king of Thrace, and was in turn
the mother of three kings, Rhoemetalces of Thrace, Polemo II of
Pontus, and Cotys of Armenia.[107] Little is known of this dynasty,
and nothing of their later relations with their city of origin. Cyzicus
claimed Tryphaena and her sons: an inscription of AD 37 acclaims
their visit to their mother there, and exalts their greatness as
receiving their kingdoms by the gift of a god, Caligula (*IGRR*
IV. 145; cf. 144, 146-47).

Meanwhile a branch of the family continued to live in Laodicea, and figures prominently on its coinage. Polemo Philopatris (*BMC Phrygia*, Laod. Nos. 145-46) may have been the nephew of King Polemo I. From his time representatives can be traced in every generation until about the Domitianic period. A probable genealogy can be reconstructed from the coinage, despite its scarcity in the years after the earthquake.[108] The sophist Polemo flourished under Hadrian; he resided primarily at Smyrna, but continued to favour his native Laodicea, and was buried there. Philostratus' account of him gives a remarkable picture of the arrogance of phenomenal wealth, influence and success (*Vit. Soph.* 1.25).[109]

The general appropriateness of Rev. 3.21 to the church in a city which had provided a dynasty of kings is apparent, especially as we have reason to think that its character was much influenced by this family. The application of the background is still questionable. Did the city owe its affluence in some degree to royal favours, or did the royal branch perhaps sever its links with its city of origin for estates in Cyzicus or Iconium?[110] The arrogance of the local branch and its influence on the fortunes of the city is attested: Polemo the sophist, according to Philostratus, treated kings as his inferiors. The Laodicean branch certainly appropriated imperial and royal names from the other (cf. *CB* I.45): perhaps the ultimate status-symbol at Laodicea was to boast a connection with royalty evidenced by the use of its names and attributes (cf. *CRE*, p. 384n.). Such a boast had no real content. The 'god' who granted a client-king his realm would as readily deprive him of it. Polemo's elevation had been, in a sense, the prize of a victory: this was no longer true of his successors. And they were not likely to share their actual power with any aspiring commoner, even a kinsman from Laodicea. But the throne of Christ will not be his exclusive possession.[111]

c. *Some Observations on the Interpretation of Rev 3.20.* Two principal views are held: (1) that this is a call to the individual heart in the present;[112] (2) an eschatological interpretation is preferred by many recent commentators.[113] Some see in addition a eucharistic flavour.[114]

Beckwith maintains the eschatological view strongly and exclusively. He writes: 'The popular representation of Christ knocking at the door of men's hearts, though containing a great truth (Lk. 19[10]), is not what is intended here.' He emphasizes the close connection of vv. 20 and 21, the similarity with eschatological passages elsewhere, especially the striking parallel with Lk. 22.29-30 (where eating and drinking in the heavenly kingdom is linked with thrones and judgment), and the analogies with other letters.

Charles connects the verse more closely with v. 19, and observes that whereas Christ there admonishes the church, he turns here explicitly to the individual (ἐάν τις). On this personal view the significant Biblical background is in Cant. 5.2 rather than in the eschatological parallels in the New Testament. In this case 'we have the beginning of the spiritual interpretation of the Song in terms of the relation of Christ to the soul' (Anderson Scott).

An exhaustive treatment of the problem is beyond our scope and purpose. In any case the alternatives need not be regarded as mutually exclusive. But there are some points which favour the personal view and accord with the approaches impressed on me by the whole bearing of the present study. (1) The eschatological parallels of Rev. 3.20 are parallel in diction, but the thought differs (so Charles, p. 101).[115] John may have known Lk. 22, but if he uses it, he does so in a characteristically independent way. (2) Conversely, Deissmann (*LAE*, p. 463) quotes a Syrian inscription of uncertain date, probably from a door, as a Christian citation of the LXX of Cant. 5.2 connected with Rev. 3.20 and interpreted allegorically of Christ. This points at least to the current recognition of this background in the early church. (3) Analogy with the other letters can be misleading. Similarity of form and repetition of phrase and symbol often mask the individuality of their character, context and background. Rudwick and Green consider that whereas the message of the other letters is essentially didactic, the Laodicean is kerygmatic; the call to repentance elsewhere admonitory, but here promissory.

These suggestions seem to be reinforced by the present study. The emphasis in v. 20a is upon the individual and his voluntary act: the promise of v. 20b seems meaningful within the setting of his contemporary life. He needed the fellowship of Christ in the present as the antidote to the self-sufficiency of a Christless church. Christ would not abuse and exploit his hospitality as Roman potentates did. Only with the personal presence of Christ would he conquer. It is an easy transition to the promise of the conqueror's future hope in terms which in Laodicea would surely recall the distinctions conferred on the Zenonids as the prize of victory.

7. *Summary of Conclusions*

1. There is reason to believe that an influential Jewish community existed in the Lycus cities, but that it was closely assimilated to the character of pagan society.

2. The Laodicean letter stands somewhat apart from the others of the series. It is also less distinctly echoed in other sections of the Revelation itself. Some phrases have an Old Testament background, but these are pointedly applied to the recipients, and some striking symbols which have no apparent Jewish background are widely recognized as containing local allusion.

3. The reference to 'the Amen', the most Jewish phrase in the letter, has close parallels in Colossians. The Colossian heresy was compounded of a 'nonconformist Judaism' and an incipient Gnosticism. Such a philosophical syncretism accommodating Christianity to current thought-forms probably centred and persisted at Laodicea. The relationship of Col. 1 to Rev. 3.14 is more than literary: the two passages are addressed to related situations.

4. The 'lukewarmness' of Laodicea is to be related to the local water-supply, as suggested by Rudwick and Green. Their interpretation of the term as denoting ineffectiveness rather than half-heartedness is to be accepted. Further study confirms their suggestion that 'hot' and 'cold' allude respectively to Hierapolis and Colossae. Some details of the background and its application remain obscure.

5. It is also accepted that the words 'I am rich . . . ' (v. 17) allude to the aftermath of the great earthquake of AD 60. It is further suggested that this ostentatious self-sufficiency reached a climax when the reconstruction was completed by the erection of great public buildings at the expense of individual citizens in the years immediately preceding the Domitianic date of the Revelation. The monumental triple gate thus donated may have been in mind in the writing of Rev. 3.20.

6. The formal evidence for the often repeated statement that an eyesalve was manufactured in Laodicea seems inconclusive. There are however considerations which support the idea: it can be shown that the local medical school produced influential specialists in ophthalmology, and there are tentative reasons for identifying the 'Phrygian stone' or 'Phrygian powder' with a substance found locally.

7. The contrast between 'white raiment' (v.18) and the clothing made from the wool of the local breed of black sheep is accepted and further illustrated.

8. We cannot follow Ramsay in relegating vv. 19-22 to an epilogue. They are an integral part of the letter and are related to the local situation.

9. The 'door' (v. 20) was a significant symbol in Phrygia, and might be variously applied. It seems that the verse is best explained against a scriptural background of Cant. 5.2 and may be related also to the local setting. The exploitation of local wealth by corrupt Roman officials and the enforced hospitality for their staff fell heavily and persistently on Laodicea as an affluent *conventus* capital. Christ in contrast pleads for the willing hospitality of the individual heart.

10. The connection between vv. 20 and 21 confirms the hypothesis of an allusion to the Zenonid dynasty, the Laodicean family which became the greatest in Asia Minor after Polemo shut out an invader and received a throne as the prize of victory.

11. It is argued from the thought of the passage and confirmed from the background that the reference of Rev. 3.20 is primarily personal and present rather than eschatological.

12. It may be added that this letter makes little contribution to the wider understanding of the problems of the church in Asia. It offers no light on persecution or on racial and religious tensions. The reason may perhaps be found in the easy integration of the church here with its surroundings. The trials and conflicts were only acute when Christians stood apart from Judaism without compromising with pagan standards. Here they were evidently open to sectarian Judaism and syncretistic influences.

EPILOGUE

Where, after all, does this study lead? The basic driving force through the preceding pages has been the contention that the symbolism of the letters was forcibly applicable to the original readers. It is, if you will, 'audience-criticism', the attempt to determine the *Sitz im Leben* in the recipient churches. But I am sometimes troubled when settings are offered which seem but tenuous constructs based on varying conjectures about the theological motivations of a Biblical writer. I have endeavoured, more simply, to put my text in context. To do that requires rigorous and balanced historical study. It is essential to that balance to recognize the pervasive Old Testament influence on the mind of the writer while focusing more particularly on the application to the needs of the churches in their Gentile environment. I am not setting out to oppose a 'Hellenistic' to a Jewish style of interpretation. Nor am I excluding the validity of other approaches, unless they are held in forms which seem to overrule discussion of the contextual evidence. The heart of the matter is that I have tried to document the setting. There are many uncertainties, and I have sometimes made my own guesses. But I want to make their status clear, to present evidence, acknowledge its limitations, and exhibit its possibilities fairly.

I have offered specific conclusions in their place. In this final summary I append some reflections on the implications for further study.

First, then, I have suggested a number of new interpretations and refinements or reassessments of old ones. Many of them are no doubt slight enough, but I believe they illuminate some important passages and collectively represent a fruitful approach to the interpretation of the book.

Second, the thrust of the whole case points towards a larger argument for the date and setting of the Revelation. My view is not novel. It is rather that I think more pieces of the jig-saw may be assembled. If their placing is accepted, they may enlarge and extend a widely received picture and help in understanding an obscure phase of Christian history.

Third, the possible light on the post-70 situation of the church raises larger critical issues elsewhere. Directly this is a stimulus to historical study, indirectly another challenge to the facile methods by which critical questions of far-reaching import are often foreclosed. The very important, if sharply debatable, recent work of J.A.T. Robinson, *Redating the New Testament* (London, 1976), is salutary here in its exposure of the fragility of many critical structures. This is not to endorse his conclusions uncritically: I differ from him, as it happens, on the central point here, his early dating of Revelation.

This study also relates to trends and directions which have taken clearer shape since the original research was completed. I see a high significance in the recent work of E.A. Judge, whose earlier monograph *The Social Pattern of Christian Groups in the First Century* (London, 1960) has sometimes been cited as the starting-point of the 'sociological' approach to New Testament study. But Judge writes rather as a social historian than as a sociologist proper. His seminal article 'Paul and Classical Society'[1] surveys the state of our knowledge of Paul's context, the quality of our primary texts against the scantiness of secondary tradition, and charts the possibilities for fruitful exploration. This book aspires in part to offer a modest contribution to the study of the social context of the Revelation in the course of the attempt to realize the writer's concern for a rigorously argued context.

Recent years have been marked by the publications of such scholars as G. Theissen, J.G. Gager, A.J. Malherbe, H.C. Kee, R.F. Hock, J.H. Elliott, and now notably W.A. Meeks in *The First Urban Christians* (Yale, 1983). While warmly welcoming this explosion of interest in the New Testament context, I am anxious that the focus shall remain on what I have chosen to call 'social history', as a rigorous discipline directed to the specifics of place and time, rather than on a concept of 'sociology' which may be tempted to impose a theoretical model on the essentially fragmentary evidence. 'The theories', according to Judge, 'have usually been hammered out in the laboratory of a South-Seas-island anthropologist, and then transposed half-way around the world, and across two millennia, without adequate testing for applicability in the new setting: so powerful is the assumption of the indelible pattern of human social behaviour.'[2] The complex culture of the Asian cities was a far enough cry from our common stereotypes of Romans, Greeks and Jews, and we must strive to handle representatively the idiosyncrasies and the silences of our evidence.

NOTES

Notes to Chapter 1

1. The usual 'contemporary-historical' view which links the book with a Domitianic persecution has however been challenged by B. Newman, 'The Fallacy of the Domitian Hypothesis: Critique of the Irenaeus Source as a Witness for the Contemporary-historical Approach to the Interpretation of the Apocalypse', *NTS* 10 (1963-64), pp. 133-8. Newman sees in the Revelation an anti-Gnostic polemic. I agree with his criticism of the use often made of apocalyptic parallels, but would not rest the argument for a persecution setting upon such premises. The historical problem of a Domitianic persecution merits close study in its own right.

Some of the ablest of most recent studies have further renewed questions which had previously commanded a measure of agreement, the Domitianic dating and the persecution setting. J.A.T. Robinson in particular has championed an earlier dating in his *Redating the New Testament* (London, 1976), J.P.M. Sweet, *Revelation* (London, 1979), pp. 25-34, and P. Prigent, *L'Apocalypse de Saint Jean* (Lausanne and Paris, 1982), p. 375, have played down the persecution factor under Domitian, while A.A. Bell, *NTS* 25 (1978-79), pp. 93-102, argues from denial of the persecution to rejection of the Domitianic dating.

The difficulty of Rev. 17.10 for the dating must be conceded. If unsolved in any case, it is difficult to fit the verse to a Domitianic date without evident special pleading. Yet the possibilities remain diverse. I am reluctant to postulate the inclusion here of an unassimilated earlier oracle in a book marked overall by an intricate structure, merely to avoid a difficulty.

This book will seek to explore the situations of the letters with due regard to the dimensions of the problems. I suggest that 'persecution' is not a simply defined term, to be discovered by clear criteria, but that complex pressures existed in the historical situation, and might be activated by authorities not necessarily predisposed to 'persecute', but adopting policies which impinged on a vulnerable group. It is important to stress the complexity of the setting, and the wide variations of local circumstance, where some views of a background of Gnosticism or some other generalized opposition are too simply conceived. I prefer to visualize a varying impact of often opposite pressures sharpened by the incidental outworking of public policy. Such a view may differ from Sweet and others less in substance than in perspective and degree; I want to stress the severity of the trial present and impending, and not to deny it the title 'persecution' from the Christian viewpoint, whatever the official view.

2. Cf. S. Neill, *The Interpretation of the New Testament 1861-1961*, p. 346, where in his concluding assessment of modern scholarship he criticizes the lack of the scientist's self-criticism in the rigorous testing of hypotheses.

3. There is however no ground for considering the book pseudonymous in the manner of earlier apocalypses. The writer's name was admittedly John: the question is 'Which John?' A recent important discussion of the complexities of the origin of the Johannine literature is in E.S. Fiorenza, 'The Quest for the Johannine School: The Apocalypse and the Fourth Gospel', *NTS* 23 (1977), pp. 402-27.

4. For general discussions of the issues of dating see H.B. Swete, *The Apocalypse of St. John* (2nd edn; London, 1907), pp. xcix-cv; I.T. Beckwith, *The Apocalypse of John* (New York, 1919), pp. 197-208; R.H. Charles, *A Critical and Exegetical Commentary on the Revelation of St. John* (Edinburgh, 1920), I, pp. xci-xcvii. Subsequent references to these authors will relate to these commentaries and editions unless otherwise specified, in the case of Charles to the first volume of his commentary unless otherwise specified. See now also Robinson, *Redating*.

5. The emphasis on the reconstruction rather than the original disaster meets J. Moffatt's objection that the incident lay too far in the past ('The Revelation of St. John the Divine', *The Expositor's Greek Testament*, ed. W. Robertson Nicoll [1910], V. 371). Subsequent referrences to Moffatt will relate to this commentary.

6. C.C. Torrey recognizes the postulated reference of Rev. 6.6 to this decree as a strong argument, but argues that parallel action might have been taken by other rulers (*The Apocalypse of John* [1958], p. 79). This however seems to misapprehend the situation. The literary authorities make it clear that this edict was an unprecedented outrage which violated accepted principles of agriculture (see on Philadelphia, Chapter 8).

7. W.M. Ramsay, 'Some Inscriptions of Colonia Caesarea Antiochea', *JRS* 14 (1924), pp. 179-84, No. 6. See further on Philad., pp. 158ff. Despite Rostovtzeff, however, it is not certain that this famine was more than local, or that some unrecorded famine might not underlie the present situation.

8. *Coins of the Roman Empire in the British Museum*, II.311, Domitian, No. 62; cf. the *denarius*, No. 63; see also E. Stauffer, *Christus und die Caesaren*, p. 165 (ET p. 152), and cf. Rev. 1.16, 20; 2.1; 3.1.

9. See the work of W.M. Calder, discussed under Philad., pp. 170-74.

10. There is nothing in the letters which might serve, for instance, to support an unambiguous determination whether or not the Temple yet stood in Jerusalem. But I should argue that as a whole they imply a situation which presupposes the distant and complex outworkings of its fall. If Rev. 11.1-2 be invoked, I must reply that this passage seems to me open to diverse explanation. It is not necessarily a proof of the contemporary existence of the Temple. Charles and others, following Wellhausen, regard the passage as an unassimilated quotation of a pre-70 oracle. See however G.B. Caird, *The Revelation of St. John the Divine* (London, 1966), p. 131.

11. See e.g. A.H. M'Neile, *The Gospel according to St. Matthew*, pp. 257-58; D. Hill, *The Gospel of Matthew*, pp. 271-72.

12. A. Plummer, *An Exegetical Commentary on the Gospel according to St. Matthew*, p. 247; W.C. Allen, *St. Matthew* (ICC), p. 191. G.D. Kilpatrick, *The Origins of the Gospel according to St. Matthew*, pp. 41-42, accepts this view of vv. 24-26 but regards v. 27 as a Matthean addition alluding to a pressing problem of AD 70-96, which ceased to be applicable when Nerva abolished the tax for the *fiscus Iudaicus*. But (1) there is no textual or exegetical reason for isolating v. 27 from its context or for supposing the setting of a different tax; (2) Nerva did not abolish the tax but only abuses in its enforcement: numerous second century receipts are extant (*Corpus Papyrorum Judaicarum*, Nos. 194-229), and there appear to be literary references in the third and fourth centuries (Origen, *Ep. ad Africanum* 14; Julian, *Ep.* 51.396D-397A). Objections may be directed against the relevance of both Kilpatrick's termini, and the value of the passage for dating the composition of the Gospel must be questioned. The *fiscus Iudaicus* raises important issues which will be discussed in the next section. See further C.J. Hemer, 'The Edfu *Ostraka* and the Jewish Tax', *PEQ* 105 (1973), pp. 6-12.

13. 'The Fall of Jerusalem and the "Abomination of Desolation"', *JRS* 37 (1947), pp. 47-54, reprinted in *More New Testament Studies* (Manchester, 1968), pp. 69-83.

It is beyond the scope of our present study to attempt to work out the implications of these observations. The relation of these passages with Mt. 24, for example, is important, and the indications for a later setting of that chapter are stronger. I suggest merely (1) that the passages from Matthew and Luke alike offer illustrative examples of the historical doubts implied in the preceding paragraph, and (2) that even the Matthean evidence is capable of very diverse reading. The orthodox dating may well be right, but the arguments for it are not cogent. Yet much is built on them.

14. A summary of the opinions of some modern scholars is given by S.G.F. Brandon, *The Fall of Jerusalem and the Christian Church*, pp. 12-14. His own book focuses attention on an important question.

15. It is sometimes necessary to point out common misconceptions. For a typical and instructive instance see Caird, p. 21n. He notes that many

commentators invoke the authority of Pliny for something he never says. It is my aim to state the facts. But this may often entail the acknowledgment of uncertainty after detailed study. This is not so telling as to repeat assumptions which support my case. But if the case sometimes appears inconclusive, that need not be a fault of the case, but a recognition of the difficulty of the matter.

16. Jos. *BJ* 7.6.6.218; cf. Dio Cass. 66.7.

17. If rigid alternatives were intended we might expect *aut . . .aut*. For discussion of the passages see G.W. Mooney (ed.), Suetonius, *De Vita Caesarum, Libri VII-VIII*, pp. 567-68.

18. Cf. Juvenal's sneering attacks on the many destitute Jews living by begging and fortune-telling in Rome (*Sat.* 3.13-16; 6.542-47).

19. G.F. Moore, *Judaism in the First Centuries of the Christian Era*, I.291-92; cf. III.97n. The whole topic has been treated by D.R.A. Hare, *The Theme of Jewish Persecution of Christians in the Gospel according to St Matthew* (Cambridge, 1967), pp. 49ff. See however the cautions in E.E. Ellis, *NTS* 26 (1979-80), pp. 490-91, and the very important study by W. Horbury, 'The Benediction of the *Minim* and Early Jewish-Christian Controversy', *JTS* n.s. 33 (1982), pp. 19-61.

20. Ignatius's experience at Philadelphia may underlie his warnings to the Magnesians (*ad Magn.* 8-11). The subject will repay further study. He opposes for instance the attempt to combine a Christian profession with Jewish practices (10.3; cf. 9.1; 10.1).

21. For Jewish hostility at Smyrna cf. *Martyrdom of Polycarp*, 13, 21; *Acta Pionii* 4.14-15.

22. No Domitianic edict against Christianity is extant. Much is often built on the prosecution of Flavius Clemens for *atheotes* (Dio Cass. 67.14). On the background generally see D. McFayden, 'The Occasion of the Domitianic Persecution', *AJT* 24 (1920), pp. 46-66. He dismisses the relevance of the Jewish tax with the comment that the Christians would not have made its imposition on them a *casus belli* (p. 46n.). Later however he observes that Domitian might on this ground have punished them as tax-evaders (p. 63). His account of Domitian's policies seems generally true, but it is here suggested that a more subtle complexity of factors brought the issue to the notice of the authorities. The historicity of the 'persecution' is not to be decided on simple criteria.

23. Perhaps at Sardis many Christians had made terms for inclusion in such a list, while the few who scorned compromise were alone excluded. Some such situation might underlie the reference to the 'book of life' (Rev. 3.5), seen as a citizen-register of the heavenly kingdom.

24. This pattern differs widely from that argued in the influential work of W. Bauer, *Rechtgläubigkeit und Ketzerei in ältesten Christentum* (see ET *Orthodoxy and Heresy in Earliest Christianity*, ed. R.A. Kraft and G. Krodel from 2nd German edn. [1971], pp. 77ff.). Bauer makes extensive use of the

argument *ex silentio* in areas where our information is severely limited. For criticism on a wider front see H.E.W. Turner, *The Pattern of Christian Truth*, pp. 39-94.

25. The reading is in doubt. The MS *viginti quoque* (A, a) has been conjecturally emended to '...*viginti. Hi quoque*...' (Keil) and to *viginti quinque* (Rittershaus). See the apparatus of R.A. Mynors in *OCT* of Plin. *Ep.* 10.96.6. For recent discussion of this correspondence see A.N. Sherwin-White, *The Letters of Pliny* (1966), pp. 691ff., and cf. pp. 772ff.

26. Cf. Suetonius's use of the verb *deferebantur* (*Dom.* 12.2) with the noun *delator*. To the objection that Roman governments were not likely to be so concerned to advertise their magnanimity toward despised minorities, we may cite the obsessive popular fear of *delatores* and suggest that the Jewish tax had provided the occasion for intensive activity on their part. Cf. further E.M. Smallwood, 'Domitian's Attitude toward the Jews and Judaism', *CP* 51 (1956), pp. 1-12; Hemer, *PEQ* 105 (1973), pp. 6-12.

27. Tos. Yadayim 2.13 and Tos. Shabbat 13.5 both set them apart from the scruples associated with scripture. The former passage excludes also Ben Sira and other later books, while the latter repudiates the Christian writings directly.

28. This must be taken in conjunction with *Philad.* 6.1, which portrays a situation where Gentiles were apparently making proselytes of Christians to Judaism. This is very strange, as noted by A.A.K. Graham ('Their Word to our Day. IV. Ignatius of Antioch', *ExpT* 80 [1968-69], p. 103). Graham offers no explanation. He sees the Docetism combatted by Ignatius as having a Gnostic basis whose terminology is reflected in Ignatius's own language. But this does not account for the peculiar strength of the Judaistic aspect of the opposition.

29. The study of the use made of both OT and NT scriptures in early Christian writings outside the New Testament would be very interesting in this connection. See D.A. Hagner, *The Use of the Old and New Testaments in Clement of Rome* (*NovT*Sup, 34; Leiden, 1973), esp. pp. 120-32.

30. For this view of Montanist origins see W.M. Calder, 'Philadelphia and Montanism', *BJRL* 7 (1923), pp. 309-54, further discussed in our treatment of Philadelphia.

31. So especially in Justin's Dialogue with Trypho, itself perhaps located in Ephesus (Justin, *Dial.* 1.217B, ed. Otto, with Euseb. *HE* 4.18.3). Justin repeatedly urges the claim of the church to be the family of the spiritual descendants of Abraham and Jacob (11.229A; 47.266D; 135.365D). He sometimes connects this with the reiterated charge that the Jews curse Christian believers in the synagogues. The details are sometimes instructive: see 16.234B-C; 96.335D.

32. This passage is very difficult and we do not exclude the likelihood that John is here using a Jewish source. This however appears to be his meaning, and the identification is elsewhere woven into the structure of the book (14.1; 21.12; cf. Beckwith, pp. 534-36).

33. See Caird, pp. 10-11, for a caution on this score. J. Kallas, 'The Apocalypse—An Apocalyptic Book?', *JBL* 86 (1967), pp. 69-80, denies that the Revelation is apocalyptic at all. He considers that the form is essentially characterized by a limited dualism which attributes evil to Satanic forces, whereas the Rev. returns to the OT view that it is punitive. On p. 78 he applies this criterion to the letters. His arguments however do not take account of all the evidence: they will not for example naturally fit the letter to Smyrna, which he does not mention.

34. Cf. e.g. Rev. 2.26-28 with Ps. 2.7-9 and Num. 24.17, noting also the echo of Ps. 2.7 in Rev. 2.18. Cf. also the Philadelphian letter with Isa. 62 and Ezek. 48.35.

35. Thus Num. 31.16 with 25.1-2 as underlying Rev. 2.14; cf. Jos. *Antiq.* 4.6.6.126-13.158.

36. So perhaps again Ps. 2.7-9 with Num. 24.17.

37. Thus Isa. 62 as a whole seems reflected in the terms of his conception of the Philadelphian situation. We may note 'Jerusalem' (vv. 1, 7), a new name for the forsaken city (vv. 2, 4, 12), the crown (v. 3), corn and wine under alien control (vv. 8-9), the gates and highway (v. 10). We argue that for John this relationship is situational, not literary, and that relevant parallels may be found in the Rev. not only in 3.7-13, but in 6.6, chs. 21–22, and perhaps elsewhere.

38. Bowman in *IDB* IV. 59; see Rev. 1.3; 10.11; 19.10; 22.7, 9, 10, 18, 19: only once is the book styled 'apocalypse' (Rev. 1.1). Perhaps these factors underlie the presentation of the letters in a shape recalling the eight oracles of Amos against the nations (Amos 1–2; cf. A. Feuillet, *L'Apocalypse: l'état de la question*, pp. 40-41).

39. See e.g. E.F. Scott, *The Book of Revelation*, pp. 18-21. His view leads him to say: 'In some respects it is the simplest and most intelligible of all the New Testament writings, for the general meaning of it lies on the surface'. Perhaps not many would feel so confident! Contrast Beckwith, pp. 213-15. The whole subject is discussed at length by Charles, pp. civ-cix: his view that the seven letters were originally Vespasianic introduces an unnecessary and unjustified difficulty.

40. C.H. Parez, 'The Seven Letters and the Rest of the Apocalypse', *JTS* 12 (1911), pp. 284-86, notes that Ramsay's view tends to a dichotomy of the book, and sees its basic unity of theme in the presentation of the victory of the ideal church. Ramsay need not however have left himself open to this objection.

41. J. Chapman, *Expos* 6th ser. 9 (1904), pp. 257-63, argued that these were the only seven episcopally constituted churches in the province (see also Ramsay's reply, *ibid.*, pp. 263-65). Others have thought John had a special relation with these seven, or that they were specially suitable to his purpose (see Beckwith, p. 436). M. Goguel, 'Les Nicolaïtes', *Revue de l'histoire des religions* 115 (1937), p. 18, following W. Bauer, argued that

these were the churches where John might gain the most favourable hearing. Those theories which find a literary pattern in the sequence of letters are the least acceptable. J.W. Bowman, *The Drama of the Book of Revelation*, p. 23, likens the geographical arrangement of the cities to a *menorah*, and in *IDB* attempts to illustrate the idea with an ingeniously arranged map. N.W. Lund, *Chiasmus in the New Testament*, pp. 331-55, develops an interrelated series of chiastic arrangements whose symmetry is achieved by conjectural alteration of the text.

42. His contribution will be evaluated below. The unhappy neglect of his work has been noted in the Preface. The topography of the churches can scarcely be treated without close reference to him.

43. Bauer, *Orthodoxy and Heresy*, p. 78; Goguel, p. 18.

44. Note the use of the article in ταῖς ἑπτὰ ἐκκλησίαις (Rev. 1.4). This implies that the grouping was recognized, but not necessarily that these were the only churches in the province.

45. The point may be abundantly illustrated. All the sites except Pergamum are now on the railway, and the road connecting them lies almost wholly over lowland and gentle contours. Only the section between Philadelphia and Laodicea requires a sharp climb above 2000 feet.

46. Cf. Parez, p. 285.

47. The tacit assumption is often made that (1) and (2) necessarily coincide. Thus E.H. Plumptre, *A Popular Exposition of the Letters to the Seven Churches of Asia* (London, 3rd edn, 1884), p. 135, rejects a local reference of *chalkolibanos* in 2.18 with the words: 'The imagery had already been used without reference to any local colouring'. It is then assumed that the introductory addresses of the letters are drawn, even arbitrarily, from the vision, and they are explained at their first occurrence in isolation from their conceptual and interpretative context. This criticism is applicable to most of the commentators, including Swete, Charles, Moffatt, Beckwith and Lohmeyer, though their arrangement is necessarily influenced by the reader's convenience.

48. It may however be argued that the identity of the star with Christ was a further primary concept there first revealed to the original readers.

49. The account of the beginnings of the Asian church in Acts, however incomplete, is indispensable. British scholarship has stressed the archaeological confirmation of numerous details in the travel narratives. The Roman historian A.N. Sherwin-White writes: 'Any attempt to reject its basic historicity even in matters of detail must now appear absurd. Roman historians have long taken it for granted' (*Roman Society and Roman Law in the New Testament*, p. 189). Of the Pauline epistles perhaps only Colossians throws much specific light on the situation in an Asian community. On any view of Ephesians it is too general to be pressed here. Philemon is brief and personal, but underlines Colossians. Such other writings as the Petrine and Johannine epistles are, or may be, addressed to destinations in Asia Minor, but present problems of date or provenance.

50. For the dating see A.A.K. Graham, *ExpT* 80 (1968-69), p. 101.

51. The recent discussion by Graham does not raise the point, though he argues that Ignatius was deeply imbued with the language and thought of several other NT books.

52. Note for instance the recurring theme of resurrection and life (Polyc. *Phil.* 1.2; 2.1-2; 5.2; 7.1; 8.1; 9.2; 12.2). If the Philippians did not share Polycarp's awareness of the inner meaning of the Smyrna letter, he might naturally appeal to longer-established writings, especially the Pauline correspondence, with which the recipients were familiar. The most quoted book is actually 1 Peter.

53. The point might be abundantly illustrated. Note e.g. *Mart. Polyc.* 17.1; 19.2; or the analogy between the death of Polycarp and that of Christ (*ibid.* 6; 14). The martyrdom of Pionius is placed impossibly on a Jewish sabbath 17 days after the sabbath of his arrest (*Acta Pion.* 2 with 23), a confusion evidently due to assimilation with Polycarp's martyrdom on a sabbath. Pionius's arrest was also represented as happening on the anniversary of Polycarp's death. And the pseudo-Pionian Life of Polycarp, however dubious as a historical scource, testifies clearly to continuity of the same tradition.

54. It is debatable how far this material has been invented by Philostratus or his professed source Damis (*Vit. Apoll.* 1.3). The difficulty in assessing the historicity of the account is partly due to the scarcity of earlier and independent references to Apollonius. There is only Lucian, *Alexander* 5, and Apuleius, *de Mag.* 90.580. In the latter case the mere occurrence of his name hinges on the correctness of a doubtful reading.

55. I imply a distinction between the unstudied accuracy in incidentals of a careful record and a conscious attempt to carry conviction by allusion.

56. Ramsay's speculation in *SC*, pp. 101-103, that the Revelation actually refers to Apollonius under the guise of the false prophet of 19.20 is unwarranted. In any case Philostratus represents Apollonius as an outspoken opponent of the tyranny of Domitian (e.g. *Vit. Apoll.* 7.6, 8ff.). His evidence may well be tendentious, but is simply set aside by Ramsay.

57. Verbal changes of an OT text may be worth weighing as possible evidence of its adaptation to a local application. The introduction of the unparalleled *chalkolibanos* in Rev. 1.15 and 2.18 is a case in point.

58. Cf. F.F. Bruce, 'The Crooked Serpent', *EQ* 20 (1948), pp. 283-88, for a rather different application of a comparable idea in treating the imagery of the Revelation.

59. The rigid and repetitive form is apparent to the casual reader and need not be again analysed here. John nevertheless achieves deeply divergent portrayals of his churches with economy of phrase. The differences of content which animate the interrelated parallels of word and structure must claim attention, and this content must be seen in the independent context of the historical situation.

60. On the difficulties of referencing to this author see the prefatory note on abbreviations and references.

61. Both writings are of uncertain date, though now recognized to be much earlier than formerly supposed. The setting of Achilles' tale is vaguely drawn, but its point turns on the fact that the temple was famous as a place of asylum, and this may be relevant to Rev. 2.7. Xenophon's local knowledge is of value (see Xénophon d'Ephèse, *Les Ephésiaques ou le roman d'Habrocomès et d'Anthia*, ed. G. Dalmeyda, pp. ix-xii).

62. See further C.J. Hemer, 'The Sardis Letter and the Croesus Tradition', *NTS* 19 (1972-73), pp. 94-97.

63. Note M. Clerc's Latin dissertation *De Rebus Thyatirenorum* (Paris, 1893) and C.J. Cadoux, *Ancient Smyrna* (Oxford, 1938). The welter of detail in the latter emphasizes the fragmented state of the evidence. Despite its copious unselectivity, Cadoux's work is far from exhaustive, and I have to seek in a different place the publication of a significant inscription first known to me through personal observation and copying *in situ* (L. Robert, *Hellenica* V. 81-82).

64. *Aegean Turkey. An Archaeological Guide* (London, 1966); *Turkey Beyond the Maeander* (London, 1971).

65. For an interesting and previously unnoticed comment see C.J. Hemer, 'Unpublished Letters of Sir William Mitchell Ramsay in the Cambridge University Library', *EQ* 45 (1973), pp. 166-71.

66. *The Apocalypse of St. John I–III* (London, 1908).

67. *L'Apocalypse* (Paris, 2nd edn, 1921).

68. For a perceptively critical review of his *Seven Churches* see J. Vernon Bartlet in *ExpT* 16 (1904-5), pp. 205-207. Bartlet rightly draws attention to his neglect of Jewish sources.

69. 'The Laodicean Lukewarmness', *ExpT* 69 (1957-58), pp. 176-78.

Notes to Chapter 2

1. Pliny says no more than this about it, dismissing it in a phrase, yet Swete (p. 12) implicitly, and Charles (p. 22), Moffatt (p. 341) and others explicitly, quote his authority for the unfounded, though very possible, supposition that it was a penal settlement (cf. Caird, p. 21). The island receives only one incidental mention in classical history (Thuc. 3.33.3). Strabo only lists its name (10.5.13 = p. 488).

2. For a description of the town see J.T. Bent, *JHS* 7 (1886), p. 144. The article by J. Schmidt in Pauly–Wissowa–Kroll includes a useful map (*PW* 18.4.2174-91).

3. The traditional 'cave of the Apocalypse' is located on the northern slope of this hill, midway between the present town and Skála.

4. Three interpretations of διὰ τὸν λόγον have been suggested: (1)

(suffering) 'because of'; (2) 'for the sake of' (preaching it there); (3) 'for the purpose of' (receiving the visions). Linguistically and contextually the first must be accepted. For the expression cf. Rev. 6.9 and 20.4. Cf. also the discussions in Charles, pp. 21-22, and Beckwith, pp. 434-35. But even accepting (1) we cannot dogmatize about the circumstances.

5. Iron-bearing rocks and some modern mining are recorded (Schmidt, cols. 2179-80), so the supposition is not improbable.

6. I cannot accept the view of J.N. Sanders, 'St. John on Patmos', *NTS* 9 (1962-63), p. 78, that John need not previously have been personally familiar with Asia. The content of the letters is not, I believe, convincingly explicable otherwise.

7. So especially '*In insulam relegare praesides provinciae possunt, sic tamen, ut si quidem insulam sub se habeant (id est ad eius provinciae formam pertinentem quam administrant) et eam specialiter insulam adsignare possint inque eam relegare*' (48.22.7). The previous paragraph denies the provincial governor the right of *deportatio* without the emperor's sanction. Cf. also the use of the term *relegatur* by Tertullian, *de Praescr. Haer.* 36. See most recently J.P.V.D. Balsdon, *Life and Leisure in Ancient Rome* (London, 1969), pp. 182ff.

8. No specimens from Patmos appear to be included in *IG* XII. *CIG* 2261 and 2262 are uninformative. Comment on a new text in *SEG* 27 (1977), No. 509, attributes Patmos to the territory of Miletus.

9. On the other hand, if John suffered exile in Domitian's reign, and the emperor was remembered as a persecutor, it is easy to account for the growth of the tradition.

10. 'What St. John Saw on Patmos', *The Nineteenth Century* (1888), pp. 813-21. He cites impressive correspondences with recorded accounts of later eruptions. But we cannot suppose that Thera was the *thērion* rising from the sea (p. 813; Rev. 13.1), or that the beast's seven heads and the two horns of its successor (Rev. 13.11) represented peaks of the island.

11. Cf. Exod. 7.17 with Rev. 16.4 (rivers of blood); Exod. 9.9 with Rev. 16.2 (boils); Exod. 9.22-25 with Rev. 8.7; 16.21 (hail); Exod. 10.4 with Rev. 9.3 (locusts).

12. The greatest disaster in human memory, according to Pliny, *NH* 2.86.200.

13. Thus cf. Rev. 8.8-9 with *NH* 2.89.203 (submarine phenomena); Rev. 8.5 with the sounds of earthquake in *NH* 2.82.193. The influence of the Patmos scene on the book has been traced in passages like 12.18–13.1. The reading ἐστάθην is attractive here and conveys a vivid personal touch: John himself stands on the shore on Patmos to see the great vision which follows (cf. Swete, pp. 160-61). Several other expressions mention the sea as an element in the visions. Swete (p. 70) refers to Patmos in his discussion of Rev. 4.6 (cf. also 10.2, 5; 15.2; 18.17; 21.1).

14. Cf. ὁ ὤν . . . in 1.4, 8 with 4.8; the seven spirits of 1.4 with 4.5; 5.6 and 3.1; 1.6 with 5.10.

15. This may best be argued in the case of Laodicea. The opening address of that letter (3.14) has no parallel in the Patmos vision, but some of the phrases in the vision may have conveyed a pointed message to the church in Laodicea (e.g. 'white wool', 1.14; 'many waters', 1.15). Cf. also 3.14 with 1.5.

16. It is remarkable that Ignatius, in combatting Jewish opponents in Asia, sets the 'Lord's day' against the Sabbath: Christians are characterized as μηκέτι σαββατίζοντες, ἀλλὰ κατὰ κυριακὴν ζῶντες (*ad Magn.* 9.1) Such points of opposition further illustrate the picture of a double Roman and Jewish threat to the church in Asia. Foerster in *TDNT* III.1096 maintains that the term 'Lord's day' has no Semitic equivalent. This would support the suggested parallelism with the imperial cult.

17. See on Pergamum, p 87.

18. F. Bleek, *Lectures on the Apocalypse* (London, 1875), p. 162, rules out (2); Trench (pp. 53-59), Tait (pp. 104-108) and others dismiss (1).

19. See further Grundmann in *TDNT* I.74. He notes that in the NT the meaning 'messenger' is often conveyed by a periphrasis, the word ἄγγελος being generally reserved for the sense 'angel'.

20. See E.C. Selwyn, *The Christian Prophets* (London, 1900), pp. 208-209.

21. Cf. however 1.11, where John is instructed to write 'to the churches', with the individual letters to 'the angels of the churches'.

22. It is Ramsay's distinctive merit here to have attempted to illustrate this kind of thinking from contemporary Anatolian evidence (*SC*, pp. 62-69). He concludes in similar terms, and deals with the problem of postulating blame in the heavenly 'angel' by suggesting that John simply dropped the artificial allegory when absorbed in the particular circumstances of the churches (pp. 70-72).

23. *Christus und die Caesaren*, pp. 197-98 (= ET pp. 175-76).

24. 26.519 (Dindorf) = 335.595 (Jebb).

25. *IG* XII.iii.445, 933-74, 1056-57. These inscriptions may be compared with another class of pagan epitaphs from the same island (*IG* XII.ii.886-932). These either describe the deceased as ἥρως (ἡρῷσσα) or, more commonly, use a formula giving the name of the dedicator in the nominative, the deceased in the accusative, and the verb ἀφηωΐζειν in varying itacisms. It seems likely that the ἄγγελος inscriptions are intended as a Jewish or Christian counterpart of these expressions of the native religion. The letter-forms used by both classes are however in some instances apparently late (Nos. 893, 909, etc.). Both types are often adorned with rosettes, supposedly Christian emblems. No. 942 may represent a pagan specimen partly erased and Christianized.

26. 'Spuren des Urchristentums auf den griechischen Inseln?', *ZNTW* 1 (1900), 87-100; cf. Deissmann, *LAE*, pp. 279-80n. An inscription of Melos (*IG* XII.iii.1238) which refers to the guardian angel of a tomb is certainly Christian, but cannot be dated so early (note its explicit formulae and advanced itacism).

Notes to Chapter 3

1. The sequence of the text dictates the treatment of this letter first, and from the standpoint of the original recipients its priority was natural. The present case might better be introduced to the modern reader through the Laodicean letter, where the element of detailed local allusion is most easily demonstrable, or the Philadelphian, where the local situation is more illuminatingly related to a historical reconstruction of the problems of the contemporary church. The *prima facie* reason for exploring the relevance of local background here is that its importance is better shown elsewhere and may then be presumed in some degree here also. Its ultimate justification is the weight it contributes here to a cumulative argument whose stronger strands are elsewhere.

2. Details of the excavations and new inscriptions have been published regularly for many years by J. Keil and others in *Jahreshefte des österreichischen archäologischen Instituts in Wien*.

3. See Ramsay, *SC* Chapter 17, pp. 210-36; Bürchner, *PW* V.ii.2773-2822; J. Keil, 'Zur Topographie und Geschichte von Ephesos', *Jahreshefte* 21-22 (1922-24), pp. 96-112; G.E. Bean, *Aegean Turkey*, Chapter 7, pp. 160-84. All these accounts include sketch-maps of aspects of the subject.

4. Cf. Paus. 7.2.8 and the foundation legend in Athenaeus, *Deipn.* 8.361c-f.

5. Evidence on this subject is extensively tabulated by R.H. Charles (pp. lxviii ff.) and by H.B. Swete (pp. cxxxix ff.). Both writers confine their parallels to v. 7 of this letter, and Charles derives even that from the traditions embodied in the Pseudepigrapha rather than direct from Genesis.

6. Both in sections likely to be pre-Christian: *Enoch* ?c. 100 BC; prototype of *Test. Levi* now known from Qumran.

7. So e.g. Jos. *Antiq.* 14.7.2.112; Acts 19.10.

8. So e.g. W.W. Tarn, *Hellenistic Civilization* (London, 3rd edn, 1952), p. 222.

9. *Nouvelles Inscriptions de Sardes* (Paris, 1964). See on Sardis, pp. 136-37. Part of the difficulty in the earlier materials consists in the ambiguity of terminology in the papyri, coupled with the suspicion that Josephus is ready to exploit tendentiously anything which lends colour to a claim for Jewish citizenship.

10. A different account of the dispute before Agrippa appears in Jos. *Antiq.* 16.2.3-5.27-60, where the Jewish spokesman was wholly concerned with practical privileges. R. Marcus in *LCL* Josephus, Vol. VII, Appendix C, pp. 741-42, finds an irreconcilable conflict between the two accounts, and therefore doubts the reality of Jewish citizenship. But there is no need to draw this conclusion. It seems more likely that the very fact of Jewish citizenship was the underlying cause of the friction. If these people claimed to be citizens they must conform. Their privilege of being treated differently could not then be tolerated, and every opportunity of pressure was exploited

to force them into line. In any case a Jewish advocate was not likely to bring into question the existing rights of his people. He was concerned with the practical abuses consequent upon resentment at their possession of those rights.

11. *Antiq.* 14.10.13.228-30; cf. 14.10.16.234; 14.10.19.238-40 (Lentulus); 14.10.12.225-27 (Dolabella).

12. 'Neue ephesische Chiliastyen', *Jahreshefte* 46 (1961-63), Beiblatt 19-32. The name of the postulated Seleucid tribe is still unknown, and the assignment of indeterminate *chiliastyes* to it still conjectural. Ramsay had supposed that this was a sixth tribe which had later been renamed 'Sebaste'. It is now clear from newly assigned *chiliastyes* of 'Sebaste' that that originated only in early Imperial times and was a seventh tribe. The number of unassigned *chiliastyes* with names of other earlier types confirms the preexistence of a sixth tribe which may well have been instituted by Antiochus.

13. Acts 19.1ff.; cf. the case of Apollos, Acts 18.24ff. The word μαθητής is used absolutely, as elsewhere of disciples of Jesus. There is therefore no reason to suppose they represented a sect of followers of John (see F.F. Bruce, *The Acts of the Apostles*, 2nd edn, p. 353).

14. See e.g. J.B. Lightfoot, *Ignatius* I.438, 440.

15. Perhaps even the element of racial reconciliation implicit in Paul's gospel appealed to some of the civic leaders (cf. Eph. 2.11-22). This might help to explain the friendship of some Asiarchs (Acts 19.31) and the favourable view of the town-clerk (Acts 19.37).

16. Cf. J. Keil in *Jahreshefte* 27 (1932), Beiblatt 54-60; M.P. Charlesworth in *CAH* XI.40. The remains of the building may be seen on a prominent site south of the street of Curetes, and a gigantic forearm of the cult-statue is on view in the archaeological museum in İzmir. There seems to be little reference to this temple, and we can believe that on the cancellation of the emperor's acts its association with him was carefully obliterated. A vivid picture of the cult is painted by E. Stauffer in *Christ and the Caesars*, tr. K. and R. Gregor Smith (London, 1955), pp. 166ff. = *Christus und die Caesaren* (Hamburg, 1952), pp. 182ff. This however is not closely documented, and should be used with caution.

17. See pp. 49-50.

18. The only external evidence which might otherwise assist us is the Ignatian letter to the Ephesians, which confirms their resolution in rejecting false teaching (6.2; 9.1), and exhibits other parallels, while apparently an independent composition. It does not however give clear guidance here. There are strong warnings against a Judaistic danger in the letter to nearby Magnesia (Ign. *Magn.* 8-10), but the parallels with the Trallian epistle are much closer, and that letter is more suggestive of the force of pagan pressures (e.g. Ign. *Trall.* 6.2; 7.2; 11.1).

19. So J.G. Eichhorn, *Commentarius in Apocalypsin Joannis* (Göttingen,

1791), p. 72, renders the word here as *humanitas*.

20. Callimachus, *ad Demet.* 40, describes a certain δένδρον as a ἱερὸν ξύλον.

21. A.J.B. Higgins in *ExpT* 57 (1945-46), p. 294, notes that עץ means 'gallows' in Est. 5.14.

22. We need not follow Charles, II.222ff., in treating the passage as an interpolation.

23. Again see Higgins, pp. 293-94. He argues from the Aramaic underlying Jesus' words in Luke that here also 'the Cross was uppermost in His mind, and the word took special significance'.

24. Modern Greek seems to maintain a clear distinction between the two words. Cf. A. Kyriakides, *Modern Greek-English Dictionary*, p. 511.

25. δένδρον is used four times in Rev. It must be emphasized that the primary reason for the use of ξύλον here is its occurrence in the LXX of the Genesis prototype.

26. 'The Tree of Life', *ExpT* 25 (1913-14), p. 332.

27. *The Meaning of Salvation* (London, 1965), pp. 210ff.

28. φηγός is strictly the Vallonia oak (*LSJ*). The word is used of the oak at Dodona.

29. Cf. recently R. Merkelbach, 'βρέτας', *ZPE* 9 (1972), p. 84.

30. Cf. C. Pickard, *Ephèse et Claros* (Paris, 1922), p. 14; W.R. Lethaby, *JHS* 37 (1917), pp. 8, 10.

31. The term used of coins issued under Attalid rule typically depicting snakes issuing from a box or chest (*cista*).

32. No. 260, of Septimius Severus, etc. The type is first found under Vitellius, and was often used under the Flavians with reference to the conquest of Judaea.

33. For the significance of sacred trees in Anatolia cf. W.M. Ramsay, *Pauline and Other Studies*, pp. 173ff. Cf. also Sir J.G. Frazer, *Adonis*, p. 86; Jer. 2.27 LXX.

34. The quail (ὄρτυξ) was associated with Artemis, and is notable both for its migratoriness and for the number of its eggs. The name Ortygia was applied to other places sacred to Artemis: to Delos, or Rhenea (Strab. 6.2.4 = p. 270), and to the place where she killed Orion (Hom. *Od.* 5.123).

35. Strabo locates this site in the valley of the Cenchrius (Sazlı Pınar). The shrine of Meryemana ('Mother Mary' in Turkish), which has become so popular a centre of pilgrimage and tourism in recent years, stands at the head of this valley. For a critical view of the claims made for this site see W.M. Ramsay, *Pauline and Other Studies*, pp. 125ff.

36. D.G. Hogarth, *Excavations at Ephesus. The Archaic Artemisia* (London, 1908).

37. The Ephesian case before Tiberius (Tac. *Ann.* 3.61) was that the temple inherited a sanctity transferred from Ortygia. So Hogarth, p. 1.

38. Such other great Ionic temples of western Asia Minor as those of

Sardis and Didyma are however sited on relatively low ground.

39. The presence of springs is seen in the repeated flooding of Wood's excavation. Or might the site have marked the falling of a meteorite in early times (cf. διοπετές in Acts 19.36)? The term διοπετές however is not necessarily to be taken literally, but was often applied to ancient wooden images (cf. Suidas; Plin. *NH* 16.79.213ff.; L. Ross Taylor *BC* V.251ff.). Suidas says the sculptors were often killed to silence their testimony that their work had no supernatural origin. With the star motif however cf. coinage (*BMC* No. 146, a cistophoric emblem, and on imperial period issues); Rev. 9.11; and note the Hittite story of the star which fell at Apasas (O.R. Gurney and J. Garstang, *The Geography of the Hittite Empire* [London, 1959], p. 88).

40. E.L. Hicks, *BMInscrs* 522-24 and cf. 525.

41. *Jahreshefte* 28 (1933), Beiblatt col. 43. The reference in *CAH* XI.40n. to the 'Archäologische Anzeigen' in the *Jahrbuch des deutschen archäologischen Instituts* is incorrect.

42. *CIG* 2646, of Mylasa in Caria; *AJA* 16 (1912), p. 13, of Sardis (c. 300 BC).

43. Cf. πᾶν ξύλον βρώσιμον (Ezek. 47.12 LXX), underlying the 'tree of life' passage in Rev. 22.2.

44. For this idea as applied to the Ephesian temple cf. W.R. Lethaby, 'The Earlier Temple of Artemis at Ephesus', *JHS* 37 (1917), p. 15.

45. τὴν ἐνδώμησιν τοῦ τεμένους καὶ θεμελίωσιν ἐν τετραγώνῳ, corresponding with the collocation θεμέλιος/τετράγωνος/ἐνδώμησις in Rev. 21.16-19. The two latter words are NT ἅπαξ λεγόμενα. The very rare ἐνδώμησις is elsewhere quoted only from one other Asian inscription (*BCH* 28 [1904], 78, of Tralles) and as a variant of ἐνδόμησις in Jos. *Antiq.* 15.9.6.335. At Smyrna the word seems to speak of the square enclosure of a *temenos*, in the New Jerusalem of the square enclosure of its walls. Could it perhaps have been a technical term for the bounds of a sanctuary?

46. Unless we choose, with Charles, to reject ἐὰν μὴ μετανοήσῃς as an otiose gloss. I prefer to think that the repetition is original and to be explained pointedly as it stands.

47. For ἐν μέσῳ cf. Rev. 1.13; 4.6; 5.6; 7.17. R.R. Brewer notes the prominence of this aspect ('Revelation 4⁶ and Translations Thereof', *JBL* 71 [1952], pp. 227-31), but explains it with reference to the Greek theatre, supposing the Apocalypse to be a drama unfolding in successive acts from the initial sacrificial rites suggested to him by the context of Rev. 4.6. This idea seems improbable, for John would scarcely make a model of the incidental pagan ritual of the drama, even if he sometimes presents Christ as the specific counterpart and answer to pagan influences in the cities he addresses. And it does not work out well in detail. There were for instance twenty-four elders, but the theatre at Ephesus had only twelve marble thrones, as he allows. The primary background of Rev. 4.6 is to be found in

Ezek 1.5. For a comparable approach with that of Brewer see J.W. Bowman, *The Drama of the Book of Revelation* (Philadelphia, n.d.).

48. A long series of these documents, all apparently of Hellenistic date, is collected in *BMInscrs* 447-76.

49. The very similar words of 1 Cor. 3.16 were written from Ephesus.

50. The difficult passage in Ign. *Ephes.* 19 is perhaps the most striking in its unstudied parallels with the Revelation. There Ignatius visualizes the spiritual powers of magic and superstition as overthrown by the manifestation of Christ. We may see there, as in the Seven Letters, the beginnings of a conscious opposition between Christian and pagan in the terms and titles of religion.

Notes to Chapter 4

1. We may conjecture that Hermogenes' history helped crystallize local tradition by the time of the Revelation if not by that of Strabo. For his date see Cadoux, *Ancient Smyrna*, p. 233. He might be identical with the physician of *CIG* 3550, but the name was frequent in Smyrna (e.g. *BMC Ionia*, Sm., Nos. 90, 118, 289, 293).

2. Matters of local history and culture would be preserved by oral tradition rather than formal literary statement. For direct evidence we must rely largely on bald facts stated by outsiders like Strabo. In local sources we get valuable indirect allusion which would have been appreciated where explicit statement would only labour the obvious.

3. Cadoux's work is indispensable for study of the city, though burdened with excessive detail. He has assembled a mass of information from extraordinarily scattered sources.

4. As early as 242 BC, in the treaty of union with Magnesia ad Sipylum, all free Hellenes resident there became citizens of Smyrna (*OGIS* 229 = *CIG* 3137, lines 44-46; cf. Cadoux, pp. 118-27).

5. Cf. also the New Jerusalem in Rev. 21 and 22. For Jewish feeling towards Jerusalem and its Temple, while that survived, cf. Mk 13.1; Mt. 24.1; Lk. 21.5; and Philo, *In Flaccum* 7.

6. J. Rendel Harris however has actually ventured to explain the name as 'myrrh' and to infer that early colonists came from Arabia (*BJRL* 10 [1926], p. 330). Modern writers, while rejecting the etymology, have recognized its importance as an ancient view (so e.g. Bürchner in *PW*). If the Aeolic form μύρρα is the earlier term for myrrh (so *LSJ*) and is itself borrowed from the Semitic, we might reasonably follow Michaelis in his conjecture that σμύρνα was actually an adaptation of the word to the name. The local legend of the foundation of Smyrna by an eponymous Amazon, attested by many coins, reflects a real memory of a Hittite outpost on this coast, confirmed by the primitive rock-reliefs of the district (Cadoux, pp. 23-31, 33-35).

7. Her petrified form was to be seen on Mt Sipylus (Ov. *Metam.* 6.310-12), though local writers maintain that the likeness to a weeping woman was only discernible at a distance (Paus. 1.21.3; Q. Smyrn. 1.292-306). Pausanias clearly distinguishes the 'true Niobe', a natural rock-formation at the edge of the town of Manisa, from the 'false Niobe', the Hittite carving of a mother-goddess, the Taş Suret, in the rock-face three miles eastward (Paus. 3.22.4; Bean, *Aegean Turkey*, pp. 53ff.).

8. Smyrna today is not, to my mind, exactly a beautiful city, certainly not in detail. Its attraction resides now in its setting rather than in architecture or planning. It must be seen from Pagus, or from the sea or shores of the gulf at some distance. In antiquity careful planning in accordance with ideals of symmetry was thought to have embellished the natural qualities of the site. Cf. generally W.M. Calder, 'Smyrna as Described by the Orator Aelius Aristides', *Studies in the History and Art of the Eastern Provinces of the Roman Empire*, ed. W.M. Ramsay (Aberdeen, 1906), pp. 95-116.

9. Thus the *stephanephoros* was an eponymous magistrate at Smyrna (*CIG* 3386) and crowning with a golden wreath was a common way of honouring distinguished men (cf. *BMC Ionia*, Sm., Nos. 323-24, of Trajan).

10. See also F. and H. Miltner, 'Bericht über eine Voruntersuchung in Alt-Smyrna', *Jahreshefte* 27 (1932), Beiblatt 127-90. This includes a plan of the city-hill (Fig. 81) and of its neighbourhood (Fig. 93). The highest point of the hill today is said to be formed not by its summit but by the mass of the great siege-mound which had been thrown up against its NW wall. This was probably the first time Greeks had had to face this Eastern technique (J. Boardman, *The Greeks Overseas*, pp. 113-14).

11. See D.S. Russell, *The Method and Message of Jewish Apocalyptic* (London, 1964), pp. 366ff.

12. He argues (*SC*, p. 269) that the word 'again' is both superfluous and misleading, that the idea is of life persisting in and through death. The Divine Sender of the letter to Smyrna 'was dead and lived', and so likewise the city itself. He erroneously attributes this rendering to the AV.

13. Cf. Theognis 1.1103f. (Bergk): ὕβρις . . . ἀπώλεσε . . . Σμύρναν.

14. The fact is emphasized by Ramsay, *SC*, pp. 251-52, 270, and *HG*, p. 62n., and in *Asianic Elements in Greek Civilisation*, pp. 89-90; Hogarth in *CAH* III.513; Cadoux, pp. 86ff. We need not follow Cadoux in criticizing Strabo for calling this period 400 years. Recent dating confirms that it somewhat exceeded 300, and it would be normal to reckon parts of hundreds inclusively. Nor should we follow Ramsay in interpreting Aristides to mean that a town stood between the two sites during the intervening period (Arist. 15.372 = 229.401; *SC*, p. 252; Cadoux, p. 86n.).

15. ἀνιστάναι in this context must mean 'to transplant'. The same verb is used by Aristides of the rebuilding of Smyrna after AD 178 (21.431 = 265.464).

16. See Cadoux, pp. 95-97.

17. Pausanias, while referring to the legend, never mentions the destruction of the old city, nor the village-period. The omission is not significant. The point is implicit in 7.5.1-3, and clear in Aristides.

18. ἀνιστάναι, ἀνεγείρεσθαι, ἐγρήγορσις and ἀναβιῶναι are applied to the city or its present benefactors.

19. He also refers to the phoenix elsewhere in a very similar context (15.371 = 229.401): (ἡ πόλις) ἑαυτὴν ἀνανεωσαμένη, καθάπερ τὸν ὄρνιν φασὶ τὸν ἱερόν. Cf. again in his lament over the destruction of Smyrna by earthquake (20.427 = 262.459): νῦν ἔδει μὲν πάντας οἰωνοὺς εἰς πῦρ ἐνάλλεσθαι.

20. Cf. e.g. ἆρ' οὐχ ἅπας μὲν θρῆνος τούτοις ἐξαλήλιπται, καὶ μνήμη πᾶσα τῶν τε ἰδίων ἑκάστῳ καὶ τῶν κοινῶν δυσχερῶν; (20.433 = 266.466) with Rev. 21.4 and 7.17, which are themselves based on Isa. 25.8. A possible parallel may also exist with an interesting, but corrupt, passage in Sulpicia, *Satire* 58-61, written ostensibly shortly after AD 95. It at least offers prima facie evidence that the early history of Smyrna could be the subject of familiar literary allusion. See further C.J. Hemer, 'Sulpicia, *Satire* 58-61', *CR* n.s. 23 (1973), pp. 12-13.

21. He cites an inscription, apparantly *SIG*[3] 136, of 387/6 BC (not 368), which mentions Smyrna as one of the sources of the corn-supply of Clazomenae. He refers to Aristides, evidently 15.372 = 229.401, which however does not justify his theory of a town between the old and new sites. His allusion to a fragment of Pindar (evidently frag. 204 Teubner; see *Asianic Elements*, p. 62n., and Cadoux, pp. 90-91) may well refer historically to Old Smyrna, as no context is preserved. He is probably correct in arguing that 'Smyrna' in Hipponax, frag. 15 Bergk, denotes a district of Ephesus (cf. Strab. 14.1.4 = p. 633; *Asianic Elements*, pp. 146ff.), as against Cadoux, p. 88n., for it explains the poet's sequence of places convincingly as the landmarks on the traveller's route to Ephesus, not Smyrna. Two passages in Pausanias (4.30.6 and 9.35.6) are not to be pressed. Despite Pliny, *NH* 36.4.11-12, their interpretation and their application to this period are contested (see Cadoux, p. 89n.).

22. Perhaps the main centre of the new *komopolis*, or at least one of its component *komai*, occupied the site.

23. See Head in *BMC Ionia*, p. 20, and Ramsay, *HG*, p. 62.

24. Hesiod, frag. *apud* Plutarch, *Mor.* 415c; Hdt. 2.73; Tac. *Ann.* 6.28; Plin. *NH* 10.2.3-5; Ov. *Metam.* 15.392-407; Artemid. *Onirocr.* 4.47; Ach. Tat. 3.25.

25. *2 Enoch* 12.1; 15.1; 19.6; all in Text A; *3 Baruch* 6; *Or. Sib.* 8.39. The theme of renewed life is not however prominent in these Jewish writings, as it is both in the pagan and Christian sources. Charles (*Pseudepigrapha*, p. 436 *ad 2 Enoch* 12.1) derives its adoption into Jewish thought from a rendering of Job 29.18. There and in Ps. 92.12 (LXX 91.12) *phoinix* was incorrectly understood to refer to the bird. See K. Lake in *LCL* and

Lightfoot, p. 95 *ad* 1 Clem. 25. Note that the reference to Tertullian for this interpretation should be *de Resurr. Carn.* 13.

The idea of a phoenix was current in the Roman world of the first century. The supposed sighting of a phoenix in Egypt was reported in AD 34 (according to Tac. *Ann.* 6.28), or in AD 36 (according to Plin. *NH* 10.2.3-5 and Dio Cass. 58.27). Pliny says the bird was displayed in Rome in AD 47, affirming the event but denying the authenticity of its identification. For the connection of this with the simile in Clement see Lightfoot, p. 97.

26. Thus B.F. Westcott, *The Gospel according to St. John*, II.323; R.H. Lightfoot, *St. John's Gospel*, p. 321.

27. Embalming as such was not a Jewish practice: see Strack–Billerbeck, *Kommentar zum Neuen Testament aus Talmud und Midrasch*, II.53 *ad* Mk 16.1. Yet the repeated reference to preservative spices (Mk 16.1; Lk. 23.56; 24.1) is a feature of some importance (see Michaelis, *TWNT* VII.458).

28. Cf. A. Plummer, *An Exegetical Commentary on the Gospel according to St. Matthew*, p. 15. We have noted that later patristic interpreters read an allegory of the burial of Christ into the mention of myrrh in the Psalms and Canticles.

29. Cf. e.g. the condensed argument from the context and associations of OT citations in the Epistle to the Hebrews (see e.g. F.F. Bruce, *Commentary on the Epistle to the Hebrews*, pp. 45ff., *ad* Heb. 2.12-13; cf. C.H. Dodd, *According to the Scriptures*, p. 126).

30. Most of the Pauline epistles are well represented, though the most quoted book is actually 1 Peter.

31. Cadoux, pp. 303-305. One MS of 1 Macc. 15.23 gives 'Smyrna' for 'Cyrene' in the list of places informed of Roman friendship for the Jews after the embassy of Simon Maccabaeus in 142 BC, but this reading is very doubtful.

32. See also Schürer in *HDB* Extra Vol., p. 93. There is the very rare occurrence of a woman as ἀρχισυνάγωγος (*CIJ* 741) and of the Hebrew שלום, a formula common in the Jewish Greek epitaphs of Palestine, but unique in Asia Minor (*CIG* 9897 = *CIJ* 739). See further below.

33. Cf. Jos. *contra Ap.* 2.4.39 with regard to the Ionian cities generally.

34. Boeckh, *ad loc.*, renders: *Iudaei . . . qui eiurata fide in civitatem recepti sint*. So Lightfoot, *Ignatius* I.470. Ramsay's view however seems correct, and is followed by Charles, p. 56. Cadoux's idea that these were pagans who, after conversion to Judaism, had reverted to their former beliefs and wished to advertise the fact (p. 348) seems to introduce improbable complications.

35. Cadoux, in a lengthy footnote (pp. 306-10), argues for Pionian authorship, explaining omissions, notably that of all mention of the apostle John, by the supposition that Pionius, though a fervent admirer of Polycarp, was an Antiquartodeciman, and therefore suppressed his links with the opposing view. This enabled Cadoux to accept the authenticity of the document and

regard its historicity favourably without rejecting the evidence of Irenaeus, *adv. Haer.* 3.3.4.

36. If taken to mean 'we had not yet received the Gospel'.

37. *SC*, pp. 272-73; Charles, p. 57; etc. Cf. Ignatius, *ad Smyrn.* 1.2.

38. Cf. Cadoux, p. 312. Lightfoot argues that Ephesus then became, at least temporarily, 'the headquarters of Christendom' (*Ignatius*, I.438; cf. 440).

39. See now however A.T. Kraabel, *Journal of Jewish Studies* 33 (1982), p. 455.

40. So Charles, pp. 56-57; Hort, p. 25; Swete, pp. 31-32. W.W. Tarn and G.T. Griffith, *Hellenistic Civilisation* (London, 3rd edn, 1952), p. 225, offer an alternative: 'The synagogues of Satan at Smyrna and Philadelphia . . . may point to some blended worship, . . . seeing that the altar of Zeus at Pergamum figures in the "Revelation" as "Satan's seat"'. Both this interpretation of Rev. 2.13 and its relevance here may be doubted: such forms of blended worship certainly existed, probably for instance at Thyatira, but there is no evidence to support such a reference here.

41. Hort, p. 25, who upheld a pre-70 date for the Revelation, wrote: 'After the destruction of Jerusalem and God's manifest judgement on the nation this form of language lost its meaning'. It seems on the contrary that the subsequent Jewish revival brought the whole area of controversy into renewed and sharper focus.

42. The 'martyrdoms' are similarly explained by W.H.C. Frend, *Martyrdom and Persecution in the Early Church* (Oxford, 1965), p. 184.

43. The maintenance of prisoners for long terms would doubtless have seemed an unnecessary financial burden to the cities. In Bithynia prisoners were guarded by public slaves, whose reliability was evidently suspect (Plin. *Ep.* 10.19, 20). See also A.H.M. Jones, *The Greek City*, p. 213.

44. So Ramsay, *SC*, p. 275; Charles, p. 56; Beckwith, p. 454. Plumptre, pp. 95-96, like Swete, makes it a typically long period. The difference is less marked than might appear, for in either case it is emphasized that the time is limited. Beckwith also comments here on the genitive ἡμερῶν, where we might expect ἡμέρας, which occurs as a variant.

45. Perhaps the nearest thing to a Jewish parallel is found in an apocalyptic passage of closely similar date and place (*Or. Sib.* 4.45-87), where a supposed prophecy of ten generations of foreign oppression concludes with a reference to the coming of Alexander in the tenth. The computation is inept, but seems to be forced into the mould of a tradition resembling the language of Aristides about Smyrna. Comparable symbolic computations of time are frequent in apocalyptic, but the individual systems are widely diverse. Compare and contrast *1 Enoch* 91.12-17; 93.3-10; *2 Enoch* 33.1-2; and the list of significances of the number ten in *Pirke Aboth* 5.1-9. See also Russell, *The Method and Message of Jewish Apocalyptic*, pp. 226-27.

46. I photographed the stone in April 1969. The lettering, though large and fairly easily legible, is rather faint and not easily reproduced.

47. Cf. Swete, pp. lxi-lxii: 'The public games of Smyrna were noted for their magnificence, and it was one of the cities where periodical festivals were held under the authority of the "Commune Asiae" in honour of the Augusti. On such occasions Christian citizens were doubtless placed in a position of peculiar peril.' Robert infers that the inscription itself is not earlier than Caracalla, who granted the city its third neocorate: the phrase ἡ γλυκυτάτη πατρίς is elsewhere associated with the period of the third neocorate.

48. Others discount the point, or make no mention of it. Note Plumptre, p. 88; Beckwith, p. 455.

49. *CIG* 3137 = *OGIS* 229, lines 3-5, of 243 BC. Cf. Cadoux, pp. 113-15. For the resulting benefits, including that of ἄσυλον, cf. the corresponding decree of the Delphians, *OGIS* 228.

50. Cf. E.R. Bevan, *The House of Seleucus*, I.199: 'Even Smyrna, which had been so eminent for its loyalty to the Seleucid house, now changed about, swore fidelity to Attalus, and was henceforward altogether alienated at heart from the Seleucid cause'.

51. He begins: ἀξία δὲ οὐ μόνον τῆς ὄψεως χάριν ἡ πόλις σωθῆναι, ἀλλὰ καὶ τῆς εὐνοίας ἣν παρὰ πάντα τὸν χρόνον εἰς ὑμᾶς παρέσχετο, συναραμένη μὲν πρὸς 'Αντίοχον πόλεμον... (41.515 = 295.766), and goes on to enumerate later services to Rome.

52. Cf. Tait, p. 206; Beckwith, p. 454. The phrase recurs in Rev. 12.11 and Acts 22.4. Cf. the idiomatic ἄχρι τῆς ἀγνοίας ('as long as he doesn't know') in Herm. *Mand*. 4.1.5. For μέχρι cf. 2 Tim. 2.9 and Heb. 12.4. Contrast the sense of περίλυπος... ἕως θανάτου (Mt. 26.38 = Mk 14.34); μαχοῦμαι ἕως ζωῆς καὶ θανάτου (*OGIS* 266.29, of Pergamum).

53. On its possible ambiguity see A.N. Sherwin-White, *Roman Society and Roman Law in the New Testament*, p. 8, and cf. Jos. *Antiq*. 18.1.1.2.

54. The distinctively kingly significance of Rev. 19.12 is confirmed by the pointed contrast of his διαδήματα πολλά with the phraseology of 12.3 and 13.1. The dragon is a caricature of Christ (Charles, p. 347). It is unnecessary to follow Charles in his supposition that 12.3 and 13.1 might be interpolations.

55. For Trench the decisive objection to this is that 'nowhere else in the Apocalypse is there a single image drawn from the range of heathen antiquity' (p. 112). We cannot accept this, though its denial might be put differently.

56. The stephanephorate, for instance, was not peculiar to Smyrna: it is thought to have originated in Miletus, and was found in several Ionian cities (Jones, *The Greek City*, pp. 47, 310-11n.). Moreover nothing is known of the office which would give point to an allusion here.

57. Ramsay (*SC*, pp. 257-58) comments: 'Several of his highly ornate sentences become clearer when we notice that he is expressing in a series of

variations the idea of a crown resting on the summit of the hill'. The 'crown' motif appears again in the phrase ἦρος δὲ πύλαι καὶ θέρους ὑπὸ στεφάνων ἀνοίγονται (21.437 = 269.471). Ramsay sees analogy between the embattled hill-summit and the turreted representation of the city-goddess on coinage (very common at all periods from the first *cistophori*). He also alludes to the actual appearance of the hill as formerly crowned with its mediaeval castle. The point might be dismissed as subjective and anachronistic, but the testimony of Aristides makes it clear that such analogies were characteristic of contemporary sentiment, and the ancient battlements evidently had a visual impact comparable with the mediaeval.

58.   *Vellem tantum me habere otii, ut possem recitare psephisma Smyrnaeorum quod fecerunt in Castricium mortuum, primum ut in oppidum introferretur quod aliis non conceditur, deinde ut ferrent ephebi, postremo ut imponeretur aurea corona mortuo* (*pro Flacco* 31.75). It is significant that he refers to an incident in Smyrna to illustrate a general point. It was common to award an honorific crown elsewhere (e.g. Demosthenes, *De Corona*, *passim*). Such honours were occasional; here however we evidently have a regular institution, amounting to a state funeral.

59.   Note the recurrence of the athlete metaphor in Ignatius, *ad Polyc.* 1.3; 2.3; 3.1; etc. The words of 2.3, in particular, look like a reference to a shared knowledge of Rev. 2.10, and so suggest an agonistic understanding of it. Cf. Polycarp, *ad Phil.* 1.1, and *Mart. Polyc.* 17.1; 14; 18.3; 19.3.

60.   U. Wilcken, *Griechische Ostraka*, I.274-76 and 296; cf. Deissmann, *LAE*, pp. 368-73. For the unintelligible ἀλλουπαρουσίας (?) of Mahaffy's text of the papyrus Wilcken proposes to divide the word and to understand στεφάνου from the previous item, ἄλλου (στεφάνου) παρουσίας, explained as 'für einen anderen Kranz, der anlässlich der Anwesenheit des Königs geschenkt wurde' (p. 275). The unpopularity of the imposition is seen in the complaint of the priests at Philae: ἀνάγκουσι [*sic*] ἡμᾶς παρουσίας αὐτοῖς ποιεῖσθαι οὐχ ἑκόντας (*OGIS* 139; 2nd cent. BC).

61.   ἀδικεῖν is always used as 'to hurt' in the Rev. except at 22.11, which Charles rejects (II.222 *ad loc.*).

62.   Charles however regards its presence here as an editorial addition of the original writer, and in 20.14 as an interpolation.

63.   Plutarch says that after death the good lead an easy life, but are not blessed or divine ἄχρι τοῦ δευτέρου θανάτου.

Notes to Chapter 5

1.   The form of the name varies between τὸ Πέργαμον and ἡ Πέργαμος. The neuter is the commoner (Strabo, Polybius and local inscriptions). 'Pergamos' occurs in Pausanias and in Xen. *Hell.* 3.1.6, and has been familiarized in English by the AV rendering. The oblique cases in the Greek

text of Rev. 1.11 and 2.12 leave the question open. The regular Latinization of the neuter will here be preferred.

2. The unstratified finds have not permitted the clear identification of prehistoric and archaic settlements. See W. Zschietzschmann, *PW* XIX.i.1239. He includes plans of the topography and excavations (cols. 1243ff.). For a valuable general description of the antiquities of the site see Bean, *Aegean Turkey*, pp. 73ff.

3. Paus. 1.4.5f.; Strab. 13.1.69 = p. 615. The original site was named Teuthrania, a name applied both to the district of the Caicus valley (Strab. 12.3.22 = p. 551) and to its early capital.

4. *BMC Mysia*, pp. xxiii-xxix and Perg. Nos. 1-3.

5. Diod. Sic. 15.90.3ff. After receiving his authority as the reward of betraying a rebel confederation, he then refused to disband his private army and maintained himself in virtual independence (*CAH* VI.21f.). He struck coinage at Lampsacus, Clazomenae and perhaps Cisthene (B.V. Head, *Historia Numorum*, p. 597; *BMC Ionia*, Satrapal Coinage, Nos. 15-27; cf. W. Waddington, *Mélanges de numismatique, deuxième série*, pp. 19-23).

6. Restoring the text as ἐπὶ τὸν κο[λωνόν]. Dittenberger (*ad loc.*) notes however that T. Reinach read κό[λπον], and found reference to the Gulf of Elaea and the old city of Teuthrania.

7. If this man is to be identified with the first *prytanis*, whose name is restored conjecturally by Dittenberger (*OGIS* 264.3-5n.), we may infer that this event immediately preceded the activities of Orontes (cf. E.V. Hansen, *The Attalids of Pergamum*, p. 12).

In the case of 'Asklepios' I have departed from my usual practice of Latinizing Greek names. The accepted Latin form 'Aesculapius' seems as inappropriate in a Greek environment as 'Jupiter' for 'Zeus'. The form 'Asclepius', though used in *OCD*, also seems unhappy, as a hybrid with doubtful sanction in usage.

8. Plut. *Alex.* 21.4 = p. 676; Diod. Sic. 20.20.1-2; 28.1-3; Hansen, pp. 13f. A series of coins, several depicting Athena and Heracles, probably date from this period (*BMC Mysia*, p. xxix and Perg. Nos. 4-25).

9. Philetaerus had consistently put the portrait of Seleucus on his coinage (*BMC*, Nos. 26-29): his successors almost always use that of Philetaerus himself (Nos. 30-46, 48-83).

10. 'Antiochus, son of Seleucus' must be Antiochus I (died 261), and this must have been very early in Eumenes' reign. Strabo's brief summary of Attalid history is very accurate.

11. Strab. 12.4.2 = p. 624; cf. *Ath. Mitt.* 33 (1908), 403f., No. 32, for the altar dedicated to him.

12. The passage sums up Livy's view of Eumenes' policy: *Cupidus belli adversus Antiochum Eumenes erat, gravem, si pax esset, accolam tanto potentiorem regem credens, eundem, si motum bellum esset, non magis parem Romanis fore quam Philippus fuisset, et aut funditus sublatum iri, aut si pax*

victo daretur, multa illi detracta sibi accessura, ut facile deinde se ab eo sine ullo auxilio Romano tueri posset.

13. App. *Syr.* 6.31, 34, 36; Liv. 37.41.9; 43.5, 8; 44.2; all perhaps details due to a Pergamene source. Cf. Hansen, p. 83.

14. The assumption underlies the whole account in Polybius (21.18.1-24.18, closely followed by Liv. 37.52-56). All hopes for the future rested on the Senate (21.18.2), and Eumenes is shown as desiring Roman presence and as content to owe his authority to it (21.21.8).

15. Cf. the comment in Hansen, p. 92.

16. Polyb. 30.1-3; Liv. 45.19f. An account of the supposed secret negotiations of Eumenes and Perseus is given in Polyb. 29.6-8 (cf. Liv. 44.24.7ff.). Polybius admits he learnt some of the details from friends of Perseus, who may have slandered Eumenes with unfounded charges (29.8.20; cf. Hansen, p. 111).

17. A remarkable document purporting to be a confidential letter of Attalus II is extant in an inscription of Pessinus (*OGIS* 315; Hansen, pp. 124f.). This, if authentic, testifies to a yet more abject state of dependence on Rome (esp. lines 53-61).

18. No other act of an Attalid monarch is mentioned so often in ancient literature, both in the historians (Florus 1.35.2; etc.) and as a byword in the poets (Hor. *Odes* 1.1.12f.; 2.18.5f.; cf. Hansen, p. 139). See also Liv. Epit. 58, 59; Strab. 13.4.2 = p. 624; Plin. *NH* 33.53.148; Plut. *Ti. Gracch.* 14 = p. 830. Mithridates the Great is said to have accused the Romans of forging the will, but its authenticity is assured by the contemporary reference in *OGIS* 338.7.

19. Cf. *OGIS* 338.12ff. for the indications of unrest.

20. Much later bitterness may be traced back to the *Lex Sempronia de provincia Asia* of 123 BC, by which Gaius Gracchus placed the collection of tribute in the hands of *publicani* (Cic. *II Verr.* 3.6.12). The grievances of the people can be clearly traced in literature (App. *Bell. Civ.* 5.1.4; and the Cilician correspondence of Cicero).

21. For the association of these four deities as the typical and principal divinities of the city see *CIG* 3538.27-29, 31-33 (an oracle datable between Hadrian and Caracalla).

22. E.g. *OGIS* 283, 301; *IGRR* IV. 284-87. See also Hansen, pp. 400-403 for Zeus and pp. 406-408 for Athena.

23. Most of their remains have been identified and dated approximately by epigraphic and stylistic evidence (summarized by Zschietzschmann, *PW* XIX.i.1241ff.).

24. Other major Attalid structures were the temples of Dionysus on the theatre terrace (later rededicated to Caracalla, col. 1260), of Hera and of Demeter (cols. 1249-52). It is not clear whether the Nicephorium adorned by Eumenes II (Strab. 13.4.2 = p. 624) is to be identified with the temple of Athena. The question is open whether Strabo attributes the bulk of the royal building activity to Eumenes or to Attalus II. Possibly the text is corrupt.

25. Hanscn, pp. 420f.; cf. pp. 221, 228, 247f., 260f.

26. Thus one Diodorus, honoured about 130-126 BC, was to receive sacrifices, an annual holy day, and a temple of white stone (*IGRR* IV. 292-94). A permanent record of the decree was to be inscribed on a *stele* of white stone.

27. So Blaiklock, *Cities*, p. 103; Barclay, p. 46.

28. *La Province romaine proconsulaire d'Asie*, pp. 138ff.

29. So Zahn, *Offenbarung*, pp. 249ff.; E.L. Hicks, *Expos.* 8th ser., 2 (1890), p. 148; Stauffer, *Christ and the Caesars*, p. 168. P. Monceaux, *De Communi Provinciae Asiae*, p. 99, cites *CIG* 2988, 2990, 2992, but the title 'first (metropolis)' is elsewhere applied to both Smyrna and Pergamum. Ramsay himself had earlier made the same assumption (*HDB* I.720ff.).

30. Cic. *ad Att.* 5.13.1; Jos. *Antiq.* 14.10.11.224.

31. The phrase τῇ βασιλευούσῃ πόλει is apparently used of Ephesus in a mutilated inscription (*Jahreshefte* 47 [1964-65], Beiblatt 5-8, perhaps of AD 162-65). I cited the original evidence for Ephesus more extensively in my thesis (pp. 179-80).

32. ἔχει δέ τινα ἡγεμονίαν πρὸς τοὺς τόπους τούτους τὸ Πέργαμον. The τόποι appear to denote the hinterland as far as the Taurus.

33. See H. Mattingly, *Coins of the Roman Empire in the British Museum*, III, pp. clvii-clxi and Nos. 1051-1100, pp. 382-97.

34. The city mint issued many *cistophori* after 133 BC (*BMC*, Nos. 86-128), including some dated to 49/8 BC by the name of a Roman *imperator*. The names of several later proconsuls occur on coins of Pergamum (Nos. 222-23, of c. AD 77; 242; 251-56); such are found also at Smyrna and more rarely at Ephesus. A treaty of about 95 BC between Ephesus and Sardis was recorded officially at Pergamum as well as at the participating cities (*IGRR* IV. 297.92-96). There is also a remarkably long series of dedications to Roman officials (*IGRR* IV. 373-409, 428-29, 433, etc.), many of them to proconsuls, who receive such titles as 'saviour' and 'benefactor'.

35. At least nine cities eventually bore the title 'metropolis', but these do not coincide with the capitals of the *conventus*, or judicial districts, as enumerated by Pliny (*NH* 5.29.105ff.; cf. Chapot, p. 353).

36. These three cities all bore the title πρώτη. One incident required imperial intervention. Smyrna had omitted the correct titles of Ephesus from a decree. Antoninus Pius pleads with the Ephesians to accept Smyrna's apology and to reciprocate by willingness to concede her her due titulature (*BMInscrs* 489; perhaps followed by the alliance coin of the three cities, *BMC Ionia*, Eph., No. 403, of Ant. Pius). The quarrel seems to have come to a head again under Caracalla. Comparison of coin types of that time suggests a kind of numismatic 'cold war'. Ephesus celebrated her third neocorate with a pointed claim (*BMC Ionia*, Eph. No. 292, of before AD 212). The other two cities produced types whose obverse was wholly devoted to displaying their titles in rebuttal of current Ephesian claims (*BMC Ionia*, Sm., Nos. 405-406;

BMC Mysia, Perg., No. 318; all with Caracalla bearded and so later). Pergamum insists she was first to be *neokoros*, first to be twice *neokoros*, first to be three times *neokoros*, and that all three were genuine imperial neocorates, with no courtesy-title from the Artemis-cult to make up the numbers.

37.   *CIG* 3524, of Cyme; 3569, of Assos.

38.   'As being κατείδωλος beyond all Asia' (Arethas, cited by Swete, p. 35). Charles suggests a contrast between the acropolis with its heathen shrines and the 'mountain of God' (Isa. 14.13; Ezek. 28.14, 16).

39.   See P. Wood, 'Local Knowledge in the Letters of the Apocalypse', *ExpT* 73 (1961-62), p. 264. A topographical understanding of the 'crown' at Smyrna is better founded, the use of the metaphor being authenticated by ancient evidence.

40.   So Deissmann, *LAE*, p. 281, n. 3. The spectacular frieze of the battle of gods and giants, now in East Berlin, depicted the latter with serpents' tails instead of legs (cf. also Rev. 9.19 with Moffatt, p. 410 *ad loc.*).

41.   The Roman sword was aptly so described, being adapted both for stabbing and slashing. ρομφαία is characteristically the sword of foreign conquest or domination. It is used in 1 Sam. 17.45 LXX of the sword of Goliath. See also *SC*, pp. 291-93; Caird, pp. 36-37.

42.   So Swete, p. 35; Barclay, pp. 54f. Contrast παροικεῖν, as in Heb. 11.9.

43.   The reading which inserts τὰ ἔργα σου καί after οἶδα (046 and many cursives) is readily explained as a harmonization, and the divergent text of the earlier MSS is to be preferred.

44.   The attempts of older writers to find a personal importance in this man or a symbolic meaning in his name are beside the point, and the legends about him valueless (Swete, p. 35; Beckwith, p. 459). The name is a shortened form of Antipatros (Antipater): cf. Jos. *Antiq.* 14.1.3.10.

45.   Early attempts at grammatical emendation are found in the MSS. א (original hand) inserts ἐν ταῖς after ἡμέραις; 046 and many cursives add αἷς; א (corrector), 025 and some cursives add ἐν αἷς. Some commentators suggest a genitive Ἀντίπα, but this has no textual authority, and the origin of the difficult reading is unexplained. It might perhaps be argued that the final ς arose from dittography with the following ο or by assimilation to the following nominative in apposition (see Swete, p. 36; Zahn, *Introduction to the New Testament*, p. 421). See however G. Mussies, 'Antipas', *NovT* 7 (1964-65), pp. 242-44, for alternative explanations of Ἀντίπας as a genitive.

46.   This difference of perspective must be noted in the discussion of e.g. 1 Pet. 4.14.

47.   Religious motifs which recall our text are very numerous on Pergamene coinage. The Asklepian serpent appears on over 150 local types, apart from the innumerable *cistophori*. Enthroned deities (Zeus, Athena, Asklepios, Sarapis and the Tyche of the city) appear at dates ranging from Philetaerus to Gordian III. For Asklepios cf. the words of Aristides: τοῦ θεοῦ σημήναντος

ἐπὶ τῆς ἐν Περγάμῳ καθέδρας (25.499 = 319.564). So also A. τὸν ἐν Π. ἐνιδρυμένον (26.519 = 335.595).

48. Αὐτοκράτορα Καίσαρα θεοῦ υἱὸν Σεβαστὸν πάσης γῆς καὶ θαλάσσης ἐπόπτην (*Inschr. von Perg.* 381, cited in *LAE*, p. 347). Contrast the attributes of God in Rev. 10.6; 14.7.

49. For the abundant evidence for Nero as 'Lord' see also *LAE*, p. 353, and cf. the expression in Acts 25.26. Momigliano calls attention to the antithesis between Christ and Nero as 'saviour' (*CAH*, X.742).

50. *IGRR* IV. 353a.32, of Perg., under Hadrian; *IGRR* IV. 451 = *OGIS* 513, of Perg., of early 3rd cent.; *IGRR* IV. 1398, of Sm., AD 124; *IGRR* IV. 1431.39, of Sm., under Hadrian; *BMInscrs* 481.191, of Eph., AD 104. The title does not occur in the text of the Rev. The word or a variant may however have been applied to John long before surviving attestations.

51. Cf. Stauffer, p. 178f. His whole chapter, esp. from p. 166, is very interesting but must be used with caution in default of clear documentation.

52. Rev. 1.8; 4.8, 11; 11.4, 8, 15, 17; 15.3; 16.17; 17.14; 19.6, 16; 21.22; 22.5, 6.

53. I believe that much difficulty has been occasioned by the usual practice of discussing the subject in the uninformative context of Rev. 2.6. The Balaam-Nicolaitan parallel, however interpreted, is surely the best point of approach.

54. The Nicolaitans are described as *vulsio eius quae falso cognominatur scientiae*. The Greek is not preserved.

55. Rev. 3.14 may be set against a speculative philosophy current in the Lycus valley since the days of the 'Colossian heresy', but there is no reason to connect this with Nicolaitanism.

56. See p. 93-94 below.

57. The modern analysis which assigns these passages respectively to P and JE is immaterial here, for ancient interpretation assumed in the narrative a unity which permitted harmonization and inferential expansion.

58. The name is presumably derived from the Zimri mentioned in Num. 25.6-15 (LXX Ζαμβρί).

59. The possibility that such a popular derivation existed is equally valid whether we suppose them to have interpreted the first element of בלעם as בעל or as בלע. In a setting of controversy either version might have done service for νικο-. A slogan would simply make the best use of available material, and it is likely that any resulting word-play or etymology would be artificial and incongruous.

60. Other documents bearing on the friendly relations of Pergamenes and Jews are concerned with matters of external diplomacy with Hasmoneans and Herods (Jos. *Antiq.* 14.10.22.247-55; *BJ* 1.21.12.425 and 1.9.3.187; 1 Macc. 15.22). None of them throws light on the number or status of Jews in Pergamum.

61. Torrey's views of the prevalence of Aramaic will be discussed in the

chapter on Sardis. The knowledge of that language is even less likely in Pergamum than in those cities where the strength of Judaism is attested.

62. R. Travers Herford in Charles, *Pseudepigrapha*, p. 709 *ad loc.*

63. Herford has collected very interesting evidence on this point in his *Christianity in Talmud and Midrash*, pp. 63ff.; cf. pp. 48, 291.

64. Here, as Herford allows (p. 67), Balaam is not exactly a type of Jesus, but the symbol is expanded into a comparison. In Epstein, *The Babylonian Talmud*, p. 261, the rendering is 'the sinners of Israel', but it is noted that the Munich Codex reads 'Jesus'.

65. This interpretation is also questioned in Epstein, TB Sanhedrin, p. 725 *ad loc.*

66. We defer for the moment the difficult problems of the dating of Jude and 2 Peter.

67. The Pergamene letter expresses Christ's hatred of the Nicolaitan διδαχή, the Ephesian of their ἔργα. It seems wrong however to press διδαχή as necessarily involving doctrine.

68. The Alexandrian text adds a prohibition of things strangled and of blood. The Western text gives the decree a purely ethical flavour. The former version is to be preferred as original; its provisions allude to pressing social issues of the Pauline churches (see F.F. Bruce, *The Acts of the Apostles*, pp. 299-300, and cf. p. 44). In either case Paul is represented as assenting to the terms, and the relevance of the fact for the history of the controversy is unaffected.

69. Cf. the promise in Rev. 2.7, where also Nicolaitanism is mentioned.

70. Some are mentioned in an edict, perhaps of Hadrian, which regulates money-changing (*IGRR* IV. 352.9-10, 24). Other examples are not of apparent importance.

71. Note for instance the ritual use of bread and wine (*passim*) and cf. Rev. 14.8-10, and also 8.3, 5; 16.19; 17.2; 18.3; 19.15.

72. Perhaps the meat in the public market was here actually dedicated to the emperor, and the conscientious Christian could not avoid such food without abstaining from meat altogether.

73. I find it easier to suppose that Peter is dependent on Jude: if Jude were secondary it would be difficult to account for its existence or preservation (see however, Bigg, *ICC*, pp. 216-24; Zahn, *Introduction to the NT*, pp. 250ff., 265ff.). If the writer of Jude had first addressed his brief but forceful letter to a church invaded by false teachers, the other writer, perceiving its relevance to the beginnings of a similar movement elsewhere, reapplied it within a letter to his own churches. There might then have been little lapse of time between the epistles. Both are related to specific situations, and are no mere generalized condemnations of heresy, but the questions of their date and destination remain very open. We might argue that 2 Peter was sent to some part of Asia Minor, if 2 Pet. 3.1 be held to refer to 1 Peter, a supposition equally possible on any view of 2 Peter.

74. The last possibility clearly hinges on a very early dating of 2 Peter. Despite the weight of contrary authority this option seems to me very open. Any dating of this letter seems to pose acute problems, and the positive reasons offered for particular hypotheses are often tenuous and incompatible. C.E.B. Cranfield, *1 and 2 Peter and Jude*, pp. 148-49, assumes an early second-century date on the basis of an inferential placing of Jude about 80, itself a conjectural evaluation of the time-lapse implied by Jude 3 and 17. B. Reicke, however, in *The Epistles of James, Peter and Jude* (*The Anchor Bible*), pp. 144-45, makes the Domitianic persecution a *terminus ad quem* and infers a date about 90 from the attitude of 2 Peter to civil authority. The historical uncertainty of such arguments and the lack of clear correlation with identifiable external data must be strongly emphasized.

75. There are several possibilities here. Possibly these traditions were based on knowledge or on assumption, right or wrong, of the identity of Jezebel or of the teachers of Jude or 2 Peter with Nicolaitanism. We cannot be sure how far these views rest on contemporary fact, how far on the colouring of later events, and how far on inferential opinion.

76. Caird (p. 41) points out that Christ's 'coming' does not necessarily refer to the Parousia. Its significance is variously applied in the letters. Here, at Ephesus and at Sardis it is a threat to the unrepentant. In the first two cases the words of the warning are identical.

77. Alternatively, (1) we might lay stress on ἐκεῖ (2.14) following a threefold emphasis on Pergamum as the place of Satanic power. Even there they tolerated a fatal compromise, where the issue between Christ and Caesar was so direct, and others might easily be misled. Or (2), the Nicolaitan compromise at Pergamum was such a standing temptation, perhaps so subtly presented that many were blind to its implications. These two suggestions might seem incompatible, and either might be pressed to exclude the other. But both might relate to potentialities of the situation, and the church might blindly entertain a view which offered an amenable *modus vivendi* in difficult circumstances, and so be open to that which John sees as a plain choice of Caesar against Christ.

78. Charles (p. 65) observes that τοῦ μάννα is the only NT example of a simple partitive genitive after δίδωμι. Cf. however ἐκ τῆς συναγωγῆς in 3.9. For the indeclinable form μάννα see R. Meyer in *TDNT* IV. 462. This form is used in Ps. 78.24 (LXX 77.24) and in the NT.

79. The OT never says this, and 1 Kings 8.9 (= 2 Chron. 5.10) is explicit that in Solomon's temple the ark contained nothing but the two tables of stone (Deut. 10.5).

80. Trench (p. 127) emphasizes the force of this form as against κρυπτόν. The act of 'hiding' might be that of preserving the sample in the sanctuary or the traditional concealment at the first fall of Jerusalem.

81. *Quis Rerum Divinarum Heres?* 39.191; *Legum Analogiae* 3.59.169; cf. 3.61.174-76.

82. So Arethas, cited by Swete, p. 39.

83. The word is rare in Biblical Greek, but common elsewhere. It is literally a 'pebble', occasionally a 'gem' (Philostr. *Vit. Ap. Ty.* 3.27), or applied to any of the numerous uses of pebbles or tablets of stone. Of these the sense 'vote' is by far the most common; the word may also by metonymy denote a 'resolution' (Pind. *Ol.* 7.87) or even a 'place of voting' (Eur. *Iph. Taur.* 945). In other cases it is used of a 'token' or 'tablet', and comes semantically close to the Greek σύμβολον and the Latin *tessera*.

The sense 'gem' has occasionally been adopted by commentators here. Artemidorus (*Onirocr.* 2.5 = p. 89) defines the word in this sense, but he is concerned to draw symbolic significance from the different derivative usages. The word should be taken here in one of its more natural senses unless it can be shown that the readers were likely to have recognized a more specialized allusion.

84. I have discussed other suggestions more fully in the original thesis from which the present work is abridged.

85. Other views, not discussed here, are: (1) the white stone as an emblem of good fortune. Pliny derives this usage from the Thracian custom of marking every happy day thus (*NH* 7.40.131; also Aesch. *Pers.* 305; Tibull. 3.3.25; and near the date of the Rev. in Pers. *Sat.* 2.1; Mart. *Epig.* 8.45.2; 9.51.4-5; 11.36.1-2; 12.34.5-7; Plin. *Ep.* 6.11.3). A variant explanation is given in Plut. *Pericles* 7.2. (2) A calculating counter for God's favourable 'reckoning' of the victor (contrast Rev. 13.18): an artificial analogy, mentioned by Swete, p. 40. (3) The stone as the conqueror himself (Charles, p. 67): a forced allegory which cannot be sustained as allegory.

86. Yoma 75a; mentioned by Bousset, p. 250; Charles, p. 66; Swete, p. 40; Moffatt, p. 358. The alternative views of this kind see allusion (1) to the engraved jewels of the high priest's breastplate (Exod. 28.17-21): thus M. Stuart, 'The White Stone of the Apocalypse', *Bibliotheca Sacra* 1 (1843), pp. 472ff.; or (2) to a conjectural identification of the Urim (Exod. 28.30) as a diamond inscribed with the divine name (Trench, pp. 135-38, refuted by Plumptre, pp. 126-27).

87. In recent discussion similar considerations weigh with Hendriksen (*More than Conquerors*, pp. 67-71), who rejects other types of background without discussion. One other Jewish parallel has been noted by Charles (p. xxxii) on a detail: the 'new name' in *Test. Levi* 8.14, where it is applied to the priesthood of the Maccabees. There is nothing further to favour a connection of thought.

88. It is immaterial whether the votes of the human judges were equal (cf. Eur. *Iph. Taur.* 1469-72) or whether Athena's vote made them equal and the equal vote constituted acquittal (so Aesch. *Eumen.* 744, 756 may be read; see G. Thomson, *The Oresteia of Aeschylus*, II.298-99).

89. The increasing distinctness of these senses is emphasized by the fact that in the court practice of the fourth century BC ψῆφοι were not stones at

all, but metal discs with a central cylindrical column, solid for acquittal (πλήρης ψῆφος), hollow for condemnation (τετρυπημένη ψῆφος). See Aeschin. *Contra Timarchum* 79 and *DGRA* II.516.

90. Athena Nicephorus was identified with Nike Apteros at Athens. The altars to 'unknown gods' at Athens (cf. Acts 17.23 with Paus. 1.1.4; Diog. Laert. 1.110; Philostr. *Vit. Ap. Ty.* 6.3) are paralleled by the unique survival of such an altar from Pergamum (as restored in Deissmann, *Paul*, pp. 287-92). Generous donations were made by the Pergamene kings to Athens.

91. Swete, p. 40; Moffatt, p. 358. The latter appears to regard it as a token securing admission to a feast.

92. So lines 97-99:

> *Ille tamen faciem prius inspicit et trepidat ne*
> *Suppositus venias ac falso nomine poscas:*
> *Agnitus accipies.*

This might be consistent with the use of a token bearing the name, which the patron checked with the features of the claimant.

93. Thus Nero (Suet. *Nero* 11.2); Agrippa (Dio Cass. 49.43.4); Caligula (Suet. *Calig.* 18.2); Domitian (Suet. *Dom.* 4.5; Stat. *Silv.* 1.6.66). Cf. Mooney, *Suetonius*, p. 530n.

94. Hepding in *Ath. Mitt.* 32 (1907), p. 294. The preserved fragment grants a concession in entrance-fee (εἰσηλύσιον) to the sons of members of five years' standing. That word is rare, but occurs with varying itacisms in inscriptions of Pergamum and Smyrna which refer to the imperial cult (*CIG* 3173 = *IGRR* IV. 1393, of Sm., under Titus; *IGRR* IV. 353.d14, of Perg.; *CIG* 3278, of Sm.). See further M.N. Tod, 'Notes on some Inscriptions from Asia Minor', *CR* 29 (1915), p. 2.

95. Thus Ζεὺς σωτὴρ καὶ νίκη before Cunaxa (Xen. *Anab.* 1.8.16).

96. The granting of such awards to athletic victors is abundantly attested, but I have found no other authority for the use of a *tessera* in this connection, as in e.g. Stuart, pp. 470-71; Beckwith, p. 462.

97. The *tessera frumentaria* entitled the poor in Rome to a regular supply of corn (Suet. *Aug.* 40.2; 42.3), and schemes of food distribution by wealthy benefactors are recorded in abundance from the cities of Asia. The *tessera nummaria* (Suet. *Aug.* 41) entitled the recipient to cash.

98. Thus the Paris Magical Papyrus of c. AD 300 mentions a φυλακτήριον in the form of a sheet of tin inscribed with a list of potent secret names and to be hung on the person of the devil-possessed (lines 3014-17, cited in *LAE*, p. 256). Cf. the Jewish use of 'phylacteries' (Mt. 23.5, a practice based on Deut. 6.8).

99. Beckwith however combines this idea with the individual view of the 'new name'.

100. Ramsay further observes that in *CIL* VI.631 most of the gladiators are characterized as either '*VET(erani)*' or '*TIR(ones)*', the former being

listed first. The two 'SP' names, while receiving neither designation, are positioned with the *tirones*.

101. The objection that gladiatorial exhibitions were not popular in the Greek East has been greatly overrated. See L. Robert, *Gladiateurs dans l'Orient grec* (1940). There are extant numerous gladiatorial inscriptions from the cities of Asia. At Pergamum there was a large amphitheatre, and the most famous citizen, Galen, actually made his name as surgeon to the gladiators there (*PW* VII.i.579). The gladiatorial theory of the present passage has been mentioned favourably as recently as by Barclay in *The Daily Study Bible*, 2nd edn (1960), pp. 119-20.

102. Ramsay insists that this was the most common date on them. This is in fact hardly established by the texts, though the *Kalendae* of various months are frequent. This fact, however, might have many explanations.

103. The occurrences of *incubatio* at Pergamum are independently attested by the many votive offerings on altars of white marble Ἀσκληπίωι Σωτῆρι κατ' ὄνειρον (*Ath. Mitt.* 24 [1899], 169-70, Nos. 8-10, etc.).

104. *OCD*, p. 887; cf. K. Regling, 'Spectator', *PW* II Reihe VI.1568-69.

105. The very common theophoric names 'Apollonius' (727) and 'Demetrius' (748) are not significant exceptions.

106. A record on stone was permanent. The desire of innumerable city officials in Asia to immortalize their names is reflected in the thousands of surviving honorific inscriptions. Cf. Horace's allusion to his lyrics as *monumentum aere perennius* (*Od.* 3.30.1).

107. Plin. *NH* 13.21.70, quoting the authority of Varro. Parchment was in use earlier: examples from Dura on the Euphrates have been dated between 196 and 190 BC. Probably it had not previously been a regular material for literary texts, and may not have extensively replaced papyrus until the early 4th cent. AD (F.G. Kenyon, *OCD*, p. 142).

108. Honorific decrees of the city repeatedly stipulate that the record of its benefactors shall be engraved on λευκὸς λίθος.

109. So Abram became Abraham. Cf. the early establishment of the custom of taking a new name at baptism (*SC*, p. 305), and also Aristides' assumption of his new name at Pergamum. Such parallels give insight into current forms of thought, which might equally find Christian or pagan expression.

Notes to Chapter 6

1. The materials are much scattered and duplicated. Some are collected in a useful Latin monograph, M. Clerc, *De Rebus Thyatirenorum* (Paris, 1893). The most important epigraphic sources elsewhere are Clerc, 'Inscriptions de Thyatire et des environs', *BCH* 10 (1886), pp. 398-423; G. Radet, 'Inscriptions de Lydie', *BCH* 11 (1887), pp. 445-84, Nos. 18-33; E.L. Hicks,

'Inscriptions from Thyatira', *CR* 3 (1889), pp. 136-38; A. Conze and C. Schuchhardt, 'Die Arbeiten zu Pergamon 1886-1898', *AthMitt* 24 (1899), pp. 97-240, Nos. 75-85; W.H. Buckler, 'Monuments de Thyatire', *Revue de Philologie* 37 (1913), pp. 289-331; the most convenient collections of the inscriptions are in *CIG* 3477-3520 and *IGRR* IV. 1189-1286.

2. Strabo merely calls it 'a colony of the Macedonians' (11.4.4 = p. 625). The early dating is confirmed by the lettering of a dedication to an unidentified Seleucus (*OGIS* 211). The two other earliest epigraphical fragments are both dedications by Macedonians, and probably of similar age (*BCH* 10 [1886], p. 398, No. 1, and 11 [1887], p. 466, No. 32). Clerc (p. 13) argues that Seleucus never controlled Lydia until after the battle of Corypedium (281 BC) in the closing months of his life. The colony would then be dated 281/80. At that time however Philetaerus in Pergamum had already rebelled against Lysimachus and was already under Seleucid protection.

3. See S. Reinach in *RA* 2 (1889), p. 158, and Ramsay, *HG*, p. 114n. Stephanus derives the name from θυγάτηρ, because Seleucus was said to have received news of his daughter's birth there. Without countenancing this grotesque etymology E.R. Bevan suggests the coincidence may have induced Seleucus to retain the old name rather than naming the colony from a member of the royal house (*House of Seleucus*, I.167n.). But the etymology might be more natural under influence of the itacistic pronunciation of Stephanus's day than in Seleucid times, though the *gamma* in fact retains a palatal sound, the fricative [γ], before a back vowel even in Modern Greek.

4. Cf. Plin. *NH* 5.31.115, and an inscription published by E.L. Hicks in *CR* 3 (1889), p. 136, No. 2.

5. For its sufferings from Philip V in 202/1 BC see Polyb. 16.1.7, and cf. Diod. Sic. 28.5. For its part in the Magnesia campaign of 190 BC see Liv. 37.8.8 (cf. Bevan, II.95); Liv. 37.37.6, 9, and 44.4 (cf. Bevan, II.111). Even after this extinction of Seleucid power in the area Prusias of Bithynia despoiled the district in 157/6 (Polyb. 32.15.10).

6. Robert argues that Thyatira was Pergamene at least by the second year of Eumenes II (196 BC), finding no trace of an era in 190 and observing that dating by regnal years was normal in the Pergamene kingdom. The Seleucid occupation during the Magnesia campaign would then have been only temporary.

There are many chronological problems. Head gives the impression of thinking Thyatira was never Pergamene before 190: Ramsay (*SC*, p. 324) writes as though it then became so securely part of the inner kingdom that it ceased to be of military importance. Both are probably artificial simplifications. It probably changed hands often and it was a focal point of military disturbance as late as the Mithridatic wars. Its possession was militarily crucial for the masters of Pergamum as early as 262 and as late as 85. The difference was perhaps that before 190 it was the scene of constant border wars, and after 190 it enjoyed comparative security except in troubled interludes.

7. Thyatira is not mentioned in the corresponding account in Appian, *Mithr.* 9.60, who locates Fimbria's subsequent suicide at Pergamum.

8. So A.H.M. Jones (*Cities of the Eastern Roman Provinces*, Oxford [1937], p. 54) actually argues from the presence of ἱεραὶ φυλαί of shoemakers and woolworkers at Philadelphia that that city must be older than its assumed foundation as an Attalid colony.

9. So e.g. Ramsay, *SC*, pp. 324-26; cf. pp. 329-30, 346-53; Swete, pp. lxiii-lxiv, 41; Charles, pp. 68-72.

10. The following examples are recorded: οἱ ἱματευόμενοι (*CIG* 3480 = *IGRR* IV. 1209), οἱ ἀρτοκόποι (*CIG* 3495 = *IGRR* IV. 1244), οἱ βυρσεῖς (*CIG* 3499 = *IGRR* IV. 1216), οἱ κεραμεῖς (*CIG* 3485 = *IGRR* IV. 1205), οἱ λινουργοί (*CIG* 3504 = *IGRR* IV. 1226), οἱ λανάριοι (*IGRR* IV. 1252), οἱ τοῦ σταταρίου ἐργασταὶ καὶ προξενηταὶ σωμάτων (slave-dealers; *IGRR* IV. 1257), χαλκεῖς χαλκοτύποι (*IGRR* IV. 1259), and, most commonly and characteristically οἱ βαφεῖς (*IGRR* IV. 1242, perhaps Augustan or shortly after; IV. 1239, of perhaps c. AD 100; *BCH* 11 [1887], pp. 100-101, No. 23; etc.). The attribution to Thyatira of a guild of σκυτοτόμοι by Clerc, p. 93, followed by Ramsay, *SC*, p. 325, is however erroneous. An improved restoration of the relevant inscription shows that it belongs to the closely related neighbouring city of Attalia (Schuchhardt in *AthMitt* 24 [1899], pp. 224-25, No. 55 = *IGRR* IV. 1169).

11. The Areni and Nagdemi (*CIG* 3488) and the Tabireni (*IGRR* IV. 1245).

12. Cf. for instance 'the craftsmen in the Shoemakers' Street' (*IGRR* IV. 1790, of Apamea). Cf. *IGRR* IV. 788-89, 791, also of Apamea, and IV. 424 and 425 (= *OGIS* 491), both of Pergamum. See also *CB* II.462. In the light of such evidence we may understand the words ἐργεπιστατήσαντα ἱερᾶς πλατείας in an inscription of Thyatira (*IGRR* IV. 1248) to refer to the president of a localized trade-guild rather than a 'superintendent of works' (*LSJ*).

13. Traditional crafts are not peculiar to Akhisar, even if their continuance is well exemplified there. In any case they play a much smaller part in the economy of the much larger modern town.

14. See especially 'The Permanence of Religion at Holy Places in Western Asia' in *Pauline and Other Studies*, pp. 163-88. There is specific evidence for the long persistence of certain guilds: those of Laodicea in the life of 14th century Denizli (Ibn Baṭṭūṭa, *Travels*, transl. H.A.R. Gibb, p. 426) and perhaps some at Smyrna and Galatian Ancyra (Ankara) into modern times (Ramsay in *AJA* 1 [1885], pp. 140-42; *CB* I.106).

15. The words πορφυροπώλης and πορφυρόπωλις are mentioned together in an inscription of Cos (*IGRR* IV. 1071).

16. It was then also still abundantly produced in the district of Kara Taş,

somc 50 m. E of Thyatira. There had been great demand for it in the carpet making of Kula until cheap European dyes replaced it (*HG*, p. 123).

17. Perhaps the same was true here, though Foucart's assertion of this in *BCH* 11 (1887), p. 101, seems to rest on a misreading of Strabo.

18. προσευχή is to be rendered 'prayer'. The inference is not affected by the textual problem. See F.F. Bruce, *The Acts of the Apostles*, p. 314.

19. The vivid and circumstantial narrative of Acts at this point and the presumed presence of the writer in Philippi between the 'we-passages' (16.17 to 20.5) confirm that the information about Lydia is well-founded.

20. Perhaps 'Lydia' was not her personal name, but an ethnic nickname (cf. Bruce, *Acts*, p. 314). It is conceivable that some subsequent mention of her real name in the Pauline correspondence escapes us.

21. Such a colony could have been established at the original foundation, a possibility noted by Ramsay, *SC*, pp. 322, 445n., referring to Jos. *Antiq.* 12.3.1.119. It seems very doubtful whether it could have been among those cities of Lydia where Antiochus III settled Mesopotamian Jews (Jos. *Antiq.* 12.3.4.149), for it was probably never under effective Seleucid control even in the earlier years of his reign.

22. Apart from the matter of the 'Sambathe' cult, the worship of Theos Hypsistos is recorded from Thyatira more than elsewhere in Lydia. See Keil and von Premerstein, *Zweite Reise*, pp. 17-18, Nos. 28, 29 (both of 2nd or 3rd cent. AD), and cf. J. Keil, '*Die Kulte Lydiens*', in *Anatolian Studies Presented to Sir W.M. Ramsay*, p. 255.

23. The former is exemplified by the cult of Artemis Anaeitis at neighbouring Hierocaesarea (Paus. 3.16.8; cf. 5.27.5 and Tac. *Ann.* 3.62; also Keil, p. 250). Egyptian dating occurs on an inscription (*IGRR* IV. 1190), and coinage testifies to a local cult of Isis (*BMC Lydia*, Thyat., No. 53, of Alexander Severus or later; cf. No. 109, of Geta).

24. Thus, among the few inscriptions assignable to the Flavian period, *IGRR* IV. 1194 = *CIL* III.7191-94; *IGRR* IV. 1193 = *CIL* III.470.

25. Acceptance of the difficult reading πεπυρωμένης in 1.15 (A, C, etc.), rather than πεπυρωμένῳ (ℵ and some cursives) or πεπυρωμένοι (many cursives), implies that the nom. form is χαλκολίβανος, feminine, (τῆς χαλκολιβάνου) being here understood.

26. Thus Oecumenius's alternatives (6th cent.), 'bronze from Mount Lebanon' or 'bronze-coloured frankincense' are both evidently based on etymological speculation (ed. H.C. Hoskier, p. 42). An objection to the first, as to some modern explanations, is that it would require the elements to be compounded in the reverse order: the inappropriateness of the second is only underlined by the prolix attempt to allegorize a spiritual meaning from the supposed reference to frankincense.

27. He takes the term to be an invention of John's own compounding. His words seem remote from a realistic appraisal: 'In this word on a small scale, as in the Apocalypse itself on a larger, the two sacred tongues, Greek and

Hebrew, will thus be wonderfully married' (p. 39). A similar view has recently been defended by C.G. Ozanne in a thesis, *The Influence of the Text and Language of the Old Testament on the Book of Revelation* (Manchester, 1964), pp. 14–17.

28. Dan. 10.6 LXX reads ὡς ὅρασις χαλκοῦ στίλβοντος. In a close parallel (Ezek. 1.4, 27 and 8.2) the rare word חשמל (LXX ἤλεκτρον) is rendered 'amber' in AV, but 'gleaming bronze' in RSV.

29. Contrast E.H. Plumptre's words in rejecting the suggestion of local reference here: 'The imagery had already been used without reference to any local colouring' (p. 135). This seems to me to misapprehend the integrated structure of the whole. For the anticipatory use of a phrase later explained more fully, cf. in another connection Beckwith, p. 426.

30. Copper may be distinguished as ἐρυθρὸς χαλκός (so perhaps in Hom. *Il.* 9.365). In Latin it is sometimes distinguished as *(aes) Cyprium* (Plin. *NH* 34.20.94), later *cuprum*.

31. He points out that the metal boils at a lower temperature than the reduction point of its ore. If then it is exposed to the air at its reduction, it immediately oxidizes. Its production is therefore dependent on the perfecting of an apparatus to distil the metal at its formation into an airless receiving vessel. He suggests that brass must have been a fortuitous discovery, and that it was reproduced by the deliberate repetition of a process not understood. It was obtained, in his view, neither from metallic zinc, nor from mixed copper-zinc ores, for these do not occur with more than a slight proportion of zinc except in Spain, and their use would also have been precluded by technical difficulties. He considers therefore that brass was made by heating copper with calamine, the principal ore of zinc. If calamine, charcoal and copper are ground and mixed, brass will form at 800°C, a temperature not higher than the melting-point of the copper.

32. See M. Farnsworth *et al.*, 'Metallographic Examination of a Sample of Metallic Zinc from Ancient Athens', *Hesperia* Suppl. VIII (1949), pp. 126–29; E.R. Caley, *Orichalcum*, pp. 14–16. This may have been made at the Laurium mines, where Pliny's *lauriotis* (*NH* 34.34.132) was probably a zinc compound. Caley suggests it was originally coated with a protective layer of another metal, cleaned away before the core was recognized as of zinc. The only other finds of undoubted zinc are attributed to prehistoric Dacia, but were surface finds of uncertain date and origin. The metal was probably never common, and its liability to corrosion would not favour its preservation.

33. A small town near the watershed between Thyatira and Pergamum is today named Bakır, the Turkish for 'copper', and the river of the Pergamum valley is the Bakır Çay, the ancient Caicus. Either or both of these however may simply be descriptive of colour, as very commonly in Turkish place-names. If the current form of the river name correctly represents the original, the interpretation 'copper-coloured river' is confirmed by the occurrence of the element in the 'adjectival relationship'. The 'qualifying

relationship' would strictly require the suffixed form 'Çayı', and this might be rendered either 'the river of copper' or possibly 'the river of (the town) Bakır'. I am indebted for confirmation of these points to my friend Dr A. Orhan Yeşin.

34. The problems of their identification are discussed by W. Leaf, *Strabo on the Troad* (Oxford, 1923), pp. 266-67 (Cisthene) and 284-87 (Andeira). Cisthene was on the coast SW of Adramyttium, Andeira in the spurs of Trojan Ida NW of Adramyttium. There may have been another Andeira E of Adramyttium (Plin. *NH* 5.33.126; cf. Leaf, pp. 326-27), and Strabo's misplacing of Pionia is evidently due to his confusion of the two (contrast 13.1.56 = p. 610 with 13.1.67 = p. 614 and Paus. 9.18.4). The essence of the case is unaffected by these problems. The principal mines were in or near the Troad, and the names are attached to localities bearing a similar geographical relation to Adramyttium and Pergamum.

35. The prominent clothing and dyeing trades would have received impetus from the same cause. Clerc, noting the recent replacement of the madder-root dye, mentions that the cultivation of madder would have disappeared also in southern France in his day apart from the action of the authorities in ordering its use for dyeing military uniforms (p. 94n.).

36. The work of M. Rostovtzeff is highly instructive here. He emphasizes that the Attalids considered themselves to have restored the entity ruled by Orontes, the rebel satrap of Mysia (*OGIS* 264.4ff.; 'Notes on the Economic Policy of the Pergamene Kings', *Anatolian Studies Presented to Sir W.M. Ramsay*, p. 363). See also his contributions in *CAH* VIII.608-13 and *The Social and Economic History of the Hellenistic World*, I.553-66.

37. Rostovtzeff, 'Notes', pp. 365-67.

38. Important discussions of it are in Forbes, p. 286; Leaf, *Strabo on the Troad*, pp. 287-89; H. Michell, 'Oreichalkos', *CR* n.s. 5 (1955), pp. 21-22; E.R. Caley, pp. 18-25. Cf. also Magie, pp. 44 and 804n.

39. These references have been discussed by Caley (pp. 25-31) and by Michell. See Hes. *Scut.* 122; Hom. *Hymn Aphrodite* 6.9; Schol. *ad* Apoll. Rhod. 4.973 (referring to Stesichorus and Bacchylides); Plato *Critias* 114e, cf. 116c, d (in description of Atlantis); Ps.-Arist. *de Mirab. Auscult.* 49 = 834a.

40. Rostovtzeff, *Social and Economic History of the Hellenistic World*, III.1448n.; cf. I.554, 556.

41. It is notable that metallurgy probably developed earlier in the Troad than anywhere else in the Aegean, and that the earliest examples of tin-bronze in the area are recorded from that district. See C. Renfrew, *AJA* 71 (1967), p. 14.

42. Cf. e.g. the remarkable engineering feat of cutting a waggon-road through the Cilician Gates at an unknown early date (Ramsay, *Cities of St. Paul*, pp. 114-15). On the decline as coupled with degradation in religion, cf. Ramsay, 'Religion of Greece and Asia Minor', *HDB* Extra Volume, esp.

p. 110. There is moreover an interesting parallel in the recent discussion of finds of arsenical bronze of the Aegean Early Bronze Age in C. Renfrew, 'Cycladic Metallurgy and the Aegean Early Bronze Age', *AJA* 71 (1967), pp. 1-20, and J.A. Charles, 'Early Arsenical Bronzes—A Metallurgical View', *AJA* 71 (1967), pp. 21-26. The latter argues that the inclusion of arsenic in the alloy was certainly deliberate and gave advantages over tin-bronze, though much arsenic would have been lost in toxic fumes, and the technique may eventually have been discontinued for that reason. The finds however illustrate the remarkable sophistication of primitive technology in reducing a metal which presents in lesser degree the same difficulties as zinc.

43. For the loss of first-century technical writing see E.A. Judge, *Jahrbuch für Antike und Christentum* 15 (1972), p. 31.

44. It is immaterial whether we render χαλκο- as 'copper' or 'bronze', or whether the alloy was precisely brass or zinc bronze. The procedure for excluding air may not have been efficient enough to eliminate considerable wastage of zinc. The point is that some zinc was made, and then incorporated in the alloy.

45. The suffix -ανος is frequent in forming a noun or adjective from a verb (cf. πίθανος, βοτάνη, δρέπανον). The sense 'frankincense (tree)' is also apparently thus derived from λείβω. λίβανος in that sense can sometimes be feminine, as is probably our χαλκολίβανος. ψευδάργυρος in Strabo is also, surprisingly, feminine. Possibly the gender might be explained by analogy between the synonyms. Tait (p. 78) refers to a suggestion of Wordsworth deriving χαλκολίβανος from λείβω, but stipulating a meaning 'liquid (or molten) brass'—again problematic etymologically.

46. R.H. Charles however points out that the title is presupposed elsewhere where God is spoken of as the Father of Christ (p. 68, referring to Rev. 1.6; 2.27; 3.5, 21).

47. Mattingly and Sydenham, *Roman Imperial Coinage*, Domitian, No. 213; cf. Nos. 209a, 440.

48. σου has already occurred four times in 2.19-20 (cf. Charles, II.251, and Beckwith, pp. 471-72). The reading κατὰ σου ὀλίγα, followed by AV, rests on very slight foundation. Charles cites only the 12th-13th cent. cursive 1.

49. Beckwith actually suggests an early belief in this theory as an alternative explanation of the insertion of σου. Swete (p. 43) thinks it may have been due to the influence of the LXX of 1 Kings (3 Kgdms) 19.1 and 20(21).5, 7, 25 (not 26). Ramsay, however, inclining to accept σου, sees a great temptation for a copyist to omit it from his copy (*SC*, p. 341).

50. E.C. Selwyn, *The Christian Prophets*, p. 123n., suggested she was the wife of an Asiarch, a speculation without apparent foundation or probability. Nor is there any justification for equating her with Lydia.

51. Blakesley, *SDB* III.1495; Schürer, 'Die Prophetin Isabel in Thyatira, Offenb. Joh. 2,20', *Theologische Abhandlungen Carl von Weizsäcker zu seinem siebzigsten Geburtstage . . . gewidmet*, pp. 39-58, and summary in *TLZ* 18 (1893), cols. 153-54.

52. He cites the unique and doubtful σαββαθεῖον in a decree of Augustus in favour of the Jews of Asia in Jos. *Antiq.* 16.6.2.164.

53. See Tcherikover, *CPJ* III.43-87. Of various names of the group the masculine Σαμβαθίων and the feminine Σαμβάθιον are characteristic. On any view the provenance of this Hebrew name is difficult to explain. There are hints that it originated in syncretistic contexts, in association for instance with the cult of Theos Hypsistos, attested at Thyatira and often showing Jewish influence, though later the name evidently lost all religious connotation.

54. I have discussed the details and possible interpretations of this site in my original thesis. I refrain from repeating here an elaborate inferential structure peripheral to the present case though very relevant to the religious history of Thyatira. The remains of an older church may be seen beneath the end of the present building and an apparently pagan horseman-god relief is preserved within it.

55. Several circumstantial pointers favour this conclusion. Cf. for instance the pattern of Lydian religious life known from Hierapolis (*CB* I.102). The shrine lay on the side of the town towards Attalia, which shared the cult. The epithet Boreitene is of a characteristic local-ethnic formation and may have applied to the original temple village. And the only inscription which records it is a dedication said to have been found at a mosque where there was formerly a temple of the Greeks (Boeckh on *CIG* 3477). It would be interesting to know whether it were *in situ*. Cf. also the tradition cited by Ramsay, *Studies in the Eastern Roman Provinces*, p. 290.

56. Clerc (p. 71n.) explains the word in *CIG* 3493 as '*urbis tutor*' on the ground that a localized sense would require πρὸ (τῆς) πόλεως as in Acts 14.13 (Lystra). *CIG* 2963, of Ephesus, is ambiguous in form (τῆς . . . Ἀ. προπόλεως or πρὸ πόλεως), but here and in some other cases an adjective πρόπολις is suggested by the syntactical form (not e.g. τῆς πρὸ πόλεως), and the meaning 'before the city' by the known position of the Artemisium. The adjective πρόπολις, certainly occurring in *CIG* 3493, is not mentioned in *LSJ*.

57. The inscription refers to the proconsulship of Catilius Severus. No man of this name is known among the recorded proconsuls of Asia, but Schürer (pp. 48-49) identified him with the legate of Syria who took office in AD 117. This man was twice consul, the second time in 120 (*CAH* XI.327 with E.J. Bickerman, *Chronology of the Ancient World*, p. 186).

58. The diversity may be due to the attempt to harmonize the traditions of various places which may have claimed a shrine of Sambathe. The σύνοδος Σαμβαθική of Naucratis (*IGRR* I.1106), for example, may testify to the existence of the cult in Egypt. See however *CPJ* III.47-48.

59. The permissive nature of Jezebel's teaching disposes incidentally of Epiphanius's supposition that she was the forerunner of the rigorist Montanist prophetesses (*Haer.* 51.33). The Alogi are said to have objected to the authenticity of the Revelation on the ground, *inter alia*, of its error of fact in

ascribing a church to Thyatira where no such body existed. Epiphanius's reply that the church there had gone over to Montanism is confirmed by the discovery of a χριστιανὸς χριστιανῷ epitaph in the district (Keil and von Premerstein, *Erste Reise*, p. 58, No. 118, of Hierocaesarea). This later development savours more of a reaction against Jezebel. For the Alogi cf. Epiphan. *Haer.* 51.3 and see Charles, p. c, and Swete, pp. cx-cxi.

60. So Swete, p. 44; Beckwith, p. 467. Cf. Also Ps. 41.3 (LXX 40.3); Mt. 9.2; Mk 7.30.

61. 'She should have her last great sacrificial meal at one of these assocations. I set her on a dining-couch, and her vile associates with her, and they shall have opportunity to enjoy—great tribulation: unless they repent, for she has shown that she cannot repent!'

62. This however is probably put in implicit contrast with some feature of the guild feasts and their attendant immorality. Deissmann, *LAE*, p. 351n., notes that κλίνη was a cult-word of pagan feasts and was transliterated into Latin. He refers to *P.Oxy.* I.10 (an invitation to dine at the *kline* of the lord Sarapis) and the similar words of III.523. Cf. 1 Cor.10.21.

63. Ramsay does not mention the provenance of this inscription, and Blaiklock (*Cities*, pp. 110-11) assumes incorrectly that it came from Thyatira.

64. There is other evidence for the particular influence of women in other aspects of the life of this city. The dyers, for instance, honoured a 'life high-priestess of the city' who was also priestess of the Augusti and had exhibited games (*IGRR* IV. 1242; cf. IV. 1225, 1247, 1254). The prominence of the priestess doubtless reflected that of the goddess in the native cult.

65. See further Ozanne, pp. 13-14. He argues against Charles's interpretation of the word in this sense in Rev. 6.8a and 18.8.

66. In the first three letters ὁ ἔχων οὖς precedes the promise to the conqueror; in the last four it follows. There is no apparent tendency in the MSS to harmonize the order by transposition. The formula is omitted from Primasius in 2.29; 3.6, 13; and by Codex Gigas in 3.22.

67. The corresponding promises in the other letters, even when complex, as at Philadelphia, are developments of a single concept.

68. It seems unwarranted however to follow Charles in postulating a distinction in John's uses of ἐξουσία with or without the article as denoting respectively full and limited authority. This idea seems to break down in view of 9.10 and 22.14, and perhaps 11.6, unless John is there using a source verbatim. Cf. however Lohmeyer, p. 29 *ad loc*. The distinction would in fact be apt here, where the word is anarthrous and refers to a particular power.

69. For the OT background of ποιμαίνειν cf. Ozanne, pp. 6-7. In the Vulgate of Mic. 5.6 and 7.14 *pascere* is likewise used in the sense 'destroy'. A possible parallel is cited by Lewis and Short from Liv. 25.12.10, where however the text is evidently corrupt.

70. The parallelism here would be more explicit if we adopted the AV or RVm renderings, understanding τὰ ἔθνη as the subject of συντρίβεται. We

should however expect the future ουντριβήσεται to conform with the future ποιμανεῖ. The occurrence of this form in P, Q and many cursives is evidently a correction made in the light of this interpretation. Lohmeyer accepts this rendering and explains the tense of συντρίβεται as a Hebraism. The parallelism in Ps. 2.9 might support this but is not decisive for the present passage. It seems best to take the whole clause as a simile closely with the preceding. τὰ σκεύη is then the subject, and the promised power is seen to comprise destruction of the hostile order.

71. The term was probably used originally of the shepherd's staff (cf. Mic. 7.14), and so both of a royal sceptre (Ps. 45.6 [LXX 44.7]) and of a means of punishment (Exod. 21.20; Isa. 10.24; cf. T.K. Cheyne in *EB* IV. 4317). Ramsay (*SC*, pp. 230-31) attractively links the expression with the military origin of Thyatira to suggest the power of the legions or the warrior-god of the city. This thought evidently underlies his description of the hero Tyrimnus (pp. 319-20).

72. Swete (p. 47) aptly expounds the point: 'The new order mut be preceded by the breaking up of the old (συντρίβεται), but the purpose of the Potter is to reconstruct; out of the fragments of the old life there will arise under the Hand of Christ and of the Church new and better types of social and national organisation'.

73. So Charles, p. 77; Swete, p. 47; Trench, pp. 154-55; Plumptre, pp. 149-50; following Tyconius (ed. Lo Bue), p. 58.

74. Cf. again the references to Balaam in Jude 11 and 2 Pet. 2.15. In the present connection we may also note the references to φωσφόρος in 2 Pet. 1.19 and raise the question whether it alludes to the use of Num. 24.17 in the setting of a similar controversy. Balaam's words were not spoken θελήματι ἀνθρώπου (2 Pet. 1.21), but he was moved by the Spirit to bear witness despite himself. Note also that the word ἅγιοι, not aptly applicable to Balaam, is probably an insertion (ἀπὸ Θεοῦ B, P, etc.; ἅγιοι Θεοῦ א, K, L, etc.; ἅγιοι τοῦ Θεοῦ A; ἅγιοι ἀπὸ Θεοῦ C).

75. In a closely contemporary poem celebrating Domitian's entry on his seventeenth consulship (1 Jan. AD 95) Statius compared the emperor with the morning star:

Laeta bis octonis accedit purpura fastis
Caesaris insignemque aperit Germanicus annum
Atque oritur cum sole novo, cum grandibus astris
Clarius ipse nitens et primo maior Eoo. (*Silvae* 4.1.1-4)

Cf. the coinage portrayal of Domitian's infant son (Mattingly and Sydenham, Dom. No. 213, etc.).

76. Cf. Mt. 13.32; 1 Cor. 15.40-44; see Bousset, p. 221; Moffatt, p. 363; Goodenough, *Jewish Symbols*, VIII.203.

77. (a) Some early commentators refer to Lucifer in Isa. 14.12. This title in context was tauntingly applied to the pretensions of the king of Babylon. It

was later used of Satan, apparently under the influence of such passages as Luke 10.18 and Rev. 9.1. (b) A symbol of brightness and beauty (Kepler, p. 65). (c) Lohmeyer (p. 30) tentatively proposes to equate Ishtar with the Holy Spirit, and to see here a promise of the gift of the Spirit. To the objection that every believer already possesses the Spirit he argues that this would not be decisive in the thought of this seer in view of Rev. 22.17. (d) Literal reference to the planet Venus as part of an astrological scheme assigning a planet to each letter (J. Lepsius; see *Expos.* 8th ser. 1 [1911]).

78. Allusion to Lucifer in the battle of the stars (*Or. Sib.* 5.516, 527) does not help here. The title 'Bar-Kokhba' reflects a Messianic claim. Other references in the Revelation itself seem to relate to different backgrounds of thought.

79. Merchants had grown rich through her (18.3, 11-17), and some of the merchandise listed was characteristic of Thyatira. No craftsman should henceforth be found in her (18.22). Her sorceries (18.23) recall the deceptions practised by the second beast (13.13-15). Lucian attributes to Alexander of Abonutichus a technique of ventriloquism by which an image appeared to speak (*Alex.* 26-27): Ramsay speculated that similar impostures were practised at the shrine of the Sibyl.

80. Deities and rulers are commonly represented holding in their right hands the emblems of their activity, and in their left those of their status. Charles (pp. 362-63) regards this symbol as a Satanic travesty of the Jewish practice of wearing phylacteries on the left hand.

Notes to Chapter 7

1. Numerous reports on the current work have appeared in *AS*, *BASOR* and elsewhere. I have used extensively a valuable article by D.G. Mitten, 'A New Look at Ancient Sardis', *BA* 29 (1966), pp. 38-68. A deep sounding in the lower city has revealed there later Bronze Age occupation levels forty feet below the modern surface (Mitten, p. 39). No foundation legend seems to be recorded, but the position of Sardis at the western terminus of the old highway leading through the Hittite capital of Hattusas (Boğazköy, Classical Pteria) is sufficient confirmation of its primitive greatness. See *HG*, pp. 27-35, for a remarkable insight into the significance of this route before its verification by excavation of the Hittite sites. Strabo's statement (13.4.5 = p. 625) that Sardis, though ancient, was later than Trojan times is probably an erroneous inference from the Iliad (20.385), where the only city in the neighbourhood is named Hyde. Hyde however was probably identical with the acropolis of Sardis (*SC*, p. 356).

The comparative stability of the mountain is evidently partly due to the horizontal strata and horizontal laying of particles. Dr J.E. Nixon has suggested to me from personal observation that the numerous tiny shining crystals in the conglomerate are double salts of magnesium and calcium, or possibly mica. Either of these would act as a binding material. The looseness of texture nevertheless makes the material liable to erosion in an astonishing degree. The hill is likely to have suffered both continual rapid weathering and occasional dramatic collapse.

3. Perhaps ancient observation of the phenomenon explains the local saying which aroused the ridicule of Apollonius of Tyana: ὡς πρεσβύτερα τῆς γῆς εἴη τὰ δένδρα (Philostr. *Vit. Ap.* 6.37).

4. Mitten (p. 55) estimates that the citadel has now eroded to perhaps one-third of its extent in the time of Cyrus. Only one fragment has been found to remain of the triple ring of fortifications famous as late as Alexander's time (Arr. *Anab.* 1.17.4). Today the lower slopes of the mountain near the temple of Artemis are one mass of hummocky debris.

5. Cf. Ἀθῆναι, Μυκῆναι.

6. At its greatest extent the area probably exceeded four square miles, stretching in a huge arc round the acropolis from the east round the north to the south-west (Mitten, p. 39). At least in the western quarter the Lydian city covered a larger area than either its Hellenistic or early Roman successors (*AS* 10 [1960], p. 24).

7. The Turkish name of the neighbourhood, Bin Tepe, means 'a thousand hills'.

8. Extensive plundering of the area early in 1966 diverted more urgent efforts to it. See G.M.A. Hanfmann, *BASOR* 186 (1967), p. 38.

9. In the caption of Ramsay's Plate XI in *SC* this mountain is wrongly identified as the Acropolis. The reprint by Baker Book House, Grand Rapids, in 1963, does not reproduce the original plates.

10. On revisiting the site in April 1969 I noted great changes since my first visit five years earlier. Extensive areas had been uncovered south of the Salihli road and in the Pactolus valley, and the gymnasium-synagogue complex was being ambitiously reconstructed. Much more extensive reconstruction has been completed since 1969.

11. Study of the gold-refining installations found in the 'Pactolus North' area suggests that the industry began there as early as 580 BC (*AS* 20 [1970], p. 25). The discovery of gold specimens with fragments of impressions of lion and incuse square designs suggests that production here was controlled by the royal mint (*AS* 26 [1976], p. 59).

12. A number of details differing from the Herodotean account are cited by later writers from the lost *Lydiaca* of Xanthus (see Jacoby, *FGH*, Dritte Teil C XX, pp. 750-57, No. 765). Xanthus was himself a Sardian born in the mid-6th century BC (Suidas), and his work, in four books, was highly valued in antiquity. An attempt to harmonize and tabulate identities of the kings was made by Leigh Alexander, *The Kings of Lydia* (Princeton, 1913). See also throughout G. Radet, *La Lydie et le monde grec au temps des Mermnades* (Paris, 1893).

13. Recent discovery of a period of Greek influence in pottery from about the 12th cent. BC has occasioned the suggestion that the Heraclid period might reflect a Greek settlement. See Hanfmann in *BASOR* 186 (1967), p. 37 and *AS* 17 (1967), p. 39.

14. The personality of Gyges has attracted legend. Herodotus gives little more than an account of his killing of his predecessor Candaules (1.8-12). Other versions of that appear in Nicolaus of Damascus (*FGH* 2A.90.47, pp. 349ff.; cf. Alexander, pp. 34-35) and in Plutarch (*Quaest. Graec.* 45 = 302A). Later Gyges' sudden rise was attributed to his possession of a miraculous ring and cap of invisibility (Plat. *Rep.* 359D-360B; Lucian, *Bis Accus.* 21; etc.). He was considered the first barbarian except Midas to have dedicated offerings at Delphi (Hdt. 1.14; cf. Athen. *Deipn.* 6.231e, f).

15. A.H. Sayce, *HDB* II.224; E. Meyer, *Geschichte des Alterthums*, 1st edn, I.558.

16. Mitten, pp. 46-48. He writes: 'These circumstances also suggest an association with Gyges, whose sudden death in battle could have required the immediate use of his tomb, followed by enlargement of the mound in tribute to his heroism'.

17. A meeting between Solon (archon at Athens in 598) and Croesus (accession 561/60), for instance, is improbable even on chronological grounds. It is characteristic of ancient feeling that Plutarch (*Solon* 27.1) acknowledges that some in his day attacked the story for this reason, but as it suited Solon's character so well he will not reject it for such slight cause. Herodotus's version (1.29-33) is a classic case of pride before a fall and the wisdom of humility. The fragments of the ninth book of Diodorus generally follow it closely (so 9.2, 28, 31, 33-34), but greatly elaborate an interview between Croesus and several wise men (9.25-27).

18. See further R.C. Jebb, *Bacchylides. The Poems and Fragments*, pp. 195-97. Jebb argues for a native Lydian origin of this version and suggests that the poet derived his knowledge of it from Delos.

19. So Croesus as a proverbial type of fallen wealth and pride is sometimes linked with Sardanapalus, the semi-mythical king of Assyria, who was said to have sought death by fire at the fall of Nineveh (see esp. Lucian, *Dial. Mort.* 2.336-37; 20.413-14, 419). Possibly tradition may have connected the two kings even in the manner of their overthrow. For the identity of 'Sardanapalus' see Weissbach in *PW* II.i.2436ff. and Hommel in *HDB* I.189. The Greeks seem to have confused the great Ashurbanipal with the last king Sinsharishkun, who perished thus in 612 BC.

20. So Lucian, *Merc. Cond.* 13: ἔστεψαι τὰ Ὀλύμπια, μᾶλλον δὲ Βαβυλῶνα εἴληφας ἢ τὴν Σάρδεων ἀκρόπολιν καθῄρηκας. Cyrus had performed both the latter tasks.

21. The versions of Herodotus, of Ctesias, frag. 29, Xen. *Cyrop.* 7.2.4 and Polyaen. *Strat.* 7.8.1 and 7.6.2-3 are set out together for comparison in Radet, pp. 251-53. Ramsay (*SC*, pp. 360-62) supposed from Herodotus that

the besiegers found a temporary weakness which permitted the climbing of the precipice.

22. 'To the student of the past it seems still to echo through history, as one of the most startling and astonishing reverses of all time' (p. 358).

23. See C.J. Hemer, 'The Sardis Letter and the Croesus Tradition', *NTS* 19 (1972-73), pp. 94-97. It will be noted that this literary evidence includes Jewish and Christian writings, sources close to the Revelation in time and place, and the Sibylline Oracles and the Letters of Apollonius of Tyana, perhaps the points at which Jewish and pagan literature respectively touch our epistle most nearly in date, provenance and genre.

24. The circumstances are carefully reported by Polybius (7.15-18). A Cretan Lagoras found a weakness at a precipitous and unguarded point where a daring ascent might be made with ladders to open the gates from within. The historian sums up the moral lessons of the case, not to trust too readily, and not to be boastful in prosperity, πᾶν δὲ προσδοκᾶν ἀνθρώπους ὄντας (8.21.11). Cf. new possible evidence for this sacking of the acropolis in *AS* 25 (1975), p. 44.

25. *Eodem anno duodecim celebres Asiae urbes collapsae nocturno motu terrae; quo improvisior graviorque pestis fuit . . . Sedisse immensos montes, visa in arduo quae plana fuerint, effulsisse inter ruinam ignes memorant. Asperrima in Sardianos lues plurimum in eos misericordiam traxit* (*Ann.* 2.47.1-3; cf. Strab. 13.4.8 = p. 628; Dio Cass. 57.17.8; Vell. Pat. 2.126.4; Suet. *Tib.* 48.2; *Anth. Graec.* 9.423; Solinus 40.5; *CIL* X.1624. See also H. Furneaux, *The Annals of Tacitus*, I.340-41).

26. Mt. 27.51; Oros. 7.4.13, 18, dating the Asian earthquake in the 17th year of Tiberius.

27. Cf. Oros. 7.4.13: *Saxa in montibus scissa, maximarumque urbium plurimae partes plus solita concussione ceciderunt*. Erosion by mere weathering would surely have softened the contours, whereas the fragmentary modern summit terminates abruptly on the south-west at the brink of an immense precipice beneath which lie great piles of debris. I cannot relate the topography of Polybius to the present condition of the hill. The feature Prion connecting the ἄκρα with the city (Polyb. 7.15.6) can hardly be the edge overhanging the present citadel-approach. Could the whole configuration of this face and its flanking pinnacles be as recent as AD 17? The possibility now gains support from the report of a soil study on the site mentioned by G.M.A. Hanfmann in *AS* 21 (1971), p. 56: 'Large landslides after earthquakes covered parts of the city in the first and ninth centuries AD'.

28. The first coins after the disaster actually seem to be an improvised issue of AD 37/8 (*BMC*, Nos. 106-109).

29. The problems of the identification of Sepharad are already reflected in the early versions of Obadiah, which tend to alter it to known, but unsuitable, places (so LXX Εφραθά = Bethlehem; Vulg. *in Bosphoro*, evidently incorporating the prepositional prefix of בספרד). See further D.

Neiman, 'Sefarad, The Name of Spain', *JNES* 22 (1963), pp. 128-32. The inscription, first published by E. Littmann and used by him to decipher some features of the Lydian language (*Sardis*, ed. H.C. Butler, VI, No. 17), has been further discussed by S.A. Cook in *JHS* 37 (1917), pp. 77-87, and by C.C. Torrey in *AJSL* 34 (1917-18), pp. 185-98. All these writers agree in identifying Sepharad in Obadiah with Sardis. The opening words of the Lydian version of the bilingual, which may have contained the Lydian form, are not preserved. That form however is elsewhere recorded as *Sfard* or *Sfarvad*; cf. *Sfardak Artimuū* (= 'Artemis of Sardis', Cook, p. 223 and note).

30. Torrey, *The Apocalypse of John*, pp. 29ff.; cf. 'The Aramaic Period of the Nascent Christian Church', *ZNTW* 44 (1952-53), pp. 205-23.

31. Strabo is explicit that Lydian was extinct in Lydia itself by the early first century AD (13.4.17 = p. 631). For a criticism of the linguistic basis of Torrey's case see the review by G.R. Driver in *JTS* n.s. 11 (1960), pp. 383-89.

32. In an official document we should expect the language of government to be placed first, followed by a rendering in the vernacular. Thus even allowing that the Persians used Aramaic officially in Sardis, this usage will not readily explain the present private epitaph, which is of a class extremely common in the later Greek epigraphy of Anatolia, erected by the family of the deceased though it might invoke the sanctions of human or divine authority. In the ordering of the versions it differs also from its nearest parallel, the Aramaic-Greek fragment from Limyra (*CIS* II.109): even an isolated family of Semitic settlers might naturally use their own tongue followed by a translation in the normal medium of the place.

33. There is of course no certainty that Aramaic-speakers in Sardis were necessarily Jews.

34. Thus a commercial colony in Damascus was authorized by Benhadad (1 Kings 20.34).

35. W.W. Tarn and G.T. Griffith, *Hellenistic Civilisation*, 3rd edn, pp. 221-23, read the evidence in the light of their assumption that Jewish citizenship was everywhere and in all circumstances impossible.

36. See L. Robert, *Nouvelles Inscriptions de Sardes* (1964), No. 14, p. 55: [Σ]αρδιανὸ[ς βουλε]υτής; cf. Nos. 13, 16-18 and discussion on pp. 56-57. See also Mitten, pp. 64-65.

37. A.H. Detweiler has suggested that it was originally built to serve as a basilica, and was later given to the Jewish community (*AS* 17 [1967], p. 29). If so, it is still remarkable that the Jews were so far accepted in a pagan city as to benefit, and that the numerous Jewish dedicatory inscriptions date from as early as the start of the third century, little later that the supposed date of the structure itself.

38. Thus apparently pagan gem designs have been found in the prosperous adjoining shop of a Jewish presbyter of early Byzantine times (*AS* 13 [1963], p. 25), and a statue of Dionysus in the basement of the 'House of Bronzes',

the residence of a family which may have included prominent members of the contemporary Christian clergy (Mitten, pp. 66-67).

A remarkable detail is the attestation of a tribe of 'Leontii' (Robert, *Nouv. Inscr.* No. 6). Robert argues that this is not a citizen-tribe, but a Hellenization of the tribe of Judah (cf. Gen. 49.9). A lion however was also the emblem of the city and its goddess, and a citizen-tribe containing Jews could have been so named because the symbol was significant to Jew and pagan alike. The lion is a recurring motif in the decoration of the synagogue, and ancient pagan representations of it were re-used there (Robert; Mitten, pp. 51-52). Cf. also 'the Lion of the tribe of Judah' as a Messianic title in Rev. 5.5 with the almost contemporary 4 Ezra 12.32.

39. One cannot justify from them the tempting supposition that the mention of Gog in Rev. 20.8 might have applied the text of Ezekiel to the preservation of a local tradition among Sardian Jews of his identity with Gyges.

40. Philo, *Joseph* 23.133, and perhaps Jos. *contra Ap.* 2.11.131, where however the reference to Croesus may be a gloss. See further Hemer, *NTS* 19 (1972-73), pp. 94-97.

41. Λυδοί in Jer. 46.9 (LXX 26.9); Ezek. 27.10 and 30.5. Λούδ however appears in Isa. 66.19.

42. Herodotus 5.102 calls the Sardian goddess Cybebe. The conventional portraiture of Cybele with *tympanum* and lions appears only on a late coin (*BMC* No. 210, of Salonina). The Cybele-Attis cult was however characteristic of Lydia as of Phrygia. I was shown a relief of a goddess holding a tympanum and attended by a lion by a villager of Sart in April 1964.

43. In fact the only representations of Artemis on the Sardian coins in *BMC* are on a series of pre-Imperial times (Nos. 53-59). Types of Demeter and of Persephone are however very numerous.

44. From *BMC* Nos. 90-93, undated; 145, of Commodus; becoming much commoner later and characteristically representing the city on alliance-coins (Nos. 215-16, 218).

45. Thus a serpent is seen issuing from the ground beneath the horses of Hades (No. 89, Imperial, undated, obv. city-goddess), or Demeter is shown thrusting a torch into the mouth of the underworld chasm, above which rises a coiled serpent (No. 138, of Antoninus Pius). In these cases native cult has apparently been expressed artistically by an approximation to a Greek myth which outwardly resembled it.

46. For this function of Cybele cf. Ov. *Fast.* 4.219-21.

47. Hanfmann points out that the bull-man representation became very popular at Gordium, the traditional city of Midas, during the Lydian period. The immortality motif is apparent in later Mithraism, where however it might contain elements derived from Christianity. Cf. esp. a Roman inscription of AD 376, which includes the words *taurobolio criobolioq. in aeternum renatus* (*ILS* 4152).

48. These themes are illustrated in the coinage of Sardis, for example where the hero Heracles drags a humped bull, perhaps to sacrifice (*BMC* No. 154, of Caracalla); or where a similar bull stands before two altars, each surmounted by a coiled serpent (no. 87, Imperial, undated).

49. Διὸς ἄνθος in Nonnus = *balis* in Pliny. The games celebrated in honour of the goddess at Sardis were called Chrysanthina (*IGRR* IV. 1518 = *LBW* 624; *BMC* No. 150). Frazer's suggestions about the identification of the plant (*Adonis*, p. 99n.) are based on hearsay about the spring flowers of other parts of Asia Minor, and he is quite mistaken in his impression that they are few. I suggest as a possibility a large and showy yellow spurge (*Euphorbia ? biglandulosa*), which is characteristic of the mountain slopes at Sardis in early April. This would fit the coinage portrayal of a 'golden bough' rather than a flower. For medicinal properties attributed to species of spurge in antiquity see Theophr. *Hist. Plant.* 9.11.7ff. He uses τιθύμαλλος and several other words without clear distinction.

50. *Adonis*, pp. 94-98. Cf. the pyre depicted on many Tarsian coins (*BMC Cilicia*, Tarsus, Nos. 105-106; etc.).

51. See Xanthus *ap*. Athen. *Deipn*. 8.346e-f = Xanth. frag. 17 in *FGH* IIIC.xx.No. 765, p. 755; Nicolaus of Damascus, frag. 16 in *FGH* IIA No. 90, p. 340. Hanfmann (p. 85n.) and L. Alexander (*The Kings of Lydia*, p. 40) are probably right in locating Xanthus's Ascalon in Lydia, though Alexander's place-name parallels will not stand scrutiny, being transparently modern Turkish. The story may enshrine a primitive tradition of a struggle of two settlements and religious centres at Sardis and at the lake. Alexander cites two inscriptions found nearby which confirm the continued sanctity of the lake to a goddess equated with Atargatis.

52. The portrayal of the place of eternal punishment as a lake (λίμνη, Rev. 19.20; 20.10, 14, 15; 21.8) seems to be unparalleled in the OT and the apocalyptic writers. The nearest approaches I have found are the 'abyss of fire' in 1 Enoch 10.13 etc., and the 'river of fire' in 2 Enoch 10.2.

53. Both the early cemeteries of Sardis were separated from the city by rivers, the Hermus and the Pactolus. We can only speculate whether this fact was thought to represent the division of the worlds of living and dead by a river-barrier. Rev. 16.12 is set in a context otherwise meaningful in Sardis.

54. Charles, p. lxxxiv n. Cf. Rev. 3.3 with Mt. 24.42; Rev. 3.5 with Mt. 10.32. Charles also inserts Rev. 16.15 into the letter and compares Mt. 24.43, 46 and 1 Thess. 5.2.

55. Otherwise there is only the recurring formula ὁ ἔχων οὖς ἀκουσάτω. Cf. Mt. 11.15; 13.9, 43; Mk 4.9, 23; Lk. 8.8; 14.35.

56. In both the church was faced with the prevalence of a celebrated Anatolian mother-goddess cult, and there was evidently close commercial and religious contact between the cities from early times. Cf. for instance the coupling of the two goddesses on the Artaxerxes bilingual, and their later representation together on alliance coinage.

57. Actually sixfold in Isaiah. The sevenfold reckoning evidently arose from the LXX, which adds πνεῦμα φόβου Θεοῦ in Isa. 11.3. Cf. Swete, p. 6. For this view see also Charles, p. 11; Beckwith, pp. 425-26; and cf. Justin Martyr, *Dial.* 87.

58. ἡ στρατηλασίη ... οὔνομα μὲν εἶχε ὡς ἐπ᾿ Ἀθήνας ἐλαύνει.

59. The normal Greek equivalents of *reliquus* are κατάλοιπος or ὑπόλοιπος (Hort, p. 32). Cf. κατάλοιπος in Acts 15.17, quoting from Amos 9.12 LXX.

60. For the aorist infinitive after μέλλειν see Blass–Debrunner, p. 174, and cf. Rev. 3.16; 12.4.

61. σοῦ τὰ ἔργα ℵ, P, Q and most cursives; σοῦ ἔργα A, C.

62. Cf. Rev. 3.12, where τοῦ Θεοῦ μου is four times repeated.

63. Hemer, *NTS* 19 (1972-73), pp. 94-97.

64. I cannot find any parallel for this usage. Beckwith's citations of οὕτως in 1 Cor. 15.11 and Eph. 4.20 seem quite inadequate. Moffatt, p. 364, makes πῶς 'practically equivalent to "that",' a usage of later Greek (Blass–Debrunner, p. 203) and found occasionally in the NT (Mk 2.26 = Mt. 12.4; Acts 11.13), but lacking force here.

65. So e.g. in the Phrygian-Greek cultic inscriptions of Dionysopolis in W.M. Ramsay, 'Artemis-Leto and Apollo-Lairbenos', *JHS* 10 (1889), pp. 216-30; *MAMA* IV. 279-90. I have found comparable examples in the epigraphy of Sardis itself (Robert, *Nouvelles Inscriptions*, No. 2, p. 23; Keil–von Premerstein, *Erste Reise*, No. 25, p. 16). The original readers may have seen some allusion to local cult where insistence on ceremonial purity was conjoined with immoral rites. Cf. Moffatt, p. 364; Charles, p. 81.

66. Trench, p. 168, Swete, p. 51, and others make much of the literal force of μολύνειν here (as against μιαίνειν). Cf. also Jude 23, from Zech. 3.4, 5, where, however, the thought is rather different. For μολύνειν cf. Rev. 14.4 and Arr. *Epict.* 2.8.13.

67. J.B. Lightfoot, *Colossians and Philemon*, p. 22n., refers to βάμμα Σαρδιανικόν (Ar. *Pax* 1174; *Acharn.* 112) and to φοινικίδες Σαρδιανικαί (Plato Comicus *ap.* Athen.*Deipn.* 2.48b). Moffatt, p. 365, sees allusion to the local woollen trade.

68. Trench distinguishes the contemporary significance of 'white garments' in v. 4 from their future meaning in v. 5.

69. Cf. 2 Cor. 2.14, where however the debated sense of θριαμβεύειν affects the meaning.

70. *Nam et rursus innumera multitudo albati et palmis victoriae insignes revelantur, scilicet de Antichristo triumphantes, sicut unus ex presbyteris, Hi sunt, ait, qui veniunt ex illa pressura magna et laverunt vestimentum suum et candidaverunt ipsum in sanguine Agni* (*Scorpiace* 12).

71. Perhaps, however, the verb is not to be pressed. It can mean simply 'go about (wearing)': ἐν κοκκίνοις περιπατεῖν (Arr. *Epict.* 3.22.10; cf. Mk 12.38 = Lk. 20.46; 1 Clem. 17.1).

72. So esp. ἀξίως περιπατεῖν (Eph. 4.1). Cf. Col. 1.10; 1 Thess. 2.12; Swete, p. 51.

73. The evidence of spelling in inscriptions and papyri suggests that the distinction of vowel length in this case had already disappeared in the NT period, even if other itacistic changes were incomplete.

74. Passages like Acts 20.11, 27.17 and Jn 4.6 are not however syntactically parallel (see Beckwith, p. 476).

75. I accordingly doubt Kiddle's distinction: 'All the faithful have before them this glorious destiny; but to one class of men it was assured without any shadow of uncertainty—to those who proved their faithfulness by dying the martyr's death' (p. 46). Nor does Kiddle seem justified in his insistence that the victor is here exclusively the martyr (pp. 61-65). This equivalence is a commonplace later, but appears neither necessary nor plausible here.

76. *Pseudepigrapha*, p. 216n. Cf. e.g. Jub. 36.10; 1 Enoch 108.3.

77. Titles include πολ(ε)ιτογράφος, γραμματοφύλαξ νομοφύλαξ. See *IGRR* III.63, 179; IV. 860; *OGIS* 229.52; Jones, *The Greek City*, pp. 239 and 357n.

78. Thus the copy of a decree at the temple of Apollo at Didyma is to be lodged εἰς τὰς βασιλικὰς γραφὰς τὰς ἐν Σάρδεσιν (*Revue de Philologie 25* [1901], p. 9, ll.23-24; cf. Bevan, *The House of Seleucus*, I.151 and 324-25n.).

79. Dio Chrysost. 31.84; cf. the case of Theramenes, Xen. *Hell.* 2.3.51; also Ar. *Pax* 1180-81 and on inscriptions from Decelea in Attica and from Ilium.

80. It is termed βίβλος τῶν ζώντων in Hermas *Simil.* 2.9 and 1 Clem. 53.4. The latter quotes Exod. 32.32.

81. Contrast the negative form of this saying (ὃς γὰρ ἐὰν ἐπαισχυνθῇ . . .) in Mk 8.38 and Lk. 9.26. Swete comments on its absence here: 'Even in the message to Sardis the last note is one of unmixed encouragement and hope' (p. 52).

82. Contrast Rev. 2.13, to Pergamum.

Notes to Chapter 8

1. The form of the name is attested by a coin (see *BMC Lydia*, p. xci). It appears as 'Cogamus' in Plin. *NH* 5.30.111 (cf. Ramsay, *CB* I.196n.).

2. The principal epigraphic sources are *CIG* 3416-37, *IGRR* IV. 1614-52; *LBW* 641-66, 1669, 1669a; Keil and von Premerstein, *Dritte Reise*, pp. 15-48, Nos. 18-57; *OGIS* 488, 526; *SIG*³ 883, 985.

3. See *OGIS* 308.15 for evidence that Attalus was styled Philadelphus before 159 BC. The existence of a 'Macedonian' colony near outlying Bebekli, 17m. NE of Alaşehir, on territory later belonging to Philadelphia, in the 35th year of Eumenes (163/62 BC) is attested by an inscription (Keil and von Premerstein, *Zweite Reise* p. 116, No. 223; cf. Magie, p. 982n.). We should have expected the settlement of the more focal site of Philadelphia to have been earlier. Perhaps Strabo's τῶν κτισάντων may imply a tradition that the brothers were joint founders (13.4.10 = p. 628). The later Johannes Lydus,

himself a native of the city (*de Magistr. Pop. Rom.* 3.26; *de Ostentis* 53), supposed it an Egyptian foundation (*de Mensibus* 3.32), perhaps through confusion of Attalus with Ptolemy Philadelphus.

4. Herodotus's Callatebus (7.31) and Xenophon's Καστωλοῦ πεδίον (*Anab.* 1.1.2; 1.9.7) must be assigned to other parts of the Cogamis valley, though Callatebus may have been an older *polis* supplanted by the Attalid city. See J.G.C. Anderson, *JHS* 18 (1898), pp. 86-89. Castolus was evidently at Bebekli (cf. *OGIS* 448), and belonged to Philadelphia in the Imperial period, though at an unknown earlier date it had been independent, as shown by the ethnic in *IG* II.ii.3059 and 3233. See L. Robert, *Études anatoliennes*, pp. 159-60.

5. The only evidence is one early electrum coin found at Alaşehir (*BMC Lydia*, Early Electrum, No. 4, of 7th-6th cent. BC.

6. The mention of ἡ παλαιὰ πόλις in an inscription of AD 85/6 might refer to a pre-Attalid settlement, or equally to some quarter abandoned as recently as the earthquake of AD 17 (Keil and von Premerstein, *Dritte Reise*, p. 22, No. 20).

7. The earliest coins, attributed to the second century BC (*BMC Lydia*, Philad., Nos. 1-4; cf. p. xc), depict a Macedonian shield, and this points to the presence of a Macedonian garrison. Imhoof-Blumer, however, followed by Ramsay, *SC*, pp. 396, 446n., assigns this coinage to the reign of Augustus.

8. Of the relevant coinage, most—on Ramsay's view all—belongs to the Roman period, and its value as testimony to the intentions of the founder is dubious. The disappearance of the Lydian language from Lydia (Strab. 13.4.17 = p. 631) cannot fairly be attributed to the influence of Philadelphia. In any case its 'open door' was towards Phrygia rather than the homeland of Lydia. See further W. Barclay, *Seven Churches*, p. 95, though some of his statements also go beyond the evidence. There is no warrant for thinking that Sardis was successful, and Philadelphia unsuccessful, in missions of Hellenization to Lydia and Phrygia respectively.

9. So e.g. Polyb. 24.5; 28.7; Diod. Sic. 29.22; Liv. 42. 55. 7; 57.4; 58.14; 65.14; 67-68; all of events in 171 BC.

10. At Philadelphia itself the games Δ(ε)ῖα Ἄλεια later received the epithet Φιλαδέλφεια (*CIG* 3427). G. Lafaye on *IGRR* IV. 1761 suggests that this was conferred to honour the brotherly concord of Caracalla and Geta. Its use here might then pointedly identify their harmony with the proverbial loyalty of Eumenes and Attalus.

11. The facts are abundantly attested by coinage; e.g. cornucopiae (*BMC*, No. 54, of Caligula, etc.), ears of corn (No. 56, of Claudius), Demeter (No. 71, of M. Aurelius), Dionysus, variously portrayed (No. 66, of Trajan, etc.), and bunches of grapes (No. 64, of Domitia) are all typical.

12. *Ne provincias quidem liberalitate ulla sublevavit, excepta Asia, disiectis terrae motu civitatibus* (Suet. *Tib.* 48.2).

13. So Skopje in Yugoslavia is said to have experienced some hundreds of

tremors in the two years following the earthquake of 1963. In March 1964 I observed and photographed there large estates of prefabricated houses on the plain outside the city, a striking modern parallel for the situation described in the words of Strabo.

14. A yet more remarkable illustration of the situation of first-century Philadelphia was provided by an experience of April 1969, when I revisited that city in ignorance of the occurrence of a major earthquake in the district a few days previously. The first indication of the disaster was provided by the sight of the total collapse of many scattered farmhouses in an area about the Salihli road about 6m. NW of Alaşehir. I then saw and photographed many tents erected by the Red Crescent for the homeless in the streets and the stadium-site of the damaged town and around the neighbouring village of Baklacı. I was informed that the earthquake struck at 4 a.m. on 29th March and that thirty-one people were killed in the neighbourhood. The epicentre apparently lay NW of Alaşehir.

15. In most cities of Ionia, Lydia and Aeolis there is an extended gap between the autonomous and the Imperial coinage. Evidence for the whole Julio-Claudian period is so scanty that it is hazardous to draw conclusions from the almost complete absence of Tiberian specimens.

16. Coins dated precisely to AD 37/8 (C. Asinius Pollio *procos.*) are restruck from an older die portraying Drusus and Germanicus (*BMC Lydia*, Sard., Nos. 106-109). The issue looks like an improvisation: Germanicus, long since dead, was probably the original agent for the emperor's disaster relief.

17. Cf. also various numismatic representations of Germanicus and the elder Agrippina with divine attributes (Nos. 52, 53, 55, all of Caligula). The name Neocaesarea for a time actually replaced the old one, as on the coins noted, though the double designation 'Philadelphia Neocaesarea' also occurs (Head, *BMC Lydia*, p. lxxxvi). Sardis temporarily assumed the epithet 'Caesarea': Hieracome became Hierocaesarea, the name by which it is generally known.

18. Note further that Philadelphian magistrates of the period style themselves φιλόκαισαρ (*BMC Lydia*, p. lxxxv and No. 54) and φιλόπατρις (p. lxxxv; cf. the much later *CIG* 3422.4). They seem to express a dual loyalty to their city and to the emperors whose generosity had given them the hope of its reconstruction.

19. This too seems to have fallen into disuse after the death of Domitian, but was resumed under Caracalla, and the title appears regularly on the richer later coinage.

20. For the severe sufferings of Asia Minor generally in the first two Christian centuries see e.g. Friedlaender, *Darstellungen aus der Sittengeschichte Roms*, 9th edn, III.29-30; J.B. Lightfoot, *Colossians and Philemon.*, p. 38, and cf. the Sibylline Oracles, *passim*.

21. M. Rostovtzeff, *The Social and Economic History of the Roman*

Empire, 2nd edn, I.145-47, 201; II.599-600n. An inscription of Cibyra shows that Vespasian sought to encourage local corn-production in Asia (*IGRR* IV. 915.10-13).

22. See esp. Suet. *Dom.* 7.2: *Ad summam quondam ubertatem vini, frumenti vero inopiam, existimans nimio vinearum studio neglegi arva, edixit, ne quis in Italia novellaret, utque in provinciis vineta succiderentur, relicta ubi primum dimidia parte; nec exequi rem perseveravit.* Cf. G.W. Mooney, p. 540 *ad loc.* The literary sources suggest that the act was an unprecedented outrage: Philostratus, *Vit. Soph.* 1.21, describes the successful embassy of Scopelianus against it. For a more favourable view from a pro-Imperial source see Stat. *Silv.* 4.3.11-12 and cf. perhaps 4.2.34-37, both of c. AD 95.

23. See S. Reinach, 'La Mévente des vins sous le Haut-Empire romain', *RA*, 3rd ser., 39 (1901), pp. 350-74. He quotes interesting evidence of a huge overproduction of wine in the previous years: see Mart. *Epig.* 3.56, 57, relating to Ravenna; so perhaps Stat. *Silv.* 1.6.33, 41, 95.

24. *JRS* 14 (1924), pp. 179-84, No. 6. See esp. lines 34ff.: *Cum autem adfirmatur mihi ante hanc hibernae asperitatis perseverantiam octonis et novenis assibus modium frumenti in Colonia fuisse et iniquissimum sit famem civium suorum praedam cuiquam esse excedere sing. denar. sing. modios pretium frumenti veto.* Cf. Dio Chrysost. 46.8ff. on the famine riots at Prusa in Bithynia a few years before.

25. There is no record that Domitian's decree threatened olive-cultivation, nor that olives were grown at Philadelphia. Both vines and olives, however, require years to mature, and their destruction could mean lasting ruin. It was an unwritten law of Eastern warfare to spare these crops (Ramsay, *Cities of St. Paul*, pp. 430-32; cf. Deut. 20.19-20; Thuc. 2.72.3). Domitian's action had transgressed this principle and represented the ultimate savagery of a foe. For the importance of fruit-trees see M. Cary, *The Geographical Background of Greek and Roman History*, pp. 19-20.

26. C.C. Torrey, *Apocalypse*, p. 79, acknowledges the strength of Reinach's argument on this point, but objects: 'This is just the sort of edict that might be given out by successive rulers. It is anonymous as it stands in Rev., and Domitian was not necessarily the first to have made such an edict.' This however seems to misapprehend the situation. The imperial act was regarded as an unprecedented outrage, and the literary authorities clearly reflect this contemporary feeling.

27. For the celebrity of the wines of Tmolus cf. Verg. *Georg.* 2.98 and Plin. *NH* 14.9.74.

28. This phrase might equally apply to temporary food-shortage or long-term economic hardship. For the magistracies cf. *IGRR* IV. 1631, 1637, 1638, 1640, and note διὰ βίου σειτοδότης (*IGRR* IV. 1630).

29. Cf. the evidence of coinage. One coin of Domitia depicts a bunch of grapes (*BMC*, No. 64). Almost alone among the specimens of the dynasty, it omits the epithet 'Flavia'. Coinage of the empress may have been early or

late in the reign, before or after her repudiation by her husband. The coin illustrates the importance of the vineyards to Philadelphia, but cannot be placed with relation to the edict.

30. The temple of the Germanicus-cult may have fallen derelict with the passing of his kinsman Claudius, while retaining an exemption from profane use. Cf. a similar case involving a temple of Claudius at Prusa in Bithynia: *Nam si facta est [aedes], licet collapsa sit, religio eius occupavit solum* (Trajan *apud* Plin. *Ep.* 10.71). Cf. *SC*, pp. 410-11.

31. Other sources fail us here. Nothing is recorded of confiscations of temple-tax in the *conventus* of Sardis, and the Attalids, unlike the Seleucids, did not commonly establish a Jewish *katoikia* in their foundations.

32. Charles derives both direct from the Hebrew text, while supposing that the former may have been influenced by a Greek rendering resembling that of Theodotion (pp. lxix, lxxx).

33. So e.g. the open gates (Isa. 60.11 with Rev. 3.8 and 21.25); the establishment of the weak and rejected over their persecutors (esp. Isa. 60.14, 15, 22 with Rev. 3.8b, 9b), and especially the concept of the city of the Lord (Isa. 60.14 with Rev. 3.12 and Rev. 21 *passim*).

34. The distinction may perhaps be upheld in the Fourth Gospel (cf. ἀληθής in 3.33; 4.18; 5.31-32 with ἀληθινός in 1.9; 4.23), but not in the LXX, nor in the Rev., in both of which ἀληθινός alone is used. Again, in the NT generally ἀληθής is commonly used predicatively (but see 1 Pet. 5.12; 2 Pet. 2.22); ἀληθινός is usually, but not exclusively, attributive. A consistent distinction on these lines cannot however be maintained in any of the writers under consideration, and most of the attributive occurrences of ἀληθινός require the sense 'genuine'.

35. Contact with pagan religion is less likely in view of the thrust of the opposition here from Judaism. An inscription of Philadelphia of about 1st cent. BC (*SIG*[3] 985) is remarkable in its record of the high ethical regulations imposed on those, free or servile, who approached a private shrine of Aggdistis. The occurrence of nobler aspirations in pre-Christian paganism is interesting in the city where the Apocalyptic letter proclaimed a 'holy' Messiah. See now S.C. Barton and G.H.R. Horsley, 'A Hellenistic Cult Group and the New Testament Churches', *Jahrbuch für Antike und Christentum* 24 (1981), pp. 7-14.

36. Neither Moffatt, nor Kiddle, who favours an eschatological view, exclude the common missionary interpretation. It is is not likely that there is allusion here to the 'door' portrayed or inscribed on Phrygian tombs (Moffatt, referring to *CB* II.395), and the context does not support Barclay (p. 103) in his additional suggestion of allusion to prayer as an open door of access to God.

37. Contrast Ramsay's view in his earlier article in *HDB* III.831, where he suggests only that the church was a recent foundation, and therefore not yet strong, though it had a a brilliant opening before it.

38. *The Apocalypse of John*, pp. 80-81. This view is inseparable from his whole historical reconstruction. See further his article 'The Aramaic Period of the Nascent Christian Church', *ZNTW* 44 (1952-53), pp. 205-33. His argument takes into account the Christian presence in the synagogues and the exclusion of their writings from the Jewish canon, but he seems to force the evidence into an unrealistic historical framework. My own suggestions may be seen as offering an alternative reconstruction relating these factors to a Domitianic setting of the 'synagogues of Satan'.

39. Cf. Smyrna. There however it is not so clear whether the Jewish hostility took the form we may infer here.

40. For the form and accentuation of this word see Blass–Debrunner–Funk, p. 47, §94. The readings δίδωμι in B, P, and δέδωκα in ℵ look like early emendations, or in the latter case dittography.

41. He notes that this use is frequent in the LXX, and quotes parallels in Acts 10.40; 14.3; 2.27, the last a LXX citation.

42. Torrey, *Apocalypse*, pp. 91, 99-100, conjectures the meaning 'the presumptuous ones' from the supposition of a corruption in a hypothetical Aramaic original. A. Pallis, *Notes on St. John and the Apocalypse*, p. 51, conjectures ἐκδικῶ σε = 'I avenge thee on the synagogue', comparing Rev. 6.10 and 19.2 and Deut. 18.19 LXX. His insertion of σε is without manuscript authority.

43. The partitive with ἐκ expresses the object of a verb in 2.10 and the subject in 11.9 (cf. John 6.39; John 21.10, with ἀπό; 2 John 4, all in 'Johannine' writings. For the whole anacoluthic structure and the incorporated accusative ἑαυτούς with infinitive, cf. the Smyrna parallel (Rev. 2.9). τῶν λεγόντων is in apposition with συναγωγῆς.

44. 'The Hour of Trial, Rev. 3.10', *JBL* 85 (1966), pp. 308-14.

45. For the Hebrew background cf. Charles, pp. 289-90. The evidence is fully treated by Brown, pp. 309-10.

46. Cf. 7.1b, 3, with 6.6. Cf. the 'twelve tribes' in 7.4-8 with 21.12 and the background of 3.12.

47. Beckwith, p. 483, entertains the possibility that the two nouns might be treated as a single compound = 'my steadfastness-command'.

48. Charles renders: 'the Gospel of the endurance practised by Christ'. This is to be 'at once as an example and as a power' (Hort).

49. See Charles, pp. 264-65 on Rev. 10.7 and Blass–Debrunner–Funk, p. 181, §356.

50. Charles, p. 90, finds difficulty in reconciling this verse with the later chapters of the Rev. This passage presupposes the continuance of the church to the Second Advent, whereas the writer's final view is that all the faithful will suffer martyrdom in the last persecution. Caird however explains the problem in the framework of the different atmosphere of parts of the book: the present concern is all 'practical, pastoral and personal' (p. 54).

51. Victors are recorded from three different sets of games held there, τὰ

268   *The Letters to the Seven Churches*

μεγάλα Δ(ε)ῖα Ἄλεια (Φιλαδέλφεια) (*CIG* 3416, 3427, 3428), τὰ μεγάλα
Σεβαστὰ Ἀναείτεια (*CIG* 3424) and τὰ κοινὰ Ἀσίας ἐν Φιλαδελφείᾳ
(*CIG* 3428), all of uncertain date, though at least the last is presumably later
than the reception of the neocorate under Caracalla. This group of local
inscriptions exemplifies with unusual clarity the importance attached to
athletic prowess, especially perhaps as publicity for a small city. The rare
term περιοδον(ε)ίκης in *CIG* 3425 and *IGRR* IV.1643 denotes an itinerant
prize-hunting sportsman (cf. Arr. *Epict.* 3.25.5 for the idea in a literary
source). The stadium site may still be seen in Philadelphia, though little
reference to it exists. See however the old plan in E. Le Camus, *Voyage aux
Sept Églises de l'Apocalypse*, p. 209.

52. Cf. also 1 Clem. 5.2 and see Charles, p. 91, for classical and Jewish
parallels.

53. Farrer, *Revelation*, p. 81; a view attributed to Vitringa and rejected by
Trench (p. 187) and Swete (p. 57) as inappropriate to this context.

54. Cf. related passages in Rev. 7.3; 14.1; 22.4 and contrast 17.5. This view
is mentioned by Charles, p. 92; Moffatt, p. 369.

55. The idea is favoured by Charles, pp. 91-92, Moffatt, p. 369, Kiddle,
pp. 53-54, and is discussed by Beckwith, p. 485. The earliest traceable source
appears to be Bousset (p. 269 *ad loc.*), who refers to an unspecified work of
Hirschfeld. It is certainly the kind of practice whch might have existed, but I
know no precise parallel from elsewhere, nor anything resembling it in the
epigraphy of Philadelphia. The cutting of inscriptions on columns was a
common practice. For connections of the 'pillar' with Philadelphia cf. *CIG
3431* = *LBW* 642; Arundell, *Seven Churches*, p. 170.

56. Rev. 3.9, 10, 11; cf. *SC*, pp. 406-408; Moffatt, p. 369. Other suggestions
need not detain us. See discussions in Charles, pp. 91-92; Moffatt, p. 369;
Kiddle, p. 54; Beckwith, p. 485; Swete, p. 57.

57. Cf. also Isa. 65.15. The point here is well expressed by Hendriksen,
p. 75: 'To the conqueror will be given the assurance that he belongs to God
and to the New Jerusalem and to Christ, and that he will everlastingly share
in all the blessings and privileges of all three'.

58. 'Not however, a νέα Ἰ. like Hadrian's Aelia, but a καινή, instinct with
the powers of an endless life . . . and of heavenly origin.'

59. We cannot follow Charles, II.150-52, in his hypercritical distinction of
two cities confused by his hypothetical editor. In any case parallels with
features of both are present in our text.

60. *SC*, pp. 409-12; Peake, p. 251; Swete, p. 58; Blaiklock, p. 121.

61. *Tobit* 13.7-18a (naming Jerusalem); *1 Enoch* 10.17-22; *1 Enoch* 24-25;
2 Baruch 73.2–74.4; *Or. Sib.* 3.743-61; 5.420-7. Cf. Beckwith, pp. 54-57.

62. Countless inscriptions attested people's preoccupation with σωτηρία.
Artemidorus of Daldis, a city in the same seismic region, presents ἀποδημία
as a specific misfortune to be feared, symbolized in dreams by visions of
earthquake (*Onirocrit.* 2.41; 4.1), but averted by such names as Meno and

Menecrates (3.38). (Names of this type are in fact strangely common in villages of the district, though I have no record of an example from Philadelphia itself.) These trivial superstitions give insight into current psychology. They afford also some guarantee that our *Sitz im Leben* is not arbitrarily imposed.

The erroneous supposition that the Turkish name Alaşehir itself means 'city of God' has been the occasion of much misplaced moralizing in the older authorities (e.g. Chandler, p. 246n.; Arundell, p. 169). The Turkish *Allah* is distinguished by the lengthened pronunciation of the doubled consonant and the sounding of final 'h', features which might easily escape a western traveller whose language made no phonemic discrimination of these points. The manner of compounding should moreover strictly require the use of the suffixed form -şehri. The word here is *ala*, meaning either, (1) 'of mixed colour', or (2) 'light chestnut in colour', 'reddish' (Mehmet Ali Ağakay, *Türkçe Sözlük*).

63. Local character is remarkably persistent in Anatolia. We shall see that there is sometimes valuable light to be shed by the discriminating use of later evidence.

64. See esp. Ign. *Philad.* 6-8. For his route and the background of the letters see Lightfoot, *Ignatius*, I.33-37.

65. This understanding of Ignatius would overcome the objections in Charles, p. 92, but is itself a mere possibility. The two words were probably very close even in contemporary pronunciation. There may have been wide local variation in the progress of itacism. In Asian inscriptions ει and ῑ are commonly interchangeable. My impression of vulgar orthography is that there is widespread confusion of η, ι, ει and of υ, οι, υι under the Early Empire, but that confusion across the boundaries of these groups is usually a mark of very late date. Perhaps the latter coalesced as 'ü' before the sound lost its rounding and became 'i'. The common MS confusion of ἡμεῖς with ὑμεῖς might have occurred before their pronunciations became identical, but more easily after. It is questionable whether the colloquial language would ever tolerate the identity of such basic words when contextually inter-changeable in the oblique cases (unlike e.g. German *Sie/sie*). Perhaps a phonetic distinction existing in NT times disappeared very soon afterwards, thus making confusion easy when MSS were reproduced from dictation. The date of origin of the modern ἐσεῖς might here be illuminating. Cf. ἐσοῦ for σοῦ twice in the papyrus letter of the bad boy Theon (2nd-3rd cent. AD; *POxy* 119 = Deissmann, *LAE*, pp. 201-202). See generally R. Browning, *Medieval and Modern Greek* (London, 1969), pp. 32-33, 67.

66. ἄμεινον γάρ ἐστιν παρὰ ἀνδρὸς περιτομὴν ἔχοντος χριστιανισμὸν ἀκούειν ἢ παρὰ ἀκροβύστου ἰουδαϊσμόν. A similar situation appears to underlie Ign. *Magn.* 8-11. Ignatius had not visited Magnesia, and he may have written in the light of his experiences in Philadelphia. His warning is directed against Jewish practice (9.1) and the attempt to combine it with a Christian profession (10.1, 3).

67. The variant ἀρχαίοις occurs only here, where it is readily explained as an easier reading (see Lightfoot, *Ignatius*, II.271).

68. Alternatively, the ἀρχεῖα, interpreted as the Gospel autographs, might be opposed to a supposedly corrupt Gospel as written and preached in Ignatius's time. The metaphorical use of 'archives' seems to be unparalleled in any case. S. Reinach, 'Ignatius, Bishop of Antioch, and the ΑΡΧΕΙΑ', *Anatolian Studies . . . W.M. Ramsay*, pp. 339-40, has argued for the literal sense, 'public archives'. The linguistic and cultural background of this passage merits close study. The word at issue is not discussed in *LSJ* or in G.W.H. Lampe, *A Patristic Greek Lexicon*.

69. Alternatively, 'Unless I find it (the Gospel) in the archives, I do not believe in the Gospel'. This, however, destroys the balance of the clauses, and the usage of πιστεύω ἐν in this way is rare.

70. 'Philadelphia and Montanism', *BJRL* 7 (1922-23), pp. 309-54.

71. There are isolated examples from Trajanopolis (Uşak) on the route from Philadelphia into western Phrygia, from near Thyatira, and doubtfully from Apamea (Dinar) in central Phrygia. Calder (pp. 310-17) gives a valuable sketch of the usual veiled-profession type of Christian epitaph with which these documents contrast so strangely.

72. Ramsay's derivation of the phénomenon from a more rigid form of Christianity, supposedly originating in Bithynia and exemplified in a remote district outside the attention of Roman officials ('Early Christian Monuments in Phrygia', *Expos.*, 3rd ser., 8 [1888], pp. 246-48, 263-64; cf. *CB*, II.510), breaks down on both counts, for (1) there is no reason to support the assumption of an unusually rigid Christianity in Bithynia, and (2) much of the Tembris district actually belonged to an imperial estate of the kind whose tenants were sometimes organized in an anti-Christian religious association. See generally J.G.C. Anderson, 'Paganism and Christianity in the Upper Tembris Valley', *Studies in the History and Art of the Eastern Provinces of the Roman Empire*, ed. W.M. Ramsay, esp. pp. 188-90, 196-202; and W.M. Ramsay, 'The Tekmoreian Guest-Friends', *ibid.*, pp. 305-77. See now E. Gibson, *The 'Christians for Christians' Inscriptions of Phrygia* (Harvard, 1978).

73. When Calder wrote the known third-century Christian epigraphy of the district round its reputed centre at Pepuza was solidly and discreetly orthodox. Later discoveries have compelled a modification of his views at this point (Gibson, Nos. 42, 43, from Üçkuyu and Bekilli respectively).

74. Ramsay attractively suggested that the correct form of 'Ardabau' was 'Kardaba', to be identified with Callatebus (Hdt. 7.31; *CB*, II.573). This however is quite uncertain, and we might equally advance the claims of Adruta, a place in the territory of Philadelphia (Keil–von Premerstein, *Dritte Reise*, p. 35, No. 46; cf. Magie, p. 982n.). The peculiar geographical expression may be more helpful, for Ramsay has shown that a detached district of Mysia lay on the Phrygian border south of Philadelphia and was

reckoned to the *conventus* of Ephesus (*CB* I.195-99, explaining the Mysomacedones of Plin. *NH* 5.31.120). The phrase might well specifically denote this district (so *CB* II.573-74). So, while the identification of Ardabau must remain conjectural, there is reason to reinforce Calder's suggestion that it was near Philadelphia.

75. Note such themes as the dispute about authority and the validity of new revelation, or even the lyre metaphor (cf. Ign. *Philad.* 1 with Epiphan. *Haer.* 48.4; Bonwetsch, *Die Geschichte des Montanismus*, p. 197). The connections should not be pressed, but they show some preoccupation with similar problems and concepts.

76. 'Phrygian' not here in an ethnic sense, which would not have been complimentary to the recipients in Philomelium. The Montanists were regularly termed 'Phrygians', but a 'Phrygian' movement evidently existed before the traditional date of the appearance of Montanus.

77. H. Grégoire, 'Les Inscriptions hérétiques d'Asie Mineure', *Byzantion* 1 (1924), pp. 703-10, and 'Du nouveau sur la Hiérarchie de la secte montaniste d'après une inscription grecque trouvée près de Philadelphie en Lydie', *Byz.* 2 (1925), pp. 329-35; W.M. Calder, 'Leaves from an Anatolian Notebook', *BJRL* 13 (1929), pp. 266-71, and 'The New Jerusalem of the Montanists', *Byz.* 6 (1931), pp. 421-25; H. Grégoire, 'Inscriptions montanistes et novatiennes', *Byz.* 8 (1933), pp. 58-65, and 'Épigraphie hérétique... et hérésie épigraphique', *Byz.* 10 (1935), pp. 247-50.

78. First published by W.H. Buckler in *JHS* 37 (1917), pp. 95-99, No. 8, but now shown by Grégoire to refer to a high Montanist dignitary (*Byz.* 2, 1925, pp. 329-35). Presumably an orthodox bishop lived in the city and the heretic, as often, in a village-centre outside, a situation to which the latter may have applied the terms of Rev. 3.12.

79. See Bonwetsch, pp. 140-48; E.C. Selwyn, *The Christian Prophets*, pp. 26-40; G.S.P. Freeman-Grenville, 'The Date of the Outbreak of Montanism', *JEH* 5 (1954), pp. 7-15. The differing dates in Eusebius and in Epiphan. *Haer.* 48.1 evidently refer to different dates in Montanist history.

80. Much tentative circumstantial evidence could be produced, for example the provenance of distinctively Montanist personal names.

81. Grégoire, *Byz.* 2 (1925), p. 331.

82. Thus the specifically Montanist elements are not easily isolated in the characteristic rigorism of Tertullian's later writings. See now G.L. Bray, *Holiness and the Will of God* (London, 1979), pp. 54-63.

83. Euseb. *HE* 5.17.2-3; cf. G. Salmon in *Murray's Dictionary of Christian Biography*, p. 738.

84. Salmon (p. 741) goes so far as to say: 'Christians had so far closed their NT canon that they were shocked that any modern writing should be made equal to the inspired books of the apostolic age', and again 'we still think it plain from the history that the conception of a closed NT canon was found by Montanism and not then created'. See also Epiphan. *Haer.* 48.1.402 =

Migne *PG* XLI.85b. His treatment of Montanism is worth weighing. He uses the Johannine writings, the prophets and the Revelation (1.1) in his reply to it. J.G. Davies, 'Tertullian, *De Resurrectione Carnis* LXIII: A Note on the Origins of Montanism', *JTS* n.s. 6 (1955), pp. 90-94, draws attention to the Montanists' passionate devotion to scriptural orthodoxy as against Gnosticism.

85. Calder, pp. 339-40, No. 8. Cf. p. 343, No. 12. I have here normalized the differing itacisms of the originals.

86. Cf. e.g. (συγ)κοινωνός in Montanist inscriptions (Calder in *AS* 5 [1955], p. 37, No. 7, and the Mendechora inscription) with Rev. 1.9 (see W.H.C. Frend, *Martyrdom and Persecution in the Early Church*, p. 88), and the constant polemic against Montanists with quotation from the Revelation (e.g. Euseb. *HE* 5.18.14 and 5.16.3 with Rev. 22.18).

87. Calder's suggestion of Bekilli (*Byz.* 6 [1931], p. 424) and Ramsay's of Buğdaylı (*CB* II.575, there spelt 'Boudaili') are both based on inadequate evidence, though the actual place must be near both. Calder's case is based largely on his discovery of a Montanist inscription at Bekilli; Ramsay's on a hypothetical connection of the name Pepuza, supposedly a reduplication of 'Pouza', with the modern Buğdaylı, assuming that the latter had been adapted to give a meaning ('the place of wheat') in modern Turkish. I am assured however that the Turkish name is accurately descriptive, and there is no reason to explain it away as a corruption of an older form. The other village of Montanist prophecy, Tymium, was conjecturally placed by Ramsay at Dumanlı (again from the resemblance of name) and by Calder at Üç Kuyu.

Notes to Chapter 9

1. The clearest map of the Lycus valley is that adapted from the Ottoman Railway Survey in *CRE*, facing p. 472. A wider area is shown by the smaller map in *JHS* 17 (1897), Plate XII, illustrating the article by J.G.C. Anderson. There is a useful description of the district in S.E. Johnson, 'Laodicea and its Neighbors', *BA* 13 (1950), pp. 1-18.

2. Herodotus describes it as 'a great city of Phrygia' in the time of Xerxes (7.30). Cf. Xen. *Anab.* 1.2.6; Diod. Sic. 16.80.8; Polyaenus, *Strat.* 7.16.1. The word μεγάλην is omitted from some of the MSS of Herodotus, possibly because copyists were misled by the city's later insignificance. His account of the topography is discussed by G. Weber in *Ath. Mitt.* 16 (1891), pp. 194-99, who includes a valuable sketch-map on p. 195.

3. J. Mellaert has published a pottery fragment of the Early Bronze Age from Colossae in *AS* 4 (1954), pp. 192 and 230-31.

4. *CB* I.172-74. See also A.H.M. Jones, *Cities of the Roman Provinces*, p. 73, and Magie, *Roman Rule in Asia Minor*, p. 1245. Cf. *CB* I.85. J.G.C. Anderson's map, revised by Sir W.M. Calder and G.E. Bean, *A Classical*

Map of Asia Minor (1957), equates Cydrara with Hierapolis and omits Hydrela. The texts however seem to confirm the equivalence of Cydrara with Hydrela, and the evidence of coinage indicates that Hydrela was distinct from Hierapolis under the Early Empire.

5. Pliny lists the cities of Asia according to their organization in *conventus*. Although named from Cibyra, this district had its capital at Laodicea.

6. To be distinguished from Hieropolis in the Phrygian Pentapolis, the city of Avircius Marcellus. See *CB* I.87-88 for the significance of the change of name.

7. See *CB* I.167=69; cf. I.6, 52, and B.V. Head in *BMC Caria*, pp. xl-xli.

8. Steph. Byz. on Laodicea; Eustath. on Dion. Perieg. 915. For discussion of Radet's view that Laodicea was founded by Antiochus I see *CB* I.32n. and Magie, p. 986n. See also Jones, *Cities*, p. 42. For a sketch-map of the site see *CB* I, facing p. 35.

9. For the Attalids see *OGIS* 483.24ff. Cf. Magie, p. 40. Immediately after 133 BC M'. Aquilius undertook a great rebuilding work, and the milestones bearing his name are said to be the earliest official record of Roman rule in Asia (Magie, pp. 41, 157).

10. Cic. *ad Att.* 5.21.9 with *ad Fam.* 3.8.5, both of 51/50 BC; Strab. 13.4.17 = p. 631; R. Syme, 'Observations on the Province of Cilicia', *Anatolian Studies Presented to W.H. Buckler*, pp. 299-332.

11. Laodicea in Col. 2.1; 4.13, 15, 16; Rev. 1.11; 3.14; Hierapolis in Col. 4.13; Colossae in Col. 1.2, and as the destination of that epistle and probably of Philemon.

12. The case for this identification is argued at length by J.B. Lightfoot, *St. Paul's Epistles to the Colossians and to Philemon*, pp. 274-81. See C.P. Anderson, 'Who Wrote "The Epistle from Laodicea"?', *JBL* 85 (1966), pp. 436-40, for the suggestion that it was a letter from Epaphras dealing with similar problems in the church in Laodicea. The apocryphal 'letter to the Laodiceans' was a compilation of unconnected Pauline sayings (M.R. James, *The New Testament Apocrypha*, pp. 478-80).

13. The name 'Philemon' is recorded on an inscription of Laodicea (*IGRR* IV. 864) and the rarer 'Apphia' actually on one of Colossae (*IGRR* IV. 868). The name 'Epaphras' also occurs in that form on an inscription of Laodicea (*MAMA* VI.1).

14. It is sometimes suggested that Colossae was now a mere πόλισμα (*CB* I.209; Ruge in *PW*), but the text of Strabo 12.8.13 = p. 576 has a lacuna and the inference is uncertain, especially as Colossae is grouped with so considerable a city as Aphrodisias (cf. Magie, p. 986). Pliny lists Colossae among the *oppida celeberrima* of Phrygia (*NH* 5.41.145), but he excludes the really important ones which he had mentioned previously (*NH* 5.29.105ff.). And in any case he is evidently following a much earlier authority, which refers to Apamea by its old name of Celaenae.

15. Ramsay comments on the old notion that the Colossians of the Epistle were the Rhodians and that they were so called from their famous Colossus. See O.F.A. Meinardus, 'Colossus, Colossae, Colossi: Confusio Colossaea', *BA* 36 (1973), pp. 33-36.

16. Nearly one hundred pounds weight are said to have been confiscated at Apamea. In Strabo's time however that was a commercial centre second only in Asia to Ephesus itself (12.8.15 = p. 577), and Apamea and Laodicea are coupled as the two greatest cities of Phrygia (12.8.13 = p. 576). For Apamea cf. Jones, *Cities*, p. 70. The occurrence of Noah's ark as a coin-type (e.g. *BMC Phrygia*, Apam. No. 82, with legend NΩE) indicates a remarkable degree of Jewish influence in the city.

For the calculation of Jews at Laodicea see T. Reinach, cited in *SC*, p. 420, and Blaiklock, *Cities*, p. 126. Lightfoot, p. 20, suggested over 11,000, but noted that his value for the gold-silver relation might be too high.

17. Note however *CIG* 9916, from Rome, the tombstone of Ammia, a Jewess of Laodicea—probably this Laodicea, for the name was common in the district (e.g. *IGRR* IV. 865; *CB* I.75, No. 9).

18. The laxity of the Diaspora is not however emphasized in the context.

19. The meaning here is uncertain. *The Babylonian Talmud*, ed. I. Epstein, renders the saying: 'The wine of Perugitha and the water of Diomsith cut off the Ten Tribes from Israel', and identifies the places respectively with the neighbourhoods of Tiberias and Emmaus. The context however suggests a location in the Diaspora.

20. There were a number of cities of the name. The story may be seen to fit the contemporary character of this most famous of the Laodiceas.

21. Most of the texts were first published by W. Judeich, *Altertümer von Hierapolis*, *JDAI Ergänzungsheft* 4 (1898), or in *CB*. Most of them are also conveniently found in *CIJ* pp. 775-80. It must be noted that Hierapolis, and its cemetery in particular, has been much more extensively preserved, explored and published than Laodicea.

22. F.A. Pennacchietti, 'Nuove Iscrizioni di Hierapolis Frigia', *Atti dell' Accademia delle Scienze di Torino* 101.2 (1966-67), pp. 300, 319, Nos. 14, 46.

23. Some other remarkable inscriptions mention the πορφυραβάφοι, which appear to have been here a Jewish association. Judeich No. 342 = *CB* II.545, No. 411 = *CIJ* 777 mentions annuities to be paid at the feast of unleavened bread and at Pentecost. For the same association cf. also Judeich Nos. 41, 42, and the much debated Judeich No. 227, which Ramsay supposed to be Christian. These inscriptions are not closely datable, though all appear to belong to the second or third centuries AD.

24. In the case of Hierapolis Ramsay argues a possible Christian origin for the names Prophetilla (*CB* I.118, No. 27, of c. AD 200), Maria (*CB* I.105-106, No. 413, of the early 3rd cent.) and for other later examples, Frey a Jewish origin for Maria (*CIJ* 779; cf. 780). Individual identifications of this kind turn on often speculative inferences from the incidence of names and

variations of formulae in documents which otherwise reflect current pagan patterns.

25. See J.G.C. Anderson in *JHS* 17 (1897), p. 411, and *CB* I.105-106 for Hierapolis; *CB* I.60 for Laodicea; Jones, *Cities*, pp. 73ff. for both.

26. It may be asked why Paul's problem involved Colossae rather than the other two cities, which must have possessed much larger Jewish communities. The answer is not clear. Possibly the influence of the native Phrygian religion of Colossae was a significant ingredient of the syncretistic compound. A Christianized worship of mediating powers persisted in the neighbour-hood. The archangel Michael was represented in mediaeval legend as the saviour of the upper valley from inundation (*CRE*, Chap. 19 and cf. *CB* I.214-15), and his church remained a famous shrine near the site after the city itself had disappeared. Alternatively we might suppose that a Christian deviation became strong at Colossae because the Pauline gospel itself had found a readier response in a poorer centre than in the materialistic affluence of Laodicea or the luxurious paganism of Hierapolis.

27. Rev. 3.14 with Col. 1.15ff.; Rev. 3.17 with Col. 1.27 (cf. Col. 2.2-3); Rev. 3.21 with Col. 3.1 (cf. Eph. 2.6).

28. Apart from the formula of Rev. 1.4, which resembles those of several Pauline epistles, there is only Rev. 1.5 ('the firstborn of the dead'), echoing the similar expression in the significant passage in Col. 1.18.

29. Thus the reference to white raiment in Rev. 16.15 is near the thought of 3.3, not 3.18. Compare and contrast also 'true' (3.14) with 3.7 (Philad.); 'beginning' (3.14) with 2.8 (Smyrna); 'rich' (3.17) with 2.9 (Smyrna); the love of Christ (3.19) with 3.9 (Philad.); 'door' (3.20) with 3.8 (Philad.); a promise of ruling power (3.21) with 2.26-27 (Thyat.); 'throne' (3.21) with 2.13 (Perg.).

30. This depends on the assumption of confusion between אמן and אמון (defectively written) in the related text of Prov. 8.30. Ἀμήν is never otherwise applied absolutely to a person: cf. however 2 Cor. 1.20. For the idea cf. also Hermas, *Simil.* 9.12.2.

31. The passage (9.26–10.1; translated in Vermes, *The Dead Sea Scrolls in English*, pp. 384ff.) is obscure. Finegan suggests in the light of the context that the מ alludes to 'luminaries' or 'seasons', and that the ו is shaped like a key, the א presumably being God. We note that the Colossians were cautioned against those who judged them over the observance of seasons (Col. 2.16) or who claimed esoteric knowledge (cf. Col. 2.2-4, 8, 18). We may at least suspect the widespread diffusion of similar sectarian tendencies.

32. It is questionable whether any consistent distinction can be drawn between ἀληθινός and ἀληθής, the latter of which never occurs in Rev. The Fourth Gospel differs in usage. It has both words, and uses ἀληθινός in the sense 'genuine'.

33. See especially C.F. Burney, 'Christ as the *APXH* of Creation', *JTS* 27 (1926), pp. 160-77.

34. Chandler, p. 266 and Arundell, *Seven Churches*, p. 90, connect ἐμέσαι with the supposition of volcanic eruption, but the alluvial strata of the hills are horizontal, as Fellows observed (*Journal*, p. 281). Trench cited opinions that water was never served lukewarm at feasts, and that tepid food was unpalatable (*Seven Churches*, 3rd edn, pp. 202-203), but see Athenaeus, *Deipn.* 3.123e. Today Turkish taste actually prefers food served tepid, and this may continue older custom.

35. Cf. J. Bonsirven, *L'Apocalypse de Saint Jean*, p. 125, and Blaiklock, *Cities*, p. 126, who draws attention to the nauseating lukewarm mixtures of thermal waters with cold streams in New Zealand.

36. Dr G.W. Blanchard explains the phenomena to me by suggesting that the shape of the channels on the plateau provides a great volume of water relative to its surface exposure to the air. A thin layer of carbon dioxide, a heavy gas, then seals off the surface from the air and prevents the chemical reaction leading to the wholesale deposition of calcium carbonate. At the edge of the cliff the water suddenly becomes exposed to the air over a wide front. The amorphous deposits at the west end may be due to the steepness of the original gradient, and the stepped pools were perhaps formed by deposition around pebbles on a shallower initial slope. Cf. W.C. Brice, *JSS* 23 (1978), pp. 226-27, for confirmation of the presence of a carbon dioxide layer at the water surface.

37. Strabo notes those of Carura (see next note, and cf. Athenaeus, *Deipn.* 2.43a-b). I am told of very hot springs also by the Maeander above Yenice (cf. *CB* I.194).

38. ζεστός, like χλιαρός, is a Biblical ἅπαξ. These words are usually applied to liquids, ζεστός elsewhere to waters of the present district (Strab. 12.8.17 = p. 578, of Carura).

39. Cf. however the participle ζέων in Acts 18.25 and Rom. 12.11.

40. Cf. Tait, pp. 405-12; Plumptre, pp. 198-202. The traditional interpretation is assumed by Charles, p. 96, Anderson Scott, p. 156, Swete, p. 60, Kiddle, p. 58, and by Caird, p. 57. Perhaps the modern connotation of 'lukewarmness' first arose from this understanding of the present passage.

41. ζήλευε (v. 19) might suggest, however, that their enthusiasm was at fault, and so be related to the traditional interpretation of ζεστός (so Swete, p. 63).

42. F. Lo Bue, *The Turin Fragments of Tyconius' Commentary on Revelation*, pp. 74-75.

43. For the topography see also G. Weber in *Ath. Mitt.* 16 (1891), pp. 194-99. One of the three streams, the Ak Su ('white water') has highly petrifying qualities, and is evidently that to which Pliny alludes (*NH* 31.20.29). Hamilton does not mention the pure stream. In any case the topography is peculiarly difficult to describe precisely. The facts are confused in Herodotus and in the legend, Strabo's version involves a misconception, and the modern descriptions and maps vary. Hamilton, Weber and Ramsay do not

agree wholly with each other or with my own observations. Some of the differences must be due to changes of course when the streams have become blocked with their own deposits. The salient fact for the present discussion is the existence of the *ayasma*.

44. Blaiklock, *Cities*, p. 124, and many others are incorrect in supposing that this source was near Hierapolis, which is beyond the main river in the opposite direction.

45. Presumably the Baş Pınar Çay. For the identity of the rivers of Laodicea see J.G.C. Anderson, in *JHS* 17 (1897), pp. 404-408. I here modernize his spelling and distinguish (1) Gümüş Çay (Asopus), W of Laodicea, (2) Baş Pınar Çay, E of Laodicea, 'rising in copious springs at Denizli, but diverted for irrigation and insignificant'. This flows into (3) Gök Pınar Su, = Çukur Su (Kapros), a larger tributary of the Lycus touching the eastern extremity of the city. (4) is the main river, Çoruk Su (Lycus).

46. Ramsay refers to the source, *CB* I.48, but it is not clear whether his statement rests on verified observation or only inference. I have seen fragments of masonry which suggested piers of arches crossing a steep tributary valley of the Gümüş Çay in line with the aqueduct and south of the low hill from which Hamilton traced it (*Researches*, I.515-16).

47. A Turkish water-engineer, a native of the district, Bay Mehmet Uysal, once vividly described to me carrying to the school-house in Yenice (Tripolis) water from the village fountain which seemed warm and steaming in winter and cold in summer, being in fact of a constant tepid temperature. This however was pure and therefore palatable. Cf. Vitruv. 8.3.1. Lukewarm water was sometimes used medicinally as an emetic (Cels. 1.3.22).

48. He reasons as follows. He first confirmed that the deposit at Laodicea, as at Hierapolis, was calcium carbonate ($CaCO_3$). The solution of carbon dioxide in water forms a weak acid, carbonic acid ($H_2O + CO_2 = H_2CO_3$). This may combine with calcium carbonate to form calcium bicarbonate: $CaCO_3 + H_2CO_3 = Ca(HCO_3)_2$. The latter is soluble in water but unstable. When the temperature is raised it becomes calcium carbonate (deposited) and water with carbon dioxide in solution. This is the usual condition of the warm waters of the Lycus valley. In the confined aqueduct pipe the situation is greatly complicated by variables which may be imponderable. But the visible deposit on the pipes testifies unmistakably to the basic reaction and so to the warmth of the water, though its actual temperature cannot be deduced from the uncertain data. Hot water would cool initially, but when the pipes were heated a stable condition of warmth would be created. The thermal conductivity of the stone would be low and no great change of water-temperature would be expected in the pipes.

49. Cf. such other old forms and transliterations as 'Thingozlou' (*CB* I.48n.) and the Arabic 'Dūn Ghuzluh' (Ibn Baṭṭūṭa, *Travels*, p. 425). The latter is said to mean 'the town of the swine', from a Turkish form *duñuz* (modern Tk. *domuz*) = 'swine'. 'Denizli' might then have been a later euphemism for 'Domuz-lu'.

50. It is very doubtful whether it could ever have been hidden beneath the surface (*SC*, p. 415): some sections are actually raised on arches. The only surviving section now partly embedded is that which crosses the low ground immediately south of the city-hill. This may originally have been on the surface and is excellently preserved, so that its line may be traced into the city. The type of aqueduct is not unique. J.G.C. Anderson discovered another of exactly the same kind at nearby Trapezopolis (*JHS* 17 [1897], pp. 401-402).

51. Why did the city take such trouble to obtain water of such bad and petrifying quality? Was it miscalculation, or had there perhaps been some change consequent on earthquake or the shifting course of a stream? Was the supply basic or supplementary? Do the ring-formations of the deposit in the pipes testify to a seasonal, or to a discontinuous, use? Did a structure so vulnerable survive the earthquake of Nero's reign? Is one pipe later than the other? Did a later pipe supplement or replace an earlier?

52. Caird, p. 56, argues for a close identification of church and city here. The interpretation need not hinge on the acceptance of this. Cf. the admonition to Archippus (Col. 4.17), possibly still a leader of the Laodicean church.

53. Cf. for the eyesalves Arr. *Epict.* 2.21.20.

54. The point is strongly made by Swete, pp. 61-62. Cf. also Trench, p. 207; Charles, pp. 93, 96-97; Kiddle, pp. 58-59; Ramsay, *SC*, pp. 428-29.

55. Trench however connects the ὅτι clause with v. 16 preceding.

56. Cf. R. Syme, 'Observations on the Province of Cilicia', *Anatolian Studies Presented to W.H. Buckler*, pp. 301ff.

57. An extant inscription seems to allude to the ἐνπόριον at Laodicea, probably the 'Exchange', but the context is uncertain and the restoration conjectural (*CIG* 3938, revised in *CB* I.74, No. 8).

58. *Cave ne portus occupet alter,* / *Ne Cibyratica, ne Bithyna negotia perdas* (Hor. *Epist.* 1.6.32-33, cited by Lightfoot, *Colossians and Philemon*, p. 7n.).

59. Sitalcas on *BMC Phrygia*, Laod., No. 54; Pythes on Nos. 55-56. The name or monogram of the latter as magistrate appears also on Nos. 57-59 and 61-62.

60. For the names of other benefactors cf. *CB* I.42n. Cf. also in earlier times the Lydian Pythius who entertained Xerxes at Celaenae (Hdt. 7.27ff.) and the contemporary of Zeno, Hybreas of Mylasa, who 'rehabilitated himself and his city' after the attack of Labienus Parthicus (Strab. 14.2.24 = p. 660).

61. Note esp. the account of the sophist Polemo (early 2nd cent. AD) in Philostr. *Vit. Soph.* 1.25.

62. Cf. the dedication to her at Hierapolis (Judeich No. 26 = *CIG* 3906b = *IGRR* IV. 810; cf. Cichorius, *Alt. von Hierap.*, p. 44). At Acmonia in Phrygia there was a cult of Poppaea which identified her with a goddess Eubosia

(*CIG* 3858; cf. *CB* II.637, 640). The equivalence of the two forms is confirmed by fluctuations of spelling, as in *CIG* 3385.2, of Smyrna, etc. The primary meaning is 'good pasture' (βόσκω).

63. Cf. also Tac. *Ann.* 4.55.3, recording how Laodicea was among those candidates passed over in AD 26 as of insufficient standing to receive the new provincial temple of the imperial cult.

64. There was a different dating in later Christian tradition. In Eusebius, *Chron.* Olymp. 210.4 = AD 64, it follows the fire of Rome, and Orosius, 7.7.12, makes it one of a series of judgments on the pagan world consequent upon the fire and the Neronian persecution. The testimony of Tacitus should be accepted here. The moralized chronology of Orosius is aptly seen in this confusion of the great earthquake of AD 17 with that at the time of the Crucifixion (7.4.13, 18). Both the later writers link the names of the three NT cities of the Lycus valley as victims of the disaster under Nero, a detail absent from Tacitus.

65. Hierapolis, Tripolis and (?) Carura are mentioned explicitly. I assume that 'Carura' is a correct emendation for 'Corcyra'.

66. See esp. Cichorius, *Alt. von Hierap.*, p. 24; also Magie, p. 1421n., and S.E. Johnson, *BA* 13 (1950), p. 13. Johnson observes (p. 14) that some of the great buildings of Hierapolis are dated by archaeology about AD 100.

67. For the financial incompetency of Trapezopolis under the Flavians see J.G.C. Anderson in *JHS* 17 (1897), p. 403.

68. Cf. e.g. *CIG* 3480, 3507, of Thyat. Similar types of inscriptions from the cities of Asia Minor might be numbered in hundreds.

69. Cf. M.J. Mellink, in *The Interpreter's Dictionary of the Bible*, III.71, where however the stadium and the triple gate are incorrectly stated to have been dedicated to Vespasian.

70. *CIG* 3935 = *IGRR* IV. 845 = *CB* I.73, No. 4; dedicated to the emperor Titus (ὑπάτῳ τὸ ζ´) by the proconsul M. Ulpius Trajanus, father of the emperor Trajan (procos. of Asia 79-80, *PIR* III, No. 574). The restoration of the unique expression στάδιον ἀμφιθέατρον is confirmed by a later inscription recording the institution of a public cult of the great-niece of Nicostratus. After two generations his gift of the stadium is explicitly remembered (*CIG* 3936 = *IGRR* IV. 861 = *CB* I.72, No. 3).

71. *Ath. Mitt.* 16 (1891), p. 145 = *IGRR* IV. 860; for the dating see *CB* I.50n. The expression in this case is παρ' ἑαυτοῦ. It recurs four times in one sentence. Contrast ἀγοράσαι παρ' ἐμοῦ (Rev. 3.18). Cf. also *IGRR* IV. 855.

72. *dedicante Sex.* [. . . A proconsul Sextus Julius Frontinus is known to have held office c. 88-90, and the *praenomen* is not so frequent that two men so called are likely to have occupied the post at unassigned dates under Domitian. The emperor's name, though deleted, is now said to be traceable.

73. *JHS* 17 (1897), 408n. Cf. L. Robert, *Études anatoliennes*, p. 532n. Ramsay had supposed it had come from the Ephesian gate, a monumental erection which survived in the time of Fellows (p. 282, describing a journey of 1838).

74. Perhaps the erection of a great new city gate at Laodicea was present to the mind of the writer of Rev. 3.20, though the word there used is θύρα, not πύλη. See further the discussion of that passage below.

75. E.g. *BMCPhrygia*, Laod. No.153, inscribed ΖΕΥΞΙΣΦΙΛΑΛΗΘΗΣ ΛΑΟΔΙΚΕΩΝ, with Asclepian serpent-staff.

76. ἄνθος χαλκοῦ was presumably the same as *flos aeris*, mentioned as an exedent and healing agent by Celsus 5.7, 10, 20 (cf. Plin. *NH* 34.24.107). Malachite is also a copper derivative.

77. This work is difficult of access. See C.G. Kühn, *Medicorum Graecorum Opera Quae Exstant*, VI.439.

78. He notes that Polemo, the Laodicean orator of Hadrian's time, was called simply ὁ Φρύξ (Philostr. *Vit. Soph.* 1.25). The case of a famous individual, however, is not really parallel.

79. See esp. M. Wellmann on '*Augenärzte*' in *PW* and L. Edelstein on 'Ophthalmology' in *OCD*.

80. The Hippocratic parallels are tabulated by W.G. Spencer in the *LCL* Celsus, III.pp. 624–27.

81. Cels. Prooem. 8, 11; Scrib. Larg. 'Ep. ad Call.', pp. 1, 3 (Teubner). Celsus derived his medical ideas from Themison of Laodicea (in Syria), a pupil of Asclepiades (Wellmann). He also alludes later to Herophilus's terminology for the anatomy of the eye (7.7.13B). Scribonius begins his work with a reference to Herophilus.

82. Cf. Horace's use of a *collyrium* on his journey to Brundisium (Hor. *Sat.* 1.5.30-31).

83. Cf. Wellmann, 'Demosthenes ΠΕΡΙ ΟΦΘΑΛΜΩΝ', *Hermes* 38 (1903), pp. 546-66. He considers it conclusive 'dass wir in ihm den Schöpfer des griechischen Canons der Augenheilkunde zu sehen haben' (p. 556) and that later writings are derived from him.

84. *EBr* XXIII.976.

85. Again there are many possibilities. Perhaps varieties of a *collyrium* originating there were later made elsewhere. Perhaps this was merely one of a number of centres where similar products were developed under the influence of Herophilean medicine.

86. I except the poetic *lapis Phrygius* of Horace (*Od.* 3.1.41; cf. Tibull. 3.3.13), which was probably Synnadic marble.

87. Cf. Col. 2.8, 18 for the influence on the Christians of the district by those who boasted a superior spiritual discernment.

88. Perhaps the Laodiceans themselves made the 'raven-blackness' of their woollen goods a commercial slogan.

89. These include several different types of garment, varieties of each of which are described as 'Laodicean'.

90. The Greek versions of *paenula* are very diverse. Cf. φελόνη in 2 Tim. 4.13 and φαινόλη in Arr. *Epict.* 4.8.34.

91. The Romans regarded embroidered clothing as characteristically Phrygian (Plin. *NH* 8.84.195-96).

92. Inscriptions of Laodicea refer to a shepherd (*MAMA* VI.21), a clothes-dealer (*MAMA* VI.12b), and to fullers, dyers and ἀπλουργοί (? garment-makers) (*CIG* 3938 = *CB* I.74, No. 8). At least one monument appears to portray a sheep (*MAMA* VI.1), and the goat-like animal on *MAMA* VI.3 and on coins (*passim*) may in fact also be a sheep, the two species sometimes being deceptively similar.

There is interesting evidence of the persistence of the Laodicean breed of sheep until modern times. Ramsay writes: 'Pococke in the first half of the eighteenth century saw a great many black sheep; Chandler saw only a few black and glossy in the early part of the present [19th] century; my experience agrees with Chandler's, except that I was not struck with the gloss of the few black fleeces' (*Impressions of Turkey*, p. 273; cf. *CB* I.42). Arundell, a few years after Chandler, says that before the aqueduct 'were Turcoman black tents, and thousands of goats and sheep of the same colour' (*Seven Churches*, p. 91). His comment is the more interesting as he seems unaware of any significance in the observation. The black sheep are still occasionally seen in the valley. I have seen the photograph of a goat-like specimen taken by Canon E.M.B. Green in 1957 and possess one taken by Mr T. Harpur in 1965: none were observed on personal visits to the district in 1964 and 1969. Bay Mehmet Uysal confirmed to me that they still occur, being surprised that the writer of Revelation showed such familiarity with the valley in a detail still distinctive of it. The consensus seems to be that the few survivals represent the final stage of the degeneration of a breed (cf. Ramsay, *Impressions*, pp. 272ff.). And in modern Turkey, according to my friend Dr A. Orhan Yeşin, *kara koçum* ('my black ram') is a familiar term of endearment in village life, because the black animal is rare and consequently valued.

93. Presumably deep purple, and so dyed, though Ramsay treats it simply as the colour of another breed of sheep (*SC*, p. 416). Ancient colour words are strangely used, though Pliny refers to a practice of dyeing purple or scarlet the unshorn fleeces of the living animals (*NH* 8.74.197).

94. Mediaeval and modern Denizli continues the textile trade, but now favours cotton-growing. Pamukkale, the modern name of Hierapolis, means 'cotton castle', either in allusion to this trade or to the white formations of its cliffs. Cf. Ibn Baṭṭūṭa, p. 425.

95. 2.3 = p. 88; cf. 4.2 = p. 205. Black clothing is connected with σωτηρία.

96. Beckwith (p. 490) expresses a doubt, asking why the following purpose clause points a contrast with nakedness rather than with black clothing. The difficulty does not seem serious, for the manner of allusion is habitually suggestive rather than rigid, and γυμνότης in v. 18 correlates with γυμνός in v. 17. The implication is that the white clothing which Christ bestows is the only true clothing in the spiritual sense: no human substitute can cover spiritual nakedness.

97. See further W. Michaelis, *TDNT* IV. 249-50.

98. It is questionable whether any distinction should be drawn between the

use of ἀγαπῶ in Rev. 3.9 (cf. Isa. 43.4) and φιλῶ in Rev. 3.19 (based on Prov. 3.12, where the LXX uses ἀγαπῶ). Charles, p. 99, and Swete, p. 63, argue that the more emotional word is used to Laodicea. In the Rev. ἀγάπη occurs only at 2.4, and the verb at 1.5, 3.9, 12.11; φιλῶ otherwise only at 22.15. ἀγάπη is characteristic of 1 John, but it is doubtful whether rigid distinction of usage can be maintained in the Johannine literature generally. Contrast e.g. John 15.9 with 5.20. See further J.H. Bernard in *St. John* (ICC), pp. 702-704, on John 21.15-17.

99.   Rudwick and Green (p. 178n.) are almost alone in suggesting a local relevance in the imagery of Rev. 3.20.

100.   Cf. T. Reinach, *Mithridate Eupator*, p. 210, who gives the reference incorrectly.

101.   *Ad Att.* 5.20.5-6; 5.21.5; the latter again written from Laodicea.

102.   For this law cf. Cic. *ad Att.* 5.21.2 and *Digest*. 48.11. A textual problem in the former passage makes it doubtful whether the provision of meals for official staff could be exacted legally within its terms.

103.   After Cicero's departure Scipio soon renewed the worst abuses. Caesar (*Bell. Civ.* 3.32) gives a long list of his impositions, including a tax on doors (*ostiaria*). Cf. Cic. *ad Fam.* 3.8.5, cited above.

104.   Contrast the conduct of Diotrephes (3 John 9, 10). The apparently unfounded tradition which made him an early bishop of Laodicea might be true to character if not to history (cf. *CB* I.78).

105.   At Hierapolis there are numerous imposing mausolea of the Roman period with gabled roofs and large doorways, and bearing inscriptions threatening penalties for this offence. Similar examples are found among the limited materials from Laodicea (e.g. *CB* I.74, No. 7; *MAMA* VI.19). The cases from Hierapolis include Jews, who use the same formulae as the pagans (*CIJ* 775-79).

106.   Other authorities for the events are Dio Cass. 48.26.3; Liv. Epit. 127 and Justinus 42.4.7. Only Strabo mentions the case of Laodicea, together with the similar part played by Hybreas at Mylasa. Dio records the resistance of Mylasa and Alabanda. The other writers give no details. Contrast the words of Cicero describing Asia's welcome for Mithridates, when all the cities shut their gates against the Roman consular commander (*pro Flacco* 35.61).

107.   Strabo. For Tryphaena see esp. *CRE*, pp. 382-89. She is probably the same as the queen mentioned in the *Acts of Paul and Thecla* 27ff. (M.R. James, *The Apocryphal NT*, pp. 278ff.; E. Hennecke, *NT Apocrypha*, II.353ff.), which may here contain early material. Ramsay infers that she came to Pisidian Antioch for the festival from a residence on estates at Iconium inherited from Polemo's original domain of Cilicia (*CRE*, p. 396; cf. Strab. 12.6.1 = p. 568 with *CAH* X.52). W. Schneemelcher in Hennecke (II.332-33) may be right in taking a more sceptical view of the document, though I doubt his handling of the historical data.

108.   Antonius Zeno, son of Polemo Philopatris (*BMC*, Nos. 263-64), was followed by his son, also Zeno (Nos. 265-69). His children were apparently C.

Julius Cotys (Nos. 85-86), Claudia (Nos. 87, 89) and Julia (Nos. 92-93). The sophist Polemo may have been the son of one of these last.

109. He records that Herodes Atticus esteemed 'the Phrygian' a greater orator than Demosthenes, though his fame was evidently ephemeral. For later notable representatives of the family see *CB* I.45.

110. Contrast the cognomen 'Philopatris' used by the Laodicean branch.

111. The representation of a deity enthroned is a frequent motif of Laodicean coinage. A brief survey shows Aphrodite, Hades-Sarapis, Roma (? or Athena), Cybele, and the city goddess thus depicted. Zeus Laodicenus regularly carries a sceptre (*BMC*, Nos. 85, 86, etc.).

112. So Trench, pp. 217-21; Anderson Scott, p. 158; Charles, p. 100; Zahn, p. 316; Rudwick and Green, p. 178n.

113. Swete, pp. 63-64; Beckwith, p. 491; Kiddle, p. 76; Lohse, p. 32; Farrer, p. 83.

114. Preston and Hanson, p. 68; Caird, p. 58.

115. Christ is here 'a Preacher of repentance—an office incompatible with that of Judge'.

Notes to Epilogue

1. *Jahrbuch für Antike und Christentum* 15 (1972), pp. 19-36. See further F.F. Bruce, 'The New Testament and Classical Studies', *NTS* 22 (1975-76), pp. 229-42. For Judge's own further assessment of later scholarship see now his article 'The Social Identity of the First Christians: A Question of Method in Religious History', *Journal of Religious History* 11 (1980), pp. 201-17.

2. *Rank and Status in the World of the Caesars and St. Paul* (Christchurch, New Zealand, 1982).

SELECT BIBLIOGRAPHY

A. *Works on the Revelation*

Allo, E.B. *L'Apocalypse* (Paris, 2nd edn, 1921).

Barclay, W. *Letters to the Seven Churches* (London, 1957).

—*The Revelation of John*, 2 vols. (Edinburgh, 1959).

Bauckham, R.J. 'Synoptic Parousia Parables and the Apocalypse', NTS 23 (1977), pp. 162-76.

Beasley-Murray, G.R. *The Book of Revelation* (New Century Bible) (London, 1974).

Beckwith, I.T. *The Apocalypse of John* (New York, 1919).

Bell, A.A., Jr. 'The Date of John's Apocalypse. The Evidence of some Roman Historians Reconsidered', *NTS* 25 (1978-79), pp. 93-102.

Bleek, F. *Lectures on the Apocalypse*, tr. S. Davidson (London, 1875).

Böcher, O. *Die Johannesapokalypse* (Darmstadt, 1975).

Bonsirven, J. *L'Apocalypse de Saint Jean* (Paris, 1951).

Bousset, W. *Die Offenbarung Johannis* (Göttingen, 1896).

Bowman, J.W. *The Drama of the Book of Revelation* (Philadelphia, n.d.).

Brewer, R.R. 'Revelation 4^6 and Translations Thereof', *JBL* 71 (1952), pp. 227-31.

Brown, S. '"The Hour of Trial" (Rev. 3 10)', *JBL* 85 (1966), pp. 308-14.

Burney, C.F. 'Christ as the APXH of Creation', *JTS* 27 (1926), pp. 160-77.

Caird, G.B. *The Revelation of St John the Divine* (Black's NT Comms.) (London, 1966).

Chapman, J. 'The Seven Churches of Asia', *Expos.*, 6th ser., 9 (1904), pp. 257-63.

Charles, R.H. *Studies in the Apocalypse* (Edinburgh, 1915).

—*A Critical and Exegetical Commentary on the Revelation of St John* (ICC), 2 vols. (Edinburgh, 1920).

Cosmades, T. *Nothing Else Remains* (Richmond, n.d.).

Court, J.M. *Myth and History in the Book of Revelation* (London, 1979).

Eichhorn, J.G. *Commentarius in Apocalypsin Joannis* (Göttingen, 1791).

Farrer, A.M. *A Rebirth of Images: The Making of St John's Apocalypse* (Westminster, 1949).

—*The Revelation of St John the Divine* (Oxford, 1964).

Feuillet, A. *L'Apocalypse: l'état de la question* (Paris, 1962).

Ford, J.M. *Revelation* (The Anchor Bible) (New York, 1975).

Giet, S. *L'Apocalypse et l'histoire* (Paris, 1957).

Goguel, M. 'Les Nicolaïtes', *Revue de l'histoire des religions* 115 (1937), pp. 5-36.

Harnack, A.von. 'The Sect of the Nicolaitans and Nicolaus, the Deacon of Jerusalem', *Journal of Religion* 3 (1923), pp. 413-22.

Hemer, C.J. 'The Sardis Letter and the Croesus Tradition', *NTS* 19 (1972-73), pp. 94-7.

—'Unto the Angels of the Churches', *Buried History* (Melbourne) 11 (1975), pp. 4-27, 56-83, 110-35, 164-90.

Hendriksen, W. *More than Conquerors* (London, 1962).

Hort, F.J.A. *The Apocalypse of St John I-III* (London, 1908).

Hoskier, H.C. *The Complete Commentary of Oecumenius on the Apocalypse* (Ann Arbor, 1929).

Kallas, J. 'The Apocalypse—An Apocalyptic Book?' *JBL* 86 (1967), pp. 69-80.

Kepler, T.S. *The Book of Revelation* (New York, 1957).

Kiddle, M. *The Revelation of St John* (Moffatt NT Commentaries) (London, 1940).

Lambrecht, J. *et al. L'Apocalypse johannique et l'Apocalyptique dans le Nouveau Testament* (Leuven, 1980).

Lilje, H. *The Last Book of the Bible*, tr. O. Wyon (Philadelphia, 1957).

Lo Bue, F. *The Turin Fragments of Tyconius' Commentary on Revelation* (Cambridge, 1963).

Lohmeyer, E. *Die Offenbarung des Johannes* (Tübingen, 1953).

Lohse, E. *Die Offenbarung des Johannes* (Göttingen, 1960).

Moffatt, J. 'The Revelation of St John the Divine', *The Expositor's Greek Testament*, ed. W. Robertson Nicoll (New York, 1910), V. 279-494.

Morris, L. *The Revelation of St John* (Tyndale NT Commentaries) (London, 1969).

Mounce, R.H. *The Book of Revelation* (*The New International Commentary*) (Grand Rapids, 1977).

Newman, B. 'The Fallacy of the Domitian Hypothesis: Critique of the Irenaeus Source as a Witness for the Contemporary-historical Approach to the Interpretation of the Apocalypse', *NTS* 10 (1963-64), pp. 133-38.

Ozanne, C.G. *The Influence of the Text and Language of the Old Testament on the Book of Revelation*, unpublished PhD thesis (Manchester, 1964).

Pallis, A. *Notes on St John and the Apocalypse* (Oxford, n.d.).

Parez, C.H. 'The Seven Letters and the Rest of the Apocalypse', *JTS* 12 (1911), pp. 284-86.

Peake, A.S. *The Revelation of John* (London, 1919).

Plumptre, E.H. *A Popular Exposition of the Epistles to the Seven Churches of Asia* (London, 3rd edn, 1884).

Preston, R.H. and Hanson, A.T. *The Revelation of St John the Divine* (London, 1949).

Prigent, P. *Apocalypse et liturgie* (Neuchâtel, 1964).

Ramsay, W.M. *The Letters to the Seven Churches of Asia and their Place in the Plan of the Apocalypse* (London, 1904).

—'The Date of the Apocalypse', *ExpT* 16 (1904f.), pp. 171-74.

—'The White Stone and the "Gladiatorial" Tessera', *ExpT* 16 (1904f.), pp. 558-61.

Rife, J.M. 'The Literary Background of Rev. II-III', *JBL* 60 (1941), pp. 179-82.

Roberts, R. 'The Tree of Life (Rev. ii 7)', *ExpT* 25 (1913-14), p. 332.

Rudwick, M.J.S. and Green, E.M.B. 'The Laodicean Lukewarmness', *ExpT* 69 (1957-58), pp. 176-78.

Sanders, J.N. 'St John on Patmos', *NTS* 9 (1962-63) pp. 75-85.

Schürer, E. 'Die Prophetin Isabel in Thyatira, Offenb. Joh. 2,20', *Theologische*

Abhandlungen Carl von Weizsäcker... gewidmet (Freiburg, 1892), pp. 39-58.

Scott, C.A. Anderson. *Revelation* (The Century Bible) (Edinburgh, n.d.).

Scott, E.F. *The Book of Revelation* (London, 5th edn, 1949).

Selwyn, E.C. *The Christian Prophets and the Prophetic Apocalypse* (London, 1900).

Silberman, L.H. 'Farewell to ὁ Ἀμήν. A Note on Rev. 3 14', *JBL* 82 (1963), pp. 213-15.

Spitta, F. *Die Offenbarung des Johannes* (Halle, 1889).

Stauffer, E. *Christ and the Caesars*, tr. K. and R. Gregor Smith (London, 1955).

Stuart, M. 'The White Stone of the Apocalypse. Exegesis of Rev. II 17', *Bibliotheca Sacra*, ed. E. Robinson (1843), pp. 461-77.

Sweet, J.P.M. *Revelation* (SCM Pelican Commentaries) (London, 1979).

Swete, H.B. *The Apocalypse of St John* (London, 2nd edn, 1907).

Tait, A. *The Messages to the Seven Churches of Asia Minor* (London, 1884).

Torrey, C.C. *The Apocalypse of John* (Yale, 1958).

Trench, R.C. *Commentary on the Epistles to the Seven Churches in Asia* (London, 3rd edn, 1867).

Wood, P. 'Local Knowledge in the Letters of the Apocalypse', *ExpT* 73 (1961-62), pp. 263-64.

Zahn, T. *Die Offenbarung des Johannes* (Zahns Kommentar) (Leipzig, 1924).

B. Sources for the Cities of Asia

(1) *Epigraphical, Numismatic and Archaeological*

Barton, S.C. and Horsley, G.H.R. 'A Hellenistic Cult Group and the New Testament Churches', *Jahrbuch für Antike und Christentum* 24 (1981), pp. 7-41.

British Museum. *Ancient Greek Inscriptions in the British Museum*, ed. C.T. Newton, E.L. Hicks, *et al.*, four parts (Oxford, 1874–).

—*Catalogue of the Greek Coins of Caria and the Islands*, ed. B.V. Head (London, 1897).

—*Catalogue of the Greek Coins of Ionia*, ed. B.V. Head (London, 1892).

—*Catalogue of the Greek Coins of Lydia*, ed. B.V. Head (London, 1901).

—*Catalogue of the Greek Coins of Mysia*, ed. W. Wroth (London, 1892).

—*Catalogue of the Greek Coins of Phrygia*, ed. B.V. Head (London, 1906).

—*Catalogue of Greek Coins. The Seleucid Kings of Syria*, ed. P. Gardner (London, 1878).

—*Coins of the Roman Empire in the British Museum*, ed. H. Mattingly (London, 1923–).

Buckler, W.H. 'Monuments de Thyatire', *Revue de philologie* 37 (1913), pp. 289-331.

—'Lydian Records', *JHS* 37 (1917), pp. 88-115.

—and Robinson, D.M. 'Greek Inscriptions from Sardes', *AJA* 16 (1912), pp. 11-82; 17 (1913), pp. 29-52, 353-70; 18 (1914), pp. 1-40, 321-61.

Butler, H.C. *et al. Sardis. Publications of the American Society for the Excavation of Sardis*, 13 vols. (Leiden, 1922–).

Calder, W.M. 'The Epigraphy of the Anatolian Heresies', *Anatolian Studies Presented to Sir William Mitchell Ramsay*, ed. W.M. Calder and W.H. Buckler (Manchester, 1923), pp. 59-91.

—'Philadelphia and Montanism', *BJRL* 7 (1923), pp. 309-54.

—'Leaves from an Anatolian Notebook', *BJRL* 13 (1929), pp. 254-71.

—'The New Jerusalem of the Montanists', *Byzantion* 6 (1931), pp. 421-25.

Clerc, M. 'Inscriptions de Thyatire et ses environs', *BCH* 10 (1886), pp. 398-423.

—*De Rebus Thyatironorum. Commentatio Epigraphica* (Paris, 1893).

Conze, A. and Schuchhardt, C. 'Die Arbeiten zu Pergamon 1886-1898', *Ath. Mitt* 24 (1899), pp. 97-240.

Corpus Inscriptionum Graecarum, ed. A. Boeckh. 4 vols. (Berlin, 1828–).

Corpus Inscriptionum Iudaicarum, ed. J.B. Frey. 2 vols. (Rome, 1936–).

Corpus Inscriptionum Latinarum, ed. T. Mommsen *et al.* 14 parts (Berlin, 1863–).

Deissmann, A. *Light from the Ancient East*, tr. L.R.M. Strachan (London, 1927).

Foucart, P. 'Exploration de la plaine de l'Hermus par M. Aristote Fontrier', *BCH* 11 (1887), pp. 79-107.

Grégoire, H. 'Épigraphie chrétienne. I. Les inscriptions hérétiques d'Asie Mineure. II. Inscriptions d'Éphèse', *Byzantion* 1 (1924), pp. 695-716.

—'Du nouveau sur la hiérarchie de la secte montaniste d'après une inscription grecque trouvée près de Philadelphie en Lydie', *Byzantion* 2 (1925), pp. 329-35.

—'Inscriptions montanistes et novatiennes', *Byzantion* 8 (1933), pp. 58-65.

—'Épigraphie hérétique . . . et hérésie épigraphique', *Byzantion* 10 (1935), pp. 247-50.

Heberdey, R., Keil, J., *et al.* 'Vorläufiger Bericht über die Ausgrabungen in Ephesos', *Jahreshefte* 1 (1898) Beiblatt cols. 53-82, etc. (reports extending over many years).

Hepding, H. 'Die Arbeiten zu Pergamon, 1904-1905. Die Inschriften', *Ath. Mitt* 32 (1907), pp. 241-377.

Hicks, E.L. 'Inscriptions from Thyatira', *CR* 3 (1889), pp. 136-38.

Hogarth, D.G. *Excavations at Ephesus. The Archaic Artemisia*, 2 vols. (London, 1908).

Inscriptiones Graecae, ed. A. Kirchhoff *et al.*, 14 vols. (Berlin, 1873–).

Inscriptiones Graecae ad Res Romanas Pertinentes, ed. R. Cagnat *et al.*, 3 vols. (Paris, 1911–).

Inscriptiones Latinae Selectae, ed. H. Dessau, 3 vols. (Berlin, 1902–).

Judeich, W. 'Inschriften', in C. Humann *et al.*, *Altertümer von Hierapolis (JDAI Ergänzungsheft* IV) (Berlin, 1898).

Keil, J. 'Erlass des Prokonsuls L. ANTONIUS ALBVS über die Freihaltung des ephesischen Hafens', *Jahreshefte* 44 (1959), pp. 142-57.

—See Heberdey, R.

—and von Premerstein, A. *Bericht über eine Reise in Lydien und der südlichen Aiolis, ausgeführt 1906* (Vienna, 1908).

—*Bericht über eine zweite Reise in Lydien. Ausgeführt 1908* (Vienna, 1911).

—*Bericht über eine dritte Reise in Lydien und den angrenzenden Gebieten Ioniens, ausgeführt 1911* (Vienna, 1914).

Knibbe, D. 'Neue ephesische Chiliastyen', *Jahreshefte* 46 (1961), Beiblatt cols. 19-32.

Le Bas, P. and Waddington, W.H. *Voyage archéologique en Grèce et en Asie Mineure*, 3 parts (Paris, n.d., ?1843–).

Mattingly, H. *Roman Coins from the Earliest Times to the Fall of the Western Empire* (London, 2nd edn, 1960).

—See also British Museum.

—and Sydenham, E.A. *The Roman Imperial Coinage* 4 vols. (London, 1923–).

Monumenta Asiae Minoris Antiqua, ed. Sir W.M. Calder *et al.* 8 vols. (London, 1928–).

Orelli, I.C. *Inscriptiones Latinae* 3 vols. (Turin, 1828–).

Orientis Graecae Inscriptiones Selectae, ed. W. Dittenberger. 2 vols. (Leipzig, 1903-5).

Oxyrhynchus Papyri, ed. B.P. Grenfell, A.S. Hunt *et al.* 51 vols. (London, 1898–).

Radet, G. 'Inscriptions de Lydie', *BCH* 11 (1887), pp. 445-84.

Ramsay, Sir W.M. 'Sepulchral Customs in Ancient Phrygia', *JHS* 5 (1884), pp. 241-62.
—*Cities and Bishoprics of Phrygia*. 2 vols. (Oxford, 1895).
—(ed.) *Studies in the History and Art of the Eastern Provinces of the Roman Empire* (Aberdeen, 1906).
—'The Tekmoreian Guest-Friends: an Anti-Christian Society of the Imperial Estates at Pisidian Antioch', *ibid.*, pp. 305-77.
—'Some Inscriptions of Colonia Caesarea Antiochea', *JRS* 14 (1924), pp. 172-205.
Robert, L. *Hellenica. Receuil d'épigraphie, de numismatique et d'antiquités grecques* 13 vols. (Limoges, 1940–).
—*Nouvelles Inscriptions de Sardes* (Paris, 1964).
Sylloge Inscriptionum Graecarum, ed. W. Dittenberger. 4 vols. (Leipzig, 3rd edn, 1915–).
Tod, M.N. 'Notes on some Inscriptions from Asia Minor', *CR* 29 (1915), p. 2.
Waddington, W.H. *Mélanges de numismatique*, 2nd ser. (Paris, 1867).
—See also Le Bas, P.
Weber, G. An inscription of Laodicea published in *Ath. Mitt.* 16 (1891), pp. 144-46.
Wilcken, U. *Griechische Ostraka aus Aegypten und Nubien.* 2 vols. (Leipzig, 1899).

(2) *Topography and Travel*
Anderson, J.G.C. 'A Summer in Phrygia', *JHS* 17 (1897), pp. 396-424 and 18 (1898), pp. 81-128.
—See also Calder, W.M.
Arundell, F.V.J. *A Visit to the Seven Churches of Asia, with an excursion into Pisidia* (London, 1828).
—*Discoveries in Asia Minor.* 2 vols. (London, 1834).
Bean, G.E. *Aegean Turkey. An Archaeological Guide* (London, 1966).
—*Turkey Beyond the Maeander* (London, 1971).
—See also Calder, W.M.
Bent, J.T. 'What St John Saw on Patmos', *The Nineteenth Century* (1888), pp. 813-21.
Cadoux, C.J. *Ancient Smyrna. A History of the City from the Earliest Times to 224 AD* (Oxford, 1938).
Calder, W.M. 'Smyrna as Described by the Orator Aelius Aristides', *Studies in the History and Art of the Eastern Provinces of the Roman Empire*, ed. W.M. Ramsay (Aberdeen, 1906), pp. 95-116.
—and Bean, G.E. *A Classical Map of Asia Minor* (London, 1957) (revision of J.G.C. Anderson's map).
Chandler, R. *Travels in Asia Minor and Greece*, 2 vols. (London, 3rd edn, 1817).
Davis, E.J. *Anatolica* (London, 1874).
Falkener, E. *Ephesus, and the Temple of Diana* (London, 1862).
Fellows, C. *A Journal Written during an Excursion in Asia Minor, 1838* (London, 1839).
Hamilton, W.J. *Researches in Asia Minor, Pontus and Armenia*, 2 vols. (London, 1842).
Hanfmann, G.M.A. *Guide to Sardis. Sart Kilavuzu* (Ankara, 1964).
—*A Preliminary Bibliography of Sardis*, n.d. (unpublished typescript in the Museum of Classical Archaeology Library, Cambridge).
Hasluck, F.W. 'The "Tomb of St Polycarp" and the Topography of Ancient Smyrna', *ABSA* 20 (1913-14), pp. 80-93.
Hemer, C.J. *Bibliography on the Letters to the Seven Churches of Asia, with special*

reference to their local background n.d. [1970] (unpublished manuscript in Tyndale Library, Cambridge).

Ibn Baṭṭūṭa. *The Travels of Ibn Baṭṭūṭa*, tr. H.A.R. Gibb, Hakluyt Society, vols. CX and CXVII (Cambridge, 1958).

Johnson, S.E. 'Laodicea and its Neighbors', *BA* 13 (1950), pp. 1-18.

Keil, J. 'Zur Topographie und Geschichte von Ephesos', *Jahreshefte* 21-22 (1922-4), pp. 96-112.

Leake, W.M. *Journal of a Tour in Asia Minor* (London, 1824).

Le Camus, E. *Voyage aux sept églises de l'Apocalypse* (Paris, 1896).

Lethaby, W.R. 'The Earlier Temple of Artemis at Ephesus', *JHS* 37 (1917), pp. 1-16.

Miltner, F. and H. 'Bericht über eine Voruntersuchung in Alt-Smyrna', *Jahreshefte* 27 (1932), Beiblatt, cols. 127-90.

Mitten, D.G. 'A New Look at Ancient Smyrna', *BA* 29 (1966), pp. 38-68.

Picard, C. *Éphèse et Claros. Recherches sur les sanctuaires et les cultes de l'Ionie du Nord* (Paris, 1922)

Radet, G. 'Notes de géographie ancienne. (1) Cydrara et Callatabi', *BCH* 15 (1891), pp. 373-80.

Ramsay, W.M. *The Historical Geography of Asia Minor* (London, 1890).

—*Impressions of Turkey during Twelve Years' Wanderings* (London, 1897).

Robert, L. *Études anatoliennes* (Paris, 1937).

—*Villes d'Asie Mineure* (Paris, 2nd edn, 1962).

Svoboda, A. *The Seven Churches of Asia* (London, 1869).

Wood, J.T. *Discoveries at Ephesus, Including the Site and Remains of the Great Temple of Diana* (London, 1877).

Short annual reports on current work at Ephesus, Pergamum and Sardis may be found in successive issues of *AS* and longer accounts of Sardis in *BASOR*. Dictionary articles have not been included here, though some, like those of Keil, Zschietzschmann and others in *PW* are of major importance for individual sites.

(3) *General Works*

Alexander, L. *The Kings of Lydia* (Princeton, 1913).

Blaiklock, E.M. *Cities of the New Testament* (London, 1965).

Cary, M. *The Geographical Background of Greek and Roman History* (London, 1949).

Chapot, V. *La province romaine proconsulaire d'Asie depuis ses origines jusqu'à la fin du Haut-Empire* (Paris, 1904).

Garstang, J. and Gurney, O.R. *The Geography of the Hittite Empire* (London, 1959).

Hanfmann, G.M.A. 'Lydiaka', *Harvard Studies in Classical Philology* 63 (1958), pp. 65-88.

Hansen, E.V. *The Attalids of Pergamon. Cornell Studies in Classical Philology*, Vol. 29 (Ithaca, N.Y., 1947).

Hogarth, D.G. *Ionia and the East* (Oxford, 1909).

Jones, A.H.M. *Cities of the Eastern Roman Provinces* (Oxford, 1937).

—*The Greek City from Alexander to Justinian* (Oxford, 1940).

Keil, J. 'Die Kulte Lydiens', *Anatolian Studies Presented to Sir William Mitchell Ramsay*, ed. W.H. Buckler and W.M. Calder (Manchester, 1923), pp. 239-66.

Liddell, R. *Aegean Greece* (London, 1954).

Magie, D. *Roman Rule in Asia Minor to the End of the Third Century after Christ*, 2 vols. (Princeton, 1950).

Monceaux, P. *De Communi Asiae Provinciae* (KOINON 'ΑΣΙΑΣ) (Paris, 1885).

Radet, G. *La Lydie et le monde grec au temps des Mermnades (687-546)* (Bibliothèque des écoles françaises d'Athènes et de Rome, 63) (Paris, 1893).

Ramsay, W.M. *The Church in the Roman Empire before AD 170* (London, 3rd edn, 1894).

—*St Paul the Traveller and the Roman Citizen* (London, 1895).

—*Asianic Elements in Greek Civilisation* (London, 1927).

—*The Social Basis of Roman Power in Asia Minor* (Aberdeen, 1941).

Tarn, W.W. and Griffith, G.T. *Hellenistic Civilisation* (London, 3rd ed., 1952).

C. *Ancient Literature*

Achilles Tatius, ed. S. Gaselee (*LCL*, ̄ ̣ ̣)

Acta Sanctorum, ed. J. Bolland (Antwerp, 1643–), reprinted in 18 vols. (Brussels, 1965).

Aeschines, ed. C.D. Adams (*LCL*, 1919).

Aeschylus, ed. H.W. Smyth, 2 vols. (*LCL*, 1922–).

—*The Oresteia of Aeschylus*, ed. G. Thomson, 2 vols. (Cambridge, 1938).

Apocrypha, OT. *The Apocrypha and Pseudepigrapha of the Old Testament*, ed. R.H. Charles, 2 vols. (Oxford, 1913).

Apocrypha, NT. *The Apocryphal New Testament*, ed. M.R. James (Oxford, 1924).

—*New Testament Apocrypha*, ed. E. Hennecke. ET ed. R.McL. Wilson, 2 vols. (London, 1963–).

Apollodorus, *The Library*, ed. Sir J.G. Frazer, 2 vols. (*LCL*, 1921–).

Apollonius of Tyana, *The Epistles*, ed. F.C. Conybeare (in Philostratus, *The Life of Apollonius of Tyana*, Vol. II, *LCL*, 1912).

Apostolic Fathers, The, ed. K. Lake, 2 vols. (*LCL*, 1912–). See also Ignatius.

Appian, *Roman History*, ed. H. White, 4 vols. (LCL, 1912–).

Apuleius, *Opera Omnia*, ed. G.F. Hildebrand, 2 vols. (Leipzig, 1842).

Aristides, Aelius, *Opera Omnia*, ed. S. Jebb, 4 vols. (Oxford, 1722–30).

—ed. W. Dindorf, 3 vols. (Leipzig, 1829).

Aristophanes, ed. B.B. Rogers, 3 vols. (*LCL*, 1930–).

Aristotle, *Minor Works*, ed. W.S. Hett (*LCL*, 1936).

Arrian, ed. E. Iliff Robson, 2 vols. (*LCL*, 1929).

Artemidorus Daldianus, *Onirocritica*, ed. R.A. Pack (Leipzig, 1963).

Athenaeus, *The Deipnosophists*, ed. C.B. Gulick, 7 vols. (*LCL*, 1927–).

Bacchylides, *The Poems and Fragments*, ed. Sir R.C. Jebb (Cambridge, 1905).

Caesar, *The Civil Wars*, ed. A.G. Peskett (*LCL*, 1914).

Callimachus and Lycophron, ed. A.W. Mair (*LCL*, 1921).

Celsus, *De Medicina*, ed. W.G. Spencer, 3 vols. (*LCL*, 1935–).

Cicero, *Letters to Atticus*, ed. E.O. Winstedt, 3 vols. (*LCL*, 1912–).

—*Philippics*, ed. W.C.A. Ker (*LCL*, 1926).

—*The Letters to his Friends*, ed. W.G. Williams, 3 vols. (*LCL*, 1927–).

—*The Verrine Orations*, ed. L.H.G. Greenwood, 2 vols. (*LCL*, 1928–).

—*Orationes*, ed. A.C. Clark, 6 vols. (*OCT*, 1905–).

—*The Correspondence of Cicero*, ed. R.Y. Tyrrell and L.C. Purser, 7 vols. (Dublin, 1879).

Clement of Alexandria, *The Exhortation to the Greeks*, ed. G.W. Butterworth (*LCL*, 1953).
—*Les Stromates*, ed. C. Mondésert and M. Caster, 2 vols. (Paris, 1951).
Corpus Poetarum Latinorum, ed. W.S. Walker (London, 1840).
Dead Sea Scrolls. M. Burrows, *The Dead Sea Scrolls* (London, 1956).
—*The Dead Sea Scrolls in English*, ed. G. Vermes (Harmondsworth, 1962).
Demosthenes, ed. J.H. Vince *et al.*, 7 vols. (*LCL*, 1930–).
Digesta Iustiniani Augusti, ed. T. Mommsen (Berlin, 1870).
Dio Cassius, *Roman History*, ed. E. Cary, 9 vols. (*LCL*, 1914–).
Dio Chrysostom, *Discourses*, ed. J.W. Cohoon and H. Lamar Crosby, 5 vols. (*LCL*, 1932–).
Diodorus Siculus, ed. C.H. Oldfather *et al.*, 11 vols. (*LCL*, 1933–).
Diogenes Laertius, ed. R.D. Hicks, 2 vols. (*LCL*, 1942–).
Dionysius of Halicarnassus, *Roman Antiquities*, ed. E. Cary, 7 vols. (*LCL*, 1937–).
Dionysius Periegetes. Διονυσίου οἰκουμένης περιήγησις, ed. E. Passow (Leipzig, 1825).
Early Greek Elegy, ed. T. Hudson-Williams (Cardiff, 1926).
Epictetus, ed. W.A. Oldfather, 2 vols. (*LCL*, 1926–).
Epiphanius, *Adversus Octaginta Haereses*, *PG* Vols XLI, XLII.
Etymologicon Magnum, ed. T. Gaisford (Oxford, 1848).
Euripides, ed. A.S. Way, 4 vols. (*LCL*, 1912–).
Eusebius, *The Ecclesiastical History*, ed. K. Lake and J.E.L. Oulton, 2 vols. (*LCL*, 1926–).
—*Opera*, ed. J. Dindorf, 4 vols. (Leipzig, 1867–).
—*Chronici Canones*, ed. J.K. Fotheringham (London, 1923).
Florus, ed. E.S. Forster, (*LCL*, 1929).
Fragmente der griechischen Historiker, Die (*FGH*, ed. F. Jacoby, 3 parts, 15 vols. (Leiden, 1954–).
Galen. *Claudii Galeni Opera Omnia* (*Medicorum Graecorum Opera Quae Exstant*, Vol. VI), ed. C.G. Kuehn (Leipzig, 1823).
Greek Anthology, The, ed. W.R. Paton, 5 vols. (*LCL*, 1916–).
Heliodorus, *Aethiopicorum Libri Decem*, ed. I. Bekker (Leipzig, 1855).
Heraclitus, ed. W.H.S. Jones (in Hippocrates, Vol. IV, *LCL*, 1931).
Herodotus, ed. A.D. Godley, 4 vols. (*LCL*, 1920–).
—*A Commentary on Herodotus*, ed. W.W. How and J. Wells, 2 vols. (London, 1912).
Hesiod, with *The Homeric Hymns* and *Homerica*, ed. H.G. Evelyn-White (*LCL*, 1914).
Hesychius, *Lexicon*, ed. J. Alberti, 2 vols. (Lyon, 1746).
Hippocrates, ed. W.H.S. Jones, 4 vols. (*LCL*, 1923–).
Homer, *The Iliad*, ed. A.T. Murray, 2 vols. (*LCL*, 1924–).
—*The Odyssey*, ed. A.T. Murray, 2 vols. (*LCL*, 1919–).
Homeric Hymns. See Hesiod.
Horace, *Opera*, ed. E.C. Wickham (*OCT*, 1901).
Ignatius. J.B. Lightfoot, *The Apostolic Fathers*, Part II. 'St Ignatius and St Polycarp', 3 vols. (London, 2nd ed., 1889).
Irenaeus, *Quae Supersunt Omnia*, ed. A. Stieren, 2 vols. (Leipzig, 1853).
Isidorus, *Etymologiarum Libri XX*, ed. W.M. Lindsay, 2 vols. (*OCT*, 1911).
Jerome, *Select Letters*, ed. F.A. Wright (*LCL*, 1933).
Joannes Lydus, *De Ostentis*, ed. K. Wachsmuth (Leipzig, 1863).

—*De Mensibus*, ed. R. Wuensch (Stuttgart, 1967).

—*De Magistratibus Populi Romani* (*CSHB*, Vol. XXVII), ed. I. Bekker (Bonn, 1837).

Josephus, ed. H.StJ. Thackeray *et al.*, 9 vols. (*LCL*, 1926-).

Justin Martyr, *Opera*, ed. J. Otto, 3 vols. (Jena, 1876).

Justinus, M. *Iuniani Iustini Epitoma Historiarum Philippicarum Pompei Trogi*, ed. F. Ruehl (Leipzig, 1886).

Juvenal. *Fourteen Satires of Juvenal*, ed. J.D. Duff (Cambridge, 1909).

Lactantius, *Opera Omnia*, ed. S. Brandt and G. Laubmann, 2 vols. (Vienna, 1890).

Livy, ed. B.O. Foster *et al.*, 14 vols. (*LCL*, 1919-).

Lucan, *Belli Civilis Libri Decem*, ed. A.E. Housman (Oxford, 1927).

Lucian, ed. A.M. Harmon *et al.*, 8 vols. (*LCL*, 1913-).

Lycophron, *Alexandra*, ed. G. Kinkel (Leipzig, 1880).

Manilius, *Astronomica*, ed. A.E. Housman, 5 vols. (London, 1903-).

Martial, *Epigrams*, ed. W.C.A. Ker, 2 vols. (*LCL*, 1919-).

Nemesianus, *Cynegetica*, in *Minor Latin Poets*, ed. J.W. Duff and A.M. Duff (*LCL*, 1968).

Nicetas Choniata, *CSHB* Vol. XLI, ed. I. Bekker (Bonn, 1835).

Nonnus, *Dionysiaca*, ed. W.H.D. Rouse, 3 vols. (*LCL*, 1940-).

Origen, *Opera*, ed. P. Koetschau *et al.*, 12 vols. (Leipzig, 1899-).

Orosius, *Historiarum adversus Paganos Libri VII*, ed. K. Zangemeister (Leipzig, 1889).

Ovid, ed. R. Merkel, 3 vols. (Leipzig, 1876-).

—*Metamorphoses*, ed. F.J. Miller, 2 vols. (*LCL*, 1916-).

Patrologia Graeca, ed. J.P. Migne, 161 vols. (Paris, 1857-).

Patrologia Latina, ed. J.P. Migne, 221 vols. (Paris, 1844-).

Pausanias, *Description of Greece*, ed. W.H.S. Jones *et al.*, 5 vols. (*LCL*, 1918-).

—*Description of Greece*, ed. with commentary by Sir J.G. Frazer, 6 vols. (London, 1898-).

Persius, *Saturae*, ed. W.V. Clausen (*OCT*, 1959).

Philo, ed. F.H. Colson and G.H. Whitaker, 12 vols. (*LCL*, 1929-).

Philostratus, *The Life of Apollonius of Tyana*, ed. F.C. Conybeare, 2 vols. (*LCL*, 1912).

—*The Lives of the Sophists*, ed. W.C. Wright (*LCL*, 1921).

Pindar, *Carmina cum Fragmentis*, ed. B. Snell (Leipzig, 1953).

Plato, *Opera*, ed. J. Burnet, 5 vols. (*OCT*, 1900-).

—*Timaeus, Critias*, etc., ed. R.G. Bury (*LCL*, 1942).

—*Cratylus*, etc., ed. H.N. Fowler (*LCL*, 1953).

Plautus, ed. P. Nixon, 5 vols. (*LCL*, 1916-).

Pliny the Elder, *Natural History*, ed. H. Rackham *et al.* 10 vols. (*LCL*, 1938-).

Pliny the Younger, *Letters*, ed. W. Melmoth, 2 vols. (*LCL*, 1915-).

—*The Letters of Pliny*, ed. A.N. Sherwin-White (Oxford, 1966).

Plutarch, *Lives*, ed. B. Perrin, 11 vols. (*LCL*, 1914-).

—*Moralia*, ed. F.C. Babbitt *et al.*, 15 vols. (*LCL*, 1927-).

Poetae Lyrici Graeci, ed. T. Bergk, 3 vols. (Leipzig, 4th edn, 1882).

Pollux, *Onomasticon*, ed. E. Bethe (Leipzig, 1900).

Polyaenus, *Strategica*, ed. E. Woefflin (Leipzig, 1860).

Polybius, *The Histories*, ed. W.R. Paton, 6 vols. (*LCL*, 1922-).

Polycarp. See Ignatius.

Polycarp, Martyrdom of. See Ignatius.

Propertius, ed. E.A. Barber (*OCT*, 1953).

Pseudepigrapha. See Apocrypha, OT.

Ptolemy. *Claudi Ptolemaei Geographia*, ed. K.F.Λ. Nobbe, 3 vols. (Leipzig, 1881).

Quintus Smyrnaeus, ed. A.S. Way (*LCL*, 1913).

Sallust. *Salluste, Catalina, Jugurtha, Fragments des Histoires*, ed. A. Ernout (Paris, 1960).

Scribonius Largus, *Compositiones*, ed. G. Helmreich (Leipzig, 1887).

Septuagint. *Septuaginta*, ed. A. Rahlfs, 2 vols. (Stuttgart, 7th edn, 1962).

Servius, *In Vergilii Carmina Commentarii*, ed. G. Thilo and H. Hagen (Leipzig, 1881).

Sibylline Oracles. Χρησμοὶ Σιβυλλιακοί / *Oracula Sibyllina*, ed. A. Rzach (Vienna, 1891).

—*Die Oracula Sibyllina*, ed. J. Geffcken (Leipzig, 1902).

—*The Sibylline Oracles, Books III-V*, ET, ed. H.N. Bate (London, 1918).

—*Sibyllinische Weissagungen*, ed. A. Kurfess (Munich, 1951).

—See also Apocrypha, OT.

Silius Italicus, *Punica*, ed. J.D. Duff, 2 vols. (*LCL*, 1934–).

Solinus, *Collectanea Rerum Memorabilium*, ed. T. Mommsen (Berlin, 1864).

Sophocles, ed. F. Storr, 2 vols. (*LCL*, 1913).

Sozomenus, *PG* Vol. LXVII.

Statius, ed. J.H. Mozley, 2 vols. (*LCL*, 1928–).

Stephanus of Byzantium, Ἐθνικῶν *Quae Supersunt*, ed. A. Westermann (Leipzig, 1839).

Strabo, *Geography*, ed. H.L. Jones, 8 vols. (*LCL*, 1917–).

—*Strabo on the Troad*, ed. W. Leaf (Cambridge, 1923).

Suetonius, ed. J.C. Rolfe, 2 vols. (*LCL*, 1913).

—*De Vita Caesarum, Libri VII-VIII*, ed. G.W. Mooney (London, 1930).

Suidas, *Lexicon*, ed. T. Gaisford, 3 vols. (Oxford, 1834).

Sulpicia. *La Satira di Sulpicia. Studio Critico, Testo e Traduzione*, ed. I. Lana (Turin, 1949).

Syncellus, *Chronographia. CSHB*, Vols XX-XXI, ed. W. Dindorf (Bonn, 1829).

Tacitus, ed. W. Peterson *et al.*, 5 vols. (*LCL*, 1914–).

—*The Annals of Tacitus*, ed. H. Furneaux, 2 vols. (Oxford, 2nd ed., 1896).

Talmud, The Babylonian, ed. I. Epstein, ET, 36 vols. (London, 1935–).

Tatian, *Oratio ad Graecos*, ed. J.K.T. Otto (Jena, 1851).

Tertullian, *Quae Supersunt Omnia*, ed. F. Oehler, 3 vols. (Leipzig, 1853–).

—*Apologeticus*, ed. J.E.B. Mayor (Cambridge, 1917).

—*Apology*, ed. T.R. Glover (*LCL*, 1931).

Theodoret, *PG* Vols LXXX-LXXXIV.

Theophrastus, *Enquiry into Plants*, ed. Sir A. Hort, 2 vols. (*LCL*, 1916–).

—*Characters*, ed. J.M. Edmonds (*LCL*, 1929).

—*De Lapidibus*, ed. D.E. Eichholz (Oxford, 1964).

Thucydides, ed. C. Forster Smith, 4 vols. (*LCL*, 1928–).

Tibullus, ed. J.P. Postgate (*OCT*, 2nd edn, 1915).

Velleius Paterculus, ed. F.W. Shipley (*LCL*, 1924).

Vergil, *Opera*, ed. F.A. Hirtzel (*OCT*, 1900).

Vitruvius, ed. F. Granger, 2 vols. (*LCL*, 1931–).

Xenophon, ed. W. Miller *et al.*, 7 vols. (*LCL*, 1914–).

—*Hellenica*, ed. E.C. Marchant and C.E. Underhill (Oxford, 1906).

Xenophon Ephesius, *Les Éphésiaques, ou le roman d'Habrocomès et d' Anthia*, ed. G. Dalmeyda (Paris, 1926).

D. Other Books and Articles

Achelis, H. 'Spuren des Urchristentums auf den griechischen Inseln?', *ZNTW* 1 (1900), pp. 87-100.

Ağakay, M.A. *Türkçe Sözlük* (Ankara, 1955).

Allen, W.C. *Matthew* (ICC, 3rd edn, 1912).

Anderson, C.P. 'Who Wrote "The Epistle from Laodicea?"', *JBL* 85 (1966), pp. 436-40.

Anderson, J.G.C. 'Paganism and Christianity in the Upper Tembris Valley', *Studies in the History and Art of the Eastern Provinces of the Roman Empire*, ed. Sir W.M. Ramsay (Aberdeen, 1906), pp. 183-227.

Aune, D.E. 'The Social Matrix of the Apocalypse of John', *Biblical Research* 26 (1981), pp. 16-32.

Balsdon, J.P.V.D. *Life and Leisure in Ancient Rome* (London, 1969).

Barnard, L.W. 'Clement of Rome and the Persecution of Domitian', *NTS* 10 (1963-64), pp. 251-60.

Barrett, A.A. 'Polemo II of Pontus and M. Antonius Polemo', *Historia* 27 (1978), pp. 437-48.

Bauer, W. *Orthodoxy and Heresy in Earliest Christianity* (ET, London, 1972).

Bernard, J.H., *St John*, 2 vols. (ICC, 1928).

Bevan, E.R. *The House of Seleucus*, 2 vols. (London, 1902).

Bewer, J.A. *Obadiah* (ICC, 1912).

Bickerman, E.J. *Chronology of the Ancient World* (London, 1968).

Bigg, C. *2 Peter and Jude* (ICC, 1911).

Boardman, J. *The Greeks Overseas* (Harmondsworth, 1964).

Bonwetsch, G.N. *Die Geschichte des Montanismus* (Erlangen, 1881).

Bourne, F.C. *The Public Works of the Julio-Claudians and Flavians* (Princeton, 1946).

Brandon, S.G.F. *The Fall of Jerusalem and the Christian Church* (London, 1951).

Bruce, F.F. *The Acts of the Apostles. The Greek Text with Introduction and Commentary* (London, 2nd edn, 1952).

—*Commentary on the Epistle to the Hebrews* (London, 1964).

Bruce, I.A.F. 'Nerva and the "Fiscus Iudaicus"', *PEQ* 96 (1964), pp. 34-45.

Buckler, W.H. 'Labour Disputes in the Province of Asia', *Anatolian Studies Presented to Sir William Mitchell Ramsay*, ed. W.H. Buckler and W.M. Calder (Manchester, 1923), pp. 27-50.

Calder, Sir W.M. 'The Eumeneian Formula', *Anatolian Studies Presented to William Hepburn Buckler*, ed. W.M. Calder and J. Keil (Manchester, 1939), pp. 15-26.

Caley, E.R. *Orichalchum and Related Alloys, Origin, Composition and Manufacture, with special reference to the coinage of the Roman Empire* (New York, 1964).

Carlebach, A. 'Rabbinic References to Fiscus Iudaicus', *JQR* 66 (1975-76), pp. 57-61.

Charles, J.A. 'Early Arsenical Bronzes—A Metallurgical View', *AJA* 71 (1967), pp. 21-26.

Cobern, C.M. *The New Archeological Discoveries* (New York, 1917).

Collins, A.Y. 'Dating the Apocalypse of John', *Biblical Research* 16 (1981), pp. 33-45.

Cook, S.A. 'A Lydian-Aramaic Bilingual', *JHS* 37 (1917), pp. 77-87 and 219-31.

Cranfield, C.E.B. *1 and 2 Peter and Jude* (London, 1960).

Cumont, F. *Les Religions orientales dans le paganisme romain* (Paris, 1905).

Deissmann, A. *New Light on the New Testament*, tr. L.R.M. Strachan (Edinburgh, 1907).

—*Paul. A Study in Social and Religious History*, tr. W.E. Wilson (London, 1926).

de Jesus, P.S. 'Metal Resources in Ancient Anatolia', *AS* 28 (1978), pp. 97-102.

Dodd, C.H. 'The Fall of Jerusalem and the "Abomination of Desolation"', *JRS* 37 (1947), pp. 47-54; reprinted in his *More New Testament Studies* (Manchester, 1968), pp. 69-83.

Evans, J.A.S. 'What Happened to Croesus?' *CJ* 74 (1978-9), pp. 34-40.

Farnsworth, M., *et al.* 'Metallographic Examination of a Sample of Metallic Zinc from Ancient Athens', *Hesperia* Supp. VIII (1949), pp. 126-29.

Finegan, J. *Light from the Ancient Past* (Princeton, 2nd edn, 1959).

Fiorenza, E.S. 'Apocalyptic and Gnosis in the Book of Revelation and Paul', *JBL* 92 (1973), pp. 565-81.

Foakes-Jackson, F.J., Lake, K., *et al. The Beginnings of Christianity*, 5 vols. (London, 1920–).

Forbes, R.J. *Metallurgy in Antiquity* (Leiden, 1950).

—*Studies in Ancient Technology*, 9 vols. (Leiden, 2nd edn, 1964–).

Frazer, Sir J.G. *Adonis Attis Osiris. Studies in the History of Oriental Religion* (London, 1906).

Frend, W.H.C. *Martyrdom and Persecution in the Early Church* (Oxford, 1965).

Freeman-Grenville, G.S.P. 'The Date of the Outbreak of Montanism', *JEH* 5 (1954), pp. 7-15.

Friedlaender, L. *Darstellungen aus der Sittengeschichte Roms in der Zeit von August bis zum Ausgang der Antonine*, 4 vols. (Leipzig, 9th ed., 1919–).

Ginsburg, M.S. 'Fiscus Iudaicus', *JQR* 21 (1930-31), pp. 281-91.

Goldman, H. 'Sandon and Herakles', *Hesperia* Supp. VIII (1949), pp. 164-74.

Goodenough, E.R. *Jewish Symbols in the Greco-Roman Period*, 8 vols. (New York, 1953–).

Graham, A.A.K. 'Their Word to Our Day. IV. Ignatius of Antioch', *ExpT* 80 (1968-69), pp. 100-104.

Green, E.M.B. *The Meaning of Salvation* (London, 1965).

Greenidge, A.H.J. and Clay, A.M. *Sources for Roman History. B.C. 133-70* (Oxford, 1903).

Hagner, D.A. *The Use of the Old and New Testaments in Clement of Rome* (*NovT* Supp. 34; Leiden, 1973).

Hare, D.R.A. *The Theme of Jewish Persecution of Christians in the Gospel According to St Matthew* (Cambridge, 1967).

Harnack, A. von. *The Mission and Expansion of Christianity in the First Three Centuries*, tr. J. Moffatt, 2 vols. (London, 2nd edn, 1908).

Haussoulier, B. 'Les Seleucides et le temple d'Apollon didymien', *Revue de philologie* 25 (1901), pp. 5-42.

Hemer, C.J. 'The Edfu *Ostraka* and the Jewish Tax', *PEQ* 105 (1973), pp. 6-12.

—'Sulpicia, *Satire* 58-61', *CR* n.s. 23 (1973), pp. 12-13.

Herford, R.T. *Christianity in Talmud and Midrash* (London, 1903).

Higgins, A.J.B. 'Jesus as Prophet', *ExpT* 57 (1945-46), pp. 292-94.

Huxley, J.H. and Polunin, O. *Flowers of the Mediterranean* (London, 1965).

Kilpatrick, G.D. *The Origins of the Gospel according to St Matthew* (Oxford, 1946).

Kyriakides, A. *Modern Greek-English Dictionary* (Athens, 1909).

Leaf, W. 'Some Problems of the Troad', *ABSA* 21 (1914-16), pp. 16-30.

—See also Strabo in Section C.

Lightfoot, J.B. *St Paul's Epistles to the Colossians and to Philemon* (London, 1876).

Lightfoot, R.H. *St John's Gospel. A Commentary* (Oxford, 1956).

Lund, N.W. *Chiasmus in the New Testament. A Study in 'Formgeschichte'* (North Carolina, 1942).

McCrum, M. and Woodhead, A.G. *Select Documents of the Principates of the Flavian Emperors, Including the Year of Revolution, A.D. 68-96* (Cambridge, 1961).

McFayden, D. 'The Occasion of the Domitianic Persecution', *AJT* 24 (1920), pp. 46-66.

McGregor, G.H.C. *The Gospel of John* (Moffatt NT Commentary) (London, 1928).

McNeile, A.H. *The Gospel According to St Matthew* (London, 1915).

Mayor, J.B. *The Epistle of St James* (London, 3rd edn, 1910).

Meinardus, O.F.A. 'The Christian Remains of the Seven Churches of the Apocalypse', *BA* 37 (1974), pp. 69-82.

Mellaert, J. 'Preliminary Report on a Survey of Pre-Classical Remains in Southern Turkey', *AS* 4 (1954), pp. 175-240.

Merkelbach, R. 'Βρέτας', *ZPE* 9 (1972), p. 84.

Meyer, E. *Geschichte des Alterthums*, 5 vols. (Stuttgart, 2nd edn, 1907–).

Michael, J.H. *Philippians* (Moffatt NT Commentaries) (London, 1928).

Michell, H. 'Oreichalkos', *CR* n.s. 5 (1955), pp. 21-22.

Miller, M. 'The Herodotean Croesus', *Klio* 41 (1963), pp. 58-94.

Moffatt, J. 'The Bright and Morning Star', *Expos* 6th ser. 6 (1902), pp. 424-41.

Mommsen, T. *The Provinces of the Roman Empire from Caesar to Diocletian*, tr. W.P. Dickson, 2 vols. (London, 1909).

Moore, G.F. *Judaism in the First Centuries of the Christian Era*, 3 vols. (Cambridge, Mass., 1927).

Mussies, G. 'Antipas', *NovT* 7 (1964-65), 242-44.

Neill, S. *The Interpretation of the New Testament 1861-1961* (London, 1964).

Neiman, D. 'Sefarad: The Name of Spain', *JNES* 22 (1963), pp. 128-32.

Plummer, A. *An Exegetical Commentary on the Gospel according to S. Matthew* (London, 1915).

Ramsay, W.M. 'Early Christian Monuments in Phrygia. A Study in the Early History of the Church', *Expos* 3rd ser. 8 (1888), pp. 241-67 and 401-27.

—'Artemis-Leto and Apollo-Lairbenos', *JHS* 10 (1889), pp. 216-30.

—*A Historical Commentary on Paul's Epistle to the Galatians* (London, 1899).

—'Historical Commentary on the Epistles to the Corinthians. Eating in an Idol Temple', *Expos* 6th ser. 2 (1900), pp. 429-44.

—'The Jews in the Graeco-Asiatic Cities', *Expos* 6th ser. 5 (1902), pp. 19-33 and 92-109.

—'The Book as an Early Christian Symbol', *Expos* 6th ser. 11 (1905), pp. 209-24.

—*Pauline and Other Studies in Early Christian History* (London, 1906).

—*Luke the Physician and Other Studies in the History of Religion* (London, 1908).

—*The Bearing of Recent Discovery on the Trustworthiness of the New Testament* (London, 4th edn, 1920).

Reicke, B. *The Epistles of James, Peter and Jude* (The Anchor Bible) (New York, 1964).

Reinach, S. 'La Mévente des vins sous le Haut-Empire romain', *RA* 3rd ser. 39 (1901), pp. 350-74.

—'Ignatius, Bishop of Antioch, and the APXEIA', *Anatolian Studies Presented to Sir*

William Mitchell Ramsay, ed. W.H. Buckler and W.M. Calder (Manchester, 1923), pp. 339-40.

Reinach, T. *Mithridate Eupator roi de Pont* (Paris, 1890).

Renfrew, C. 'Cycladic Metallurgy and the Aegean Early Bronze Age', *AJA* 71 (1967), pp. 1-20.

Robert, L. *Gladiateurs dans l'Orient grec* (Paris, 1940).

Robertson, A. and Plummer, A. *A Critical and Exegetical Commentary on the First Epistle of St. Paul to the Corinthians* (ICC, Edinburgh, 1911).

Robinson, J.A.T. *Redating the New Testament* (London, 1976).

Rostovtzeff, M. (Rostowzew, M.) *Römische Bleitesserae, Klio* Beiheft III (Leipzig, 1905).

—'Notes on the Economic Policy of the Pergamene Kings', *Anatolian Studies Presented to Sir William Mitchell Ramsay*, ed. W.H. Buckler and W.M. Calder (Manchester, 1923), pp. 359-90.

—*The Social and Economic History of the Roman Empire* (Oxford, 1926).

—'Some Remarks on the Monetary and Commercial Policy of the Seleucids and Attalids', *Anatolian Studies Presented to William Hepburn Buckler*, ed. W.M. Calder and J. Keil (Manchester, 1939), pp. 277-98.

—*The Social and Economic History of the Hellenistic World*, 3 vols. (Oxford, 1941).

Russell, D.S. *The Method and Message of Jewish Apocalyptic 200 B.C.–100 A.D.* (London, 1964).

Schoedel, W.R. 'Ignatius and the Archives', *HTR* 71 (1978), pp. 97-106.

Sherwin-White, A.N. *Roman Society and the Roman Law in the New Testament* (Oxford, 1963).

Smallwood, E.M. 'Domitian's Attitude towards the Jews and Judaism', *CP* 51 (1956), pp. 1-13.

—*Documents Illustrating the Principates of Nerva, Trajan and Hadrian* (Cambridge, 1966).

—*Documents Illustrating the Principates of Gaius, Claudius and Nero* (Cambridge, 1967).

—*The Jews under Roman Rule from Pompey to Diocletian* (Leiden, 1976).

Strack, H.L. and Billerbeck, P. *Kommentar zum Neuen Testament aus Talmud und Midrasch*, 4 vols. (Munich, 1922-).

Syme, R. 'Observations on the Province of Cilicia', *Anatolian Studies Presented to William Hepburn Buckler*, ed. W.M. Calder and J. Keil (Manchester, 1939), pp. 299-332.

Tenney, M.C. *New Testament Times* (Grand Rapids, 1965).

Torrey, C.C. 'The Bilingual Inscription from Sardis', *AJSL* 34 (1917-18), pp. 185-98.

—*Documents of the Primitive Church* (New York, 1941).

—'The Aramaic Period of the Nascent Christian Church', *ZNTW* 44 (1952-53), pp. 205-23.

Turner, H.E.W. *The Pattern of Christian Truth. A Study in the Relations between Orthodoxy and Heresy in the Early Church* (London, 1954).

Weber, G. 'Der unterirdische Lauf des Lykos bei Kolossai', *Ath. Mitt.* 16 (1891), pp. 194-99.

Wellmann, M. 'Demosthenes περὶ ὀφθαλμῶν', *Hermes* 38 (1903), pp. 546-66.

Zahn, T. *Introduction to the New Testament*, tr. M.W. Jacobus *et al.*, 3 vols. (Edinburgh, 1909-).

INDEX OF BIBLICAL REFERENCES

APOCRYPHA

PSEUDEPIGRAPHA

RABBINIC WRITINGS

INSCRIPTIONS

COINS

PAPYRI AND OSTRACA

SELECTED GREEK WORDS

HEBREW WORDS

LATIN WORDS

ANCIENT PLACES

ANCIENT AND MYTHOLOGICAL PERSONS
(also Nations, Dynasties, Periods)

MODERN PLACE NAMES

NOTE In the Turkish alphabet letters without diacritics precede the corresponding letters with diacritics. Thus 'Gur-' precedes 'Güm-'. 'C' is sounded as 'j' in 'jam', 'ç' as 'ch' in 'church', 'ş' as 'sh'. 'Ğ' is almost silent, a weak glide, throaty after or between back vowels. Dotless ı is sounded by saying 'u' as in 'put' with lips spread wide, dotted 'i' is like 'i' in 'machine', but short. 'Ö' and 'ü' are as in German.

INDEX OF MODERN AUTHORS

SUBJECT INDEX